Legal Executions in the Western Territories, 1847–1911

Legal Executions in the Western Territories, 1847–1911

Arizona, Colorado, Idaho, Kansas, Montana, Nebraska, Nevada, New Mexico, North Dakota, Oklahoma, Oregon, South Dakota, Utah, Washington and Wyoming

R. Michael Wilson

McFarland & Company, Inc., Publishers
Jefferson, North Carolina, and London

Library of Congress Cataloguing-in-Publication Data

Wilson, R. Michael, 1944–
Legal executions in the western territories, 1847–1911 : Arizona, Colorado, Idaho, Kansas, Montana, Nebraska, Nevada, New Mexico, North Dakota, Oklahoma, Oregon, South Dakota, Utah, Washington and Wyoming / R. Michael Wilson.
p. cm.
Includes bibliographical references and index.

ISBN 978-0-7864-4825-8
softcover : 50# alkaline paper ♾

1. Capital punishment — West (U.S.) — History. 2. Criminal justice, Administration of — West (U.S.) — History. I. Title.
HV8699.U6W55 2010 364.660978 — dc22 2010006308

British Library cataloguing data are available

Manufactured in the United States of America

McFarland & Company, Inc., Publishers
Box 611, Jefferson, North Carolina 28640
www.mcfarlandpub.com

Table of Contents

Preface

Half the world's countries have abolished the death penalty, but in the United States the administration of the death penalty persists as one of the most controversial ethical and practical issues of American jurisprudence. Capital punishment has been under attack in America for a dozen decades and one day may become an "endangered species" as more states abolish the practice of taking a human life as the ultimate penalty of the law. If the trend continues, the death penalty will become a relic, to be found only in those literary museums known as historic encyclopedias. I was drawn to an examination of these early western case histories not because documentation may be lost to future ages but because the work of documenting these thrilling events has proven so daunting that few have undertaken the task. Those who have "picked up the gauntlet," however, have limited their efforts to mere lists or to documenting a constrained geographical area. An examination of the death penalty in the early days of the West is an important aspect of the debate over capital punishment, and nothing less than 100 percent of the executions in 100 percent of the western territories gives us the basis for drawing meaningful conclusions.

In June 2009 sixteen jurisdictions among the United States had no death penalty statute in effect: Alaska, Hawaii, Iowa, Maine, Massachusetts, Michigan, Minnesota, New Jersey, New Mexico, New York, North Dakota, Rhode Island, Vermont, West Virginia, Wisconsin, and the District of Columbia. Kansas, New York and New Hampshire had not executed a person since 1976 when the U.S. Supreme Court restored the death penalty, and Illinois currently has a moratorium on death sentences. Colorado, Kansas, Maryland, Montana, Nebraska, and New Hampshire are considering statutes abolishing the practice, due at least in part to economic considerations, but these are the states which have the fewest prisoners on death row. Since 1976 there have been nearly twelve hundred executions in the United States, reaching a high of ninety-eight in 1999 but decreasing to thirty-seven by the end of 2008, and two thirds of those put to death were executed in just five states: Florida, Missouri, Oklahoma, Texas, and Virginia. It seems only a matter of time before these high rate capital punishment states begin to question the propriety of executing human beings condemned to death and opt for a term of life in prison.

The present work contains all the details of all the crimes resulting in executions in the fifteen western American territories. With this information one is able to see practices and patterns which lead to several logical conclusions: (1) The death penalty is no deterrent to murder. Regardless of the number of public executions, "cold-blooded, pre-meditated, first-degree murder with malice" proliferated in the Old West. If there is a justification for the infliction of death as a punishment it must be to prevent future murders by the same criminal; and (2) If capital punishment is to continue we must come to realize that the U.S. Supreme Court got it wrong when they said that death by hanging was "cruel and unusual."

When a hanging is done properly, death is instantaneous and any agonies perceived are in the eye of the beholder.

The research for this book relied primarily upon the newspapers of the time and we are truly indebted to those newspaper editors who relished the "sordid details" to boost subscription rates. Other sources, though less accessible, include court records, records of the territorial governors, and the diaries and personal accounts of early settlers. The work has been arranged with the researcher in mind, with case histories presented by territory alphabetically, case histories listed chronologically, and each case history headed by the name of the condemned and the date of execution. Specific sources are listed at the end of each case history and a general bibliography is provided. Even the best laid plan can go awry, and several last minute discoveries have been included in an Addendum. While this affects the perfect order of the executions, the omission of these events would leave this work forever defective. Searching the contents for something specific has been enhanced by the compilation of a comprehensive index.

Introduction

The oldest profession after hunting and gathering, despite the cliché, was probably crime. Before men in a male dominated society could turn their attention to the opposite sex, their basic needs — food, water, and shelter — would have to be satisfied. Some men would have the skills, the means, and the motivation to satisfy those needs by their own efforts, while a few would resort to intimidation, theft, and even murder to ensure their survival. Punishment for criminals identified and caught would have followed quickly and death would have been a most probable consequence. At first the means of inflicting death would have been rudimentary; but hanging, both as an effective method of execution and as a deterrent, may have evolved as one of the earliest innovations. Before the Romans began their conquest of the world the Persians were hanging criminals, but it was perceived as a peculiarly Persian custom and the Romans preferred crucifixion to any other form. When the Romans first encountered the Germanic tribes they found them using the rope and limb as their primary means of execution. From the mainland of Europe the practice of hanging criminals spread to England with the Anglo-Saxons, and there it was refined almost to an art form.

The earliest English gallows was a crossbeam between two posts or tree limbs against which a ladder was propped. The condemned person climbed or was pushed to the required height and the noose slipped over his or her head. The hangman would turn over the ladder, so there was no drop and the person strangled. Although ladders worked well for small numbers of hangings, death sentences proliferated; so the gallows naturally evolved into a long beam on top of two sturdy posts with multiple ropes dangling beneath. The condemned were crowded into tumbrels — two-wheeled carts pulled by a horse — and rode to the gallows seated upon their coffins. The tumbrels were pulled beneath the beam and the nooses adjusted, and then the carts were driven away leaving the condemned dangling. After a suitable period of time the dead were removed and, if there were more condemned waiting, the procedure would be repeated. This method meant that the drop was short, or there was no drop, so the time allotted had to allow for the slow strangulation of each convicted criminal.

Spectators might try to relieve a subject of their agony by pulling on their legs or raising them up and then abruptly dropping them, trying to break their neck. The success of this latter technique prompted a change in English law in 1760 when the "trapdoor" method of hanging was instituted to provide a drop sufficient to dislocate the cervical vertebrae.

The English custom of hanging criminals came to America with the Pilgrims and the first murderer hanged in America was John Billington, who was executed in Plymouth, Massachusetts, on September 30, 1630. The practice of hanging criminals moved west with the pioneers and the laws regarding the methods of inflicting death remained unchanged throughout America's territorial period. The sentence of death was imposed exclusively for the crime of murder in the first degree with only a few exceptions, and hanging was the most common form of execution. Death by firing squad was used as an alternative to hanging in Utah and Oklahoma, and it was left to the condemned to choose his manner of death. A firing squad could consist of as few as one man or as many as nine men.

During the early days executions were thought to be a deterrent, so gallows were built a distance from the jail, allowing for a solemn procession exhibiting the condemned man on his way to his execution. Soon it became apparent that this caused a variety of difficulties, so scaffolds were built closer to the place of confinement. When the law changed to require that gallows be built inside an enclosure, and the hanging be a private affair, scaffolds were consistently built adjacent to the jail. The sheriff of each county was responsible for executions and he invited at least one physician and also might invite, as witnesses, the district attorney, lawmen, a coroner's jury of six to twelve reputable citizens, ministers of the gospel, and a number of relatives or friends of the condemned man. The condemned was provided access to religious comfort and many condemned men chose to be baptized into a religion during their final hours. Before the fatal moment arrived, the condemned was offered a hearty meal; he washed, shaved and dressed in a new dark suit or other attire of his choosing provided by the county; and the death warrant was read to him in his cell or on the gallows. He was often provided an alcoholic beverage or drug before walking to the scaffold and again as he stood on the trapdoor. The prisoner was escorted by several men who provided support in case he faltered, and he was followed closely or led by his religious advisor. The condemned was placed on the trapdoor and his wrists and arms, knees and ankles were pinioned. At some point during the proceedings he was given an opportunity to speak to the crowd and once his speech was finished the rope was adjusted and the black cap was pulled over his face. It was then but a moment before the trap was sprung and the body dropped. A hanged man remained suspended until an attending physician pronounced him dead and the time varied with each individual.

How It Feels to Be Hanged

In the latter part of the nineteenth century there was a preoccupation with what it felt like to be hanged. Of course there was no opportunity to ask the subject of a legal hanging, as the law required that they be "hanged until dead." However, failed suicides by hanging and scientific study provided insight into the sensations and as early as April 16, 1869, the *Walla Walla Statesman* in Washington Territory published an article entitled "How it feels to be hanged":

> We are told that hanging, if successful — that is, if it breaks the person's neck — is the most sudden death he can die. It ruptures the spine in the immediate neighborhood of the *medulla oblongata*, and thus breaks up communication of the nerve force, or vital power, to the organs that carry on the human machinery. If the man's neck is not broken the first action of the cord is to close the trachea, or windpipe, and thus stop the supply of air. It also compresses the large veins in the neck which return blood to the heart — the jugulars — but does not entirely compress the large arteries that carry blood to the brain, for these lie deep. The immediate physiological effect is congestion of the brain — a congestion not dissimilar in its commencement from the congestion of drunkenness, which is generally regarded as agreeable, and the consequences of this congestion — a consequence that perhaps follows in three minutes after the pressure of the cord is felt — is the total abolition of conscious sensation. The man may struggle and writhe in a way terrible to see, but these struggles are like those of convulsions generally — painful only to the beholder. Therefore, if a man is hanged successfully, he feels only the one sickening sensation of the plunge before he gets to the end of the rope — three seconds of horror. If he is hanged successfully, by strangulation, he feels the same three seconds, and in addition, between the pressure of the cord and the deep congestion of the brain, three minutes of

swimming, drowsy, uncertain uneasiness — at worst, three minutes and three seconds; and this is all we give of misery to murderers. Compare with this the pain that man suffers before he dies from an ordinary illness — the drawn out wretchedness of his three weeks of fever, the days of agony with rheumatism, and the bent-forward, restless nights before this rheumatism finally brings his damaged heart to a standstill; the months of slow death entailed by a cancerous stomach; in fine, compare the history of any disease with the short shrift of hanging, and then reflect that our humanity now obliterates the murderer's three minutes and three seconds by the use of chloroform. Really it is a fine age, and if a man is tired of this world and wants to get out on easy terms, the thing for him to do is to cut his neighbor's throat and be hanged under chloroform.

Theodore Baker was legally hanged in New Mexico on May 6, 1887, but on December 23, 1885, he had been lynched by a vigilance committee. He was rescued by lawmen, cut down, and resuscitated. As he awaited the date of his legal execution he told a reporter of the *Daily New Mexican* about his experience with the lynch mob:

I went with them, and at the door I began to curse at them, when one of them put the muzzle of his pistol to my ear and said, "keep still or I'll put a bullet through you." I knew him by his voice, and knew he would do it, and I kept still. A little further on we came to a telegraph pole. From the crossbar swung a new rope. On the end was a big slip-noose. They led me under the rope. I tried to stoop down and pull my boots off, as I had promised my folks not to die with my boots on, but before I could do it the noose was thrown over my head and I was jerked off my feet. My senses left me a moment, and then I waked up in what seemed to be another world. As I recollect now, the sensation was that everything about me had multiplied a great many times. It seemed that my five executioners had grown in number until there were thousands of them. I saw what seemed a multitude of animals of all shapes and sizes.

Then things changed and I was in great pain. I became conscious that I was hanging by the neck, and that the knot of the rope had slipped around under my chin. My hands were loosely tied, and I jerked them loose and tried to catch the rope above me. Somebody caught me by the feet just then and gave me a jerk. It seemed like a bright flash of lightning passed in front of my eyes. It was the brightest thing I ever saw. It was followed by a terrible pain up and down and across my back and I could feel my legs jerk and draw up. Then there was a blank, and I knew nothing more until 11 o'clock the next day.

One of the main criticisms of hanging as a means of execution was that the condemned's neck was, all too often, "unbroken and he would perish by the long and painful process of strangulation." John Burns, however, spoke from personal experience in refuting that perception. He recalled the situation:

Some time during the [Civil] war ruffians, who desired to be thought [bush] whackers, came upon me at my house, intending to compel me to give up some money I was supposed to have. I had none, and told them so, but they did not believe me and their next move was to cut a cord out of a bedstead, tie one end around my neck, throw the other over a joist overhead, and pull me up till my feet were clear of the floor. This they did four times, questioning me between whiles. I lost consciousness every time as soon as my feet left the floor but felt no pain at any time, and after the second hoist I meant to sham continued insensibility when they let me drop again, since to lower me they just let go the rope and I fell to the floor, but this was beyond my power. My first consciousness was that I had raised my body to a sitting position, which put shamming out of the question. I experienced no pain when the rope tightened, nor when I was suspended, nor after I was released, except the soreness caused on my skin by the chafing of the rope. I weighed about two hundred pounds, which insured that the rope was fully tightened each time.

Dr. D.S. Lamb, an ex-surgeon of the United States Army, studied the subject of hanging and in 1894 reported in the *St. Louis Globe-Democrat*:

DEATH BY HANGING —

The Three Different Stages Through Which the Victim Passes

> I have made the subject of death by hanging a long study. From my observations during my experience in the army I feel justified in saying that death by hanging is the most exaggerated of all modes. It may be immediate and without symptoms but the subject must pass through three stages before death.
>
> In the first stage the victim passes into a partial stupor lasting from thirty seconds to two minutes, but this is generally governed by the length of the drop, the weight of the body, and the tightness of the constriction. There is absolutely no pain in this stage; the feeling is rather one of pleasure. The subjective symptoms described are intense heat in the head, brilliant flashes of light in the eyes, deafening sounds in the ears and a heavy numb feeling in the lungs. In the second stage the subject passes into unconsciousness and convulsions usually occur. In the third stage all is quiet except the beating of the heart. Just before death the agitation is renewed, but in a different way from that in the second state. The feet are raised, the tongue has a peculiar spasm, the chest heaves, the eyes protrude from the orbits and oscillate from side to side, and the pupils dilate. The pulse can, in most cases, be felt ten minutes after the drop.
>
> I once knew a man who was desirous of ascertaining if there was any suffering by hanging and in order to find out he placed a rope around his neck and stepped off a bench, intending to step back again, but he became immediately unconscious and would have died in a few minutes had it not been for the timely arrival of a friend. He said he experienced all the feelings that I mentioned in the first stage.

This three stage process depended upon the rope being properly knotted and adjusted. The knot was carefully positioned on the left shoulder just behind the jaw so that it would press upon the carotid artery, cutting off blood to the brain which resulted in unconsciousness in a few seconds. This positioning of the knot forced the head to snap backward and dislocate the vertebrae. Ideally, during a legal hanging, the spine would be dislocated between the first and second or the second and third cervical vertebrae and the spinal cord would be severed, or at least severely compressed, cutting off all sensation to the torso and extremities.

The Apparatus

Before one execution by hanging the trapdoor gallows was described as "ready and in fact every detail for the execution has been carefully arranged. The gallows is of the regulation pattern, very strong built, and has a drop of six feet. The rope is of best quality hemp, and 1½ inches in size." In fact, there was no regulation design for gallows. Each sheriff, when required to do so, hired a local carpenter to design and build a gallows for his county. The trapdoor and release mechanism were of particular concern and the drop, the distance a man would fall, had to be calculated correctly. The distance a particular man should drop was determined by a mathematical formula, based upon weight, where a one hundred ninety-six pound man required a six foot drop and, for each deduction of seven pounds in weight, two inches were added. Scaffolds of the trapdoor design, paid for with county funds, were usually disassembled and stored for reuse. Another type of gallows used a heavy weight as a "counter-poise" so that when the weight was dropped the condemned man was jerked up with such suddenness it dislocated the man's vertebrae.

Hemp was used almost exclusively for a hangman's rope because the strands were longer and stronger than flax, the other commonly available material at that time. The hemp material was beaten until soft and then twisted into strands, and three strands were then twisted around a central strand called "the heart" to form a rope. A very thick rope was ordered from the manufacturer so that even after stretching it was still thick enough to prevent it from cutting into the neck of the condemned person. Upon its arrival the rope was soaked in water and stretched to remove elasticity and then it was tested for the condemned's weight, usually by dropping a comparable weight through the trapdoor the required distance or by jerking up the equivalent weight of the condemned man. The loops of a hangman's noose were not a set number; but seven loops were most often used, though on occasion a hangman might use as few as five or as many as thirteen loops. The point where rope grated on rope was lubricated with grease, soap, or wax to make the strands slide more easily and cinch tightly.

When execution was by firing squad, rifles were used; and, when three or more, a portion of the arms were loaded with powder only so that each shooter could later rationalize that his weapon did not fire the fatal bullet. This accommodation was intended to steady the shooter's aim.

The Changing Perception of Crime in the Wild West Territories

The perception of crime changed with the times. In the earliest days it was believed that more crimes should be included as capital offenses and the *Sacramento Herald* recommended the following:

> Hang Them! That is what nearly every one says of that class of scoundrels who lay in ambush along remote highways and accost the wayfarer suspected of having valuables in his possession, and drivers of express coaches with 'Halt! Pass over that box! Shell out quick!' the peremptory demand being backed up by several very unpleasant looking shooting-irons, all cocked and primed, aimed at an undesirable short range.... [T]he Legislature (should enact) a law declaring highway robbery to be a capital offense, punishable in the same manner that the crime of murder in the first degree is punished.

These sentiments prevailed throughout the West, but after only a few men had been hanged in Nevada the effectiveness of the death penalty was already being questioned. Virginia City's *Territorial Enterprise* expressed the following opinion:

> Death or Imprisonment. No matter how vile the murderer, how clear his conviction, how just the sentence, how willing people may be, while the horror of the homicide is fresh upon them, to execute summary vengeance, when the day of execution draws near a morbid sentiment of sympathy takes possession of a certain portion of the community. They follow the creature to the gallows, and before and after death pay him more attention than they would an honest but poor man in sickness — more than they would his corpse in death. It is, in the light of these and other facts which are apparent enough, doubtful whether, as a preventative of crime, the execution of criminals does any good.

Crime, it was thought, might be hereditary and one expert concluded as follows:

> When the study of heredity reveals the fact that even the nature of vagabondage is perpetuated; when the surprising revelations of Margaret (Jukes), mother of criminals, from whose loins nearly a thousand criminals have thus far been traced, are considered, common sense will ultimately recognize that the imprisonment of a criminal for ten or twenty years is not simply to punish him or to relieve the public of his lawless acts, but to restrain him from perpetuating his kind. He is to be quarantined, in just the same way that a case of the plague might be, that his kind may not increase. With these plain facts thoroughly understood men high in authority must find some other excuse for the exercise of their pardoning power, and other reasons for allowing so large a proportion of criminals to go free.

Some families, it was believed, simply had "bad blood" and it was supposed that the physical characteristics of criminally oriented individuals were distinct from those of a law abiding citizen. But by the mid–1880s the scientific community began questioning the ability of law enforcement and the courts to address the problem of crime. Basic premises about the nature of crime suggested that the basis for crime might be deeper than a social or environmental cause, and *Popular Science News* asked, "Is Crime a Disease?":

> In recent times the idea has become very prevalent among a certain class of sentimentalists that crime is not an indication of innate depravity, but a symptom of mental and physical disease, or an inheritance from some criminal ancestor and, therefore, the much-abused murderer or robber is not a bad man but only an unfortunate one, deserving of pity and care

rather than punishment. A sick man, they say, ought not to be imprisoned and one who is staggering under a load of homicidal tendencies bequeathed to him by his grandfather is not worthy of death, even if he does occasionally send some of his less unfortunate fellow-beings into the next world. A man physically and mentally sound is less likely to commit acts than ones with a diseased body or abnormal mental action, and the history of the notorious Jukes family proves beyond question that from a single criminal ancestor may spring a long line of descendants, a majority of whom will be enemies to the welfare of society. But, granting that a tendency to crime may be inherited, it must originate somewhere, and if a man's ancestor may have been a spontaneous criminal, as it were, another man of the present day may also be laying up on his own responsibility a heritage of crime for his unborn descendants. If the abnormal tendencies can be eradicated and the criminal made a useful member of society, every effort should be made to that end; but if crime is a disease, it seems — at least in its more serious manifestations — to be an incurable one. The percentage of reformed criminals is discouragingly small, and that of those convicted for subsequent offenses disproportionately large. The best treatment of such persons is a perplexing question, but the right of self-preservation is paramount to every other consideration, and the morbid unwholesome sympathy shown by an increasing class of people toward those who are so much out of harmony with their social environment will only result in great injury to the orderly and law-abiding classes of society, without causing any decrease of crime or conferring any permanent benefit upon the criminals themselves.

After thirty-five years of unchecked crime in the West the editor of San Francisco's *Argonaut*, in 1896, reasoned that "Kindness to criminals is cruelty to the innocent and cruelty, too, to all who, but for the fear of punishment, would become criminals. The interests of society in the United States at this time demands an aggressive public opinion in favor of speedier trials, the withdrawal of right of appeal in criminal cases, and the rigorous enforcement of the laws against those who break them."

Frequency of Executions

In the Old West defendants were condemned to death only when they were convicted of murder in the first degree, with few exceptions, but even then many convicted murderers were sentenced to prison terms. Other murderers eluded the hangman through suicide, by escaping from imprisonment never to be heard of again, or by obtaining a second trail on appeal and being acquitted, or convicted of or pleading to a lesser degree of crime. In numerous instances death sentences were commuted to a life term in prison and, even when the evidence clearly showed every element necessary for a conviction of murder in the first degree, juries might bring in a peculiar verdict such as murder in the second degree or manslaughter.

Most hangings were successful, according to newspaper accounts, and even when the prisoner strangled to death the condemned was reported to be unconscious within seconds after the jerk or drop. There were some exceptions, however, and the decapitation of Thomas Ketchum in New Mexico is often cited. However, one of the earliest instances of bungling was the hanging of Pablita Sandoval in New Mexico when the sheriff failed to bind her limbs. It was not the embarrassment of bungling, however, that promoted privacy in executions. Early executions were intentionally as public as possible as this was believed to deter other would-be murderers; but in the mid–1870s the phenomenon of "private executions" swept through the west, and territories required that gallows be constructed within a wall or enclosure of high board fencing, or a special building be erected or selected for the purpose. The laws were often very specific in excluding and including citizens of the jurisdiction, and the number of witnesses was greatly limited. However, there was no federal guideline requiring executions to be private, and a public hanging occurred in the "civilized east" as late as August 14, 1936, when Rainey Bethea was publicly hanged in Owensboro, Kentucky.

The Case Histories, by Territory, in Chronological Order

ARIZONA

The region that would become Arizona was explored and settled by Spain between 1536 and 1821, when it became a part of an independent Mexico. The area was acquired by the United States as a concession in the Treaty of Guadalupe Hidalgo on February 2, 1848, following the war with Mexico, but was under American control for many months previously. The region became the New Mexico Territory as part of the Compromise of 1850. In 1854 a large tract of land was purchased from Mexico in the Gadsden Purchase and annexed to the New Mexico Territory, a significant portion of which would later be within Arizona's borders. On February 24, 1863, Arizona became a separate territory and in 1866 ceded the northwestern triangle, known as Pah-Ute County, to Nevada, thus establishing the borders which exist today. On February 14, 1912, the Arizona Territory was admitted as the 48th state, the last territory within the continental United States to achieve that status.

Fernandez, Manuel
May 2, 1873

Michael "Rawhide" McCartney was an eccentric, solitary in his habits, but an honest man and a first-class businessman and well liked throughout Yuma County. McCartney occasionally drank to excess but while under the influence of liquor he refused to transact any business and while on a spree would lock himself in his store. Those who knew McCartney were not surprised to see his place of business closed for days at a time; but his absence from his boarding room was suspicious, and the other boarders at the Colorado Hotel decided to investigate. They went to McCartney's store and attempted to rouse him, supposing him to be asleep, but no sound came from within. Suspecting foul play they made entrance by removing a log in the back wall of the store, lit a lamp, and found the mutilated body of the storekeeper lying on the counter with his head resting upon a bolt of calico, besmeared and surrounded by a pool of blood.

The murder had been committed with an axe and the sharp edge had been buried in the man's left temple its full length. There were no indications of a struggle and the body appeared to be positioned as if McCartney was asleep when killed. McCartney was known to have on hand a large sum of money, so robbery was the motive; but the safe's lock baffled the robber and he got nothing but the few dollars he found in the till. Coroner Carr held an inquest and, though the jury found that the "deceased came to his death at the hand of some person or persons to them unknown," three men were arrested: Manuel Fernandez, Canuto Soto, and Jesus Maria Ballestros. At their preliminary examination Manuel Fernandez was identified as the murderer and charged with first degree murder, while

Canuto Soto was identified as his accomplice and charged with second degree murder. Jesus Maria Ballestros proved an alibi and was released.

Though heavily ironed the two murderers managed to escape from Yuma's flimsy jail on January 5, 1873, by digging through a wall with a broken file. The fugitives went to a nearby Indian settlement and asked to have their irons removed, but one Indian ran for help and the prisoners were soon back in their cell. At their trial in March both men were found guilty as charged and on March 28 Fernandez and Soto were brought into court for sentencing. Canuto Soto, who had pleaded guilty, received ninety-nine years at hard labor to be served in the territorial prison at Yuma, which then was actually the county jail as no prison had yet been constructed. Fernandez' sentence was "that he shall be confined in the County jail, or some other place of safety, until the 2nd day of May 1873, on which day between the hours of 10 A.M. and noon he shall be hanged by the neck until he is dead."

Fernandez was attended during his last days by John Maria Chaucot, Father Confessor, and by his assistant, the Rev. P. Bourgade, who encouraged the condemned man to confess publicly. A woman who had been to see Fernandez on Thursday, before the Holy Communion was administered, also begged him to confess his crime; but he said, "I cannot, it pains me so." Before being led to the gallows Fernandez said to sheriff Francis H. Goodwin that he could not confess at that moment but, "We will see when we get outside." However he never braced up sufficiently to confess. On Saturday, May 2, at 10:00 A.M. a party of seventy citizens surrounded the gallows, armed with shotguns and other arms, under the order of Sheriff Goodwin, and several armed men were posted on housetops overlooking the jail yard. The prisoner was led out at 10:30 A.M. and, after taking his position on the platform, he said, "Good-bye, ladies!" and while waving his hand at several senoritas present continued: "Long live Mary, the Most Holy! I salute you all. To my Mexican friends present I give this advice: May you never occupy the place that I do today. I would rather be shot. It is an honor for a man to die in battle; but I am in your Territory, and have to die. God gives life; God takes it away. God gave me life. I have only to die. But I am better off dead than that poor Indian," meaning Canuto Soto.

The Catholic service for the condemned was read and followed by the reading of the death warrant. The condemned man then commenced a speech, which he repeated several times and became confused, so the Reverend Bourgade stepped forward and said, "Think of God." Fernandez then knelt with the Fathers and prayed for several moments. He arose and while the sheriff was pinioning his arms he said impatiently, "Quick! Why are you tying me?" One of the priests then distracted him by repeating, "Jesus, Savior of the World" as Fernandez said, "Why tie me so fast? We are all born to die!" When the black cap was placed over his head he yelled out, "I want to die with my eyes uncovered!" The sheriff told him that such was the law and the prisoner bowed his head, apparently in prayer, then suddenly straightened up and said, "Ah! What a disgrace this is!" At 10:45 A.M., while Fernandez was reciting the "Confiteor after the Confessor," the trap was sprung and Drs. George S. Rose and C. Arnaba advanced and pronounced him dead of a broken neck. The body was cut down at 11:10 A.M., placed in the coffin provided by the county, and afterward buried in the Catholic cemetery.

Arizona City (Yuma) Arizona Sentinel: December 7, 1872; January 11, 1873; March 29, 1873; May 3, 1873.

Abiles, Manuel
August 6, 1875

On April 23, 1875, several men were drinking together, one of them a man commonly known as "Pinto." Manuel Abiles had some difficulty with Pinto and during the argument Abiles took a large ash stick and struck Pinto on the head and body. The blow to the head killed him. William Malone, who disliked

Pinto and owed him money, stood nearby and watched but took no action. Abiles and Malone were arrested for murder, Malone as an accessory only. But Malone was acquitted as he had done nothing to aid or encourage Abiles. Abiles was arraigned in Yavapai County on May 7, 1875, his trial commenced on May 11, and two days later he was found guilty of murder in the first degree. He was ordered to appear in court for sentencing on May 29, and the judge then ordered that Manuel Abiles be "hanged by the neck until dead" on July 23, 1875. An application for a commutation of sentence or a respite was forwarded to the office of governor Anson P.K. Safford; but the governor, after carefully considering the matter, concluded that the arguments were not sufficient and declined to intervene.

On the evening of August 5 Abiles dictated a statement to four men who had served on his jury:

> Believing that these are my last words on earth I make this statement: Bill Melone [*sic*] killed Gregorio with an ash stick. A lot of us were drinking and some hard words passed. Gregorio picked up a stone and hit another man in the mouth; this commenced the row. Gregorio had worked for Melone and Melone owed him four dollars. Melone struck him because he had hit the other man in the mouth with a stone. I saw him hit Gregorio with the ash club. It was this blow which killed Gregorio. Melone was drunk. I went to protect Gregorio, but when I got there it was too late. Melone and Jesus Eridia both went out after him before I did. I saw Melone strike him as I was running up.

In the morning Abiles was marched to the gallows, positioned on the trapdoor, and his wrists and ankles were pinioned. He was given an opportunity to speak to the crowd but said nothing new, and then the noose of ¾ inch hemp was positioned and cinched and the black cap was pulled over his face. In but a moment the trap was sprung and Abiles dropped five feet, breaking his neck. The attending physician, after monitoring his vital signs, pronounced him dead and he was cut down, placed in the pine coffin provided by the county, and buried that evening.

Prescott (AZ) Daily Miner: May 13–14, 1875; May 26, 1875; May 31, 1875; July 23, 1875; August 6, 1875.

De Hay, Michael
January 14, 1876

In 1856 Michael De Hay married Esther Menstock at La Crosse, Wisconsin, and in 1869 they settled in the Parahnegat Valley in Lincoln County, Nevada. In August 1875 De Hay found employment in the Groom District, sixty miles from his ranch. He was determined to move his family to some place where he could educate his children and had become a member of a committee trying to get a school started at Hiko. The committee hired a teacher and De Hay made arrangements to remove his family to Hiko. However, just at that time his wife abandoned him, taking with her the children, team, and a wagon loaded with most of their household goods. While at his work he learned that she had started for Arizona with a Mr. Suttenfield, a stranger who had camped on the De Hay ranch for a few weeks during his absence. When De Hay returned to his empty house the constable served a summons in favor of storekeeper Wilson for $51, most of which his wife had obtained in supplies for the trip to Arizona.

De Hay started in pursuit the next day but passed them at Chloride, where they had camped six miles from Mineral Park. De Hay went on to Mineral Park and laid his case before an attorney and, following his advice, swore out a process and had the entire party brought into Mineral Park. However, nothing came of it so De Hay rented a house, went to work, and provided for his family. He tried by every means to induce his wife to live with him as before and forgave her infidelity, but to all his appeals she turned a deaf ear and continually declared that she never would resume their marital relations. De Hay learned that his wife, from time to time, was meeting with Suttenfield at a house Suttenfield had rented near Mineral Park and in late 1875 De Hay, crazed with jealousy, murdered his wife.

He was tried at the November term of the 3rd Judicial District of Arizona by Judge Charles A. Tweed. De Hay claimed insanity, testifying that Esther's continued infidelity affected him day and night and he was troubled with horrid dreams and at times was nearly insane with jealousy. He said that on the night of the murder he was suddenly awakened from a deep sleep and thought he saw his wife standing over him with a butcher knife in her hand. She had been sleeping in another room in their only bed with the children while he was sleeping on the floor of an adjoining room. De Hay said that he jumped up and grabbed his revolver from beneath his pillow, then rushed into the bedroom. Esther jumped into bed and "curled down," but he fired at her and pulled her out onto the floor. He testified that when he saw the blood and realized what he had done he was horror stricken and rushed out of the house. Then, determined to take his own life, he placed his pistol to his breast and fired twice without effect, so he ran downtown and hid in the hay loft where he was found. His claim of insanity was rejected by the jury. He was convicted of murder in the first degree, and sentenced to hang on January 14, 1876. Neither appeal nor application for executive clemency would delay the proceedings.

Before noon on Friday, January 14, 1876, the prisoner was conducted onto the gallows where Sheriff A. Comstock read the death warrant. De Hay was asked if he had anything to say and his answer was, "As it is the will of the people that I should die, so let it be. The Lord have mercy on my soul." He then thanked the jailors for their kindness, shook hands with those on the platform, and bid all good-bye. His arms and legs were pinioned as he remarked, "I am the first of my name to die on the gallows." The black cap was pulled over his face, the noose adjusted, and a prayer offered up by the Reverend Blakslee. When "Amen" was uttered the prisoner exclaimed, "I'm gone! I'm gone!" and the trap was sprung. There was not a quiver of a muscle and after the body had hung twenty minutes Dr. Reese pronounced him dead. The body was cut down and lowered into the coffin provided by the county. De Hay was buried that evening a dozen yards from the courthouse.

Prescott (AZ) Daily Miner: January 21, 1876; February 5, 1876.

Malone, James
March 15, 1878

On January 10, 1876, a group of soldiers from Company K, 19th Infantry, gathered in the post trader's store at Fort Mojave and were drinking heavily. Among them were Richard L. Lawler, James Malone, Leopold Eith, James Henry, and J. Wilcox. The soldiers became drunk and rowdy, so they were asked to leave, but they purchased a supply of whiskey and continued their drinking outdoors. Lawler imbibed to excess and finally became stupefied from the liquor and, though unsteady on his feet, managed to walk around the building and find a place to lie down.

Lawler was unpopular among the men of Company K, particularly with Malone, because of his obnoxious manner in discharging his duties while a noncommissioned officer. Also, considerable animosity existed because of his appearance as a witness against some men of the 19th Infantry who had been tried by court-martial. Malone, Eith and the other soldiers found Lawler asleep and collected stones and adobes and stacked them nearby. When all the ammunition was in place the disabled man was stoned to death by Malone and Eith, his head crushed in and his body horribly mutilated. The victim offered only slight resistance because he was too drunk to rise, and after the first blow he was entirely helpless. The soldiers removed the dead body to the Colorado River, relying upon the swift current to carry away the corpse and all evidence of their deed. They were confident that, if the body were not found near the store, they could not be implicated in his death as it would be supposed he had deserted. Malone and his companions then returned to the fort and slept, certain that they were free from discovery and arrest.

However, Lawler's body was swept into a slough of the river, where it was trapped until discovered. The dead body was reported to authorities, who recovered it and ordered an inquest.

The coroner's jury found that a murder had been committed and an investigation began that pointed to Malone and Eith but also implicated the others. Malone, Eith, Henry and Wilcox were arrested and brought to trial at the June 1877 term of the district court. Henry turned state's evidence against Malone and Eith and was released in consideration of his testimony. There was not enough evidence to try Wilcox, so he was released as well. Malone and Eith were found guilty of murder in the first degree and on June 30, 1877, both defendants were sentenced by Judge C.A. Tweed: "that you be removed hence to the county jail or other place of confinement and there securely kept until the day hereafter be fixed for your execution and that on that day you will be taken to the place of execution and then and there be hanged by the neck until you are dead, and may you through sincere penitence and contrition obtain forgiveness and pardon for your great sin."

The cases were appealed to the U.S. Supreme Court, which affirmed the decision of the lower court. But the evidence in Eith's case was not as strong as in Malone's case, so, when applications for commutation of their sentences were submitted to President Rutherford B. Hayes, Eith's application was granted and Malone's was denied. The killing of one soldier by another was a federal offense, so Eith was sent to a prison outside the Arizona Territory, which was under contract with the U.S. government, to serve out his life term.

On Friday, March 15, 1878, at 1:35 P.M. Malone arrived at the county jail, having been brought from the Fort Whipple guard house by U.S. marshal Wiley W. Standifer and deputy U.S. marshals J.W. Evans and E.P. Raines, and attended by Father Becker, the Rev. Alexander Gilmore, and the Rev. D.B. Wright. The gates to the jail yard were thrown open at 1:40 P.M. for those holding tickets and sixty witnesses filed in; but the jail fence and the adjacent rooftops were covered with several hundred spectators. At 1:45 P.M. the prisoner entered the yard holding his crucifix, with Marshal Standifer on his right, Father Becker on his left, and deputy marshal Evans and the Reverends Gilmore and Wright following. Malone ascended and took his place on the trapdoor facing north and then Marshal Standifer read the sentence of Judge Tweed and the death warrant.

Malone's wrists and arms, knees and ankles were pinioned and the noose was adjusted. Malone then requested the reading of his confession, written the previous night, and the Reverend Wright read the statement claiming he was innocent of any participation in the crime and merely knew of its commission at the time by accident; he blamed Henry and Wilcox for the murder, emphasizing the irony that the two guilty men were free, and concluded that he made this statement knowing he was going to die and rested his hopes for the hereafter on its truthfulness. When the Reverend Wright concluded, the black cap was pulled on; but Malone asked that it be removed so he could shake hands with the soldiers from Fort Whipple. The cap was removed and he called to a sergeant and several troopers and they ascended the stairs and shook hands with the prisoner. He next shook hands with deputy marshal Evans and Marshal Standifer and asked the latter to be careful to adjust the noose properly and "make a good job of it." He asked for a drink and an alcoholic stimulant was provided. Then Father Becker performed the last rites of the Catholic Church. The black cap was again drawn over the prisoner's eyes, the noose was readjusted and cinched tight, and at exactly 2:15 P.M. the trap was sprung. There was a slight convulsive movement of the chest and left arm before the body hung motionless. Dr. John Goodfellow pronounced him dead at 2:24 P.M., nine minutes after the trap fell. The body hung a total of twenty-one minutes before it was cut down and deposited in the coffin provided by the government. Malone was buried in the Citizen's Burying Ground that evening.

Prescott (AZ) Daily Miner: February 5, 1878; March 15–16, 1878; March 22, 1878; *Florence (AZ) Enterprise*: March 16, 1878.

Dominguez, Demetrio
November 26, 1880

William C. Ayers drove a stagecoach southward out of Prescott at 8:30 P.M., with William Thomas of Gillette, an ex-foreman of the Tip-Top Mine, the only passenger aboard. The coach was ascending a hill two miles north of Gillette when Ayers saw three men running toward the stage shouting to one another: "Pronto! Pronto!" When they reached the head of the lead horses they divided, two men running down the right side of the coach and one to the left. The first man on the right rushed to the coach door, placed his pistol so close to Thomas as to burn his clothing, and began firing at him while the man on the left did the same, one man firing in from each door. The second man on the right covered Ayers with his revolver, caught hold of the wheeler lines, and in English ordered Ayers to get down. He then called out in Spanish to the man on the left to cease firing, "as the third Mexican had been blazing away at Ayers pretty lively with his revolver" but without effect. After the man on the right discharged his pistol several times he drew a bayonet and repeatedly stabbed Thomas until the passenger fell to the floor of the coach. The two shooters then left Thomas, returned to Ayers, and robbed him of his revolver, watch and money. While they were occupied with the driver, Thomas opened the stage door and fell on his face in the road; but he got to his hands and knees and crawled to one side of the road where he collapsed and was robbed of all his valuables. The trio of robbers then ordered Ayers to take Thomas' trunk from the boot, get the key, and open it. Ayers asked why they attacked the man in the stage and they replied: *Este Hombre es no bueno*! (That man is no good!). After rifling the trunk the robbers ordered Ayers to unhitch the horses, which they mounted and rode north. Ayers made the wounded man as comfortable as possible and ran into Gillett for another team, then returned to the scene of the robbery and hauled the coach and wounded man into town. On November 28, the day following the attack, Thomas died of his wounds. The three murderers were pursued, but by December 12 Prescott's *Weekly Miner* announced that the robbers had escaped into Sonora, Mexico.

Robert N. Paul, Wells, Fargo & Co.'s special detective, followed the three murderers for several days before he lost the trail. He continued to watch for clues and, in February 1880, he learned that one of the murderers was at Maricopa. On February 3 Paul found that the fugitive had just left town for Davidson's Springs with D.F. Harshaw. Paul overtook his prey twenty miles out on the Patagonia road, with the fugitive driving Harshaw's team. Harshaw had arrested the Mexican named Demetrio Dominguez and when captured Dominguez had on him the watch taken from Thomas. It was a four ounce, stem winding silver watch of ordinary description except that the stem, rings and hinges were gold; the watch had been repaired at the jewelers in Prescott shortly before the murder and the jeweler was able to describe it.

Dominguez was jailed at Tucson and then taken to Prescott where, on February 13, the prisoner waived his examination before Judge Fluery and was held to answer to the grand jury. The prisoner was indicted, convicted of murdering Thomas, and sentenced to hang on September 14. In anticipation of his execution, Dominguez wrote his confession, saying he was forced to accompany the other two men and identifying Fermin Fiembres of Suaqui Grande, Sonora, and Umecino Moraga of Babraera, Sonora, as the murderers. In a postscript he wrote, "I did commit the crime. It is a bad example. I was seduced by those bad men, and now I repent of the bad example that I have given to the world. I want to be pardoned of this bad example that I have set, and want you to believe that I have repented of all my crimes and bad acts. I offer my life as a ransom."

Dominguez slept very little his last night and spent the time writing and talking. Shortly after daylight he arose and dressed in the light gray trousers and checkered woolen shirt furnished by the county, and after breakfast he spent his remaining time in prayer with Father Gerard. At 12:30 P.M. Dominguez was escorted from his cell by the priest, Sheriff Reuben S. Thomas and Deputy William Blankenship. At the door of the courthouse the party mounted a carriage, accompanied by a guard of thirty men on horseback and afoot; the guards were armed with shotguns to prevent a rumored rescue. Upon their arrival at the gallows the guards formed a square around the base and were surrounded closely by a crowd of two hundred persons gathered to witness the execution. Dominguez dismounted the carriage without assistance, but needed help ascending the stairs, and took his place on the center of the trapdoor. Sheriff Thomas read the death warrant, which was translated into Spanish by M.L. Peralta, and next came the last benediction given by the priest. The doomed man bid farewell to those around him as his wrists and arms, knees and ankles were pinioned; then the black cap was drawn over his face and the noose adjusted around his neck. Deputy Sheriff McDonald sprang the trap and the body fell eight feet; except for a few convulsive jerks and a quivering of the flesh in the first three minutes, no sign of life was apparent. After hanging for nearly thirty minutes, the body was examined by Dr. Conyers and Dominguez was pronounced dead. The body was cut down and the black cap removed. The face of the deceased appeared turgid and black, the tongue protruding, the eyes staring and bloodshot, the lips black, and the nostrils pinched and tinged with blood. Dominguez' body was at once deposited into the coffin provided by the county and given to undertaker John Averish. Several Mexican ladies later arranged for a private burial.

Tucson Arizona Daily Citizen: November 26, 1880; *Prescott (AZ) Miner*: November 28, 1879; December 1, 1879; December 5, 1879; December 12, 1879; February 13, 1880; November 6, 1880; November 26, 1880; December 3, 1880; *Phoenix (AZ) Herald*: November 28–29, 1879; February 3, 1880; April 20, 1880; November 7, 1880; November 26, 1880; *Yuma (AZ) Sentinel*: December 6, 1879.

Voolo
January 14, 1881

On November 10, 1880, Keokun, Pierka and Voolo, Pima Indians, were visiting Papago Indians near the Indian village of Pepick when Arthur Muncy rode by at sunset. Voolo said to Keokun, "I will follow you and kill you," meaning Muncy. Pierka and Voolo went into the brush with Keokun close behind, and Keokun asked Voolo what he meant by the remark. Voolo replied, "It has been my desire to do an act of that kind for a long time." Pierka then scolded Voolo: "You have wasted all your ammunition," and Voolo replied, "Well, let us go and get some at an Indian house." Pierka said the Indian would not give them ammunition but Voolo said he would tell him they were going to shoot crows.

However, they decided not to go for the ammunition and Keokun, at Voolo's request, went to Juan Largo's pasture and got their horses. The three Indians caught up with Muncy and rode along with him a short distance, Pierka speaking in Spanish, which Muncy spoke also. Muncy told them he had come up from Tucson on the stagecoach, got off at old Casa Grande, and was going to Phoenix. Voolo and Pierka watched for a chance to knock Muncy off his horse, where they could kill him with a rock or stick, but the opportunity never arose. Muncy stopped where a party of whites was camped, so the three Indians continued ahead to a place where they thought they could ambush Muncy, and then Keokun counseled against the plan.

When Muncy did not appear the Indians rode to their homes and on the way Voolo said they would track Muncy the next day; but in the morning Keokun refused to go. Voolo and Pierka followed the road toward Saccaton and passed the wagons where Muncy had stopped the previous evening. They then started looking for Muncy's tracks. They could not find his trail, so they crossed the river and found the trail heading for Santana Village. They started for that place when they saw Muncy coming toward them; but he appeared asleep in his saddle so they hurried ahead to Sweetwater, a place they thought would be good for an ambush. They chose a large bush to hide behind and waited for Muncy to appear; but when he came into view they decided it was not a good place and let him pass, then continued ahead again. The two Indians saw a dust cloud on the road so they hid. Soon Doctor Ernest of the Pima Agency met Muncy, and they stopped to talk. They dismounted and, when the doctor rode on, Muncy laid down to smoke and relax. Voolo said, "Let me shoot," but Muncy was standing sideways and it was not a favorable shot.

Muncy finally mounted and continued on with the two Indians still stalking him. Finally Voolo told Pierka to ride up beside Muncy to distract him and, just as Pierka came abreast of Muncy, Voolo shot him in the back. Muncy fell from his horse and was lying on the road talking very excitedly, so Pierka said, "You didn't wound him very badly." Voolo replied, "Why don't you dispatch him." Pierka said, "I am not doing that business," and while the Indians were arguing Muncy arose and walked toward Casa Blanca. The Indians became frightened and fled, and the next day Muncy's body was found.

The three Indians were arrested but Keokun had not been involved in the killing and was released, and Pierka turned state's evidence, so both Keokun and Pierka testified against Voolo. The trial lasted two days. On November 23 Voolo was found guilty of first degree murder and on November 29 Judge Charles Silent sentenced Voolo to hang on January 14, 1881. There was no delay in carrying out the sentence of death for Voolo.

The scaffold was erected south of town, a sturdy affair built of large beams. The condemned man showed no fear during his confinement and marched to the gallows resigned to his fate. He took his place on the trapdoor, where his limbs were pinioned, the black cap was pulled on, and the noose adjusted with the greatest efficiency. In a moment the trap was sprung and, after the body had hung a sufficient time to ensure that he could not be resuscitated, the remains were cut down and given to members of his tribe for burial. Later that day the gallows was carefully disassembled and stored away for later use.

Globe (AZ) Arizona Silver Belt: January 16, 1881; *Tucson (AZ) Daily Citizen*: January 16, 1881; *Phoenix (AZ) Herald*: November 15, 1880; December 4, 1880; January 15, 1881; *Pinal City (AZ) Pinal Drill*: December 4, 1880.

Esicio, Miguel
May 20, 1881

Jesus Corrales operated a store from his house on the west side of Florence in Pinal County, Arizona. He stocked a number of items of interest to the Mexican population, and patrons could order liquor over the counter by the bottle or glass. On the morning of August 29, 1880, Miguel Esicio came to the store at 9:00 A.M. and started drinking whiskey; by early afternoon he was joined by William Gray and his sister Agnes. Esicio did not appear intoxicated when he invited Gray to join him for a drink several times during the day, and Gray gladly accommodated the friendly Mexican. Just before 4:00 P.M. Esicio was joined by his Mexican friend Nevis Montaño, but in a short time Esicio shouted out, "Don't try to make a fool of me." Corrales immediately intervened and told them that if they were going to quarrel they must go outside. They left with Gray following closely behind, and before the quarrel could continue Gray stepped between them saying, "It's no use quarreling."

The two men turned and started walking away from each other while Gray returned to the house. Montaño, after taking only a few steps, turned toward the house and looked toward Gray, who stood in the doorway next to his sister. Esicio had also taken only a few steps when he whirled, pulled his pistol and, without warning or hesitation, shot at Montaño once. The bullet entered Montaño's right side under his arm and went into his chest but did not exit. He fell mortally wounded and bled to death in a few minutes. Esicio then aimed at Gray and fired once, the bullet striking the heel of his boot as his sister, seeing his predicament, pulled him onto his back inside the house. Corrales, gun in hand, rushed out and got the drop on Esicio, disarmed him, and marched him to jail.

A doctor was called but Montaño was already dead when he arrived. Esicio's trial commenced in Judge Charles Silent's courtroom at the November term. He was convicted of first degree murder and sentenced to hang on January 14, 1881. However, a stay was granted while an appeal was before the supreme court; the appeal was denied, and Justice Stillwell set the day of execution at May 20, 1881.

Esicio was disliked by the Mexicans in Florence because he was a large powerful man — six feet tall and weighing over two hundred pounds — and he bullied his countrymen. He often said the Americans were his only friends, but he said he wanted everyone to turn out to see how bravely he died. He was pleased when five hundred persons attended, including a number of Indians from the reservation and a large number of Mexican residents. The same scaffold on which Voolo had been hanged four months earlier had been erected on the same spot south of town. On Friday, May 20, 1881, Miguel Esicio was taken from the jail and conducted to the scaffold. He took his place on the trapdoor, where his wrists and arms, knees and ankles were pinioned, the black cap pulled over his eyes, and the noose adjusted. In but a moment the trap was sprung and he fell to his death, not disappointing those who came to see that he died "game." He hung for several minutes after the attending physician pronounced him dead and then he was lowered into the casket provided by the county and buried that evening.

Tucson (AZ) Daily Citizen: December 2, 1880; *Prescott (AZ) Miner:* May 21, 1881; *Phoenix (AZ) Herald*: May 21, 1881.

Harper, Thomas
July 8, 1881

Thomas Harper settled near Tombstone, Cochise County, Arizona, during the boom period, ran with the "cowboys," and became a particular friend of Curly Bill Brocius. One day Harper mentioned he was going to Huachuca and a man named John Talliday asked him to collect a debt. Harper obliged but then spent the money. Talliday was enraged and on September 18, 1880, he confronted Harper at Ramsey's Canyon in the Huachuca Mountains. Talliday demanded the money Harper had collected but Harper, who was offended by Talliday's tone, shot him and Talliday died on the spot. Harper was arrested, jailed at Tucson, and indicted by the Pima County grand jury. He was tried, found guilty of murder in the first degree, and sentenced to hang on July 8, 1881. The condemned man had been hoping that something might intervene to prevent, or at least postpone, his impending doom; but the Thursday evening before his execution a telegram arrived from acting governor John J. Gosper, who refused to interfere and ordered that the execution proceed.

As Harper began to prepare for his death Father Antonia ministered to his religious needs, and he finally became reconciled to his fate. On the fatal day two hundred people gathered at the gallows by 2:15 P.M. when the prisoner was escorted to the scaffold and seated in a chair. The death warrant was read and other formalities completed and the prisoner then arose, removed his hat, and was positioned on the trapdoor. He said, "Good-bye to the United States," and then shook hands with the undersheriff, saying, "Boy, I always liked you." Next Father Antonia offered a prayer and shook hands with the prisoner. Harper insisted on placing the rope on his own neck but Sheriff Robert Paul changed it, and the prisoner said, "That won't do, that's wrong." The prisoner made a change but the sheriff changed it back and Harper's arms and legs were immediately strapped by the sheriff, undersheriff and chief of police to prevent further interference. Harper exclaimed, "Boys, well here goes." Anticipating the drop, he lurched forward, but he was steadied by the sheriff and Father Antonia, who distracted him by speaking in an undertone. Harper smiled as the sheriff pulled the black cap over his head and complained, "I have something to say before I die," but he was not given the opportunity to speak. The spring release was touched by the sheriff at 2:30 P.M. and the body fell with a dull thud. Harper died without a struggle, his neck broken. After he was pronounced dead by the attending physicians he hung a while longer before being cut down and deposited in the coffin provided by the county. He was buried before sundown.

Prescott (AZ) Daily Miner: July 9, 1881; *Phoenix (AZ) Herald*: July 9, 1881; *Phoenix (AZ) Gazette*: July 14, 1881.

Berry, John W.
February 3, 1882

On April 21, 1881, the body of Michael P. "Old Tex" Shores was found in an early state of decomposition along the trail seven miles from Tiptop, Yavapai County, Arizona, where his ranch was located. The murderer had shot Shores from behind on the previous day, the bullet entering left of the spine and exiting at the left nipple. The motive was robbery as Shores was known to have a number of gold pieces on his person; they were not with the body, and the bridle from his horse had also been stolen. The murderer, after committing the deed, fled southward, taking to the rocks and horse ranges to make it impossible to follow his trail. An inquest revealed that Shores had been killed with a .44 caliber bullet fired by a man of full height on horseback, judging by the point of entry and exit.

Shores was a cautious man who would not let his guard down unless he was familiar with his attacker, and suspicion fell upon an old friend named John W. Berry. Berry had been a former employee of the Tiptop Company but recently had a disagreement with the mine's manager and left. In addition, Berry carried a .44 caliber six-shooter. Berry was arrested in Phoenix and charged with possession of a saddle claimed by a man at Frog Tanks; he also had in his possession the bridle belonging to Shores. For want of evidence he was discharged on the theft charge, but was immediately arrested by deputy sheriff M. Rodgers of Phoenix and charged with murdering Shores. Berry was taken to Prescott and at his examination he was held over for action by the grand jury, indicted, tried and convicted of first degree murder. The evidence was wholly circumstantial but "so well connected link by link that it proved beyond a reasonable doubt that Berry was the man who had committed the murder." Berry was sentenced to hang on February 3, 1882, and neither appeal nor application for executive clemency would delay the proceedings.

When the fatal day arrived a large crowd assembled in and around the jail yard an hour before the execution. A few minutes before the scheduled time, Berry was taken from his cell and driven to the scene of his execution in a barouche. Forty-year-old Berry, neatly dressed in a dark suit, white shirt, collar, and black necktie, was led to the gallows by Father Duraches, who had attended to the prisoner's religious needs for several days. Following were Sheriff Joseph R. Walker, deputies Long, Herbert, St. James, and Mulvenon and deputy marshal Dodson. On reaching the scaffold Berry ascended the stairs with a firm step and took his place in front of the trapdoor. Deputy sheriff Herbert read the death warrant in a solemn tone, during which time Berry showed no sign of wavering. When the reading concluded Berry was placed on the trapdoor by the sheriff and a glass of whiskey was provided. As the officers were binding his limbs he turned to the sheriff and requested that the business be done quickly as possible, and these were the only words spoken before the black cap was pulled on and the noose adjusted. At 12:08 P.M. the trap, which worked with a lever, was sprung and Berry dropped six feet. His neck was broken by the fall and, except for a slight contraction of the muscles, no movement was perceptible. At 12:24 P.M. Berry was pronounced dead; the body was cut down, placed in a rough pine coffin, and given to the city undertaker for burial.

Prescott (AZ) Miner: April 1, 1881; February 3, 1882.

Hall, William H.
February 10, 1882

On the morning of September 24, 1881, several men were drinking and carousing in Prescott, Yavapai County, Arizona. At 7:00 A.M. they went to H.J. Bishop's store and saloon to continue their spree, but Bishop refused to admit them. Without warning someone in the party shot at Bishop, wounding him. Bishop fired three shots in self-defense and wounded two men, one named William H. Hall and the other a man named McBride. After wounding the two men Bishop dropped to the floor and bled to death. McBride was wounded by two bullets, one in his arm and the other in his shoulder, while Hall was seriously wounded by one bullet.

Hall and McBride were believed to have fired the shots killing Bishop, but it was thought they would die of their wounds. When both men survived the matter was investigated and evidence proved that Hall had fired both shots which killed Bishop, while McBride had been an innocent bystander who happened by Bishop's Saloon at the same time as the revelers. Hall was indicted, tried and convicted of first degree murder at the fall term of the district court and sentenced to hang at Prescott on February 10, 1882.

On Friday, by invitation of the condemned man, representatives of the press were present at 11:30 A.M. for the reading of the death warrant by Sheriff Joseph R. Walker. Immediately afterward the procession formed and Hall was marched out, and at 11:52 the condemned man ascended the scaffold, knelt at the rear of the platform, and silently prayed. When he arose he requested that the reporters come forward and report what he had to say, and as he talked his limbs were pinioned. He spoke as follows:

> I wish to return thanks to my Attorney Charles B. Rush, and my heartfelt thanks to those who have extended to me kindness. I forgive those who have ever in anyway wronged me, and hope God will also forgive them. I had no ill feelings against Bishop. He was my friend and I have been convicted through malice. I have not the language at my command with which to properly express my thanks to Mr. C.B. Rush. I forgive everybody in this world and hope God will forgive us all. At best life is short, and it is but a little while until we all will be on the other shore.

The prisoner shook hands with those on the scaffold and Colonel Bigelow, who was reporting for the *Democrat*, asked him his real name as it was understood Hall was an alias. He replied that he had left it with his attorney, who would attend to it, and then to the colonel he made his last remarks on earth, which were, "Good-bye, old boy." At this moment the black cap was drawn over his face, the noose adjusted, and the spring immediately activated. Hall fell, dislocating his neck between the two upper vertebrae, and after eleven minutes he was pronounced dead by Drs. Ainsworth and McCandless. Hall was left hanging one additional minute and was then cut down, placed in the coffin provided by the county, and buried in the local Catholic cemetery. The condemned man had claimed that his real name was H.H. Hill and that he had assumed the alias because, during his lifetime, he had killed eighteen men. But his confession, in which he named his victims, was made to a priest so the details could not be published.

Prescott (AZ) Daily Miner: September 27, 1881; February 10, 1882; *Phoenix (AZ) Herald*: February 10, 1882.

Dandy Jim; Dead Shot; Skippy
March 3, 1882

A lesser medicine man of the White Mountain Apache tribe suddenly rose to prominence. Nock-ay-dit-klin-na, who was but five feet six inches tall and weighed one hundred twenty-five pounds and with a ghostly complexion, attended a school where he was exposed to various precepts of the Christian religion. Upon his return, he became the center of Apache revivalist gatherings during which he taught his followers a new and peculiar dance which incorporated the sacred pollen of the tule plant, called hoddentin. He preached resurrection of the dead and expulsion of whites from what was formerly an Apache domain, and promised better times for Indians in all respects.

The "Prophet" first held his gathering some distance from Fort Apache but by mid-summer of 1881 he moved to Carrizo Creek, only eighteen miles above the fort. After troops reconnoitered the gathering the Prophet moved further away, choosing Cibecue, which was forty-six miles from the fort. There was a great deal of concern among the military and settlers that these gatherings were a precursor to war, so twice the Prophet was summoned to attend a meeting, once by the Indian agent and once by General Carr; twice he ignored the order. Finally, on August 15, Indian agent J.C. Tiffany telegraphed the general that he wanted the Prophet "arrested or killed or both."

After considerable discussion, General Carr, on August 29, left Fort Apache for Cibecue with five officers, a surgeon, seventy-nine soldiers, a guide, an interpreter with five assistants, the general's fifteen year old son, nine civilians, and twenty-three Indian scouts. Midday of August 30 the force of one hundred thirty-nine men entered the Cibecue Valley and rode directly to the Prophet's wickiup, took him prisoner, and then retreated across Cibecue Creek, where they prepared to camp. Several times groups of Indians approached and each time they were turned back. Finally all the troops had gathered at the preselected site when one of the scouts suggested that there were too many anthills for a camp. When told to go beyond the anthills and find another site, twenty-two scouts lowered their weapons and began firing at the troops. The sergeant of scouts, Dead Shot, signaled with war whoops. Privates John Sonderegger and Edward D. Livingstone were killed by unknown Indians and Captain E.C. Hentig was killed by Dandy Jim. Half the herd of horses and mules were driven off as the remainder of the Indians took to the brush and continued the fusillade, which killed Privates William Miller and John Sullivan and wounded three others, two of whom died later. The Prophet tried to flee and was shot but not killed, and when he continued his efforts to escape he was hacked to death with an ax. The dead soldiers were buried beneath the general's tent and the remainder of the troop returned to Fort Apache two days later following a grueling march led by Sergeant Mose, the only Indian scout who remained loyal.

It was estimated that eighteen Indians had been killed, including six of the treacherous scouts, and all of the Indians scattered, with most of the mutinous scouts fleeing into Mexico. Some guilty Indians tried to quietly return to their families, including Dead Shot, Dandy Jim, Skippy and two others known by their numbers. These five Indians were arrested, lodged in the guardhouse at Fort Apache, and tried by a military commission. The two Indians known by their numbers were sent to Alcatraz, while the three mutinous scouts were sentenced to hang, which was approved by President Chester A. Arthur, who set the date at March 3, 1882. Upon receipt of the sentence and the president's endorsement, every precaution was taken to prevent an escape or suicide. Each condemned prisoner was confined in a separate cell, which was securely locked, and they were only allowed out one at a time when they could be closely guarded. Notwithstanding the vigilance and precautions, Dandy Jim succeeded in separating his leg shackles three weeks before his execution and made a desperate attempt to escape; but he was fired on by the guard. After running five hundred yards he was wounded in the left arm, the effects of which still caused him suffering on the date of his execution.

On the morning of March 3, 1882, the three Indians ate sparingly of their breakfast and afterward were handcuffed, the first time since their confinement. At 12:20 P.M. the shrill note of the trumpet proclaimed that the hour for the execution was at hand and the troops assembled in front of their quarters, under arms, and marched to within twenty yards of the gallows. The orders detailing the sentences were read while the three condemned Indians looked out from their cell windows and then were conducted to the gallows. The platform was reached by stairs at the rear and the height from the ground was six feet, allowing for a four foot drop and two feet of clearance. The trapdoor was twelve feet long and the prisoners were aligned beneath the nooses, one soldier posted behind each Indian to steady him. The Indians' limbs were securely pinioned before they were told they could speak, and all gave much the same speech: that it was not right to hang them; the white man had given them good clothes and food, but now were going to take it all away from them; but they were satisfied to die as they would meet all their friends who had gone before them. Dead Shot added that he had suffered a good deal in this world but would be happy soon. The post chaplain offered a prayer for their souls and then the black caps were drawn over their faces, the nooses were adjusted, and at 1:05 P.M. the trap was sprung. After the bodies had hung ten minutes, the attending physicians felt for a pulse and pronounced them dead. Seven minutes afterward, the bodies were cut down, deposited in their coffins, and buried in the vicinity of the fort.

Tucson Arizona Weekly Star: March 9, 1882; *Virginia City (NV) Territorial Enterprise*: March 4, 1882; *Tombstone (AZ) Epitaph*: March 6, 1882; *Tucson (AZ) Weekly Citizen*: September 2, 1881; March 5, 1882.

Ah Jim; Ah Queen; Poh Ah Dock
December 28, 1883

Poh Ah Dock, a Chinese man, was charged with murdering another Chinese man in Graham County, Arizona, on June 9, 1883. He pled not guilty but produced no witnesses in his defense and waived written instructions for the jury. On November 19 the jury found him guilty of murder in the first degree and the judge read the sentence: "It is therefore ordered adjudged and decreed that the said Poh Ah Dock be remanded to the custody of the Sheriff of the County of Graham and be by him kept in close confinement until Friday the 28th day of December, A.D. 1883 on which said day between the hours of 8 o'clock and 10 o'clock A.M. you be hanged by the neck until you be dead, and may God have mercy on your soul."

The trial of Ah Jim and Ah Queen commenced the following day in Graham County, Arizona, and the two Chinese men were charged with murdering a fellow countryman on May 2, 1883. Their trial lasted one day and they were found guilty of murder in the first degree. Both defendants were sentenced to hang on December 28 in the company of Poh Ah Dock. Neither appeal nor application to Governor Frederick A. Tritle for executive clemency delayed the proceedings.

On Friday, December 28, the only three Chinese men hanged in the Arizona Territory were "swung into eternity."

Phoenix Arizona Gazette: March 2, 1882.

Delaney, William; Dowd, Daniel; Howard, James; Kelly, John C.; Sample, Omer W.
March 28, 1884

Just past 7:00 P.M. on December 8, 1883, five men rode into the small mining town of Bisbee in Cochise County, Arizona. They walked to the store of Goldwater & A.A. Castaneda and, while two men remained outside the store to watch the street, three men entered. Inside was the owner's wife and six patrons making their final transactions before the store closed. The three robbers, with guns drawn, forced Joseph Goldwater to hand over the money in the cash drawer. The robbers then searched the living quarters of Jose Maria Castaneda, who was confined to his sickbed, and they found his money and watch beneath his pillow. They opened the safe expecting to find the payroll for the Copper Queen Mine but were disappointed when they learned it had not yet arrived by stagecoach.

Outside, J.C. Tappenier, assayer at the Copper Queen Mine, and D.T. Smith, a well known rancher on the San Pedro River, were walking toward the store when the two robbers posted outside each fired a single round from their Winchester rifles. Tappenier fell with his head inside the Bon Ton Saloon while Smith fell but a short distance from Tappenier, both dead, as each man had been shot in the head. At the sound of gunfire the town's people began to run toward the scene or peeked out of their windows. As the town's citizens converged on the store, the two lookouts panicked and began shooting indiscriminately at any movement. J.A. Nolly was shot in the breast and lingered a few hours before expiring, while Mrs. R.H. Roberts, a young pregnant woman, peered out of her door and was shot through the spine, dying a short time later and bringing the death toll to four persons.

The murderers completed their robbery within minutes and, once the shooting started, they hurried out of Bisbee with $3,000 and two gold watches. Rewards were posted of $1,500 for each man "dead or alive," and posses were formed. Deputy sheriff William Daniels was put in charge of the investigation and he led the pursuit of the murderers. Texas-born John Heith was a dance hall and saloon keeper at Bisbee and he and another man were hired as trackers; but Heith led the posse in circles and during the time he was with the posse suspicion began to form. Heith and the other tracker trailed the murderers as far as Soldier's Hole but then returned to Tombstone, where both men were arrested at gunpoint and lodged in Tombstone's jail. As soon as Heith was behind bars he informed on his fellow conspirators and named the five perpetrators of the "Bisbee massacre"—William E. Delaney, Daniel Dowd, James Howard, John Kelly, and Omer Sample. Flyers were distributed announcing the names, descriptions, and rewards and these circulars were translated into Spanish and distributed below the border. At the preliminary examination Heith was held to answer to the grand jury, while the other prisoner was cleared and released.

After leaving Bisbee the five murderers proceeded eastward until they reached Soldier's Hole, where they divided their booty. Dowd and Delaney went south into Sonora, Mexico, while Howard, Kelly and Sample turned north for Clifton. While passing through the Chiricahua mountains, Howard, Kelly and Sample were mistaken for a gang of train robbers and chased by a posse, but they escaped in a terrible snowstorm. Kelly then left Howard and Sample at the railroad line and stole a ride on a freight train bound for Deming, New Mexico. He grew his beard and let his general appearance deteriorate, hoping to pass as a tramp; but at Deming Kelly went to the barber shop. Barber Augustin Salas, upon shaving his brushy client, immediately identified him as a wanted man and held him with a razor at his throat while a lawman was summoned. Kelly was arrested on suspicion of being a train robber; but soon he was on his way to Tombstone in irons and was turned over to sheriff Jerome L. Ward on December 11.

Sample and Howard continued to Clifton, where they told W.W. Bush, the night bartender at George Hill's Saloon, that they decided to go to Happy Jack's about thirty-five miles above Clifton, "where they would get a crowd together to return and serve Clifton the same as Bisbee." Deputy sheriff John Hovey was told of the plan and, with deputy sheriff A.G. Hill, made preparations to pursue and capture the murderers. The deputies found Nicolas Olguin ready for duty with a force of thirteen Mexicans and on Friday morning the posse, numbering nineteen men, headed north. A short distance beyond Arnold's Ranch a lookout with field glasses signaled that someone was approaching from behind, so the posse laid an ambush; when the man drew near, he was recognized as Howard. He was within a few yards of the ambush before he discovered the muzzles of eighteen rifles pointed at him and heard the command "throw up your hands." He recognized familiar faces and remarked, "I don't propose to walk into anybody's graveyard!" The officers realized that Howard had gone around the mountain so he would make a fresh trail, and believed that Sample could not be far ahead.

The next morning the posse continued following the Blue for three miles where the trail turned into a narrow crevice in the mountains to the left, not wide enough for two men to ride abreast. At the bottom of this box canyon was a stream of water and it was decided to proceed on foot, so Olguin proposed that his men ascend the gorge and soon the band of Mexicans was wading up the canyon. At a distance of three miles the canyon widened to a width of fifty yards and, just before it opened onto a mesa, they came upon Sample's camp. Rifles were leveled and Sample, who was busy cleaning a revolver and two rifles with not a single cartridge in any weapon, had to surrender or die. Olguin's men took their prisoner to join the remainder of the posse and the march to Clifton began.

When Dowd and Delaney left their three companions at Soldier's Hole they turned south into Sonora, Mexico, and traveled together as far south as Bavispe, where Dowd left for Janos while Delaney went to Magdalena where he assumed the alias Summers and sought work. He was directed to the town of Minas Prietas where many Total Wreck miners were working, but he was recognized so the mine superintendent gave him a job to detain him until he could be arrested. Deputy sheriff Daniels, meanwhile, was on their trail and arrived at Bavispe one hour after Dowd had left for Janos, so, with Delaney detained at the mine, Daniels followed Dowd. At Janos the deputy found that Dowd had gone on to Corralitos, so he followed, and with help from the superintendent of mines he arrested Dowd on New Year's Day. They drove their prisoner to the San Jose station on the Mexican Central Railroad, a distance of one hundred ten miles from Corralitos, locked Dowd in an express car, and brought him onto American soil without the formalities of extradition. Daniels then arrested Delaney on January 15 and also returned him to American soil without the formalities of an extradition.

With all six prisoners jailed, the grand jury indicted them on February 8 and their trial commenced immediately; three days later all six men were convicted of murder. On February 19 the five Bisbee murderers convicted of first degree murder were sentenced to hang but John Heith had been found guilty of second degree murder only and on March 21 Judge D.H. Pinney sentenced him to serve life in prison. The citizens were angered by the lenient sentence given to Heith, as men sentenced to serve life terms often served less time in prison than those sentenced to a term of years; also, pardons had been granted wholesale over the previous decade. At an early hour on the day following sentencing a mob of one hundred men, principally miners from Contention and the Grand Central Mines, went to the courthouse and entered the jail. Jailer Billy Ward, thinking it was the prisoners' breakfast being delivered, opened the door without checking and was taken prisoner. Heith's cell was opened and his shackles removed, and he was taken out to the waiting mob, which drove their prisoner down Toughnut Street at a run until they reached a certain telegraph pole. Heith requested that someone tie a handkerchief over his eyes and pleaded that they not shoot nor mutilate his body after he was hung. His hands were tied, the noose was positioned, and he was pulled up to his death; he hung for quite a while before he was cut down and delivered to the county coroner. The coroner's jury, following the inquest, found as follows: "We, the jury, find that John Heath [*sic*] came to his death from emphysema of the lungs, a disease very common at high altitudes. In this case the disease was superintended by strangulation, self-inflicted or otherwise."

On March 27 the scaffold was tested and pronounced to be one of the strongest and surest ever erected in the territory. The platform was eight feet above ground, twenty-four feet long and fourteen feet wide with a five foot drop, leaving three feet of clearance. The doomed men slept well that final night and arose the next morning in good spirits. Their morning was occupied in shaving and dressing and then came the baptism of Howard and Sample, followed by their confessions to their spiritual advisers. The death warrant was read within the jail by Sheriff Jerome L. Ward, at the request of the prisoners, and before leaving their cells the five condemned men told reporters that they forgave all and hoped everybody would forgive them. Two thousand people witnessed the execution, one half being within the jail yard and the others on rooftops in the vicinity. At 1:00 P.M. precisely the five condemned men walked onto the scaffold and, when asked what they had to say, Sample spoke first, asserting he was an innocent man and that he wanted a Christian burial, and that Heith had been innocent. Howard and Dowd merely approved his remarks but Delaney added that, although in the last stage of life, if he had a fair trial he would not have been hanged, and Kelly expressed the wish to have his religious advisor care for his remains. Dowd, when the rope was being positioned, turned to the deputy and said, "[P]ull that tight," and as the black caps were pulled over their faces all cried out, "Good-bye!" The remarks of all five men occupied only three minutes and immediately afterwards, at 1:18 P.M., the trap was sprung. All but Dowd died without a struggle and his body only convulsed for several minutes. The physicians pronounced all five men dead at 1:26 P.M. and, upon examination, it was determined that Dowd's neck had not been broken and he had strangled to death. By 2:00 P.M. the bodies had been cut down and delivered to the morgue, where hundreds of curious citizens passed through to view the corpses. The following day the bodies were turned over to the Catholic church for burial.

Phoenix (AZ) Herald: December 10–11, 1883; December 15, 1883; December 20–22, 1883; *Tucson (AZ) Weekly Citizen*: March 29, 1884.

Casey, Joseph
April 15, 1884

On Saturday evening April 28, 1883, prisoners Joseph Casey and Harry St. Clair were cleaning the top of the cells in Tucson's jail when they discovered that a bar was loose in the grating leading to the corridor. Casey said they could pull the bar out and escape. The next morning before 9:00 A.M., while the jailor was in the yard, the jail guard was in the courthouse with trusties, and deputy Vosburg was asleep upstairs, the two prisoners pulled out the bar. St. Clair went first, with Casey next, and a Mexican prisoner followed closely behind. Casey went into the office and, while looking around for the keys to the "Oregon boot" (a restraint device that featured a heavy iron band locked above the ankle and connected to the wearer's boot by a pair of braces), discovered three pistols on a small cot. Casey handed St. Clair one of the pistols but he objected saying, "No, Casey! I do not want it. There may be some harm done, and I do not want any such thing. If you will make him throw up his hands I will buck and gag him as he comes in the door." Casey insisted, "No, Harry, you take one of them," and at just that moment they saw jailor Andrew W. Holbrook coming in with a small fire shovel in his hand.

Casey told him to raise his hands but instead the jailor raised the fire shovel and was about to strike Casey when he fired the first shot. Holbrook turned around and ran for the backdoor but Casey fired a second shot; when Casey turned around he found St. Clair was at the courthouse door asking the guard to come back into the jail. After the first shot was fired St. Clair threw his pistol on the floor, so Casey, after firing the second shot, picked up St. Clair's pistol and laid both pistols on a shelf. Casey then went back into the jail through the same hole he had come out, and a few moments later St. Clair and the Mexican prisoner followed. St. Clair said, "Casey, what did you do that for? I told you before we went out that I would not have anything to do with hurting anyone." Casey replied, "Harry, you do not think I intended to do what I did?" and St. Clair said, "No, Casey. I do not." Casey and St. Clair were indicted, tried in the Pima County court, and convicted of murder in the first degree. After sentencing Casey showed a defiant recklessness and made several more attempts to escape from the Tucson jail; but six days before his execution Casey gave a full confession, hoping the details would exonerate St. Clair, and he was successful.

On Tuesday, April 15, 1884, Joseph Casey was escorted to the scaffold after noon, attended by Sheriff Robert Paul, detective Len Harris, Sheriff Jerome Ward of Cochise County, and deputy Appel. While the preliminaries were being attended to, Casey, who was still seated, said "I want to make a few remarks. I did kill Mr. Holbrook, but I did it under the impulse of the moment. I had no intentions of killing him. I believe in all my life I never did anybody any bodily injury before, and did not mean to do it to him. I forgive everybody, and hope all forgive me. I want to make a statement in regard to Harry St. Clair. He had nothing to do with the shooting. He is a young man and I hope he will get out. He got no friends to help him. I hope you will do something for him. I die Catholic, and resign my body to the care of the jury." After Casey's comments he stood up and took his place on the trapdoor, and the leather bands were placed upon his wrists and ankles. As the noose was being drawn about his neck the condemned man said, "We all got to get here sometime, boys; we all have to get to the jumping off place." When the rope tightened on his neck he said, "Very uncomfortable necktie," and just as the black cap was being pulled on he called out, "Turn her loose; good-bye!" The trap was sprung at 1:07 P.M. and Casey fell, breaking his neck. After hanging a sufficient time he was pronounced dead, cut down, placed in the pine coffin provided by the county, and buried a few hours later.

Tucson Arizona Citizen: April 16, 1884; *Florence (AZ) Enterprise*: April 19, 1884.

Dilda, Dennis W.
February 5, 1886

Brothers H.W. and J.B. Williscraft came to the Walnut Creek area of Yavapai County, Arizona, and bought farm land. H.W. Williscraft bought out his brother's interest but learned that he could not handle the work alone and was looking for someone to take over the farming business when Dennis W. Dilda appeared. An arrangement was made and Dilda moved his wife and two children into the Williscraft house. Williscraft reserved one room in the large house in which he kept a trunk containing valuables, and he secured the room with a heavy padlock. Williscraft moved off the property but left "General Grant" Jenkins, who had been with Williscraft for years, as a general caretaker for the property.

Williscraft visited the farm in early December and found Jenkins gone, and Dilda said the old man had suddenly become tired of the place and just packed up and left. Williscraft also found the padlock pried off his reserved room, the trunk ransacked, and a gold watch and two pistols missing. Williscraft swore out a warrant with Sheriff William Mulvenon charging Dilda with the theft, and deputy sheriff John M. Murphy was assigned to serve the warrant. Murphy arrived at the ranch of Charley Behm, a neighbor of Dilda, midday Sunday, December 20, 1885. Murphy declined assistance and called at the Dilda house, returning several times during the afternoon; but each time Dilda was absent.

Shortly after dark Murphy went again, this time armed with Behm's "needle gun," and Dilda's wife said her husband had not yet returned. The moon was full and the sky clear so the deputy planned to take a vantage point to watch the house, but Dilda was lying in wait behind fence and when Murphy stepped through the gate he was shot from ambush. The bullet entered Murphy's back and exited the upper part of his left breast. Murphy, although he had received a mortal wound, turned around and fired one shot from Behm's gun, then took several steps toward Dilda before he fell to the ground and bled to death. Dilda dragged the body into the yard and folded it in two so it would fit in a gunny sack. He and his wife dragged the body through the house to the back bedroom, where a trapdoor led to a cellar, and dropped the body in. Dilda followed and buried the body three feet deep beneath the dirt floor, which took nearly the entire night. When Murphy did not return to Behm's home to retrieve his horse Behm became suspicious; the two shots he'd heard concerned him, so he sent Williscraft to investigate. He warned Williscraft to be careful, so when Dilda tried to lure Williscraft into rifle range he refused to cooperate. Williscraft returned the next morning and found evidence of the murder, so he called for the authorities.

Dilda had left on foot the morning after the murder, armed with his .30 caliber Remington rifle, Behm's needle gun, a .44 caliber revolver and cartridge belt; he also took along clothing and valuables belonging to Murphy. A party of men searched the Williscraft farm but found nothing until an Indian tracker noticed a wheelbarrow track from the house leading to a garden a hundred feet behind the house. The wheelbarrow had a heavy load going but no load on its return so they concentrated their search on the garden and found Jenkins' body buried four feet deep. He had been dead two weeks, killed by a ball from a musket which had torn off the top of his head; Dilda would confess later that he killed the old man while he was bending over the wash basin "because I was tired of having him around." The search intensified and the body of Murphy was then discovered buried in the basement. Sheriff Mulvenon organized a posse and was on Dilda's trail for two days before they came upon the fugitive sleeping under a tree near Ash Fork, got the drop on him, arrested him without resistance, and lodged him in the county jail at Prescott. A grand jury was impaneled, an indictment returned on two counts of first degree murder, a pleading made, trial held, a conviction returned, and sentence passed all in just forty hours after his capture. Dilda received the news of his hanging with the utmost composure and he declined to provide a full confession up to the moment of his death. His last comment on the subject was, "You know it would be natural for a man in my position, if he could tell anything that would benefit him, he would do so, but I have nothing to say."

Dilda's last night was restless and he arose at 8:00 A.M., and took a seat in the jail corridor. He refused to see the priest and at 8:30 A.M. his hair was cut and he was shaved by a barber, then he put on the new suit of clothes provided by the sheriff. At 9:00 A.M., after breakfast, he had his picture taken and two hours later the sheriff read the death warrant in the jail corridor, with newspaper reporters present. Dilda spent the morning smoking his pipe and pacing until 11:30 A.M. when the condemned man was brought from his cell and placed aboard a barouche. As Dilda came out of the jail he said to the crowd, "Good-bye, Boys!" and from that moment until he reached the scaffold the prisoner did not speak a word.

In the barouche was Sheriff Mulvenon, Sheriff Robert Stein of Mojave County, ex-sheriffs of Yavapai County Joseph R. Walker and Jacob Henkle, and Prescott's chief of police. The vehicle containing the prisoner was escorted from the courthouse to the scaffold by the Prescott Rifles and Prescott Grays militia units and at the gallows they formed a hollow square around the scaffold to keep the eight hundred men and a dozen women from crowding in. Once on the platform Dilda was asked if he had anything to say. He asked Sheriff Mulvenon to send his body to his wife in Phoenix. Dilda was directed onto the trapdoor and he asked for more whiskey, which was given to him while George Burton pinioned his ankles and knees. Dilda's wrists and arms were then strapped behind him by deputies M. Hickey and Burton, and Hickey pulled the black cap over the prisoner's head. The noose was adjusted by James Tackett, and Sheriff Mulvenon immediately pulled the lever springing the trap, just three minutes from the time Dilda stepped onto the trapdoor. Dr. Frank K. Ainsworth, the county physician, assisted by the post surgeon from Fort Whipple, monitored Dilda's vital signs and at the end of fifteen minutes he was pronounced dead. After hanging a few minutes more the body was cut down and placed in the coffin provided by the county and an examination revealed that Dilda's neck had been broken in the fall; the doctors insisted that his death had been instantaneous and painless. The body was driven to the cemetery by the undertaker and within a half hour Dilda was buried, to await the summons from his wife to have the remains sent to Phoenix.

Prescott (AZ) Weekly Miner: January 6, 1886; February 10, 1886.

Wilson, Frank
August 12, 1887

In the spring of 1886 Samuel Clevenger and his wife, Charlotta, with their adopted thirteen year old daughter, Jessie, left Graham County, Arizona, for the Washington Territory accompanied by hired hands John A. Johnson and Frank Wilson. The Clevengers had been farming near Fort Thomas but old age and the privations of frontier life convinced the Clevengers to sell out, move north, and retire. Samuel drove the wagon outfit with his wife riding inside while Wilson and Johnson, who had been with the Clevengers for several years, drove thirty head of horses which had been acquired as part of the payment for their farm. Jessie sometimes rode in the wagon with her mother and sometimes rode her horse. At night the Clevengers slept in a tent while Wilson and Johnson spread their bedrolls and slept under the stars. In addition to the horses, the wagon, and camping outfit, the Clevengers had a stock of saddles, pistols, rifles and shotguns, clothing and other merchandise, and $500 in currency.

The party traveled north and on May 19 they reached House Rock in the Buckskin Mountains, where they camped the night. Nearby, another party, taking the same trail toward Canab, Utah, had camped and among them was a man named McAlister, who would settle at Canab. The following day the Clevenger party struck out for Navajo Wells, the next watering place on the trail. They went into camp on May 20 at 4:00 P.M., still four miles south of the Yavapai County boundary, and the next morning Wilson and Johnson arose first and started a fire near the Clevenger's tent. Samuel arose next and, only partly dressed, came to sit by the fire, and Jessie soon came from the tent and started preparing breakfast. Charlotta had been feeling ill so she remained in the tent. Johnson went to a tree where the camp axe had been laid, carried it to where Samuel sat and, from behind, struck him on the head twice, one a fatal blow. Samuel fell forward into the fire, so Johnson pulled his body out of the flames. Jessie froze where she stood and watched Wilson who, upon seeing Samuel killed, took the axe from Johnson and rushed into the tent where Charlotta slept. Jessie heard her mother call out her name and in a moment heard her death groan.

Johnson and Wilson next went to a nearby cedar grove, buried the bodies in a common grave, and built a fire on top of the site to disguise it. They sorted through the wagon and discarded everything they could not use or sell. Wilson told Jessie to get into the wagon, then threatened to kill her if she mentioned the murders to anyone. That night Wilson slept with Jessie for the first time, and the murderers and captive continued on to Canab.

In January 1887 stockmen were searching for stray cattle at the summit of the Buckskin Mountains and discovered the ruins of a deserted camp; one hundred yards distant was a pile of ashes, burnt debris, and camp items strewn about. Upon investigating, the men were surprised to find a human arm protruding from the ground, so they sent for tools and carefully exposed the entire remains of two people. A coroner's jury was summoned from Canab, the nearest settlement, and they hastened to the spot to examine the remains. Samuel was found partially clothed, with two axe wounds to his head, while Charlotta, in her night clothes, had a single wound on her head resembling the back side of an axe. The bodies were buried in a single hole, one on top of the other; but the soil at the grave was alkaline and had preserved the facial features so well that one of the jurymen, the man named McAlister, immediately recognized the Clevengers. He recalled the two men and girl traveling with them, and Johnson and Wilson were immediately suspected and the coroner's jury charged them with the murders.

Sheriff William Mulvenon took a personal interest in the case and, after investigating at the scene and at Canab, learned that the guilty parties had continued on to Bullionville, Utah, where they divided the stock, money and merchandise. Johnson had gone to Pioche, Nevada, where he was cutting and hauling wood, until he learned that officers were looking for him. He then fled to Duckwater, Nevada. The sheriff found Johnson working on a farm and arrested him. Johnson told the sheriff that Wilson had taken the girl and his share of the plunder to Oakdale, Idaho. Johnson was lodged in the Canab jail to await the sheriff's return and Mulvenon continued on to Idaho, where he arrested Wilson and Jessie. While en route to the Yavapai County seat, he picked up Johnson from the jail at Canab. He took his three prisoners to Prescott, where the district court was then in session, and within a few days a grand jury indicted the two men, Jessie being held only as a witness.

The trial of Frank Wilson was scheduled for Monday, March 28, 1887, and he was convicted and sentenced to hang; and afterward Johnson was also convicted and sentenced to hang but he continued to insist that he was innocent. He claimed that he had been feeling ill and started on the trail ahead of the Clevenger party and when the party caught up with him it consisted of only Wilson and Jessie. He could not explain the absence of Samuel and Charlotta nor his lack of curiosity about their disappearance, nor could he explain his willingness to accept a share of the plunder. When it became clear to Wilson that he would die on the gallows he confessed, claiming sole responsibility for the murders and exonerating Johnson. An application for the commutation of Johnson's sentence was submitted to Governor C. Meyer Zulick, who agreed to interview the prisoners on the morning of their execution and said he would then make a decision.

Thursday night the men slept and ate well while the death watch maintained the utmost vigilance. Father Gobitosi and the Sisters of St. Joseph attended the condemned men and gave them what consolation they could. Jessie Clevenger and Wilson had a meeting during which Wilson wanted to kiss her, but she waved him away and accused him of lying in his confession. After Jessie left, Governor Zulick and Secretary Bayard went directly to the cells of the prisoners and the governor handed Sheriff Mulvenon the death warrant, which was read by Undersheriff Waddell, first to Wilson then to Johnson. At noon Wilson and Johnson were brought from their cells and Sheriff Mulvenon informed Johnson that he had been granted a respite until September 23 because Governor Zulick had not yet considered Wilson's confession. Johnson was nearly overcome with joy when told of his reprieve and warmly grasped Sheriff Mulvenon by the hand, then shook hands with Wilson and said, "[G]ood-bye and God bless you."

Wilson, supported by the sheriff and deputy Hickey, was taken to the jail yard, where he mounted the scaffold and, on being asked if he had anything to say, stepped forward and stated that his written confession was true; that Jessie Clevenger and Johnson were innocent of any connection with the crime; that he alone killed and buried the Clevengers. Bidding everyone good-bye he stepped onto the trapdoor and asked the sheriff to go on with his work; while the straps and noose were being adjusted Wilson smiled and nodded to several men he knew in the crowd. At 12:10 P.M. everything was in readiness and the trap was sprung. The prisoner's neck was broken by the fall. At 12:27 P.M. he was pronounced dead by Dr. Robinson and after being cut down the body was put into a plain coffin provided by the county and given to undertaker Randal.

John A. Johnson's sentence was commuted to life in prison for his part in the double murder and on December 11, 1887, he was registered as prisoner 499 at the territorial prison near Yuma.

Apache County (AZ) Critic: August 27, 1887; *Phoenix (AZ) Herald*: August 12, 1887; *Prescott (AZ) Morning Courier*: August 8, 1887; August 12, 1887; *St. Johns (AZ) Herald*: August 18, 1887.

Duran, Martin
March 3, 1888

Eighteen-year-old Martin Duran left home in July 1887 and moved to Flagstaff, Yavapai County, Arizona. He met and became hopelessly infatuated with Reyes Baca, a beautiful Mexican girl eighteen years of age who lived in Flagstaff. Duran convinced her to live with him as man and wife. This arrangement continued for two months when Baca, tired of their arrangement, moved into the house of a female friend north of town and began to show interest in another Mexican youth. On the evening of September 18 at 11:00 P.M. Duran invited several Mexican friends, among them a gifted guitarist, to accompany him to the new residence of Baca and serenade the ladies; he took with him whiskey to share with his friends. Baca and her friend had retired for the night but upon hearing the music arose, dressed, and joined the quartet in the front yard. At 2:00 A.M. the ladies invited the men inside and sent for beer. After all had drunk a little, Duran asked Baca to accompany him outside, where he tried, by various pleas, to convince her to again live with him. He became neither angry nor loud when she repeatedly rejected his proposals.

The couple returned to the house, where Duran went directly to the table and commenced writing; but when Baca passed close to the table Duran calmly arose, pulled a pistol from his waistband where it had been concealed, and sent a bullet through Baca's brain, killing her instantly. He then fired two more balls into her body before anyone could intervene. The murderer, still holding the pistol, walked out of the house and headed downtown while the men in the house rushed to find Constable Donahue, who found Duran at daybreak standing on Railroad Avenue. He was arrested and disarmed without incident but told Donahue that, had the constable arrived a few minutes later, he would have killed himself with the same pistol.

Duran was taken before justice of the peace Crothers for examination, held to answer to the grand jury, and remanded to the county jail at Prescott, where he arrived by train on the evening of September 20. Duran was indicted and tried on November 14 and he was found guilty of murder in the first degree. Duran's testimony showed that the homicide was cold-blooded, premeditated murder and his only defense was that Reyes Baca, the girl he loved, had "played him dirt."

On December 17, 1887, Judge Wright sentenced Duran to hang on January 20, 1888; Judge Wright was asked to appeal to Governor C. Meyer Zulick for clemency but he declined. As the date of execution approached an application was filed pleading for commutation of sentence, and acting governor J.A. Bayard granted a respite to February 24, 1888, extended to March 3. This additional time permitted Duran's friends to organize a concerted campaign to obtain clemency but Governor Zulick refused to intervene. Father Gobitosi tried everything to convince the governor to grant clemency or a reprieve but finally, at noon, the hour set for execution, the Father requested that Sheriff William Mulvenon allow a delay of forty minutes, which was granted. The condemned man, dressed in the new dark burial suit provided by the sheriff, was still confident that the governor would save him. However, when Father Gobitosi appeared robed in stole and surplice to hear his final confession and administer absolution, he finally gave up hope. Duran and Father Gobitosi retired to an adjoining cell and the ceremony of absolution so affected the Father that he was unable to accompany the condemned man to the scaffold, so Duran exited the cell alone.

Sheriff Mulvenon read the death warrant, which was translated into Spanish by Jesus Melendrez, and at 1:30 P.M. the procession started for the scaffold with the sheriff and Melendrez in the lead, followed by deputies Hickey and Burton supporting Duran. When the prisoner passed into the sunlight he said several times, "My God! This is tough!" Deputy Tackett waited atop the gallows and when Duran arrived he was positioned on the trapdoor. He was so limp that he had to be propped up while Tackett pinioned his wrists and ankles, and the sheriff then asked if the prisoner had any remarks. The condemned man made a brief speech in Spanish before repeating one last time, "My God! This is tough!" He asked that a silk handkerchief be tied around his neck so that the rope would not hurt him and, after this was done, the noose was carefully positioned. At that point in the proceedings Duran made a supreme effort to brace up as he said good-bye to all his friends and, with a ghastly smile, said, "I guess I will go asleep now." The black cap was pulled over his head and in a moment, at 1:37 P.M., the trap was sprung by the sheriff and Duran's body dropped six feet, breaking his neck. Drs. McCandless and Halsey of Prescott and Dr. Wells of Beatrice, Nebraska, were in attendance and they timed Duran's pulse. In eight minutes they pronounced him dead, but the body was allowed to hang four minutes longer before it was cut down and delivered to undertaker Randal for burial in the Catholic cemetery.

Prescott (AZ) Daily Miner: August 24, 1887; September 24, 1887; November 19, 1887; January 28, 1888; March 3, 1888; March 7, 1888; *Flagstaff Arizona Champion*: December 17, 1887.

Firimino
May 17, 1889

In June 1888 Firimino, a seventeen-year-old Papago Indian, was hunting with a Papago Indian named Quitola. They saw a white prospector named Ford riding quietly along the road, but Ford did not see the Indians. Firimino took careful aim and fired. The bullet knocked Ford from his horse but did not kill him, so Firimino crushed Ford's skull with rocks. Firimino and Quitola were soon identified, tracked down, and arrested. The two Indians were indicted, tried, and convicted at the fall term of the district court in Pima County, and Quitola was sentenced to serve twenty-five years at the territorial prison near Yuma where he registered as prisoner 531 on October 2, 1889. Firimino was sentenced to hang but three times he was granted a respite from Arizona's Governors C. Meyer Zulick and Lewis Wolfley. Finally, on May 16, 1889, Tucson's *Citizen* announced, "The scaffold upon which Firimino is to be hung has again been put up and is now in readiness for business. He will probably be hung about noon time tomorrow."

Precisely at 12:30 P.M. on Friday, May 17, deputy sheriff Charles Kresham approached the cell door and read the death warrant, to which Firimino listened with utmost attention. He had nothing to say, knew his hour had come, and had spent the last half hour looking out of his cell door at the inquisitive faces of the onlookers. At 1:00 P.M. the jail door swung open and Firimino, led by deputies Kresham and Moore and followed by Sheriff Matthew F. Shaw, appeared in the jail yard. The prisoner presented a rather neat appearance as, when asked how he would like to appear on the scaffold, the prisoner had stated that his idea would be to appear in a pair of new red-top boots. These were furnished him and "the poor fellow whilst standing upon death's trap could not refrain from casting an admiring glance at his cowhides." Firimino displayed not the slightest fear as he walked up the gallows stairs and, as he turned around to face the upturned faces, smiled as a photographer took his picture. When the noose was being placed upon his neck he bowed his head to accommodate the party adjusting the noose. At 1:02 P.M. the trap was sprung, and Firimino broke his neck in the fall. In thirteen minutes the attending physicians pronounced him dead, the body was cut down, and Firimino's remains were given to his Papago friends for burial, at his request.

Tucson Arizona Citizen: May 16–17, 1889; *Florence (AZ) Enterprise*: May 25, 1889.

Kah-dos-la; Nah-con-qui-say
December 8, 1889

On June 3, 1887, Gon-sha, As-ki-say-la-ha and Na-con-qui-say, Apache Indians, attacked and killed a cattleman named Deihl at his ranch between San Carlos and the San Pedro River in Pinal County, Arizona, and Gon-sha admitted at trial that he had "made a good shot" with his pistol before Deihl knew he was in danger. As-ki-say-la-ha and Na-con-qui-say denied shooting at Deihl, but cartridge casings showed there were three shots fired by three different weapons so they were also convicted. Gon-sha was sentenced to death, while As-ki-say-la-ha and Na-con-qui-say were sent to prison outside the territory. However, after serving a short term in prison the two Indians were released on a writ and returned to Arizona. Gon-sha was still in jail awaiting his execution when all three Indians were arrested, taken to Florence, and granted a new trial.

Kah-dos-la and Pah-ala-gos-za were among a group of Apaches who obtained a jug of whiskey from a Mexican and then refused to pay for it. A Mr. Jones happened along going to his ranch near Dudleyville and the Mexican asked him to arbitrate the matter. While talking with several of the Indians Kah-dos-la and Pah-ala-gos-za shot Jones from his saddle, so the Mexican mounted Jones' horse and fled. The Indians went into the reservation to hide among their people but, after some time and negotiations, they were brought to Florence and tried at the same term of court as the three murderers of Deihl. Kah-dos-la and Pah-ala-gos-za were convicted of first degree murder and sentenced to hang with the other three condemned Indians.

On Wednesday, December 6, interpreters were brought from San Carlos to translate the death warrants and after that ceremony was completed the condemned men were visited by Father Monfort, a Catholic priest, and several Sisters of St. Joseph. They helped the men prepare for their deaths and baptized two of the Indians, but old chief Gon-sha stated that he would die in the Indian faith. On Wednesday night the Indians retired as usual, singing songs until they were ready to sleep, then, in the Indian fashion, they pulled their blankets over their heads. At 2:00 A.M. one of the Indian prisoners announced that the old chief was dead and upon investigation it was found that not only had Gon-sha killed himself but that As-ki-say-la-ha and Pah-ala-gos-za had also accompanied him.

The three Indians had torn strips from their breech-clouts and tied them around their necks, making a secure knot by giving an extra twist so that when drawn tight the noose could not be loosened. The ends of the garrotes were then taken by the hands of the suicidal Indians and drawn tight with a sudden jerk, and strangulation followed. The coroner later determined that the Indians had been dead five hours, which placed the time of death at 10:00 P.M., or the time they first seemed to bed down. That left only Kah-dos-la and Na-con-qui-say to hang.

Notwithstanding the heavy rain clouds hovering low and a constant drizzle falling, fifty persons assembled in the jail yard at 7:00 A.M. In the jail a prayer was offered by the Rev. I.T. Whittemore, while Father Monfort read the sacrament and then Kah-dos-la and Na-con-qui-say, wrists bound, marched out of the jail and onto the low platform of the gallows and took their places beneath the dangling nooses. Their legs were pinioned and the nooses adjusted before they said good-bye to all present, and charged the interpreter to tell their relatives at San Carlos that they had joined the Catholic church and would go to heaven. The black caps were pulled over their faces and precisely at 7:30 A.M. the rope which supported the counterpoise weight was severed with a hatchet; it took a moment for the heavy weight to take up three feet of slack. Suddenly the two men were jerked up eight feet, their heads almost touching the beam above, and then fell back with a sharp rebound. "The counterpoise was charged with seventeen hundred pounds of quicksilver in iron flasks, to offset the weight of seven hundred pounds of aboriginal humanity, and a slack of thirty inches gave the weight a sufficient impetus to accomplish the desired result in the most expeditious and humane manner." The great weight had not been adjusted to accommodate the lower weight of only two Indians. Both of the Indians' necks were broken by the first jerk of the rope and nine minutes after the weight fell Na-con-qui-say was pronounced dead, and five minutes later the pulse of Kah-dos-la ceased. The bodies were cut down, placed in coffins provided by the county and buried in the Catholic cemetery.

Florence (AZ) Enterprise: December 7, 1889.

Nah-diez-az
December 27, 1889

On November 1, 1879, the Carlisle School, the first non-reservation Indian school, opened its doors in Carlisle, Pennsylvania. Many students came north from Apache tribes banished to Florida but others came east from the San Carlos Indian Reservation near Tucson, Arizona. Among the latter was a Pinal Indian boy of fourteen years named Nah-diez-az, an only child who had helped his father farm a small allotment of reservation land. Some of the students did poorly in this new environment, turning inward or becoming hostile, but Nah-diez-az appreciated the opportunity to improve his prospects. He was a good student and had done so well that he earned the sobriquet "the Carlisle Kid," and he excelled in any curriculum dealing with agricultural matters. The father of Nah-diez-az died while he was away at school and when his mother took ill he returned to care for her. As soon as he was home he began to prepare their plot for planting but during his absence a road had been surveyed, and it passed through the family plot.

On March 10, 1887, Frank Porter, the agency's farm supervisor, went to the wickiup of Nah-diez-az to inform him that he and his mother were going to be moved to another plot, one which was far inferior to the plot upon which his family had lived throughout his lifetime. Nah-diez-az argued against the move and when the discussion became heated Porter, fearing violence, fled to the agency and strapped on his six-shooter. He went to the post and asked Captain Francis E. Pierce, 6th Cavalry, for assistance and the captain assigned Lieutenant Seward Mott to accompany Porter. Mott also wore a sidearm but there was no fear of shooting as the Indians at San Carlos were not allowed to possess firearms, except for members of the agency's Indian police force.

Mott and Porter rode to the wickiup and when Nah-diez-az saw two armed men approaching to evict him, or worse, he rushed into his wickiup and dug out the old army Colt his father had hidden years before. The two men dismounted while Nah-diez-az was about this business, so when the Indian emerged from the wickiup he immediately took aim at Porter and, without warning or hesitation, fired one shot. The boy was not familiar with firearms and his shot missed Porter but hit Mott, mortally wounding the lieutenant. Mott collapsed and Porter, fearing for his life, mounted and rushed to the police-scout headquarters where he reported the shooting.

Al Sieber detailed agency policemen Mickey Free and Haskay-bay-nay-natyl, known as "Sergeant Kid," to bring in Nah-diez-az and they rode to the wickiup. The two Indian policemen were surprised when Nah-diez-az came out with one hand raised and the other holding the pistol by the barrel. They arrested the Indian and took the unconscious Mott back to the post, where Dr. T.B. Davis cared for the lieutenant; but the wound was too severe and Mott died the following day without regaining consciousness. Nah-diez-az was taken before federal judge W.W. Porter (no relation to Frank Porter) at the May term of the circuit court and the defendant explained all the details which led to the shooting, pled guilty, and asked for mercy from the court. The judge accepted the guilty plea, the explanation, and the plea for mercy into consideration and reduced the sentence from death to life imprisonment at the territorial prison near Yuma. Nah-diez-az was delivered to the territorial prison without incident but was soon transferred to the Illinois penitentiary, which was under contract to the federal government, to serve out the remainder of his term. Other Indians, convicted of lesser crimes at about the same time, were sent to a prison in Ohio.

The Indian Rights Association became concerned with the suffering of Indians in the Ohio penitentiary and filed a case on behalf of Captain Jack. When the supreme court issued a writ of habeas corpus it was interpreted as a pardon, so the Indians at the Ohio penitentiary and Nah-diez-az at the Illinois penitentiary were released and returned to the San Carlos reservation, arriving on May 25, 1889. The citizens of Arizona were angry at the release of the Indians and the military command at San Carlos was incredulous over the interpretation of the court's action as a pardon, especially for the murderer of Lieutenant Mott. The legal officer from the post, Lt. F.B. Fowler, appeared before Globe's justice of the peace and swore out a warrant for the arrest of Nah-diez-az, charging him with murder, and on June 5, 1889, the arrest warrant was delivered to Gila County's Sheriff Glenn Reynolds for service.

Once again Nah-diez-az surrendered without incident and had his preliminary hearing at Globe on June 21. He was held for trial at the October term of the territorial district court and seventeen Indian criminals soon joined him in jail. When the trial began for Nah-diez-az the prosecution called Frank Porter, F.B. Fowler, Al Sieber and Dr. Davis for the prosecution, but Nah-diez-az was the only witness for the defense and he offered the same explanation he had told two years earlier, describing his threatened relocation by the military and the difficulties he had experienced in keeping his small patch of ground. He insisted that Porter and Mott had come armed, intending to evict him by force, and he fired in self-defense; he testified that he had not intended to shoot Lt. Mott but had fired at Porter. Defense attorney Van Wagenen delivered a touching plea for mercy, emphasizing that Mott's death was more a tragedy than a murder; nevertheless, the jury convicted Nah-diez-az of first degree murder. On October 30, 1889, Judge J.H. Kibbey sentenced Nah-diez-az to hang on December 27, 1889. The prisoner, shocked at the death sentence, tried to interrupt the Judge, saying, "No! Me good Indian," but Sheriff Reynolds ordered him to be quiet so that the judge could finish the sentencing. Once back in the jail all the Indians discussed the various sentences they had received and Nah-diez-az, familiar with the conditions at the territorial prison near Yuma, stated that death was the more lenient sentence.

At 9:00 A.M. on the fatal day, Nah-diez-az was taken to the scaffold, a "twitch-up" affair with a heavy counterpoise weight wrapped with a chain and suspended by a rope. The weight was an ingot of copper from a local mine and the distance it was to drop had been carefully calculated. The condemned man "showed not the slightest trepidation, but joked with the deputy when pinioned and the noose was being placed." His last words to the sheriff, referring to his treatment at Globe and San Carlos, were, "Goodbye, Hell!" However, Sheriff Reynolds had not figured into his calculation the very light weight of the Indian and Nah-diez-az was jerked all the way up to the cross beam, crushing his skull. He was pronounced dead seven and one half minutes after the weight dropped, and the body was cut down after hanging only a few minutes more. He was deposited into the coffin provided by the county and buried next to the graves of two men lynched at Globe in August 1882.

Tucson Arizona Citizen: December 27, 1889.

El-chees-choos
July 11, 1890

On March 2, 1890, a freighter named Herbert was murdered six miles north of Fort

Thomas in Graham County, Arizona, by six Tonto Apache Indians. He was driving a wagon loaded with merchandise for Globe when attacked, and the Indians took his horses and burned his wagon, then disrupted the telegraph by cutting a pole and stealing a length of wire. As soon as a courier informed the men at Fort Thomas, Lieutenants Powhattan Clarke and James Watson led a detachment of troops to the place of the murder and recovered the body, which they sent back to the fort. They repaired the telegraph and then started in pursuit of the Indians, who had fled northward, and after a three hundred mile chase the troops cornered the hostiles in a cave. Both officers leaped to the front with the intent of gaining control of the entrance to the cave but Lieutenant Clarke encountered one of the Indians at the mouth of the cave and received a shot through his hat and one between his legs. Indian scout Rowdy shot the hostile Indian twice through the body, killing him and saving the life of Clarke. Another Indian was also killed during the skirmish but all the others were arrested and jailed.

The prisoners were confident they could prove an alibi, and all but one Indian, named El-chees-choos, proved an alibi and were released. El-chees-choos was indicted, tried and found guilty of murdering Herbert, and he was sentenced to hang on July 11, 1890. Jimmy Stevens and Marajildo Grijalva acted as interpreters for those who cared to talk with the condemned Indian, and Father Geldorf visited the prisoner several times, urging the necessity of spiritual preparation for the next world. However, all efforts were rejected by the condemned man, who said that "[N]o doubt your religion is good for this world, and if I was to remain in it I would be willing to become a Christian, but as my time is nearly up here below I can not see that any benefit could come to me now. I will see God himself and tell Him the whole story and, if He thinks I ought to go to hell, it will be all right."

El-chees-choos protested his innocence to the last and claimed that the two Indians who were killed by the troops at the cave were the assassins of Herbert, and that he was forced to accompany them, as they fled, at the point of a rifle. Whiskey was offered on that last morning, but the prisoner refused saying, "You people are trying to make fun of me. I know that I have to die today. I don't want any whiskey and don't want to be made fun of." Later he called for a watermelon, which was provided, and he spent his last hours playing cards with the other prisoners.

At 2:00 P.M. Sheriff William Whelan, with deputies Robertson, Solomon, and McCarty, entered the jail and read the death warrant. The procession formed and the party marched into the jail yard where the scaffold had been prepared. When they arrived El-chees-choos asked permission to smoke a cigarette, which was granted. He sat on the courthouse steps and told the twenty-five witnesses, through an interpreter, "[I]f you wished to keep Indians from killing white men you had better hang all the Indians." When he finished his cigarette he arose and walked alone to the platform and took his place beneath the noose. He began humming a song, which he kept up until the noose was adjusted and the black cap was drawn over his face. Deputy J.P. Robertson cut the rope restraining the counterpoise weight, it dropped, and suddenly El-chees-choos was jerked into the air. The condemned man hardly made a struggle and in fourteen minutes he was pronounced dead by attending physician Dr. A.H. Hoeffer. The body was then cut down, placed in the coffin provided, and buried that evening.

Florence (AZ) Enterprise: March 8, 1890; March 29, 1890; April 19, 1890; July 26, 1890.

Granada, Antonio
June 19, 1891

Antonio Granada had just reconciled with his wife and daughter from whom he had been separated for over five years. The family had been living together in Morenci, Graham County, Arizona, just four days when, on Monday, July 14, 1890, Granada called on deputy sheriff J.R. Smith and informed him that he had "a lot of fresh meat over at my house which I wish you to take care of." The deputy could not quite understand his meaning so he accompanied Granada to his home and found Mrs. Granada and their daughter lying dead on the ground, mutilated and covered with dirt and blood. Smith asked Granada why he had killed them and he answered, "[B]ecause they are mine." The citizens of Morenci heard of the tragedy and assembled for the purpose of lynching Granada, but deputy Smith lodged his prisoner in the Clifton jail. In Clifton Granada was further questioned by deputy Solomon. He said that he had killed his wife and daughter "in accordance with his ascribed duties of family life." Granada was indicted, tried and convicted of murder in the first degree, the jury rejecting the proposition that Granada was insane at the time he murdered his wife and daughter, and he was sentenced to hang.

While awaiting the fatal day, Granada read his Bible constantly, occasionally praying that he hang rather than serve a life of imprisonment in the territorial prison near Yuma. On Thursday a reprieve of ten days was received from Governor John N. Irwin for Frank Nelson, who was also to be hanged on Friday, so early on Friday morning it was decided to ask the governor for a like reprieve for Granada. A message was prepared and a messenger was started on horseback for Fort Thomas with instructions to secure relays of horses and return to Solomonville by 6 o'clock in the evening; but the messenger did not return, so, with everything prepared beforehand, Granada was led to the scaffold at 5:45 P.M. The condemned man was dressed in a neat black suit and smoked a cigar as he came from the jail, and displayed not the least sign of nervousness. He climbed the stairs to the platform and was positioned on the trapdoor, where his wrists and arms, ankles and knees were pinioned before he was asked if he had anything to say. He replied that he did not as "what has been done can not be undone." The black hood was pulled over his face and the noose positioned, and in the next moment deputy sheriff Charles Gooding sprang the trap. The drop was six feet and death was instantaneous, according to Dr. A.H. Hoeffer, and the attending physician pronounced him dead in twelve minutes. He was then cut down and placed in the coffin provided by the county. On Saturday a dispatch was received from Governor John N. Irwin respiting Granada for ten days but it was more than eighteen hours late.

Tucson Arizona Citizen: July 19, 1890; June 17, 1891; June 27, 1891.

Nelson, Frank
June 30, 1891

In July 1890 Frank Nelson, a twenty-seven-year-old Negro soldier in Company C of the 24th Infantry at Fort Grant, killed his mistress and her child and wounded another girl. The murders were committed in the presence of officers and men of Company C. Nelson was arrested, tried, convicted of first degree murder, and sentenced to hang. He confessed some of the circumstances before his death, saying, "It's true that I killed her because I was jealous of her and did not want her to leave me. I was aggravated and whiskey helped the aggravation.... I never had any trouble with anyone except only where this woman was concerned.... [S]he was the wife of a soldier in Company A, and she was a public woman." Nelson had been reprieved four times and had been scheduled to hang with Antonio Granada on June 19 when Governor John N. Irwin granted him a fifth respite. Nelson had a total of one hundred fifty-seven days respited but the governor refused to interfere further.

At 10:30 A.M. on June 30, 1891, Father Geldorf entered Nelson's cell and performed the ceremony of baptizing the condemned man into the faith of the Holy Catholic Church. The condemned man read the Lord's Prayer and repeated the Apostles' Creed in a clear voice. After the priest left, Nelson dressed himself in a neat suit of black, a white shirt, and a pair of slippers, and when asked how he felt, he said, "I am fully prepared to die. I feel that the great sin that I have committed has been forgiven.... I want to say, too, that Sheriff Olney and his brother Dan and all the deputies and jailers have treated me as well as any man can expect. They treated me good. So have all the good people of Solomonville, to all of whom I am going to return thanks to in my last words on the scaffold." He was then offered whiskey but he refused the drink, saying, "I am well braced and do not need any spirits. I am through with whiskey in this world."

At 3:00 P.M. Nelson was escorted into the jail yard where he ascended the scaffold and proceeded at once to address the witnesses, presenting a semireligious and advisory tone. He knelt and repeated the Lord's Prayer and arose with tears in his eyes, which he wiped away with jailor Goodwin's handkerchief. He took his position on the trapdoor and the straps were applied, the noose adjusted, and the black cap pulled over his face. The trap was sprung by Sheriff George A. Olney and in three minutes Nelson was pronounced dead, though he was kept hanging for twelve minutes more by order of Dr. A.H. Hoeffer. Nelson's body was then cut down and turned over to Father Geldorf, who buried him in the Catholic graveyard that evening.

Tucson Arizona Citizen: July 1, 1891. *Phoenix (AZ) Herald*: July 2, 1891.

Lashley, Philip
July 9, 1897

At 6:00 P.M. on April 19, 1896, Philip Lashley entered the officer's clubroom at Fort Huachuca, Cochise County, Arizona, and found John Sanders eating ice cream while talking with a young waitress named Maggie Jenkins. When Sanders finished his ice cream and was about to leave, Jenkins asked him to accompany her home and handed him a plate with ice cream and cakes for her mother; Sanders walked to the door to wait. Lashley was lying on a bed in the clubroom but, jealous that he had not been asked to accompany the young lady, he suddenly sprang to his feet and confronted Sanders. Before a word could be spoken Lashley pulled his revolver, pressed it against Sanders' breast, and pulled the trigger. However, it misfired and Sanders backed away, still holding the plate. Lashley pulled the trigger again but again it misfired, but on the third attempt the round exploded. Sanders fell to the ground and soon died from the wound. Lashley was arrested, jailed, indicted, tried, convicted of first degree murder, and sentenced to hang. He was held at the territorial prison, arriving on June 22, 1896, and registering as prisoner 1194. Various appeals were denied and the date for execution was finally set for April 9; but it then was delayed until Friday, July 9, 1897.

Lashley was returned to Tucson from Yuma in preparation for his execution and he tried to make "a sort of picnic occasion" of the event. During the entire morning Lashley exhibited the utmost unconcern, chatting freely with visitors and occasionally singing songs, but he was abusive to all the officials and declared he would die "game." The death warrant was read to him in his cell at 2:15 P.M. and an hour later he was led out by Sheriff Robert N. Leatherwood, accompanied by deputy marshal Compton. Lashley ascended the scaffold and made a long rambling speech filled with profanity, in part reading from notes, which occupied twenty minutes, which he had asked the sheriff to limit him to. He had refused all efforts at religious counsel and no clergymen were present. He then took his place on the trapdoor and his limbs were strapped. Throughout the entire ceremony he danced and sang, and when the black cap was pulled over his face he shouted, "Let her go, Gallagher!" The trap was sprung at 3:43 P.M. and his neck was broken in the fall. He was pronounced dead at 4:00 P.M. and the body was cut down a few minutes later. His remains were lowered directly into a coffin and given to the undertaker.

Prescott (AZ) Daily Miner-Journal: July 14, 1897.

Parker, Fleming
June 10, 1898

Fleming Parker and Jim "Harry" Williams worked for the Arizona Cattle Company near

Flagstaff, Arizona. They lived in Abe Thompson's cabin and enjoyed the thrilling life of the cowboy, but there was never enough money. They decided to rob a train and in December 1896 they burglarized two cabins and took two Winchester rifles, food, and several Selsor shirts which they cut into masks. They enlisted the help of Abe Thompson and Lovell "Love" Martin, and Parker sent them for ammunition and dynamite. Martin bought .40–60, .44 and .45 ammunition at Kingman, while Thompson got two sticks of dynamite in Peach Springs. Parker and Williams were each armed with one of the stolen Winchester rifles and Martin and Thompson gave them their six-shooters. On February 7, 1897, Martin and Thompson took fresh horses to Peach Springs and, according to the plan, they would be robbed of their fresh mounts while returning to their cabin.

On the bone chilling evening of February 8, 1897, Parker and Williams went to the rock cut eight miles east of Peach Springs near mile post 457 and at 7:15 P.M. captured night watchman Edward Allen. At 8:50 P.M. the passenger train appeared. Parker forced the watchman to flag the train and engineer Bill Daze stopped at the station. Daze asked Allen to explain but at that moment a masked Parker entered the cab of engine 85 of train no. 1 and took charge at gunpoint. The two robbers took the fireman, engineer and watchman to the rear of the express car, where the fireman uncoupled the remainder of the train; then Parker took the train men back to the engine while Williams remained on the rear platform of the express car. His job was to guard against interference from anyone in the passenger cars, so he fired five shots along the side of the train to keep the passengers inside.

Parker, once back in the engine cab, ordered Daze to pull the engine forward to Nelson's Siding two miles west and then fired one shot in the air, a signal to Williams that he was still in control of the engine. The express messenger had been alerted by the unscheduled stop and gunshots so he armed himself with a .45 caliber revolver and, with his assistant, jumped from the opposite side of the express car. They ran toward the rear of the train but when they came abreast of the rear platform they came face-to-face with Williams, armed with a Winchester rifle, a revolver, and two sticks of dynamite. The messenger did not hesitate but fired two shots in rapid succession. The first bullet struck Williams' breast just above his heart and passed through his body; and as the robber slumped the second bullet struck Williams in the left eye and exited at the back of his head, killing him instantly. The train was underway so when the two express men hesitated they missed their chance to board the rear platform and were left behind. The engine, tender, express and mail cars pulled ahead two miles to Nelson's Siding. Parker took watchman Allen to the mail and express cars and found the express unguarded. He then went into the mail car and waved aside mail clerk A.S. Grant at gunpoint, went through the registered mail, and took nine packages which looked as if they contained valuables.

Parker ordered the engineer to back the engine halfway toward the passenger cars, where he fired four shots in the air and looked north of the tracks, as if expecting someone; but there was no reply to his signal so the engineer was ordered to drive the engine back to Nelson's Siding where Parker said, "[G]et out of here as soon as God will let you," and observed, "I am short two men." However, Parker made no effort to find the missing men and walked off into the brush. Daze backed his engine to the passenger cars, coupled them to the mail car, and continued on to the next station, where the robbery was reported. The most substantial clue was the dead bandit lying on the rear platform of the mail car and he was soon identified as a former employee of the Arizona Cattle Company. In Peach Springs Thompson had gone to bed after sunset while Martin went up a hill to watch, but when no one appeared Martin went back into town. He found Thompson awake and learned that Parker and Williams had made a failure of it, and Williams had been killed. They returned to Thompson's cabin and were soon arrested. Martin was not a hard case so he quickly weakened and confessed, and on March 22 he wrote out his confession identifying Parker as the second train robber.

Sheriff George C. Ruffner of Yavapai County, with deputies Martin Buglin, Ed Riley and Tom Rogers, were soon on the track of Parker; Indian trailers were employed, as Parker had chosen the most rugged terrain in that part of the country for his escape. On Sunday afternoon Ruffner, with Buglin and Riley, fell back on their trail to butcher a beef while Rogers went ahead with the Indians. Rogers' party stumbled upon Parker, took him prisoner, and set up camp to await the arrival of the sheriff; but Parker suddenly seized upon a moment of laxity, grabbed a Winchester rifle and pointed it at Rogers. The deputy retreated and, when Parker fired one shot, the Indians scattered into the brush and circled around to look for the sheriff.

The next morning Sheriff Ruffner, with Deputies Buglin and Riley, started up Diamond Creek searching for Parker. The party had not gone far when they saw the fugitive coming down the canyon. They set up a crossfire ambush and waited and when Parker came abreast of Ruffner he called out, "Hands up!" Parker turned toward the sound, rifle at the ready, when the two deputies at his back repeated the same command. Parker looked over his shoulder and saw he was covered from both sides and, realizing that resistance was futile and probably fatal, complied with the order and surrendered his Winchester. The following day Parker arrived at Prescott and was lodged in jail. On February 24 he was taken before Justice J.M.W. Moore for his preliminary hearing and held for trial. On Sunday, May 9, 1897, Parker escaped from the county jail with forger L.C. Miller and Cornelia Asarta, a Mexican charged with attempted murder.

Lee Norris, the assistant district attorney, was wounded with a charge of bird shot while assisting jailor Meador in trying to prevent the escape. That evening Norris began hemorrhaging and he died just at midnight. Governor Benjamin J. Franklin issued a Proclamation of Reward in the amount of $500 each for Parker and Miller and $250 for Asarta. The county added to those rewards, and later Wells, Fargo & Company would offer an additional $1,000 for Parker. On Tuesday, May 18, L.C. Miller was captured at Jerome and on Wednesday, May 26, just at daybreak, Parker was captured eighty miles north of Flagstaff by S.S. Preston and ten Navajo Indians. Cornelia Asarta was never found and it was thought, from all the circumstances of the escape, that he died in the wilderness from the serious wound received while escaping, from an infection, or from starvation or exposure.

While Parker awaited his trial for murder Thompson was tried as an accessory to the train robbery, convicted, and on June 28 received a sentence of five and one half years to be served in the territorial prison near Yuma. Parker and Miller were granted separate trials and Miller was convicted of murder and sentenced to serve a life term. Parker was tried and convicted of murder in the first degree and sentenced to hang on August 14, but legal motions delayed the proceedings. After nearly a year of appeals the date for the execution was set for June 10, 1898.

On Wednesday, June 8, Parker was baptized into the Catholic church. On Thursday evening the prisoner asked for whiskey to stimulate him and he fell asleep at 4:00 A.M., but was soon awake. At 10:00 A.M. Sheriff Ruffner read the death warrant to Parker in his cell and twenty-five minutes later they began the march to the scaffold. The sheriff held Parker's left arm while deputy Jeff Davis held his right, and his priest and deputies J.P. Dillon, Pete Boscha, and ex-deputy Johnny Munds followed. As Parker emerged from the jail and saw the gallows he said, "Hold on boys, I want to look at this thing; I never looked at one before." Sheriff Ruffner permitted him to go under the scaffold and examine it, and he spent several minutes showing a special interest in the release mechanism for the trapdoor. The prisoner climbed the stairs and stepped heavily upon the trapdoor, as if to test its strength, and said, "I will set my feet right on these two nails," then took off his slippers. Sheriff Ruffner commenced buckling the straps around his legs and the prisoner said, "Take your time, George, there is no use in putting them on; I am not going to straddle out; you needn't worry." After Parker's arms and legs were pinioned he was told he could speak to the spectators and he said, "I have not much to say. I claim that I am getting something that ain't due me, but I guess every man who is about to be hanged says the same thing, so that don't cut no figure; whenever the people says I must go, I am one who can go, and make no kick." The black cap was then drawn over his face but he said, "Hold on, I want to shake hands with the boys." The cap was removed and he shook hands with all those on the scaffold, saying that he had no ill feelings toward anyone. After shaking hands with everyone he motioned to the jailor and shook hands with him a second time, holding his hand for a few seconds, and remarking, "It's all off; tell the boys [meaning those in the jail] that I died game and like a man." The black cap was again drawn over Parker's face and Dillon adjusted the noose while Sheriff Ruffner stood with his hand on the lever. Parker said to Dillon, "Don't get excited," and then to the sheriff, "George, you put her on." Dillon had the rope adjusted properly but the sheriff gave it a tug and at the same moment, at exactly 10:31 A.M., he sprang the trap and Parker dropped six feet. There were several convulsive twitches of the legs but these were the only motions perceptible as attending physicians Drs. E.W. Dutcher and J.R. Walls stepped forward and monitored Parker's vital signs. After eleven minutes Parker was pronounced dead and the body was cut down; an examination showed that Parker's neck had been broken in the fall. The body was at once removed to Logan's Undertaking Parlor where it was viewed by a large number of people during the afternoon, and at 4:00 P.M. Parker was buried in Potter's Field at the expense of the county. *Prescott (AZ) Journal Miner*: February 9, 1897; February 17, 1897; February 24, 1897; April 28, 1897; May 12, 1897; May 19, 1897; May 26, 1897; June 2, 1897; June 11, 1897; June 23, 1897; June 28, 1897; June 30, 1897; July 8, 1897; *Yuma (AZ) Sentinel*: May 15, 1897.

Smiley, George
January 8, 1900

In March 1899 a section foreman for the Santa Fe Railroad named McSweeney quit his job. One of the men who worked for McSweeney was track-walker George Smiley. Smiley had just completed eight hours work but when he demanded his pay he found a new man in the position of foreman and was told that Smiley had not done the work under his supervision and had to get his pay from McSweeney. Smiley went to McSweeney but was told that, as McSweeney no longer worked for the railroad, he could not pay Smiley. Smiley was shuffled back and forth between the two men without being paid until, in his frustration, he became convinced that the two foremen were purposely making a fool of him. On the afternoon of March 28 Smiley, while making the rounds of Winslow's saloons, happened to meet McSweeney and, after a heated exchange of words over the back pay owed, McSweeney turned and walked away. Smiley shot twice at his former foreman, the second bullet causing a mortal wound in McSweeney's back, and later he would claim that McSweeney made a threatening movement so he acted in self-defense. Smiley was arrested without incident and Sheriff F.J. Wattron was telegraphed. The sheriff took custody of Smiley and jailed him at Holbrook in Navajo County. Smiley's situation was not helped by McSweeney's widow being blind, helpless and penniless while trying to raise three fatherless children. He was indicted, tried, and found guilty of first degree murder on October 14, 1899, and two days later Judge Richard Sloan sentenced him to hang on December 8, 1899. Smiley made one feeble attempt to escape but then resigned himself to his fate. Sheriff Wattron sent out invitations to the execution as required by the state's penal code, which did not prescribe any wording:

> Holbrook, Arizona, *December 1, 1899.*
>
> Mr.— — — — — — — — — —
>
> You are hereby cordially invited to attend the hanging of one *George Smiley, Murderer*
>
> His soul will be swung into eternity on December 8, 1899, at 2 o'clock P.M. sharp.
>
> The latest improved methods in the art of scientific strangulation will be employed and everything possible will be done to make the surroundings cheerful and the execution a success.
>
> F.J. Wattron,
> Sheriff of Navajo County

Some members of Arizona's press characterized the invitations as "flippant and facetious" and criticized the sheriff in their newspapers. The criticism was picked up by newspapers all over the country and was then published worldwide. An embarrassed Governor Nathan O. Murphy issued a thirty day respite for Smiley, which gave the sheriff an opportunity to issue a new, quite carefully worded, invitation:

> Revised Statutes of Arizona, Penal Code, Title X, Sec. 1849, Page 307, makes it obligatory on Sheriff to issue invitation to executions, form (unfortunately) not prescribed.
>
> Holbrook, Arizona, *1/7—1900,*
>
> Mr.— — — — — — — — — — —
>
> With feelings of profound sorrow and regret, I hereby invite you to attend and witness the private, decent and humane execution of a human being, name, George Smiley; crime, murder.
>
> The said George Smiley will be executed on January 8, 1900, at 2 o'clock P.M.
>
> You are expected to deport yourself in a respectful manner, and any "flippant" or "unseemly" language or conduct on your part will not be allowed. Conduct, on anyone's part, bordering on ribaldry and tending to mar the solemnity of the occasion will not be tolerated.
>
> F.J. Wattron,
> Sheriff of Navajo County
>
> I would suggest that a committee, consisting of Governor Murphy, Editors Dunbar, Randolph and Hull, wait on our next legislature and have a form of invitation to executions embodied in our laws.

Precisely at 2:00 P.M. on Friday George Smiley ascended the scaffold in the presence of fifteen witnesses and accompanied by Sheriff Wattron, deputy Bargman and Father Dilly. He took his place on the trapdoor and the sheriff asked the condemned man if he had anything to say. Smiley replied, "Nothing, except I thank the Sheriff and deputies for many kindnesses, and I die a Christian." He was quickly prepared and at 2:15 P.M. the trap was sprung. The body dropped six feet, breaking the prisoner's neck, and he was pronounced dead by the two attending physicians eighteen minutes later. The body was then cut down and placed in a coffin provided by the county, and Smiley's remains were buried in the town's graveyard following a brief funeral service.

Phoenix Arizona Republican: January 8–9, 1900.

Penero, Ramon
June 1, 1900

On the evening of July 21, 1899, Ramon Penero, Antonio Sanes and a third Mexican were drinking in a Morenci saloon. Penero and his accomplice lured Sanes outside and, under cover of darkness, stabbed Sanes to death and rifled the pockets of the dead man, sharing the plunder. The accomplice fled and was not heard of again but Penero was captured, indicted and tried at the fall term of the Graham County district court. On October 13 he was found guilty of murder in the first degree and six days later Judge Doan sentenced him to hang on December 1, 1899. An appeal to the territorial supreme court stayed the execution, but the lower court's decision was finally affirmed and Judge Doan resentenced Penero to hang on June 1, 1900. The prisoner's attorney applied to Governor Nathan O. Murphy for a commutation of sentence to life imprisonment, claiming that Penero was insane. The cause for believing him insane was the fact that twelve years earlier he had received a blow on the head from a hammer, but at 1:00

P.M. word was received from the governor that he declined to interfere.

A few minutes before the execution Penero dressed in his new suit and was then brought into the courtyard, accompanied by his guards and a priest. He mounted the scaffold without assistance and took his place on the trapdoor, and the straps were applied to his limbs. He was asked if he had anything to say and he replied, "Nothing, except that I would rather be shot than hung." The noose was placed around the prisoner's neck by Sheriff Ben R. Clark, the black cap was pulled on, and the trap was immediately sprung, and Penero fell seven feet, breaking his neck. Dr. Lacy, the county physician, had requested Dr. Platt to attend the execution in his stead, so the physicians in attendance were Drs. Platt, Dudley, Lindley, and Parker. Thirteen minutes after the trap was sprung the doctors pronounced Penero dead. After hanging several minutes more he was cut down and given to the undertaker, who took him to his parlor. An autopsy was performed and it was discovered that the hammer blow of years past had left a small indentation on the brain, but there no cause for insanity. Penero was buried that evening.

Solomonville Arizona Bulletin: October 20, 1899; June 1, 1900; *Tucson Arizona Citizen*: June 8, 1899; *Phoenix Arizona Republican*: June 3, 1900.

Halderman, Thomas; Halderman, William
November 16, 1900

An arrest warrant was placed in the hands of Constable C.L. Ainsworth of Pearce for service on the Halderman brothers, Thomas and William, charging them with violating a livestock law. Ainsworth, concerned about arresting the Haldermans at the Wilson Ranch on Turkey Creek or some other remote place in the Chiricahua Mountains, took the precaution of stopping at the Smith Ranch and asking one of the ranchmen to assist him. They refused to accompany Ainsworth, possibly because Smith was the complaining witness against the Haldermans, but Smith suggested that Ainsworth go to the Moore ranch three quarters of a mile away and ask Teddy Moore to assist him. Ainsworth went to the Moore ranch and got eighteen-year-old Teddy, and they went to the Wilson ranch house.

On April 7, 1900, while still in the saddle forty feet from the house, Ainsworth called out and the Halderman brothers came out. The constable told them that he had a warrant for their arrest for cow stealing and would have to take them to Pearce for an examination. They agreed to go but it was early so Ainsworth asked them if they had eaten breakfast. They said they had not, so the constable told them to eat while he and Moore waited. Moore and Ainsworth waited while the Halderman boys ate breakfast but then the brothers said they needed some clothes, so Ainsworth said, "[A]ll right, go and get your clothes, boys, and then we will start for Pearce."

The Haldermans went back into the house but when they returned, one at each door, it was with rifles in hand. The Halderman brothers owned one rifle and the other belonged to old man Wilson; when they reached the doors one of them shouted to the officer, "Hands up." However, both Haldermans immediately opened fire upon the constable and Moore. They killed Ainsworth and he fell from his horse, but Moore wheeled his horse and started toward his mother's ranch as fast as he could ride, the Haldermans shooting at him. The last shot which was fired struck Moore in the back when he was one hundred fifty yards distant, and this shot eventually proved to be fatal. Moore reached home and was helped from his horse by his mother and sister and he related all the circumstances of the attack, then bled to death in a few hours. The Haldermans, after the shooting, fled, taking with them old man Wilson's rifle and their own, and crossed the Chiricahua Mountains afoot, finally reaching a camping place on the upper Gila River in New Mexico.

The day following the murders a reward of $50 was offered for the arrest of each fugitive by Sheriff Scott White of Cochise County, and a descriptive reward poster was widely circulated. It was not long before Sid Mullen, Sheriff White's deputy, and his posse captured the Halderman brothers at their New Mexico camp and took them back to Tombstone. In early June they were tried for killing Moore, convicted of first degree murder on June 11, and sentenced to hang on August 10, 1900. An application for a stay of execution was submitted based upon new evidence which was to be produced, but Governor Nathan O. Murphy was out of the territory. The application was forwarded to President William McKinley and he granted a stay until October 5, and when the governor returned to the territory he extended the stay of execution. The new evidence, it was claimed, would prove that Moore had actually rustled and killed the cattle and that he had intended to blame it on the Haldermans as revenge for some wrong done by older brother William. The evidence never materialized, however, and a new date of execution was set for November 16, 1900.

On the date of execution a large crowd gathered early, anxiously awaiting admittance to the jail yard. All the windows in the courthouse on the second floor facing and overlooking the gallows were lined with people, and one hundred invited guests were in the enclosure. The iron door leading from the second-floor jail was swung open and the condemned men appeared, Thomas Halderman in the lead escorted by deputy sheriff Johnson and William Halderman behind escorted by deputy sheriff Bravin; Sheriff White and the Reverend Elliott followed closely. Thomas, the younger brother, said, "Hello, Hombres," and then shielding his eyes from the sun, said, "The sun's hot, ain't it?" The prisoners walked to the scaffold and mounted the steps with a firm tread and showed no signs of faltering as they advanced onto the platform. William, stepping to the front under the dangling noose, surveyed the crowd below and said, "Nice looking crowd" then smiled and remarked, "Some of you fellers are shaking already." Thomas, who was equally nervy, held the noose and looked over the crowd below, then turning to his brother observed, "Those people look alright."

Thomas examined the noose and placed it around his neck as he listened attentively to the reading of the death warrant by Sheriff White, but William paid little attention and engaged in conversation with deputy sheriff Bravin. At the conclusion Sheriff White asked if they wished to make a statement and Thomas said, "I have nothing to say and guess it would not do any good anyway. I forgive you all and hope you will forgive me." William spoke next and said, "This will be an experience that ought to benefit all of you. I hope I will meet you all. I pray for you and hope you will pray for me." The straps were secured about their waists to hold their arms and another about their ankles to hold them firmly. William then asked Sheriff White, "Kindly give us time for a little prayer?" The Reverend Elliott, who had been constantly with them, stepped forward and had the two condemned men clasp hands as they prayed, then shook their hands. The black caps were drawn over their faces and both men said in chorus "Good-bye boys! Pray for us," and when each again said "Good-bye," the crowd responded.

The trapdoor was sprung at exactly 12:40 P.M. At the end of thirteen minutes Dr. H.F. Walter, county physician, and Dr. Toney of Pearce pronounced Thomas dead, and two minutes later William was pronounced dead. The bodies were cut down twenty minutes after the trap was sprung and an examination was made by Dr. Walter and Dr. Toney, and they found that Thomas' neck was broken by the fall but William's neck had not been broken and his death was caused by "the violent shock, compression of a vital nerve, and by strangulation." The bodies were deposited in their coffins and taken to the cemetery that afternoon for burial at county expense.

Yuma (AZ) Sentinel: November 21, 1900; *Tombstone (AZ) Prospector*: August 9, 1900; August 14, 1900; August 23, 1900; September 10, 1900; September 17, 1900; November 16–17, 1900; November 24, 1900.

Ortiz, Santiago
November 16, 1900

Twenty-two-year-old Santiago Ortiz had known William S. Moffatt for several years. The young Mexican had worked at various jobs in Moffatt's store in Harrisburg, Yuma County, Arizona, and Moffatt had often helped Ortiz out of a jam. On August 11, 1900, Moffatt retired to the rear of his store, where he had his living quarters. When Ortiz was certain that his employer was fast asleep he selected from the store's stock a mining drill bit, an iron rod about three feet in length, and quietly crept up on the sleeping Moffatt. The first blow crushed the old man's skull. Ortiz then took several hundred dollars in money and checks, other valuables and the murder weapon, and fled up a canyon. A short distance from the scene of his crime he buried the drill bit, with blood and bits of hair still clinging to it. Deputies Saunders and Blair were soon on his trail, a plain track as he had three nails with large heads in one heel which made his boot prints distinguishable from any others, and it was but a short time before they captured Ortiz with the stolen property still in his possession. He made a full confession, even showing them where he had buried the murder weapon.

Ortiz was tried at the October term of the district court, convicted of murder in the first degree, and sentenced to hang on November 16, 1900. Neither appeal nor application for executive clemency delayed the proceedings. Ortiz spent his last week in a special "dark cell" where he was under a death watch twenty-four hours a day to ensure he did not commit suicide. However, he was provided an electric light and given reading materials, good food and the companionship of Father Durand, with whom he regularly read his Testament.

By 9:30 A.M. Friday morning a crowd had gathered at the courthouse and in a half hour the courtroom and nearly the entire space of the corridors on each side of the scaffold were filled with people who had come there to witness the hanging. At 10:00 A.M. Sheriff John M. Spees, with Joe Redondo as interpreter, entered the doomed man's cell and the death warrant was read, but Ortiz had nothing to say. At 11:30 the sheriff and deputies cleared the courtroom while final preparations were completed for the execution, and then the doors were reopened and two hundred men with invitations were admitted. As the bell on the Church of the Immaculate Conception tolled the hour of noon the sheriff appeared on the scaffold and formally announced that Santiago Ortiz was about to be executed for the murder of William S. Moffatt, and then he retired.

In two minutes the condemned man, neatly dressed in a new suit of black, exited his cell following Father Durand and accompanied by the sheriff, with deputies and the county physician behind. Ortiz took his place upon the trapdoor and was asked if he had anything to say, and he replied, "I forgive my enemies that God may forgive me." Straps were placed on his wrists and ankles while Father Durand prayed, the doomed man repeating after him. The sheriff put his hand on the prisoner's shoulder and gently pushed him to the center of the trapdoor where the noose was adjusted and the black cap pulled over his face and, in but a moment at 12:05 P.M., the trap was sprung. The physicians monitored vital signs and pronounced the prisoner dead at 12:21 P.M. and the body was cut down. An examination followed and the doctors reported that his neck was only partially dislocated, but they insisted that death had been painless. The body was turned over to the county coroner for burial as no friends or relations had appeared to claim it.

Yuma (AZ) Sentinel: November 14, 1900; November 21, 1900.

Chacon, Augustine
November 21, 1902

Augustine Chacon, known as El Peludo, or "the Hairy One," was known as an excellent cowboy throughout the Arizona Territory during the 1880s. In 1890 he had a disagreement with his employer, Ben Ollney, over three months' wages which were due him and Ollney, notorious for his tightfistedness, made it clear that he would not pay Chacon and ordered him off the ranch. Nelly Ollney, Ben's daughter, stepped between the men before blood was shed and Chacon rode off toward Safford. Chacon spent the night drinking, and in the morning he strapped on his guns and rode back to the ranch. Ollney not only refused to pay Chacon but also insulted him and laughed at his attempt to collect his money. Ollney then made the fatal mistake of reaching for his six-gun, because Chacon was much faster, and he shot Ollney dead. Five of Ollney's hands came to aid their employer but, instead of bringing down the Mexican or putting him to flight, Chacon stood game and killed four while wounding the last of his attackers. The wounded cowboy rode to Whitlock Springs and sounded the alarm.

Ollney's brother lived at Whitlock Springs and soon he put six cowboys on Chacon's trail. They followed him to a box canyon, cornered him and called for his surrender, but Chacon again stood game, firing two six-guns as he charged at the six men. He killed four more cowboys with only a minor wound to his right arm, then rode off. The entire Ollney family was murdered at Whitlock Springs two days later but Chacon denied having committed that heinous crime and said that at the time he was hiding at a Mexican woodcutter's camp with two other fugitives, Albert "Burt" Alvord and William "Billy" Stiles, and nursing his wounded arm.

Months passed before Chacon visited a girl near Fort Apache and was arrested. A lynch mob formed and went to the jail, but when they arrived they found the cell empty and the bars cut through with a hacksaw blade. During the next several years Chacon crossed back and forth across the international border, committing crimes on one side and then crossing to the other side until things cooled, then committing a crime there and crossing back. Many a murder and robbery were attributed to Chacon and quite probably he was responsible for at least a portion of them.

On December 18, 1895, Chacon, with Pilar Franco and Leonardo Morales, burglarized a store in Morenci and when the store's manager, Paul Becker, returned to his sleeping quarters in the rear one of the burglars stabbed him. Becker broke free and made his way to Short's Saloon where he called for help. Becker survived a horrendous wound. A posse was soon on the trail of the three burglars, which led plainly to the Contreras cabin above the town. As soon as the posse neared, Chacon, with four other men, ran into the rocks and began firing. While two of the bandits fled, the remaining three, including Chacon, kept up a withering fusillade. Pablo Salcido, a long time friend of Chacon, decided to approach the three bandits and ask them to surrender but as he came near their position a shot rang out and Salcido fell dead, shot through the head. The gun battle finally ceased and when the posse approached the stronghold they found that the other two men had abandoned Chacon, who was temporarily paralyzed from a wound to his shoulder. Chacon was lodged in the jail at Clifton and at his examination he was held to answer for the murder of Salcido and moved to the jail at Solomonville.

At the spring term of Judge Owen T. Rouse's court Chacon was found guilty of first degree murder and sentenced to hang on July 24, 1896. His case was appealed to the supreme court and, because of his previous escape attempt, he was moved to the jail at Tucson while awaiting the court's decision. The supreme court affirmed the verdict of the lower court and Chacon was taken back to Solomonville, where the date of execution was set for June 18, 1897. On June 9 Chacon escaped from the Solomonville jail and fled into Mexico. The jail's walls were ten inches of adobe with a double layer of two inch pine boards held together with five inch nails. He would have created quite a racket digging out, so the jailors were suspected of turning a deaf ear. Chacon was now careful not to alienate the Mexican authorities and jeopardize his safe haven south of the border.

In March 1901 the territorial legislature

created the Arizona Rangers to fight lawlessness anywhere within its borders and on the top of the list of fugitives was Chacon, followed closely by Burt Alvord and Billy Stiles. Just as the Ranger's Captain Burton Mossman was about to loose his position, due to a change in the presidency, he devised a plan to capture Chacon using Alvord and Stiles to lure the Mexican fugitive north of the border. The plan succeeded and Chacon was captured on September 4, 1901, and taken to Packard, a train station one mile inside the United States border where Mossman delivered Chacon to Jim Parks, the newly elected Sheriff of Graham County. Chacon, now forty-six years old and wrecked by years on the run, was already sentenced to death, so his appearance in court was merely for the purpose of setting his new execution date, November 21, 1902.

Chacon was resigned to his fate when the hour of execution arrived. He was conducted into the Clifton jail yard and marched up the thirteen steps of the scaffold which had been built for him five years earlier. He refused support from the sheriff's brother John Parks and Lee Hobbs, who walked on each side, while Father de Richermont led the way and conducted services of the Catholic church. Chacon stepped onto the trapdoor and assisted the men by removing his shoes and helping them place the straps on his legs. He was asked if he had anything to say to the one hundred witnesses and the prisoner replied, "Yes, I have a statement to make to my people," then he talked for thirty minutes.

He denied killing Pablo Salcido, for which he was to hang, but admitted that he had killed fifteen Americans and thirty-seven Mexicans. Several men ascended the steps to shake his hand during the time he spoke, and then turned to the sheriff and asked if the execution could be delayed until 3:00 P.M. Parks refused, so when another man began to climb the steps to shake hands Chacon said, "It's too late. Time to hang." He asked that he be allowed to die without a hood but the sheriff told him it was required by law, and as the black cap and rope were being adjusted Chacon cried out, "Adios, todos Amigos!" and in a few seconds the trap was sprung by the sheriff. Attending physicians pronounced Chacon dead twelve minutes after the drop, and he was then cut down and buried in the local graveyard.

Graham County (AZ) Bulletin: December 19, 1895; July 25, 1896; June 9, 1897; September 6, 1902; November 21–22, 1902; *Phoenix (AZ) Arizona Republican*: June 10, 1897; November 21–22, 1902.

Hidalgo, Hilario; Rentario, Francisco
July 31, 1903

The Goddards owned a successful sheep ranch in the vicinity of Cañon, an area also known as Goddard because that family was the major landowner. Each year during the sheep shearing season Charles Goddard took on extra help and in mid–February 1901 one employee was a troublesome Mexican named Francisco Rentario. A dispute arose between Rentario and another shearer and the troublemaker tried to stab his fellow worker with his shears. Goddard intervened and struck Rentario across the face with his six-shooter, the barrel of the gun causing a deep gash and knocking the Mexican to the ground. When Rentario recovered his senses his wound was bandaged and it was clear that the gash would cause a large scar on the Mexican's face. Rentario swore he would kill Charles Goddard for preventing his attack on the Mexican, and for the ugly scar. However, nothing occurred and the incident was soon forgotten as the men had many thousands of sheep to shear and were too busy to be distracted.

When the season ended, Rentario left without further incident and he did not return during the 1902 season. On February 1, 1903, as the shearing season was about to begin, two Mexican hard cases were loitering about Goddard's two-story building, which served as headquarters for his sheep ranching enterprise, the post office, and a stagecoach depot. The two men approached Francisco Rodriguez, who managed the ranch, and several times asked questions about the forthcoming shearing season: when the other shearers would arrive, if the payroll had been brought in, and general questions about the Goddards and others at the station.

That evening Charles and Rosa Goddard sat down to their Sunday supper with postmaster Frank Cox and an overnight guest named Milton Turnbull. Rosa had just gone into the kitchen when the two heavyset Mexicans suddenly burst into the room and demanded food. Charles explained, in Spanish, that the meal was finished but, if they would wait, some food would be prepared for them. One of the men shouted, "No! Now!" as both men drew their six-shooters and fired upon Goddard, Cox and Turnbull. Frank Cox was killed immediately by a bullet passing through his body, while Charles Goddard received several mortal wounds to his chest and fell to the floor bleeding. A bullet hit the chair of Turnbull, who fell over and feigned death while Rosa, hearing the shots, ran upstairs and hid. The two Mexicans ate and then ransacked the first floor looking for the payroll, but did not go upstairs. They blew out all the lamps and fled but Turnbull lay still until daylight, afraid to light a lamp in case the men should return to finish their murderous work. Rosa remained hidden upstairs the entire time, also afraid the men might return, and by dawn Charles Goddard had bled to death.

Turnbull rode to the Cordes Ranch and sent a rider to the railroad depot at Mayer, where a telegram was dispatched to deputy sheriff Joseph Campbell at Prescott. At 7:00 P.M. Campbell forwarded the message to Sheriff Joe Roberts, who was at Phoenix, and then went to Goddard. He picked up deputy George Heisler along the way, and at the sheep ranch Rosa Goddard and Francisco Rodriguez gave them excellent descriptions of the two fugitives. The deputies looked for a trail but it had been washed away by a recent rainstorm. When the next southbound stage came in Rosa Goddard boarded and rode to Phoenix where her children were in school, but the driver reported seeing two men matching the fugitives' description walking southward when he had come up on Monday, and this was relayed to the sheriff.

An indictment was returned by the grand jury in the names Richard Roe and John Doe and descriptive circulars were sent throughout the territory, especially along the border with Mexico, and soon leads were coming in. One of the first was from Frank Murphy, a railroad promoter, who came into the sheriff's office in Prescott to report that two Mexican troublemakers had been fired by the railroad on the Friday before the murders, and they fit the descriptions being circulated. Murphy provided the names of Hilario Hidalgo from Chihuahua, Mexico, and Francisco Rentario from Guanajato, Mexico. Two days later Sheriff Adelbert Lewis of Cochise County notified Deputy Heisler that the two men he was seeking were working in Naco, a border town south of Bisbee; but when Heisler arrived, Naco's deputy Billy Blankenship told him that the men were actually working in Mexico. Hidalgo was employed on a section crew for the Southern Pacific Railroad laying tracks into Mexico while Rentario was working at a mine several miles below the border. Relations with Mexico were poor at the time and there were no extradition arrangements with the Mexican authorities, and the border was poorly marked so everyone, except lawmen and the militaries of the two countries, passed back and forth freely.

Deputies Blankenship and Hiesler arranged, with the manager of the railroad, for Hidalgo's railroad section crew to work on the tracks north of the border. Hidalgo, when approached by the lawmen, believed he was still in Mexico so he surrendered without resistance, confident he could easily avoid extradition. He was lodged in the jail at Naco to await the arrest of Rentario. The deputies next arranged with the mine manager to pay his crew with drafts drawn on a bank just over the border in Naco. Rentario went to the bank but it was closed so he ran back into Mexico; but later that day, when a fellow miner signaled that the coast was clear, Rentario crossed into the United States and was arrested.

The prisoners were taken to Prescott on April 6, 1903, and lodged in the Yavapai County jail, which was located in the basement of the courthouse. On June 2 the two defendants under the names on the indictment, Richard Roe and John Doe, pled "not guilty" and trial was set for June 10. At their trial in the district court at Prescott, Rosa Goddard and Francisco Rodriguez positively identified the two defendants as the murderers. There were only seven witnesses for the prosecution and, although the two men produced several alibi witnesses, they were both found guilty of first-degree murder after only thirty minutes' deliberation. Within a week the defendants were brought into court and sentenced to hang on July 31, 1903. The gallows was built on the east side of the courthouse and walled off by a high wooden fence.

On July 31 Sheriff Joseph I. Roberts, with a reporter from Prescott's *Journal Miner* as a witness, read the death warrant to each man in his cell beginning at 10:45 A.M. Hidalgo laughed and said that he had heard it many times before, concluding, "If that were a song I could sing it to you now." The lawmen and reporter then retired while a priest administered the last rites to the condemned men and prayed with them. The condemned men bathed, shaved and dressed in the new black suits provided by the sheriff, then they were escorted up the stairs from the basement jail into the enclosure. They walked up the thirteen steps onto the scaffold at 11:15 A.M., with their priest leading the way. As Hidalgo's arms and legs were being pinioned he noticed acquaintances in the crowd of five hundred spectators and, calling to them by name, made some remarks in Spanish which were not recorded; Rentario also spoke to several people in the crowd. Just as the black caps were pulled over their faces they both shouted, "Adios! Adios todos!" and then Hidalgo said, muffled somewhat by the hood, "Good-bye, Frank" to the man who had sat the death watch with them for the past week. The trap was sprung by Sheriff Roberts at 11:24 A.M. and Hidalgo's neck was broken in the fall, but Rentario died by strangulation. Both men were pronounced dead by the attending physicians ten minutes and forty seconds after they dropped. They were cut down, deposited in the coffins provided by the county, and buried in potter's field at county expense that evening.

Phoenix Arizona Republican: August 1, 1903; Coburn, Walt; "Dual Hanging in Arizona," *Badman* (1971).

Ubillos, Martin
June 16, 1905

Martin Ubillos was mining with another Mexican in the Weaver District of Yavapai County, Arizona. One evening the two men quarreled and the argument deteriorated into a fight. Ubillos killed his partner and dragged the body onto the campfire head first, where the head was burned from the torso. He was arrested, indicted, tried in the Yavapai County district court, and sentenced to hang but the governor commuted his death sentence to life imprisonment at the territorial prison near Yuma. Simon Aldrate was also serving a life sentence at the territorial prison. The sweltering heat of August and close proximity of bodies left tempers short, and Ubillos and Aldrate fought without any clear winner. The following morning Ubillos stabbed Aldrate with a makeshift knife and Aldrate died of the wounds. Ubillos was tried in the district court of Yuma County, found guilty of first degree murder, sentenced to hang, and returned to the prison to await his execution. At 10:00 A.M. on June 16, 1905, Sheriff Gus M. Livingston, accompanied by Justice J.L. Redondo, the Reverend Father Vandermaussen, deputies Will Despain, Sex Smith, and Julio Martinez, and ranger Frank S. Wheeler, went to the territorial prison and read the death warrant to the condemned man in his cell. Ubillos was visibly affected and it appeared he would weaken at the last moment but, under the spiritual influence of the Catholic priest, he became wholly absorbed in religious devotion.

The prisoner was taken from the prison,

boarded a carriage, and was driven to the courthouse where they entered through the probate judge's office. A crowd had assembled in the courtyard and on the rooftops overlooking the scaffold. At 10:55, the sheriff and priest on either side of the condemned man, they climbed the steps to the platform, followed by Redondo as interpreter and four others. Sheriff Livingston pinioned the prisoner's limbs with straps while the prisoner clutched a small crucifix and repeated a prayer. The sheriff then positioned the condemned man in the center of the trapdoor and adjusted the noose, and deputy Despain quickly pulled the black cap over his face. At a signal from the sheriff the rope securing the trap was severed by Jack Caruth and the prisoner dropped, breaking his neck. The attending physician monitored his vital signs and when the heart ceased to beat he was pronounced dead. After hanging long enough to ensure he could not be revived, his body was cut down, placed in his coffin, and buried that evening.

Yuma (AZ) Sentinel: June 16, 1905.

Booth, Zack
September 15, 1905

William W. Berry hired Santiago Vigil to move his flock of sheep from the St. Johns area over the Mogollon Rim for winter pasturage in the Salt River Valley. With Santiago was Berry's twenty-year-old son, Wiley, and Santiago's seventeen-year-old-son, Juan, but the rest of the Berry family had gone to the warmer clime of Thatcher during the cold season at St. Johns. The flock had a hard trip and was trail weary when they reached Brushy Basin in Gila County on December 18, so Berry decided to rest the sheep there. Brushy Basin had plenty of good grass and water but the party had exhausted most of their supplies, especially sheep salt, and Brushy Basin was just eight miles from Payson and five miles from Gisela, where they could restock.

On December 21, 1903, Wiley informed the Vigils that he would go into Gisela the following day and bring back their supplies, then go to Thatcher to spend Christmas with his family. The cattlemen in the Brushy Basin area had unilaterally, and unanimously, decided that Brushy Basin would remain exclusively cattle country, and they still remembered the Pleasant Valley range war after sheep were allowed into cattle country. They were determined to keep the sheep out and held several meetings about the matter. One of the angriest of the cattlemen was Zack Booth; and Zack's brother John, usually a quiet man, was equally outraged by the invasion of "woollies." Santiago was with the flock on the morning of December 22 when two men rode out of the woods, confronted him, and ordered him to move the sheep out of cattle country. Santiago told them that the boss was in camp, but the men pulled their six-guns and again ordered him to move the sheep. Santiago again directed them to speak with Berry, so the men holstered their pistols and rode into the camp. The men dismounted, had a conversation with Berry, then returned to their horses, and Berry suspected that the men were hostile. He edged toward his carbine as they mounted, but they quickly reined about and shot Berry dead. Juan ran for cover in the brush but they shot him down.

Santiago heard the shooting and, leaving dogs to herd the flock, ran to the camp, where he found the boys lying in pools of blood, apparently dead. He mounted Wiley's horse and rode hard for Payson, but the two men were hiding in the timber watching and as soon as Santiago rode away they returned to the camp. One picked up Berry's carbine and fired several shots into his dead body, then fired a grazing shot across his saddle so he could claim self-defense if it became an issue, then placed the carbine on the ground and rolled Berry onto it. The two men then rode to the body of Juan Vigil, who had recovered sufficiently from his wounds to continue crawling toward concealment; but the boy had only managed a few feet before one of the Booths fired four bullets from his carbine into the boy's back, killing him.

Deputy sheriffs John Chilson and Ben

Pyeatt returned to the camp with Santiago. They worked for Sheriff C.R. Rogers, who fancied himself a detective, and he encouraged his men to investigate and gather evidence. The two deputies measured the horses' gaits, documented the irregularities of the hoof and boot tracks, and then followed the trail back to Gisela. Santiago had given the deputies an excellent description of the men and their horses and Chilson recognized the description of one horse as belonging to Zack Booth. The deputies went to Zack's ranch and found two horses in the corral which matched the animals described by Santiago. They searched the house without result but in the saddle shed they found a saddle with the bullet graze, a rifle in its scabbard, and a .38 caliber six-gun and cartridge belt. Both weapons had been fired recently and had not been cleaned. The deputies walked and galloped the horses over soft ground and determined that the gait and tracks matched exactly those at the sheep camp. The lawmen saddled the horses and led them to John Booth's house where one of John's sons thought they were returning loose stock, and identified one animal as Zack's horse and the other as the horse ridden by his father. The deputies learned that the Booths were working on a nearby road so they went there, arrested the Booth brothers, and on December 26 lodged them in the Payson jail.

At their hearing two days later the Booths were held to answer based solely on the deputies' testimony. Sheriff Rogers, however, was determined to build a strong case and devised a plan to get a positive identification from Santiago, who claimed he could never forget the "tiger's eyes" of one of the murderers. Rogers convinced the owner of the "16 to 1" Saloon to hold a belated Christmas party with eighty men invited, including the Booth brothers. Behind the bar hung the Booths' saddles, six-guns, rifle in its scabbard, and Berry's .30-.30 carbine. As the party continued, Santiago was brought in, given a few drinks, and then asked if he recognized any of the evidence. He pointed out Wiley's carbine. Rogers then asked Santiago if he recognized any of the men in the room and Santiago immediately identified Zack Booth as one of the murderers, but he seemed unsure of John. However, after some coaxing he identified him, saying, with his hand on John's shoulder, "This one of them who kill my son!" The Booths were again lodged in jail and moved to Globe the following day, where they were indicted and held for trial.

The bodies of Juan Vigil and Wiley Berry were exhumed, a post mortem examination was conducted by Dr. A.B. Curtis, and the nature and character of their wounds was documented. The relative positions of the bodies when found were compared in relation to various points in the camp and the direction of the gunshots was determined. However, at their examination on June 13, 1904, the Booths pled "not guilty" to a charge of murder.

The prosecution chose to try the Booths for the murder of Juan first, since the saddle would be used in a claim of self-defense in the case of Berry's death. Although there was little physical evidence to convict the brothers, Zack, to protect John, confessed to both killings to exonerate his brother but claimed self-defense. The jury retired at 6:00 P.M. on June 16 and the following morning at 9:15 returned the verdict: "We the jury empaneled and sworn in the above entitled action upon our oaths do find the defendant Zack Booth guilty of murder and fix the penalty of death, and do find the defendant John Booth not guilty." On June 18 Judge Edward Kent sentenced Zack Booth to hang on August 1, 1904. Appeals followed but the verdict and sentence were affirmed by the supreme court on March 30, 1905, and Zack Booth was sentenced to hang on August 16. Governor Joseph H. Kibbey granted a thirty day respite when new evidence was promised but the evidence was never produced, and the governor then declined to grant an additional respite or commute the sentence to life imprisonment.

An effort to have the condemned man declared insane failed, so, on the morning of the execution, a petition for a writ of habeas corpus was submitted citing the same grounds already reviewed by the supreme court, which was denied though it delayed the proceedings for a few hours. When informed that his case was hopeless, and that he must meet his doom, the condemned man remarked to the deputies that he would "have to go the route." After supper he wrote letters until 4:00 A.M., then retired and slept three hours. The death warrant was read to Booth at 10:15 A.M. and, at his request, the 24th Psalm was read at the same time. With him were the Rev. R.I. McKee and officers of the Salvation Army; Booth joined in the prayers, but refused to give a full confession. He dressed entirely in black and remained in his shirtsleeves until called by Sheriff W.G. "Ed" Shanley. The procession formed and Booth walked onto the platform between the sheriff and undersheriff Heron. He said, "Good-bye, boys; good-bye, everybody; a lot of people are here to see Zack go the route." He then noticed the height of the platform and remarked to the sheriff, "You're going to give me a big drop there, Ed," then to the crowd, "Remember me to all the people up around St. Johns. I'm an innocent man; what I did was to protect my property and rights — my life and my home. I'm going to meet my dear old mother in heaven."

Booth stepped onto the trapdoor and the straps were adjusted around his wrists and arms, knees and ankles. After prayer and the reading of the 90th Psalm he said good-bye to those near him. He then took a pocketknife from his pocket and handed it to the sheriff, saying, "The devil gave me quite a hunch to cheat you out of this job, Ed, but I thought I'd go the route." He was then asked if he wanted to speak to the crowd again and he claimed that one of the witnesses committed perjury; he blamed the Mexicans for his death, and then expressed concern about the doctors and asked them to be certain the "work was done well." He thanked the officers for their kindness and assured the reverends that he would meet them in heaven. The noose was placed about his neck but he complained that it was too tight, so it was loosened while the black cap was adjusted. He was talking in fragmentary sentences when, in the midst of a half uttered word, the trap was sprung and the body fell nearly seven feet, breaking his neck. A faint heartbeat could be detected for ten minutes and in sixteen minutes Dr. A.F. Maisch pronounced him dead. The body was cut down and prepared for the casket, but claim had been made by relatives for the body so later that day it was buried in the city cemetery.

Globe Arizona Silver Belt: August 17, 1905; September 14, 1905.

Leigh, Clement
January 19, 1907

Clement Leigh and Jennie Bauters, a prostitute, lived together in Jerome, Arizona, but moved to the Gold Road mining camp in Mojave County. They had been associated for a long time but Bauters had grown tired of Leigh's companionship and his frequent demands for money, so she abandoned him and began bestowing her favors upon others in the camp. This excited jealous rage and Leigh, a man known for his vicious character, went to Bauter's home early on the morning of September 3, 1905. Leigh was in a quarrelsome mood when he entered and spoke only a few harsh words before pulling his revolver. He chased Bauters into the street as he shot at her, causing a serious wound. As she lay helpless at the roadside he casually reloaded his gun, approached, rolled her over to get a better aim at her face, and fired one bullet into her brain from point-blank range. He then feigned attempted suicide, inflicting a slight wound to his left side.

Leigh was arrested, indicted, and tried for the murder of Bauters and was easily convicted on the evidence. The case was appealed to the supreme court upon the premise that one of the members of the indicting grand jury was a rival for the favors of Bauters; but the justices affirmed the district court's decision, and the application for a commutation of sentence was made to Governor Joseph H. Kibbey. The governor, after carefully considering the case, refused to intervene. The day before the execution Leroy Anderson, attorney for Leigh, applied to the governor for a reprieve so that he might have time to prepare an application for a commutation on the ground that Leigh was insane at the time the crime was committed. Anderson proposed that he needed the time to secure evidence to support that proposition, so a reprieve was granted until January 18, 1907. Early in the final week the case was brought before the governor alleging that Leigh was addicted to liquor and drugs and because of his lifestyle was insane at the time of trial, but twenty-four affidavits were also filed by reputable citizens who had known Leigh for years and refuted the allegations. The governor considered the matter and declined to intervene.

The prisoner prepared, dressed in the suit of black clothes, white shirt, collar and tie provided by the county, and then said farewell to his friends. The sheriff appeared at the cell door and read the death warrant, and Leigh asked if they had come for him. When they answered "yes" he lurched forward against the bars of the cell where a metal projection cut a deep gash on his head, but before he could fall to the floor the officers caught him and laid him down. He had partially revived when the officers carried him onto the scaffold and hurriedly prepared him for the drop. As they raised him up his eyes partly opened but he did not seem to know what was going on, and not one word was spoken. He was a ghastly sight as the officers adjusted the noose around his neck, with blood trickling down his face and white shirt front. After the trap was sprung, there being no perceptible movement, the doctor declared him dead in ten minutes, but the body was allowed to hang for thirty minutes before it was cut down. It was placed in the cheap coffin provided by the county and buried that evening.
Phoenix Arizona Republican: January 18, 1907.

Baldwin, William
July 12, 1907

William Baldwin had been employed as a laborer on the Roosevelt Dam in Gila County, Arizona, but was not working Thursday, January 31, 1907. Under the pretense of going hunting Baldwin left Roosevelt in the direction of the Morris ranch but returned about 11:00 A.M., running and breathless, and said he was passing the Morris ranch when he saw two Mexicans attack Mrs. Morris and her daughter. He said he ran to the women's assistance and beat off the Mexicans, who escaped, but in the fight he had been severely wounded by knife slashes. On investigation the bodies of Mrs. Morris and her daughter were found several hundred yards from the ranch house and investigation of the scene convinced the authorities that Baldwin was the murderer, that no other persons had been there, and that his wounds were self-inflicted to lend color to his story.

Baldwin was arrested and taken to Globe where a lynch mob quickly formed; but Judge Nave addressed the men and, being armed at the time, announced that he would defend the prisoner with his life, and promised a speedy trial. While the judge was distracting the mob, Sheriff John H. Thompson hurried the prisoner to a train which had been pressed into service and took his prisoner to the jail at Tucson for safekeeping. The mob, upon learning of Baldwin's departure, disbanded. Judge Nave kept his promise and called a special session of the grand jury, which indicted Baldwin, who in a few weeks was returned to Solomonville and tried. He was convicted and sentenced to hang in May but the case was appealed to the supreme court. However, Baldwin's attorneys became convinced of Baldwin's guilt and, having discharged their duty to do all in his defense, refused to appear at the supreme court hearing. The justices allowed sufficient time for the appeal to be argued, then affirmed the lower court's conviction and sentence. On the Monday following the supreme court's decision Judge Nave set the date for Baldwin's execution at Friday of that week, but newly assigned attorneys filed an application for a stay in the proceedings so that an application for a new trial could be prepared. Governor Joseph H. Kibbey found the application wanting in merit and declined to intervene.

During the week before his execution the prisoner espoused the Catholic faith and, if any confession was made, it was under the seal of the church. He refused to tell the whereabouts of the knife with which Mrs. Morris and her little daughter were murdered, but he persisted in telling a rambling story of a Mexican tramp, differing in each rendition in many details from his original statement. When the moment arrived Baldwin mounted the scaffold bravely, and the *Arizona Republican* reported that "The Negro Went to His Death Without Manifestation of Fear and Without Making a Public Confession of His Guilt." Graham County's Sheriff Alphie A. "Pap" Anderson sprang the trap at 8:45 A.M. and death was pronounced in sixteen minutes. For the first time in Arizona two young girls were among the witnesses to an execution — a daughter and niece of the murdered woman — Eunice Morris and Maggie Nelson. They had come one hundred and fifty miles and begged for the privilege.

Phoenix Arizona Republic: July 12, 1907.

Groce, H.J.
July 17, 1908

The Groce family lived in Texas but H.J. Groce's wife abandoned him in July 1906 and moved to Tucson in Pima County, Arizona. Groce followed his wife and begged her to return home but she refused so he returned to Texas. In November 1907 Groce arrived in Tucson and again tried to convince his wife to return with him, and again she refused to reconcile. On the day he was planning to return to Texas Groce bought a revolver and went to his wife's house. He asked her to mix his favorite drink, which she could do more to his satisfaction than any other person, and she accommodated him. She then started toward the depot with her husband to say good-bye, and they seemed to be on the friendliest terms as they walked along. Suddenly Groce drew his new revolver and shot his wife dead and then tried to kill himself, but failed.

Groce later admitted that he had bought the gun to kill a Pullman porter named Jenkins, whom he blamed for his wife's estrangement, but in a fit of jealous rage he had killed his wife instead. An investigation later revealed that Mrs. Groce had not met Jenkins until she arrived in Tucson so he had played no part in her decision to leave her husband. Groce was indicted, tried, convicted of murder in the first degree, and sentenced to hang. A vigorous fight for a new trial began in the district and supreme courts and, when all hope of relief through the courts failed, an appeal was made to Governor Joseph H. Kibbey for a commutation of sentence. Groce's attorney was in Phoenix on the Thursday before the execution, pleading for clemency based on the extenuating circumstance that H.J. Groce was provoked by his wife's desertion and her unfaithfulness. However the governor, in refusing to intervene, said that the extenuating circumstances had been left to the jury to weigh and, since there was no new information or evidence, he refused to act. Word of the governor's decision was withheld until the condemned man started to the scaffold, so Groce did not abandon hope until the last moment. Though ill for some time Groce appeared strong enough to make the march to the gallows and even smiled at the audience within the enclosure. His only remark was "[T]his is an awful death to die." The condemned man was attended by Father Timmerman of the Catholic church, a religion Groce had embraced during his confinement. He stood firmly upon the trapdoor while his wrists and ankles were pinioned, the black cap drawn over his face, and the noose adjusted. At exactly 1:00 P.M. Sheriff Nabor Pacheco sprang the trap. In eighteen and one half minutes Groce was pronounced dead and the body was cut down, placed in the pine coffin provided by the county, and buried in the Catholic cemetery.

Phoenix Arizona Republican: July 18, 1908.

Hawkins, Edwin W.
August 14, 1908

Twenty-two-year-old Edwin W. Hawkins moved west from Chicago and began a life of crime. He spent a brief term in California's Folsom Prison and when released in mid–1907 he and his wife moved to Arizona. In November Hawkins, assisted by his wife, attempted to rob Albert Leonhardt in Pima County but Leonhardt was an athletic young man and offered a vigorous resistance. Hawkins, without warning or hesitation, shot Leonhardt dead. In February 1908 Hawkins was arrested on suspicion of a number of burglaries, but thought the matter trivial and asked why they did not question him about the murder of Leonhardt. He then confessed to the killing, but said he murdered Leonhardt in defense of his wife when their victim put up a terrible struggle. He was indicted, tried, convicted of first degree murder, and sentenced to hang on August 14, 1908. Neither appeal nor application for commutation delayed the proceedings. As the time for his death approached Hawkins embraced the Catholic faith and, at the urging of the priest, made a full confession. After giving the details he concluded, "I must have been crazy," then expressed regret and afterward asked everyone who called on him to pray for his soul.

The hanging of Hawkins had been set for 1:00 P.M. but he was expecting a message from his mother and it had not arrived so, at his request, Sheriff Nabor Pacheco delayed the execution for twenty-five minutes. There was still no message at 1:30 P.M. so there was a further delay, but at 2:00 P.M. the murderer was led onto the scaffold. Just as Hawkins was about to step onto the trapdoor the message was received over the telephone in the sheriff's office and it was handed into the enclosure. It read, "Be brave; I can say no more. Bessie." Hawkins read it with a smile and then took his place beneath the noose. During the brief religious ceremony his wrists and ankles were pinioned, then the black cap was pulled on and the noose adjusted. The trap was sprung at 2:02 P.M. and Hawkins dropped, rebounding sharply once, but his neck had not been broken. In fourteen minutes the attending physicians announced that strangulation had been complete and pronounced him dead, and the body was cut down. Immediately afterward the body of Hawkins was removed to a morgue where brief services were held. The body was then buried in the Catholic cemetery.

Phoenix Arizona Republican: August 13–14, 1908.

Lopez, Jose
January 5, 1910

Maria Espinoza's ranch was four miles west of Florence on the north side of the Gila River. She lived with six of her small children and one grown daughter. At 11:00 P.M. on August 1, 1909, Jose Lopez, a nineteen-year-old boy, aroused the family from their slumbers and demanded payment of $8, a debt owed his adopted father, Antonio Lopez. Espinoza ordered him to leave the premises and said she would pay Antonio the next day, but Lopez used harsh language toward her and finally left with a threat that he would return. The family, not anticipating further trouble that night, retired; but two hours later Lopez returned with a shotgun, pulled off his shoes one hundred yards from the house, and slipped up on the sleeping family. When he was within ten feet of Espinoza a little boy awoke and, seeing Lopez with gun in his hand, called out, "What are you going to do with that gun?" Lopez replied, "I know what I am going to do with it," then pointed it at the boy. At that instant the boy's mother awoke and sprang to her feet and the murderer deliberately fired at her, the entire charge of heavy buckshot entering her chin and killing her instantly.

At the sound of gunfire the children scattered through the dense mesquite and undergrowth surrounding the house, with the murderer pursuing the grown daughter. She succeeded in eluding him, although he searched for an hour. As soon as the murderer left, the older of the little boys ran several miles to the house of Jesus Feliz and reported the murder. Feliz mounted a horse, hurried to town, and notified Constable Margarito Rameriz. Constable Ramirez went directly to the ranch of Antonio Lopez, where the murderer lived, and scouted the area. He found the murderer lying under a tree several hundred yards from the house and arrested him. When he asked why he had shot Maria Espinoza the only reply the prisoner would make was, "Well, I have done what I done."

The murder so incensed the community that Sheriff James E. McGee had the prisoner removed to the new territorial prison at Florence. He had been removed only a short time when a large party of men broke into the jail intent on lynching the murderer, but they found his cell empty. Lopez was examined by Justice E.B. Devine and held for action by the grand jury. He was indicted, tried, convicted of first degree murder and sentenced to hang.

An execution chamber was built at the new territorial prison at Florence when the legislature shifted responsibility from the county, and Lopez would be the first man executed at the new prison. The execution was scheduled for 10:30 A.M. on January 5, 1910, and thirty persons invited by Superintendent Rynning were admitted to witness the solemn affair. At the appointed time the condemned man, neatly attired in a black suit and wearing a purple spray on his left lapel, came from the death watch cell walking between the Rev. Father Henry Heitz, pastor of the Catholic church, and the captain of the guards. The prisoner ascended the iron stairway leading into the execution room and when he reached the platform he walked directly onto the iron trapdoor and took his place at the center. His wrists had been bound in his cell and it took two guards but a moment to bind his ankles with leather straps. Father Heitz asked if he had a last message to deliver and he replied in Spanish, "[I]f I have offended anyone present I ask their forgiveness." The noose was then adjusted about his neck and the black cap was drawn over his face. The Holy Crucifix was pressed to his lips beneath the hood by Father Heitz and, the moment it was removed, Rynning touched the lever and the body dropped into the chamber below. The drop was six feet and, although the condemned man was of light weight, his neck was broken by the fall. Dr. Ketcherside of Yuma and Dr. Brockway of Florence went into the chamber beneath the scaffold and, with instruments, recorded vital signs until they pronounced the prisoner dead in sixteen and one half minutes. Relatives were waiting and the remains were placed in a coffin and turned over to them for final disposition.

Florence Arizona Blade-Tribune: August 4, 1909; January 10, 1910.

Barela, Rafael; Sanches, Cesario
December 2, 1910

On September 27, 1910, at the cinder pit near Flagstaff, Arizona, Rafael Barela and Cesario Sanches murdered Gregorio Conejo, an aged Mexican, and robbed him of $210 he was known to carry. They hacked Conejo's body to pieces. They were arrested almost immediately and within eight days they had been indicted, tried, convicted, and sentenced to hang. Barela's mother, Mrs. Julia Trujillo de Barela, who lived in El Paso, Texas, made every effort to have her son's sentence commuted to life imprisonment, but she failed. Friends of both men and the consular representative of Spain, on behalf of Sanches, also asked for clemency but the crime was deemed too terrible to warrant any interference by Governor Richard E. Sloan. A death watch was maintained over Rafael Barela and Cesario Sanches in their steel-bound cell at the territorial prison in Florence, where they had been lodged pending their execution.

On Friday morning, December 2, 1910, twenty witnesses were escorted into the execution chamber and at 10:30 A.M. the two condemned man were brought from their cells by the warden, accompanied by Father Joseph Colombe. The death warrant had been read to them in their cells and both men declined to speak to the witnesses. The gallows would accommodate only one man and Sanches had been selected as the first prisoner to be placed on the trapdoor. Thirty-six-year-old Sanches had nerved himself for the ordeal and stood firmly as the guards strapped his ankles together, pulled the black hood over his face, and adjusted the noose around his neck. Father Colombe pressed a cross to the condemned man's lips beneath the hood and knelt before him in silent prayer. At the conclusion of the prayer the trapdoor was sprung and the body shot downward into the death chamber under the scaffold. Sanches' neck was broken and Drs. George M. Brockway and Edward S. Godfrey Jr. pronounced him dead in twelve and one half minutes. The body hung a few minutes more before the corpse was removed and deposited in its coffin.

Twenty-five-year-old Barela watched the execution of Sanches and, when the gallows was ready, he was led onto the trapdoor. His ankles were pinioned and, when the noose had been adjusted about his neck, the attending priest pressed the holy cross to Barela's lips beneath the black hood and then knelt in prayer. When the priest arose the trapdoor was sprung and Barela fell, but his neck was not broken and he strangled to death in twenty minutes. Both he and Sanches were buried in the Catholic cemetery later that evening.

Florence Arizona Blade-Tribune: December 3, 1910; *Phoenix Arizona Republican*: December 3, 1910.

Franco, Domingo
July 7, 1911

On March 18, 1911, Domingo Franco and Francisco Amado attended a dance at Harshaw in Santa Cruz County, Arizona. After the dance Amado and another man were arguing when Franco made a comment that caused Amado to call him a fool. Heated words were exchanged, followed by a struggle, during which Amado severely scratched Franco's face. The next morning Franco armed himself with a pistol and visited a store where several men usually congregated, including Amado. When Franco left, Amado followed and the two men walked down the road a short distance before Franco drew his pistol and shot Amado in the stomach. When the wounded man was found he had a pocketknife in his hand but the blades were closed, so Franco's later claim of self-defense was refuted. Amado was rushed to Patagonia for medical treatment but the wound was severe and he died a few hours later. Franco was arrested, indicted, tried, convicted of murder in the first degree on April 19, and sentenced to hang on July 7, 1911. A few days before Franco's execution his relatives applied to Governor Richard E. Sloan for a commutation of sentence but the executive did not find sufficient cause for interfering.

On the fatal morning, Franco was escorted from his cell to the execution chamber and took his place on the trapdoor. He stepped onto the trapdoor shortly after 11:00 A.M. and thanked the prison officials for their kind treatment during his confinement. His wrists and ankles were pinioned, the black cap was drawn over his face, and the noose was adjusted. At 11:15 A.M. the trap was sprung and fifteen minutes later Franco was pronounced dead by the prison physician. Though the usual formal invitations had been issued to officials and those entitled to be present only a few prison officials, a few convicts, a physician, and one newspaper reporter attended.

Phoenix Arizona Republican: July 8, 1911.

Gallegos, Alejandro
July 28, 1911

Louis D. Yaeger was one of the best known and best liked flock masters in Arizona. On the morning of May 9, 1911, he arrived in Humboldt, Yavapai County, Arizona, a half mile from where his flocks were grazing. He found that a band of his sheep had mixed with a band of Hutchinson's sheep and the herders of neither man seemed able to separate them. Alejandro Gallegos, a sheepherder in the employ of C.C. Hutchinson but a former employee of Yaeger, was in the party; Gallegos was drunk and armed with a rifle. Yaeger disarmed Gallegos, removed the cartridges from his gun, and handed the weapon back. Yeager called to the others to help him separate the sheep and all responded but Gallegos, to whom Yaeger paid no attention. After a few minutes Gallegos reloaded his rifle with cartridges from his pocket and, slipping around to one side of Yaeger, fired twice, killing him instantly.

Gallegos fled on foot but was pursued on horseback by two men from Humboldt, and he was captured before sunset. He raved like a madman when captured but later wept, and said he did not know why he had killed Yeager, as his former employer was his best friend. Yeager's body was taken to Phoenix and buried. A special grand jury was convened by Judge E.M. Doe and, when arraigned, Gallegos pled guilt; but the court formally heard the evidence before sentencing the man to hang. He was taken to the penitentiary and during his confinement was in utter despair and torment. A few days before Gallegos' execution Yeager's father filed an application pleading for a commutation of sentence on behalf of the condemned man, but Governor Richard E. Sloan had left the territory and Acting Governor Young would not act because the matter was being considered by the governor. The governor finally declined to intervene.

Once all hope was lost the ministrations of Father Heitz helped Gallegos resign himself to his fate. On his final morning Gallegos was brought to the gallows in the execution room at 10:30 A.M. and hardly a word was spoken once the prisoner appeared, except such words as the last ceremonies made necessary. The prisoner's wrists and arms, knees and ankles were bound with straps, the black hood was pulled over his face, the noose was cinched in place, and at 10:45 A.M. the trap was sprung. Eleven minutes later Dr. Brockway, the prison physician, pronounced him dead. The view of the witnesses had been obstructed because the base of the gallows was surrounded by a black curtain so the spectators only saw the rope suddenly become taut with a jerk that shook the scaffold. Next came the rebound and the rope became taut with less violence, and then for a few moments swayed, with each sweep shortening until it became still. The witnesses were then admitted beneath the scaffold and afterward the jury signed the death certificate. The body was cut down, deposited in its coffin, and buried that evening.

Florence Arizona Blade-Tribune: July 29, 1911; *Phoenix Arizona Republican*: July 29, 1911.

Colorado

The first explorer to enter the region which would become Colorado was Spaniard Francisco Coronado in 1541, but it was not until 1706 that Spain claimed Colorado and was in conflict with France over ownership. In 1803 the eastern portion was acquired from France by the United States in the Louisiana Purchase. The remainder of the state passed from Spain to Mexico in 1821 and hence to the United States as a concession in the Treaty of Guadalupe Hidalgo in 1848, following the war with Mexico. The Colorado Territory was formed in 1861 and Colorado was admitted as the 38th state on August 1, 1876.

Stoefel, John
April 7, 1859

On April 7, 1859, John Stoefel went out from their camp at Vasquer's Fork with his German father-in-law and two brothers-in-law to look for stray cattle. Stoefel soon returned alone and his behavior was so peculiar that he was restrained and questioned. He readily admitted that he and one brother-in-law had left the others and he said he had murdered him. A search was made and the body of the man was found, shot through the head. Stoefel was tried before Judge Seymour W. Wagoner and found guilty based on his own confession. He was taken forthwith and hanged from a tree.

Denver (CO) Rocky Mountain News: April 23, 1859.

Young, Moses
March 15, 1860

William West and Moses Young left their families in Leavenworth, Kansas, and traveled to Denver, Colorado, in 1859. West was employed by and lived with Young for several months but before January 1860 West had moved into his own house situated sixty-six feet from Young's house on the same line. Young still owed West money but could not pay him so he gave West several deeds to city lots as security, and while at Young's house the deeds lay around without any particular effort made to secure them. Shortly after West moved out he returned to Young's house and collected the deeds. In January Young outfitted West to go to the mines in the mountains but West returned after a few days, never having reached his destination, and this angered Young. The two men argued over the matter. On Monday, March 12, Young went to West's house and demanded return of the deeds held as security, and offered West an order on goods from Doyle & Company, which equaled the money owed. West refused and demanded money, but Young had no money so no arrangement could be made. West was then outfitting to go into the mountains on March 14 and Young told him to leave the deeds behind.

During the forenoon of March 13, 1860, J.M. Hunter was at West's house while the owner was away, and Young appeared carrying a double-barreled shotgun. He came to the house looking for West and said he wanted his papers. Young fired his gun into the air and then asked Hunter for buckshot, but Hunter had none so Young went to Dunn's store and bought $.25 worth of the largest buckshot, eighteen to the load. After noon Young returned to West's house without his gun and found West sitting on the bed while Hunter sat on the floor. West and Young tried to reach some agreement but none could be made and as soon as Young left West arose and bolted the door, saying that he was afraid of Young.

Soon Hunter arose, unbolted the door, and started for Young's house. West followed but took a course as far from Young's house as he could. When West was opposite Young's door, and Hunter just a short distance from it, Young appeared with his shotgun. Hunter called out, "Mose, don't shoot," and Young replied, "I said I would," as he fired one barrel. West, hearing Hunter's warning, turned partly around to retreat to his house when fifteen large buckshot struck him in the right side. He fell and cried out three times that he was killed and called on someone to arrest Young. West bled to death within minutes. Young fled and hid beneath a pile of harness in the attic of Stag Hall on Blake Street, but he was discovered by John O'Neill and William Byers at sundown, arrested, and held for trial. The following morning a people's court was convened and the first order of business was the appointment of a presiding judge and two associate judges, a secretary, and a sheriff who appointed five deputies. A jury of twelve men was empanelled and the charge was read, which set forth that Moses Young was being tried for murder in the first degree. This process took the entire morning, so the court recessed for dinner and reconvened at 2:00 P.M. Twelve witnesses were called before the evidence was summed up by the attorneys and the case was submitted to the jury, which deliberated a few minutes before returning a guilty verdict. The presiding judge, after conferring with his associates, sentenced Young to hang the following day, March 15, and detailed twenty-five men to take charge of the prisoner.

Early on the morning of March 15 men were busy erecting a gallows on the spot where

William West had died, and they completed every detail by noon. At 3:00 P.M. the Jefferson Rangers, a local militia unit, marched to Denver Hall to escort the prisoner to the scaffold, but found Young engaged in fervent prayer with the Rev. J.H. Kehler, so there was a brief delay. The party then started for the gallows, the prisoner within a hollow square of rangers. Young was supported by the Reverend Kehler and T.J. Bayard, Esq., with the sheriff and his deputies in front and rear. The steady tap of a drum paced the solemn procession and, upon their arrival, the Jefferson Rangers surrounded the scaffold to hold back the large crowd.

Young climbed the stairs onto the platform and Oscar B. Totton read the statement and resolution of the committee, and then Young's "statement of forgiveness" was appended. The prisoner and the Reverend Kehler knelt in prayer, after which Young shook hands with everyone on the platform as each man retired, leaving only the sheriff and one deputy. The prisoner stepped onto the trapdoor, where the black cap and noose were adjusted, his wrists and ankles were tied, and the sheriff and his assistant retired, leaving the condemned man alone. The trap was sprung at 4:21 P.M., with the prisoner dropping three feet, which broke his neck. At four minutes the body hung lifeless and in eleven minutes more the attending physicians pronounced him dead, and in another five minutes Young's body was cut down. The body was delivered to friends who buried his remains the following day at 11:00 A.M.

Middletown (NY) Banner of Liberty: May 2, 1860; *Janesville (WI) Daily Gazette:* March 23, 1860; *Golden (CO) Western Mountaineer:* March 21, 1860.

Gredler, Marcus
June 15, 1860

In June 1860 Marcus Gredler was traveling with the Roeders, a German family, and he had developed a great dislike for Jacob Roeder, whom he found quarrelsome. Many others shared Gredler's opinion of Jacob so the Roeders usually camped some distance from other parties to avoid difficulties. Jacob, his wife, Marcus Gredler, Frank Pampuch, and another man had left Denver on Tuesday, June 12, and that evening Jacob and Gredler quarreled about the choice of a campsite. They had settled their differences before going about their camp duties, when Gredler approached Mrs. Roeder and said that Jacob "would not last more than two or three days."

After supper Mrs. Roeder retired while Pampuch was busy spreading his bedroll, the second man was out of camp on some duty, and Gredler and Roeder sat by the fire. Mrs. Roeder was nearly asleep when she was aroused by a strange noise and looked out of the wagon to see Gredler standing over her husband, a bloody axe in Gredler's hands and her husband lying on the ground with a mortal gash on his head. But Roeder was still alive when Gredler yelled, "Damned Dutch s__ of a b___!" and struck a second blow with the axe. Gredler then dragged Roeder's dead body a short distance from camp saying, "Damn you, you'll never trouble me any more." Gredler returned shortly and took Roeder's revolver from the wagon, which he fired twice in the air as he threatened Mrs. Roeder, Pampuch and the other man with death if they revealed his crime. He insisted the killing was in self-defense and had them swear an oath to testify to that version. The third man tried to escape during the night but Gredler threatened him and he returned to his bedroll. The following morning Pampuch and the second man buried Roeder's remains while Gredler started for Denver. Four miles from camp Gredler met a Mr. Par and related his version of self-defense, then submitted to arrest. The prisoner was taken into Denver and held by a force of men under the direction of Sheriff John H. Kehler.

A people's court was convened on Thursday, June 14, 1860, and at 7:00 A.M. the prisoner was removed to Apollo Hall; but by 10:00 A.M. more than one thousand people had assembled, so the court reconvened at an open place beneath several shade trees. William M.

Slaughter was elected presiding judge with John W. Kerr and Charles P. Marion associate judges and the trial commenced, but as only five witnesses were called the case was concluded shortly after noon. Testimony was followed by closing arguments and the prisoner was given an opportunity to address the jury, but he only spoke of his good character and did not address the evidence. Judge Slaughter charged the jury, they retired at 4:20 P.M., and in forty minutes they returned a verdict of guilty of murder in the first degree. The judges conferred for several minutes before reading their judgment: "We the judges chosen by the people to try the case of Marcus Gredler for murder, of which crime a jury of his countrymen has found him guilty, do hereby, on behalf of the people, pass the following sentence: that the prisoner shall be hanged by the neck until dead on Friday the 15th day of June 1860 between the hours of 2 and 5 o'clock P.M."

A vote of the people present was proposed but the prisoner was first allowed to appeal his case to the multitude and he claimed innocence; said he was provoked; then spoke of his wife and child in the old country; his fond hope for a successful future in mining for gold when he emigrated to America; and his desire for an early return to his family. He spoke for ten minutes before announcing "I am done" and retaking his seat. The vote was then taken and the approval of the verdict and sentence was nearly unanimous. The prisoner was remanded to the custody of the sheriff at 5:30 P.M. and the crowd dispersed. The prisoner was closely guarded throughout the night and at dawn he was taken to the Broadwell House for a hearty breakfast, shaved, and given materials to write letters to his wife and friends.

At an early hour workmen had begun construction of the gallows on Cherry Creek bottom at the foot of Certia Street, only a short distance above the heavily populated part of the city. The scaffold was enclosed within a rope barricade two hundred feet in diameter to keep the crowd from rushing the gallows, and nearly four thousand people had gathered at the site by 2:55 P.M. when the procession began. The condemned man walked between the Reverends Kehler and Cormack, followed by a few friends and escorted by a strong police force on foot and horseback. Once upon the platform Gredler made a few remarks and then had Mr. Newman read his confession. The reverends conducted services and offered prayers before Gredler said good-bye to all and warned them to govern their passions. The noose was adjusted and a black cap was drawn over the prisoner's face before his wrists and ankles were bound and, at 3:30 P.M., the trap was sprung. Attending physicians pronounced him dead in twenty minutes and ten minutes later the body was cut down. Sheriff Kehler took charge of Gredler's remains and had them placed in the coffin provided by the county, and he was buried before sundown.

Denver (CO) Rocky Mountain News: June 13–15, 1860 (extras); June 20, 1860.

Gordon, James A.
October 13, 1860

On August 15, 1860, twenty-three-year-old James A. Gordon was on a spree at the Denver Hall when he brandished his revolver and threatened to kill someone; when he left the hall he shot at a stray dog, but missed. He then went to the Louisiana Lunchroom and ordered a drink but when served he shattered the bottle on the shelf behind the bar. As John Gantz left he was seized by the hair and dragged back into the lunchroom by Gordon, who pinned Gantz to the floor at the foot of the bar, then deliberately snapped his pistol at him at point-blank range. The first four cylinders were either empty or expended but the fifth time his weapon exploded in Gantz' face, killing the German instantly. Gordon fled but the following morning he was found by his friends, who told him he had killed a man and a lynch mob would hang him if he was found.

Gordon fled to Leavenworth, Kansas, but William H. Middaugh pursued the fugitive after he procured a warrant from Kansas judge Pettit and a special commission as a deputy U.S. marshal so he could cross territorial and state borders. He started with deputy sheriff Marshall Armstrong and secured the assistance of the sheriff of Coffee County, Kansas, as they trailed Gordon to Humboldt, where they were only a half hour behind the fugitive. When the lawmen were two miles out of Humboldt they saw a man, grazing his mule, who fit the description of Gordon. Middaugh, who was well known to the fugitive, remained in the wagon while the Coffee County sheriff and deputy Armstrong went for Gordon. They approached Gordon on foot with shotguns cocked and loaded with heavy buckshot. As Gordon saw the men coming he hurriedly tried to unpicket his mule, but they got the drop on him and he had to surrender or die. They took from him a large and small revolver and pinioned his arms, then took him into Humboldt where a blacksmith double ironed the prisoner before he was taken to Leavenworth.

At Leavenworth Judge Pettit held over the prisoner for his return to Denver and Middaugh was assured that there would be no obstacle to Gordon's extradition. However, on September 17 Judge Pettit, chief justice of the Kansas supreme court, held a hearing in which he erred in finding Denver to be in Montana County and not in Arappahoe County and he released Gordon. Before Gordon could make his escape from the city a large mob of Germans, incensed at the injustice, took Gordon to the nearest tree to lynch him. He fought so desperately that his clothes were torn off during the struggle, but the men managed to get a noose around his neck three times and hoist him up twice before Middaugh, Mayor McDowell and others were able to rescue him and lodge him in jail. Middaugh took his prisoner to Denver, arriving early on Friday, September 28, and turned Gordon over to Sheriff Kehler.

The following morning a people's court was convened and A. Hunt, Esq., General Larimer and Colonel William Person were appointed judges and it was agreed to proceed according to matters of fact and the circumstances of the case and not according to forms of law. The facts of the case were then proven during hours of testimony which continued until late into the night, and the trial continued until Sunday evening when it closed with forceful statements by counsels. Gordon made a lengthy statement which detailed his flight and attempted lynching, but insisted he remembered nothing of the crime. He was convicted of murder in the first degree and, after consultation by the three judges, he was sentenced to hang on Saturday, October 13, and by a unanimous vote the people affirmed the decision and sentence. Gordon's friends then stirred sympathy during the week and on the Thursday and Friday before the execution they circulated petitions to have Gordon released and banished from the community. They acquired more than eight hundred signatures, many from people new to the city who knew little of the crime, and on the strength of these petitions a meeting was called to consider the matter of a pardon. Judge McLure, Colonel J.D. Henderson and John C. Moore spoke for Gordon, while Dr. Rankin and Judge Bennett spoke for the people. When the statements concluded the question was proposed: "Shall the verdict of the jury, and the sentence of the court, endorsed by the people on Sunday last, be endorsed, sustained, and carried out?" This query was followed by one thundering shout of "Aye!" and not a single "Nay!" was heard.

During his final night Gordon was guarded by fifty men resolved to prevent escape or rescue by his friends. Early Saturday morning, October 13, 1860, the gallows was erected on Cherry Creek bottom at the foot of Certia Street, only a short distance from the heavily populated part of the city. Rope barricades were strung several hundred feet from the scaffold, as had been done when Gredler was hanged at that location on June 15, 1860, and by 3:00 P.M. over three thousand people had gathered. Gordon, riding in a closed carriage with Sheriff William Middaugh, arrived at 3:30 P.M., guarded by three hundred armed men; the infantry formed a hollow square around the gallows while the cavalry took its position by the rope barricades. Gordon and

Middaugh, with the Reverend Rankin and several assistants, ascended the stairs, where the reverend offered a prayer. Gordon called for Peter Doran to come to the scaffold for a brief conference and then the prisoner addressed the crowd, thanking his friends for trying to reprieve him and those who had visited him during his confinement. He turned to Sheriff Middaugh and said, "Remember to fix the rope so that it will break my neck as soon as it possibly can. All I want is to have you remember me to my old friends and parents; don't forget that—remember me to those old friends. Oh! If some good friend here would shoot me, I would be happy; but it is all well; good-bye; fix the rope so that it will break my neck the quickest possible. Good-bye. Oh! God have mercy!" Gordon's wrists and ankles were tied, the black cap was pulled on and the noose carefully adjusted and, in a moment, the trap was sprung. In twenty minutes he was pronounced dead, the body was cut down and given to friends of the deceased, and he was buried on Sunday.

Golden (CO) Western Mountaineer: August 30, 1860; September 13, 1860; September 27, 1860; October 4, 1860; October 11, 1860.

Watters, Patrick
December 20, 1860

Patrick "Patsy" Watters emigrated to America and finally settled in Colorado. He agreed to accompany Thomas R. Freeman down the Platte River to buy hay at Hamet's, and look over a piece of land that interested Freeman. Watters was to be paid $1 per day for his work loading hay; but before they left, Freeman borrowed a double-barreled shotgun from a Mr. Neely and $10 from Joseph Johnson. They started on Sunday, November 25, 1860, and the following day arrived at Hamet's and loaded their hay. Afterward Freeman looked at the plot of land and negotiated a deal, and the next morning they headed for Cole's to have the land claim recorded. Watters was riding next to Freeman because the bed was full of hay and he carried the shotgun across his lap. With the trip coming to a close Watters, who had from the beginning planned to rob Freeman, shot his employer in the back of the head with one charge of buckshot. Freeman fell backward into the wagon bed and Watters grabbed the reins and drove the wagon two hundred yards off the road into the brush. He pulled Freeman's body from the wagon and, after taking $11 from his pockets, covered the body with hay. He took the horse and several items of personal property, which he sold along the road as he fled toward Cottonwood Springs.

The wagon was found under such suspicious circumstances that a warrant was immediately issued and Mr. Shortridge was deputized to pursue Watters. The deputy found his man at Cottonwood Springs, where he had arrived only a few hours earlier, but the prisoner had none of Freeman's property with him and the body had not yet been found. Along the trail deputy Shortridge found Freeman's horse, overshoes, powder flask, and the double-barreled shotgun; the men who bought these items would later place them in the possession of Watters. The prisoner insisted that he knew nothing of Freeman's disappearance, so a committee of men proposed a ruse to convince Watters he was about to be lynched, but only after the men promised deputy Shortridge they would not raise Watters' feet off the ground. As soon as the noose was in place the prisoner agreed to show them the body and led them to the grave thirty miles from Denver. John Wanless examined the body and found one buckshot just under the skin of the cheek, but Watters said Freeman had been shot from behind, and this proved to be true when the doctor discovered two buckshot in the head, as the rest had exited through the face. Watters said the killing was accidental, but as he stood over the body he said, "Poor fellow; I'm sorry I killed him." Several other admissions proved that he had intentionally killed Freeman and refuted his claim that it was accidental, so Watters was taken to Denver and jailed.

On Wednesday, December 19, 1860, in

response to a published summons, a large meeting of citizens assembled near Criterion Hall for Watters' trial. Colonel Person was elected presiding judge with General Marshall and E.H. Hart associate judges and at 2:00 P.M. the indictment was read: "The People of the Pike's Peak Gold Region *vs.* Patrick Watters. The People of the Pike's Peak Gold Region, assembled at the City of Denver, the 19th day of December, A.D. 1860, do find and present that on or about the 30th of November 1860, at the said Pike's Peak Gold Region, one Patrick Watters did make a felonious assault on one Thomas R. Freeman, then and there being, and him the said Thomas R. Freeman, with premeditated malice did murder and slay, contrary to all laws of God and man."

The case was opened with ten witnesses appearing for the prosecution and three for the defense, and the prosecution then waived a closing argument while the defense reviewed the evidence in the best light possible for their client. The jurors were then charged by Judge Person and they retired for ten minutes' deliberation before returning a verdict of guilty as charged. Judge Person asked if Watters had anything to say about why a sentence of death should not be pronounced and Watters said he did not, so he was sentenced to hang the following day. The prisoner spent the remainder of Wednesday and Thursday morning arranging his worldly affairs and making a full written confession of his guilt. A little before 3:00 P.M. Sheriff E.W. Wynkoop, deputy Shortridge and a posse of special deputies formed in front of Criterion Hall and in a few minutes the prisoner appeared. He was escorted to the gallows, where he spent several minutes in prayer and communion with his priest and, when given the opportunity to speak, confessed the murder to the crowd of thousands. The condemned man was prepared, placed on the trapdoor, and at 3:09 P.M. the trap was sprung. Watters broke his neck in the fall, but was allowed to hang for several minutes after he was pronounced dead. Watters' remains were cut down, placed in a plain pine coffin, and buried at county expense that evening.

Denver (CO) Rocky Mountain News: December 19–21, 1860; *Golden (CO) Western Mountaineer*: December 20, 1860.

Van Horn, William S.
December 18, 1863

Mrs. Squires, a "woman of the lowest character," had come to Colorado from Kansas with William S. van Horn in late August 1863. They leased the Exchange at Gregory Point and opened a whiskey shop. In her capacity as operator of the shop, Squires became intimate with Josiah Copeland and van Horn was openly jealous, but he took no aggressive action. On October 17 Squires went to Central City and met Copeland, who invited her to supper and that evening accompanied her on the road to Gregory Point. The couple took Casey Road and reached the powder magazine before they became aware of a man following them, so Copeland went back to investigate and discovered van Horn. The two men exchanged heated words and van Horn, without warning or provocation, pulled his six-shooter and fired three bullets at Copeland. All three bullets struck Copeland in the head or body and two bullets inflicted mortal wounds. Copeland turned, ran past Squires and collapsed, and van Horn then carefully selected several large rocks and crushed the skull of the helpless man.

The body was found and, the relationship between the three parties being known, van Horn was immediately suspected. He was arrested and confined at the courthouse to appear before a justice of the peace, and at his examination he was held to answer to the grand jury. When the prisoner was being moved to the jail a large crowd nearly took him from the officers, intending to lynch him, but Sheriff William Cozens convinced the mob to disperse and allow the law take its course. On November 23, 1863, the trial of van Horn commenced before Judge Charles L. Armour of the U.S. court at Central City. The jury was empanelled and the indictment read before the court adjourned for dinner. When the court reconvened the testimony was heard and the attorneys from both sides made eloquent speeches before the judge charged the jury and sent them to deliberate. Shortly after supper they returned a guilty verdict. The defense filed a motion for a new trial on the grounds that this court lacked jurisdiction but the motion was denied and the prisoner was sentenced to hang on December 18. The condemned man was confined in the Central City jail but he tried to escape so he was moved to Denver and lodged in the Larimer Street jail, a far superior facility. On December 17 he was returned to Central City under escort of Squadron D, First Cavalry, commanded by Lt. Dickerson, and the Methodist Reverend Vincent was summoned. The reverend learned that the prisoner was unrepentant; nevertheless Vincent returned the next morning and prayed with the condemned man. But still van Horn showed no remorse and would not confess nor even admit he had done wrong.

The scaffold had been built on the hill overlooking Mountain City from the north side and within a few rods of the spot where the crime occurred. Soon after breakfast the crowd began to gather and by 10:00 A.M. more than fifteen hundred men, women and children had gathered at the scaffold and on the adjacent hillsides. A rope barricade protected the gallows, a black wooden coffin was stored by the scaffold, and a grave had been dug on the hill overlooking the site. At 10:30 A.M. the prisoner, dressed in a grey suit and hat, was taken from his cell and seated in a carriage. Troop D, First Cavalry, surrounded the carriage to keep the crowd back and Marshal Hunt rode with the driver while inside the prisoner sat between Sheriffs Cozens and Wilson. At the scaffold the crowd parted and the prisoner ascended and took his place on the trapdoor without prompting. He was asked if he had anything to say but declined, so Marshal Hunt tied his hands behind him and his legs were bound together, the noose was positioned. After his hat was removed, the black cap was pulled over his face. The men on the scaffold turned away as a Mr. Caldwell sprang the trap and the prisoner fell four feet, breaking his neck. The body hung for twenty minutes before attending physicians pronounced him dead. Sheriff Cozens then lowered the body into the coffin and in a few minutes the remains of van Horn were buried.

Black Hawk (CO) Daily Mining Journal: December 18, 1863; *Denver (CO) Weekly Commonwealth*: October 28, 1863.

Foster, Franklin; Stone, Henry
May 24, 1866

Henry Stone enlisted in the army and in 1865 his unit transferred to Camp Wardwell on the Platte Road in Colorado. Soon afterward he met Franklin Foster and on January 5, 1866, Foster and Stone deserted. They rode toward Central City, taking a southwesterly course to the Platte River Road where it crossed Bijon Creek; after traveling one mile they came upon the camp of Isaac H. Agustus and H. Sluman. The two soldiers tied their horses to the wagons and asked if anything was broken, but Agustus explained that several of their five horses had broken loose during the night and they had spent the entire day hunting them. Stone stood near Sluman, his six-shooter in hand as he spun the cylinder, but it was Foster who suddenly pulled one of his two revolvers and shot at Augustus six times, badly mutilating his face and head, and then Stone shot Sluman twice. Foster pulled his second revolver and shot Sluman five times, killing him.

Foster and Stone went through the pockets of their victims and Foster took $100 from Agustus, who was found alive and taken to Camp Wardwell; but he died without regaining consciousness. Sluman's body was examined and found to have three fatal wounds: one through his bowels; one through the right breast; and the third bullet piercing his heart. Stone and Foster rode a short distance after the killings, camped, and made plans to go east, but they were arrested by sundown the next day, They were charged with two murders and lodged in jail. They were tried in Judge

Gale's courtroom, convicted of first degree murder, and sentenced to hang on May 24, 1866.

The Reverend Potter, a Baptist minister, attended Foster for days before his execution but as the hours dwindled Foster called for Father Macheboeuf and also called for the Baptist Reverend Clark; but only the Reverend McClure administered to Stone. Both prisoners slept soundly their last night and after breakfast the two condemned men dressed in new slacks, white shirts, brown linen coats, and slippers. The gallows had been constructed at the foot of the low bluff overlooking Cherry Creek near the southern border of the city. The location had been chosen to accommodate a large crowd, and the authorities were not disappointed when more than three thousand men, women and children attended.

At 1:00 P.M. the prisoners were driven from the jail to the site in a closed carriage, escorted by deputy sheriff Bailey, U.S. marshal Earl and jailor Hasket. They were met at the gallows by Sheriff R. Sopris and his deputies, the Reverends McClure, Potter and Clark. The Reverend McClure read scripture and led the singing of "Rock of Ages," and then addressed the Throne of Grace on behalf of Stone. The Reverend Clark did the same for Foster and, without further delay, each man had his wrists and ankles pinioned and the noose adjusted. At 1:34 P.M. each man had a black cap pulled over his face and in a moment the trap was sprung. At 1:51 P.M. the attending physician pronounced them dead and the bodies were cut down. The remains of both men were placed in plain pine coffins provided by the county and buried at county expense that evening.

Denver (CO) Rocky Mountain News: January 10, 1866; May 23–25, 1866.

Carr, Joel
November 6, 1869

On Saturday evening, November 6, 1869, Joel Carr went to Daniel Steele's hotel in Evans for his supper; but Carr had to wait a length of time he deemed excessive, so he began to abuse Steele and his family. Steele ordered Carr out of the hotel but Carr obtained a six-shooter and returned to the hotel, where he again berated Steele. The proprietor made every effort to pacify the bully but, when that failed, he tried to get away. Carr fired a single shot at Steele and the bullet struck Steele near the left ear and lodged in the forepart of Steele's brain. Steele collapsed, never regained consciousness, and died in thirty minutes. Carr threw down the revolver and started walking toward Denver but had not gone far before he was captured by H.B. Haskell, who had taken a load of lumber into town, learned of the shooting, and pursued the murderer.

Carr was taken back to Evans and a people's court was convened. Captain R. Sopris was elected judge, and a jury was empanelled. The trial lasted thirty minutes and following a few minutes' deliberation a verdict of guilty of first degree murder was returned. Judge R. Sopris sentenced Carr to be taken forthwith to the nearest stout limb and hanged by the neck until dead. The sentence was affirmed by the people and immediately carried out by a committee appointed by the multitude, all others present serving as witnesses to the execution. Carr was bound hand and foot and blindfolded. A sturdy rope with a slip knot was placed around his neck and he was pulled up, the loose end of the rope then being tied to the tree trunk. Carr died of strangulation so, to be certain he could not be resuscitated, he was left dangling overnight. In the morning the body was cut down, placed in a pine coffin, and buried in an unmarked grave.

Denver (CO) Rocky Mountain News: November 8, 1869.

Smith, George
February 18, 1870

See Addendum, pages 205–206

Miears, Theodore
January 24, 1873

In May 1871 twenty-six-year-old Theodore Miears found work on Tom Lewis' ranch, twelve miles from Denver on the Platte River and two miles from Littleton. At the end of July, Lewis and his three ranch hands visited Denver but once in town Miears quit and began looking for another job. On July 31 he went to the ranch of Mrs. Arabella "Belle" Newton near Littleton and was hired as a ranch hand. Mrs. Newton had previously taken in a man named George Bonacina and they lived together, claiming to be brother and sister; but Mrs. Newton's neighbors were skeptical and angered by their cohabitation. Miears, after being hired, started for Denver to pick up his clothes and Mrs. Newton accompanied him to spend a few days at the Tremont House.

Miears immediately returned to the ranch and, with Bonacina, started harvesting grain. As they worked Bonacina warned him of rumors that the neighbors might try to burn the grain. Bonacina said that he and Miears would have to sleep in the field as soon as the grain was stacked. Both men carried arms to protect the grain and each man had at hand a shotgun and a pistol, and Bonacina also had a rifle. Mrs. Newton had told the men she would give a suit of clothes to the man who killed the first person who came for her grain. Over the next few days the men had disagreements over Bonacina's treatment of his horses, and Bonacina swore constantly, which upset Miears. On Sunday Bonacina hitched the team, borrowed $25 from Miears, and went into Denver to get Mrs. Newton. After 8:00 P.M. on Thursday, August 10, Bonacina told Miears to go out to the stacks; Bonacina soon followed and the men made their beds. However, before they retired Miears asked for repayment of the $25 dollar loan and told Bonacina he no longer wanted to work for Mrs. Newton, but Bonacina said he did not want him to leave until the threshing and other work was done. Bonacina made no effort to repay the money so an hour later Miears said he was leaving the next day and demanded repayment of the loan, but in response Bonacina yelled, "You damned lousy s__ of a b___, I won't pay it, but I'll pay you now."

According to Miears, Bonacina reached for his rifle and in self-defense he drew his revolver and shot once. Bonacina fell backwards, wounded and helpless, when Miears shot him again, killing him. Miears went to the house to kill Mrs. Newton so that she could not sound an alarm, and called to her, saying, "They were around," meaning someone tried to burn her grain. He said, "George is chasing them," and when Mrs. Newton came to within fifteen feet of him he shot her, the buckshot causing an ugly wound in her breast. She staggered back into the house and hid during the night while Miears returned to the stacks, covered Bonacina's body with hay, and slept. In the morning Mrs. Newton rode to Lyman's Ranch and Mr. Lyman returned with a team and took away Newton's wagon. After Lyman left, Miears went into the house, ate, then went to Lyman's for a horse. By 9:00 A.M. the murderer was fleeing southward, went over the divide, and continued on to Woodbury's Stagecoach Station to wait for the coach from Denver to Pueblo.

Sheriff D.J. Cook was notified of Bonacina's murder and telegraphed Colorado City and Pueblo to watch for the fugitive, so news of the murder had already reached Woodbury's before Miears arrived. The fugitive had been drinking whiskey on the trail and at Woodbury's he continued drinking heavily, so when he slept the caps were removed from his shotgun and his revolver was taken. When the stagecoach arrived he awoke to find he was the prisoner of Sheriff Cook, who had come in on the coach. The next coach returning to Denver took the sheriff and his prisoner back to Denver and Miears was lodged in the county jail. Miears was indicted for murder and his two day trial commenced February 5, 1872, but after he was convicted of first degree murder a new trial was granted. The second trial finally began on October 21, 1872, and two days later the defendant was again convicted of first degree murder; on December 30, 1872, Judge Wells sentenced him to hang on January 24, 1873. Appeals were filed and it was believed that a writ of error might be granted staying the execution, but the judge denied the motion. A petition from citizens was then taken to acting governor Frank Hall but this was rejected. A writ of error was next taken to Judge Belford of the 2nd Judicial District, but he also refused to grant a stay. The final effort was to file an appeal with Chief Justice Moses Hallett but on January 23 he also denied the motion.

During his incarceration Miears maintained a stolid indifference to his fate and spent his time reading a German prayer book. Two Catholic priests attended him constantly those last two days. When Miears was informed that his last hope was gone he seemed perfectly resigned, but turnkey Frank Smith continued to keep a close watch on his prisoner. Miears' attorney, at 6:00 P.M. that final night, agreed to write to the prisoner's mother and sisters and took a lock of his hair to enclose in the letter; he said he would wait at the telegraph office for a last minute respite. In the morning the prisoner made a full confession while tailor Kastor measured him for his burial suit; he ordered a black sack coat, black pantaloons, vest, and a white shirt. Kastor returned in a half hour for a fitting and Miears was fully satisfied, then joked, "I will probably not need another right away." Miears said later, "I have made my peace with my Maker and I die happy in the Catholic faith, feeling that I will soon be in heaven." On being asked if he felt remorse, he replied, "Oh, yes, a little; but then, there is no use crying over spilt milk."

By 1:15 P.M. the street in front of the jail was crowded with curious spectators and the elegant closed carriage standing near the sidewalk was the focus of intense scrutiny. Miears had his dinner shortly after noon, dressed, and spent his last hour receiving spiritual consolation and absolution from the two priests. At 1:30 P.M. Sheriff Cook appeared, read the death warrant, and then announced that Miears' time had come. The prisoner said farewell to each prisoner and to turnkey Frank Smith. At 2:00 P.M. Fathers Robinson and Borg emerged from the jail, attired in clerical robes and carrying crucifixes, and entered the carriage. In a moment the condemned man, unshackled for the first time in weeks, appeared with Sheriff Cook and deputy Smith and joined the priests. The Denver Scouts, a local militia group, drew sabers and led the way to the gallows; behind was county physician Dr. Heimberger in his buggy, and the procession was flanked on all sides by a large crowd.

The gallows had been erected at the confluence of Cherry Creek and the Platte River and was constructed of heavy pine timbers well riveted together. At 3:00 P.M. the Governor's Guard arrived and formed a cordon around the gallows to prevent the crowd from closing in, and the procession arrived fifteen minutes later. The occupants of the carriage alighted as the Denver Scouts cleared a passageway through the crowd and took up positions around the scaffold. The prisoner climbed the stairs and took his place upon the trapdoor without direction; on the platform with him were the two priests, the sheriff, and deputies Frank and Bill Smith. A short prayer was offered and the prisoner kissed the crucifix before he was given his opportunity to speak to the crowd. He said only, "Farewell, I'm a-going into another world." The deputies had pinioned Miears' wrists and ankles during the proceedings so when the prisoner concluded his short remark Sheriff Cook adjusted the noose and deputy Frank Smith pulled on the black cap. The prisoner waited alone while everyone retired from the platform and at 3:19 P.M. the trap was sprung. The condemned man dropped four feet, breaking his neck, and Dr. Heimberger, coroner Dr. Mariz, and the Denver Guard's surgeon, Dr. Williams, monitored Miears' pulse, which ceased in six minutes, and they pronounced him dead. The body was allowed to hang for eleven minutes more before being cut down and placed in the pine coffin. Miears' remains were delivered to the city sexton, who placed them in an express wagon and drove them to a spot near the city cemetery, where Miears was buried next to three murderers who had preceded him to a Denver gallows.

Denver (CO) Rocky Mountain News: January 24–25, 1873.

IDAHO

Idaho was part of the "Oregon Country" when it was acquired from Great Britain in 1846. A dispute persisted over the northern boundary of the Oregon Country between the parallels of and 54° 40' and 42°, which had been under joint control of the United States and Great Britain and included the area between the northern border of California and the southern border of Alaska. Although there was a strong movement in America to claim the 54° 40' boundary for the United States — Alaska's southern boundary agreed to by Russia — President James K. Polk surprised everyone when, on June 15, 1846, he agreed to the parallel of 49° to separate the United States from Canada. This agreement gave the United States sole control over the area that would become Idaho. The Idaho Territory was established on March 4, 1863, and Idaho was admitted as the 43rd state on July 3, 1890.

Howard, William; Lowery, Chris; Romaine, Jim
March 4, 1864

In 1863 William "Doc" Howard, James Romaine and G. Christopher Lowery were in Lewiston, Montana Territory, when Lloyd Magruder left with a pack train loaded with goods for his Bannack store. They met Magruder on the trail and worked their way into his confidence but, when they arrived in Bannack, they found that miners were leaving daily for new strikes in Virginia City. Magruder stocked his store in Bannack and continued to the new boomtown, where he sold the remainder of his goods, receiving $30,000 in payment. He returned to Bannack to buy more mules but needed help with his growing pack train so, when the Chalmers brothers asked to accompany him, he agreed. The Chalmers had done well at Bannack and had accumulated more than $1600 in gold dust. Charles Allen, a long time employee of Magruder, and William Phillips joined the party and Magruder hired William "Uncle Billy" Page to complete his crew.

After traveling toward Lewiston for several days they camped in a clearing with a black rock cliff on one side and a deep ravine on the other; they released the animals to graze in a meadow a short distance from camp. Magruder and Lowery were on first watch so they went to a point where they could guard the stock and built a small campfire. Lowery took one of the camp axes with him "to cut wood or drive stakes to tether the animals." Magruder was filling his pipe when Lowery said he would gather more wood and picked up the axe. When Magruder bent over the fire to light his pipe Lowery struck him on the head, knocking him senseless, and then struck several more times, killing him.

He returned to the main camp and woke Romaine and Howard, but whispered to Page to stay in his blankets, and the three men murdered the Chalmers brothers with two camp axes. Romaine and Lowery next went to Phillips' sleeping form while Howard took a shotgun and slipped into the tent where Allen slept, and when Phillips' death groans woke the sleeping teamster Howard shot Allen in the head, blowing off the entire back of his skull. They dragged Magruder's remains into camp, wrapped all five bodies and threw them over the precipice into a ravine, and then burned or buried most of the camp outfit. They abandoned those animals of questionable value but, when the animals followed, they were driven down a canyon and shot, all except a dozen mules which ran into the brush and hid. The horses and two good mules were driven into Lewiston and left with Bishop Goodrich "until spring." Romaine, Howard, Lowery and Page then took the stage to Walla Walla, Washington, continued to Wallula, and then went to Portland, Oregon, where they boarded the *Sierra Nevada* steamer for San Francisco.

Hill Beachy, owner of the stagecoach line, recognized Lowery when he bought the stagecoach tickets at Lewiston and noticed that the names given were aliases. He investigated and found the animals left by the men; he recognized the horses belonging to Magruder. When the old teamster failed to turn up after several days, Beachy obtained extradition papers from acting governor William B. Daniels and, with Thomas "Pike" Farrell, went after the four fugitives. They missed the men by two days at Walla Walla and by one day at Wallula and at Portland, the first town with a telegraph, they missed the men by hours. They decided not to wait for the next boat and took the stagecoach southward but, before leaving, Beachy telegraphed ahead and asked that the fugitives be arrested when they disembarked; so, when Beachy arrived in San Francisco, the fugitives were in jail.

Before Beachy arrived the four men hired a lawyer to fight extradition and the attorney also filed a writ of habeas corpus with California's supreme court. Beachy sent Farrell back to Lewiston with the news while he went to Sacramento to have his extradition papers signed, and it took several days to convince the governor to endorse the extradition. He next hired an attorney to fight the writ and soon had his prisoners aboard ship bound for Portland, with San Francisco lawmen as guards and a military escort waiting at Portland to escort them to Lewiston. After a close call with a Lewiston lynch mob the prisoners were jailed at the Luna House, the hotel owned by Beachy, but were quickly moved to the Fort Lapwai guardhouse, then returned to a newly built jail in Lewiston when the time for trial neared. Page was not charged as he had not participated in the murders though he knew all the details, turned state's evidence, and after testifying was released. Howard, Lowery and Romaine were tried in January and the three defendants were convicted of first degree murder, the jury reaching a decision without leaving their seats. On January 26, 1864, Judge Parks sentenced them to hang on March 4.

Romaine and Howard slept well on the night of March 2 but Lowery was restless and often blurted out, "Damn the thing!" or just, "Damn it!" He told the other two he would "go ahead and select the first camping ground," and that he would like to "bribe some s__ of a b___ to take me up strangler's gulch two days ahead of time." On the night before the execution each man asked for, and was given, a dose of morphine so that all three slept soundly, and then spent their last morning praying with their Catholic priest. At 11:30 A.M. the infantry from Fort Lapwai arrived with the vehicle that would convey the prisoners to the gallows and forty-five minutes later the troops, under Lt. Purdy, formed a hollow square around the wagon and the handcuffed prisoners were brought from the jail. They took their seats in the wagon, with a guard on both sides of each prisoner, and were driven to the gallows. Upon arrival the troops formed a square around the gallows to keep the crowd back and the prisoners, with two guards each, the sheriff and deputy Hill Beachy and the U.S. marshal climbed onto the platform.

The condemned men sat in the chairs provided while the priest read a short prayer, and then the prisoners were asked if they had anything to say. Howard rose first, stepped forward and asserted his innocence. Lowery came next and stated that he could clear the other two prisoners, who were innocent, but to do so he would implicate seven other men "whom he loved more than life itself," then insisted that Page was the real murderer before he turned to Romaine and Howard and asked them to forgive him for killing them. Lowery then said he was ready for them to "launch the boat," and several times referred to a letter he had left. Romaine had his turn next but was unable to say his entire piece, except, "I am an innocent man, I want you to distinctly understand that." The nooses were adjusted while each man gave various instructions to the sheriff and deputy, and Howard finally asked Beachy to see that it was done right. As

Beachy examined the work, Romaine said that Beachy could have cleared him, and made other such suggestions until he finally "broke down and cried like a baby."

With all in readiness the sheriff asked if they were ready and Howard replied, "All ready!" followed by Lowery who said, "Launch your boat, she is nothing but an old mud scow now anyhow!" There was a long pause before Romaine said, "Yes!" The lever was moved, the trap was sprung, and the three men fell beneath the platform where they were hidden from view by a curtain. Dr. M.A. Kelly was in attendance and pronounced the last man dead at thirty minutes. They were immediately cut down and placed in the coffins provided. Lowery's letter was then opened by the sheriff and it was found to be a tirade of obscenities shedding no light whatever upon the crime. In May William Page led a party of men to the spot where the murders had occurred and as much of the remains and property as could be found were recovered and taken to Lewiston. Page then became a nuisance about town for the next year, until he became interested in a woman who was living with another man. One morning he broke into their house and beat the woman's paramour but, when Page returned later in the day, the man was waiting and shot him dead in self-defense.

Boise (ID) News: March 26, 1864; *The Dalles (OR) Mountaineer*: February 17, 1864; *Boise Idaho Daily Statesman*: May 23, 1896.

McBride, Anthony
January 24, 1868

On Sunday evening, August 11, 1867, Anthony McBride visited a camp in Payette Valley and noticed two Chinamen already asleep in their bedrolls. He asked the others in camp, "Are they wild Indians?" and the men answered that they were not. McBride then said, "I think I will shoot them anyway," and threatened to shoot the witnesses if they interfered. He pulled his six-shooter and shot one of the sleeping Chinese men several times, and the victim bled to death in minutes; but the witnesses managed to overpower, disarm, and arrest McBride before he could shoot the second Chinaman. The prisoner had his examination before Judge Gillespie the following Saturday and was held over for the grand jury. Deputy sheriff Cahalan took custody of the prisoner and transported him to Boise by stagecoach. While traveling McBride talked of the murder and said his only regret was that he had not killed the witnesses. He would later present, as his defense, that he was so drunk he did not know what he was doing and thought the Chinaman was a wild Indian. He was indicted, tried, convicted of first degree murder, and sentenced to hang on January 24, 1868. Neither appeal nor application for executive clemency would delay the proceedings. As the fatal day approached Fathers Poulin and Cazeau attended to the prisoner's spiritual needs.

The gallows had been erected two miles from town near the mouth of Crane's Gulch and Sheriff Lindsey detailed a guard to maintain order among the three hundred spectators gathered that morning. The sheriff, Undersheriff Yates and Father Cazeau arrived at the gallows with the prisoner at 1:00 P.M. McBride mounted the scaffold and took his place on the trapdoor. After the priest made a few remarks McBride stepped forward and made a brief speech, repeating his defense of drunkenness, and concluded that "As I am to meet God the next minute, I am innocent of the crime of murder." He then stepped back and again centered himself on the trapdoor beneath the noose. Undersheriff Yates read the death warrant as the condemned man's wrists and ankles were being pinioned and then Yates adjusted the noose. McBride said several times, "My God! My God!" and appeared to be praying, but just before the hood was pulled on the prisoner noticed a fellow trooper in the crowd and said to him, "Good-bye sergeant; we are not on the Truckee now," and then spoke his last words, "Good-bye gentlemen, All!" As soon as Yates pulled the black hood over McBride's eyes the trap was sprung by Sheriff Lindsey. McBride's neck was broken in the fall and not a twitch nor convulsive movement was seen. He was quickly pronounced dead but the body hung a while longer before being cut down and placed in the plain pine coffin provided by the county. McBride's remains were driven directly to the graveyard and buried before sundown.

Boise Idaho Daily Statesman: August 17–18, 1867; January 24–25, 1868; May 23, 1896.

Walters, Simeon
December 10, 1869

Simeon Walters was living near Silver City, Owyhee County, Idaho, in October 1868 when he made arrangements to purchase a ranch from Joseph L. Bacon that was located on Reynolds Creek on the stage road between Boise and Silver City twenty miles from the latter. On October 19 Walters hired a buggy and team from a Silver City livery and drove to Bacon's ranch to complete the sale, but found Bacon was at Ritchey's ranch. He went after Bacon, found him herding J.C. Bernard's cattle, and insisted that Bacon accompany him to Boise to complete the sale. However, Bacon declined as he was needed with the herd, so Walters, with Mrs. Bernard, continued on to Bernard's ranch on the Snake River. It was late when the two men arrived with the cattle but Walters renewed his demand that Bacon accompany him to Boise City. Bacon objected, saying it was too late and that "not a scratch of a pen nor a paper will exchange hands until I see what sort of money you will pay, good or bogus."

On the morning of October 21 Bacon told Bernard that if he made the trade he would not return, so Bernard gave a small amount of money to Walters to buy ten pounds of coffee, tea, nails, and candles. When Bacon and Walters left Bernard's ranch Bacon wore an overcoat, heavy woolen shirt and pantaloons, and a belt with a distinctive U.S. percussion cap box and a scabbard containing a revolver. Just before noon Walters and Bacon passed J.H. Jackson, who noticed them because Walters was driving from the left side, which was quite peculiar. An hour later Walters, driving alone a mile north of Dry Creek, passed Thomas Kifer, who was driving a team of oxen toward Boise City. Walters arrived in Boise before 2:00 P.M. and told liveryman J.D. Agnew to care for the horses as he would use them again that night. Walters began dusting the buggy and Agnew said it wasn't necessary as he would wash it, but Walters objected and said he wanted it dusted and would not allow Agnew near the buggy. Walters took a belt, scabbard and pistol from the wagon, which he sold to gunsmith Lewis Heyd for $12, and while there had his pistol reloaded with two cartridges. He then went to Roth's store and bought the items for Bernard and asked Roth if he could leave a trunk with him for safekeeping.

After supper Walters drove his buggy out of town but soon returned with a plain-looking trunk, and this trunk would later be identified as one Bacon had left with Sy Polk containing the deed to the ranch, account books, clothes, and a picture of Bacon's wife. Walters next drove to Bernard's, arriving at 7:00 A.M. on October 22; but the horses looked as if he had been driving all night even though the trip from Boise should have taken only a few hours. He gave Bernard his supplies but the coffee was missing; he told Bernard that he had given Bacon $1260 in greenbacks for the ranch, said that Bacon was satisfied with the exchange, and that he had left Bacon "with some muttonhead" in Boise. Walters saddled a horse from his team and rode toward Boise and was seen near Dry Creek at 4:00 P.M. On October 23 he went to the hay ranch of Meyer & Price and took possession of a horse left by Bacon, then went to Silver City to return the buggy and team. On October 25 Walters walked to Bacon's ranch and demanded possession from B. McCleary, who leased the only building and lived there with his wife. Walters showed the deeds but McCleary refused to deliver the place without an order from Bacon. Walters next went to the hay ranch of Meyer & Price and asked to borrow a rifle and skiff to shoot a deer he saw on an island but he was refused. Walters was seen several times riding along the banks of the Snake River.

On October 27 Walters went to Bernard's and it was during this visit that Bernard became suspicious so he started toward Boise City searching along the way. En route he met Joseph Babington, who joined him. At noon the following day Babington found a hat stuffed in a badger hole and Bernard identified it as Bacon's; they saw blood on the rim and a mark as if a bullet had grazed the felt. They found buggy tracks going toward a small island in the creek and traced the buggy wheels and footsteps to a place where a body had lain. Here they found clotted blood, which they collected, and then followed the buggy wheels back to the road toward Boise City. Bernard went into Boise to deliver his evidence, swear out an arrest warrant for Walters and, with deputy sheriff Forsyth, returned home and arrested Walters. The prisoner was taken to Boise, where he had a hearing before Justice A.W. Flournoy, held to answer to the grand jury, and lodged in jail.

Now the search for Bacon's remains began in earnest and on October 30 and 31 Austin Savage, Frank Corbass, Bernard, Riley and Cannon found Bacon's rough boots near the place he was killed. They traced the buggy tracks from the island to a road leading to an abandoned ferry on the Snake River. They found where the buggy had stopped and followed boot tracks leading to the riverbank. It was presumed that Walters had killed Bacon about noon of October 21 and left the body on the island, then returned that evening and took the body to the Snake River, where he threw it in. The coffee, missing from Bernard's supplies, was found scattered on the bank of the Snake River, apparently knocked from the buggy when Bacon's body was pulled out. Walters' several trips along the river during the following days was an effort to see if he could find a trace of the body, and when he had found it lodged on an island he swam out and sent it on its way downriver.

The body did not turn up for some time but finally, on December 2, as Frank Money and a man named Miller were looking for cattle along the Snake River thirteen miles below the island near Meyer & Price's hay ranch, they found the body of a man. The feet and a portion of a leg were preserved in the water but birds and coyotes had eaten away nearly all of the exposed flesh, except around the left eye socket, cheek and forehead. There were two wounds from one bullet, one an entrance wound at the rear of the head and the other an exit wound above the right eye. The dead man was dressed in a heavy woolen shirt and pantaloons and a few inches from the body Money found a brown glass eye. When the body was examined at Boise it was found that the feet had a peculiar deformity of the toes so that they turned inwards, and from the peculiarity of the feet, the glass eye, and clothing the body was identified as the remains of Bacon. The undisturbed flesh on the face was explained by Dr. Bishop, who suggested that the staring glass eye had scared off animals until some adventurous bird had, once all the other flesh was gone, plucked out the glass eye and the body had been found before significant damage was done to that area. The glass eye explained why Walters had driven the buggy from the left side, so that he would have been on Bacon's blind side.

Late in November the Ada County grand jury returned an indictment for first degree murder but the trial was held over for the spring 1869 term. The defense attorneys filed a motion for a change of venue and this was granted to Boise County, where the trial commenced in Chief Justice Bowers' courtroom on March 11. On Monday, March 15, the case went to the jury at midnight and they deliberated until Tuesday at 4:00 P.M. before returning a verdict of "guilty as charged in the indictment." The motion for a new trial was denied and the date for sentencing was set for March 24, when Walters was sentenced to hang on May 12. His attorneys filed an appeal with the supreme court asking for a new trial, but in August the appeal was denied. Walters was then sentenced to hang on December 10, 1869, and petitions were filed with Governor

David W. Ballard asking for a commutation of Walter's sentence to life imprisonment, but these were denied.

On Thursday, December 9, Walters was interviewed by a reporter from the *Idaho World*, and he said he would write out his statement for the newsman. Father Mesplie arrived and reported that the governor had refused to interfere, but the priest had sent T.M. Britten to Boise with a request for a reprieve. On the fatal morning T.M. Britten returned from Boise and reported that there was no longer hope of intervention, so the prisoner dressed in his black suit of broadcloth, white hat with the flap thrown back, and white gloves. At 1:30 P.M. Walters called for the reporter again and gave him his written statement, and once again insisted he was innocent. The reporter retired when Fathers Poulin and Mesplie arrived and at 1:45 P.M. the procession formed, with Sheriff Britten leading, Undersheriff Sayrs and deputy Howell on each side of the prisoner, and the two priests following. They walked to the scaffold erected inside an enclosure in the jail yard and Walters took his place on the trapdoor. The two priests stepped forward on either side while Undersheriff Sayrs read the death warrant and the prisoner was then asked if he had anything to say, but he declined. Father Poulin announced that he had been asked to say, for the prisoner, that he was innocent. The priests offered a prayer, administered the last consolation, and said farewell to the condemned man before retiring. Sheriff Britten and his deputies quickly adjusted the noose, secured the straps which bound his arms and legs, and pulled the black cap over the prisoner's face. The condemned man stood for a half minute while the sheriff stared at his watch and, in accordance with the court's order, sprang the trap at exactly 2:00 P.M. The prisoner dropped six feet, breaking his neck and the only movement was a slight shrugging of the shoulders. Drs. Belknap and Zipf monitored his vital signs and in ten minutes they pronounced him dead. At exactly 2:30 P.M. Sayrs had the body cut down and placed in the coffin at the foot of the gallows' stairs. Jailor Rush cut several locks of hair from Walters' head which, at his request, would be sent to his relatives and then the lid of the coffin was screwed down. The coffin was carried into the ante room of the jail, where it lay until the next morning. At 10:00 A.M. Father Mesplie conducted a service and then the coffin was taken to the public burying grounds west of Idaho City and buried.

Boise Idaho Statesman: May 23, 1896; December 9, 1869; *Idaho City Idaho World*: March 18–25, 1869; December 16, 1869.

Tambiago
June 28, 1878

The Bannock Indians believed they needed the Catnas Prairie to survive as a tribe but it had been invaded by whites; they were also unhappy with their agent at Fort Hall and with the missionary that had been sent to teach them. As a consequence they went to war with the settlers of Idaho and there were many murders, atrocities and other depredations by the Indians. They obtained at least twenty-five rifles and ammunition from a gunrunner and this enabled them to escalate the fight. When a man named Rhoden was murdered six Indians were captured; but evidence and admissions proved that the killing was accomplished by one Indian who was assisted by another, and it was proved at trial that Tambiago was the murderer and that he was aided by his brother. Tambiago's brother was sentenced to a long prison term and Tambiago was sentenced to hang at the prison on June 28, 1878.

As his execution day approached Tambiago was visited by Father Archambault and Mr. Perrault, a reporter from the *Statesman*, and the priest urged him to confess. The priest said that his statement could be written down and sent to Washington, which might bring some relief to his tribe, but Tambiago refused saying, "Washington no good. No believe us at Washington. Chief at Washington no do anything for Indians."

It had rained continuously for some time as

the date for the execution approached but the storm cleared by Friday morning, June 28, and Tambiago could see, from his window, that people were assembling nearby. When told they had come for his execution he said, "Me no die today; tomorrow die all right; one sleep more, then die with good heart." When questioned why one day should make a difference he said that Chief Tagee would come on Saturday. When told there would be no delay he became upset and paced his cell, threatened that he would not walk to the gallows, and requested that they shoot him in his cell. Before leaving his cell he admitted to the reporter that he expected the Indians to rescue him but they had "made the mistake of a day and would surely come on the morrow." However, when the fatal moment arrived Tambiago offered no resistance, walked onto the scaffold with a firm step, and glanced at the crowd as he indulged in a ghastly smile. He declined to speak to the spectators so his wrists and ankles were tied and the noose adjusted, but he resisted the black cap as it was pulled on, seeming more afraid of it than of the noose. At 1:00 P.M. the trap was sprung and Tambiago broke his neck in the fall. Dr. Treadwell pronounced Tambiago dead after seven and one half minutes but the body was allowed to hang a few minutes longer. By 1:15 P.M. he was laid to rest in the coffin provided by the county. His remains were buried immediately afterwards.

Boise Idaho Daily Statesman: June 29, 1878; May 23, 1896.

McCullough, Thomas
September 16, 1880

Thomas McCullough, a Canadian who persisted in stating that his true name was Timothy Connor, moved to Leesburgh, Idaho, in 1877. In February 1880 he had a disagreement with William Luderman and shot him dead. McCullough claimed that the shooting was in self-defense and testified that Luderman was shooting at him when he returned fire. However, the jury did not believe him and found him guilty of first degree murder. At the July term of the court Judge Morgan sentenced McCullough to hang on Tuesday, September 16, 1880. The usual appeal and petitions for commutation were submitted but to no avail, as the supreme court would not grant a new trial and Governor John B. Neil would not commute the sentence. On Sunday, September 14, Bishop Tuttle of Salt Lake City, who was on his Episcopal visitation with some of the ladies of Salmon City, visited the condemned man. After singing and praying with them the prisoner begged the bishop to remain to the end but the bishop could not, so the ladies undertook the task of his religious consolation and administered to him with singing, praying, and the reading of scripture up to his last moments.

Sheriff Young had chosen a counterpoise weight design for the gallows, using four tanks of quicksilver to jerk the condemned man upward. When the hour arrived McCullough was taken from his cell, escorted across the yard by the sheriff, and directed to stand beneath the noose. The prisoner was turned to face the crowd while deputy Nichols read the death warrant and asked the prisoner if he had anything to say, but McCullough declined except to repeat that he did not have a fair trial, was an innocent man, and that he never intended to kill Luderman. The sheriff bound McCullough's wrists and arms while a deputy bound his ankles and knees. The noose was adjusted and just before a deputy pulled on the black cap McCullough said, "Good-bye to all; praise God!" The cap was then pulled down and, while McCullough was speaking his last words, the sheriff moved to the restraining rope, picked up a hatchet, and stood poised to strike the blow that would release the weight. At 10:25 A.M. the restraining rope was severed, the weight dropped seven and one half feet, three feet of slack was taken up, and McCullough's body shot upwards and then rebounded fifteen inches. There was a slight struggle for two minutes, but at nine minutes Dr. George A. Kenney pronounced him dead. At the end of twenty-five minutes the body was cut down and lowered into its coffin. Dr.

Kenney announced that the deceased had broken his neck between the third and fourth vertebrae and the spinal column was separated half an inch. After McCullough hanged, the sheriff published, at McCullough's request, his final writing: "When I am gone and in my grave, and all my bones are rotten, these few lines will tell my name, when I am quite forgotten. Thomas McCullough."

Boise Idaho Tri-weekly Statesman: September 28, 1880.

McDonald, Henry
October 14, 1881

George Myers was born in 1821, a tough German who lived through hardships in the bleak Alleghenies and led the line of march westward. He took up freighting and it seemed that every time there was a mineral strike Myers would be there with his two sturdy wagons and mules. The *Idaho Statesman* described the life of a freighter, saying that Myers was among the best of the class:

> The life of a mountain teamster is one of continuous vicissitude. In his long and weary journey from Kelton to Boise he encounters endless privations as part and parcel of his daily existence until familiarity with danger breeds contempt of fear, and peril is accepted as a portion of his daily lot. Such are men of rough hands and occasionally soft and gentle hearts. At the call of danger they are the first to shoulder the rifle and their motto is "All for one and one for all." Large as is the price they receive for their freight, the expense of subsisting teams in the long march over the mountain and desert soon consumes the bulk of their receipts. Yet with all this drawback they are liberal to a fault and brave to a virtue, as a class.

In 1880 Myers' wagons carried freight into Boise, Idaho, and took the same out to Kelton, Wood River, Salmon River, and other towns and settlements whose residents depended upon the freighter to provide nearly everything used in their daily lives. In mid–September Myers left Boise with a big load of goods for Kelton. On the morning of September 20 Henry McDonald bought a ticket on the Overland stagecoach as far as Soul's Rest but, upon arriving, paid to extend his ticket until the stage overtook Myers' team; several days later Myers' team was driven into Kelton by McDonald. He claimed he had bought the team from Myers and explained that the old teamster had met friends on the road and decided to go with them to Willow Creek, Oregon. McDonald provided an address where Myers could be reached, received payment for the goods he delivered to Kelton, and loaded the wagon with goods for the return trip to Boise.

When McDonald arrived in Boise he tried to take ownership of a horse belonging to Myers, which was in the charge of William Marlatt, and this raised the suspicion of foul play. Myers' friends wrote to the address provided by McDonald but the letters were returned unopened. After McDonald left Boise with a load of goods for Wood River, Myers' friends went to the authorities with their suspicions and a warrant was sworn out for McDonald's arrest. He was overtaken at Dunn's Station, brought back to Boise, and lodged in jail. No one had seen Myers since late September and McDonald, when questioned, gave several conflicting stories, and during his time in jail he wrote letters to George Rodgers at Terrace, Nevada, enclosing letters to Myers' friends which were supposed to have been signed by Myers. These, it was thought, were to be forwarded to prove that Myers was alive.

While circumstantial evidence was mounting against McDonald there was not enough evidence to prove that a crime had even been committed, and the murderer might have gone free but for one of those coincidences which often upset the best laid plan. Len Lewis was in a party hunting stray stock between Pilgrim Station and Salmon Falls, at the forks of the Toano Road, when his saddle loosened and he stopped to tighten it. While on the ground he caught sight of some shreds of clothing protruding from a badger hole and, investigating, he found human hair, a beard, clothing, and, after digging further, the bones of Myers. McDonald, as soon as he heard of the discovery, began telling various stories to explain Myers' death, all of which exonerated him of any crime, and he even tried to implicate Len Lewis as a murderer. The prisoner could not be indicted until it was determined in which county the crime occurred so a survey was made placing the scene of the murder in Owyhee County. McDonald was removed to Silver City, where he was indicted and tried at the June term of the district court. He was convicted of first degree murder and Judge Prickett set the date for his execution at August 5, 1881. The usual appeal followed, which served as a stay until the supreme court, on September 12, affirmed the lower court's decision and Judge Prickett then scheduled McDonald's execution for October 14, 1881.

A terrible storm of freezing rain and heavy wind arrived the night before the execution and several inches of snow fell, so McDonald was taken from his cell to sit by the jail stove under the close guard of jailor Stoddard and Sheriff J. D. Spriner. As noon approached a large number of people from Silver City who gathered to see the hanging began to congregate at the livery stable. At 1:00 P.M. McDonald, accompanied by Father Nattini and the sheriff, went to the stable where a wagon waited to take him to the gallows, constructed between the city cemetery and the New York Mill one mile from town.

McDonald, dressed in a yellow blanket overcoat, black hat and striped cassimer pants was followed to the gallows by a long procession of spectators. The coffin was already in place at the scaffold and the grave had been dug twenty feet beyond. The rope was not yet in place but the condemned man walked up the stairs and talked with his priest while waiting for these preliminaries to be completed. When all was ready the sheriff read the death warrant and asked McDonald if he had anything to say, but the condemned man declined to speak to the crowd. He stepped onto the trapdoor and several friends were allowed to ascend and shake his hand. The officers and Father Nattini said good-bye as McDonald's limbs were being pinioned. The noose was then adjusted and as soon as the black cap was pulled on at 2:01 P.M. Sheriff Spriner, with his hand poised on the lever, sprang the trap. McDonald broke his neck in the fall and the attending physician pronounced him dead in twenty minutes. The body was then lowered into its coffin and before 3:00 P.M. McDonald was buried in the Silver City cemetery, as none of his relative had made a claim for his remains.

Boise Idaho Daily Statesman: May 23, 1896; *Boise Idaho Tri-weekly Statesman*: September 28, 1881; October 15, 1881.

Mooney, Michael
December 29, 1882

Joel Hinckley was agent for the Utah & Northern Railroad at Franklin, Idaho. On the night of October 27, 1881, a mail carrier for the office retired in another part of the building when he heard Hinckley enter, go to the corner of the office where the washstand was located, and begin washing his hands. In a minute the mail carrier saw two masked men enter the office and one brandished a revolver, saying to Hinckley, "Throw up your hands!" Hinckley, who was about to wipe his face with a towel, turned his head to see who gave the command and the robber, without hesitation or further warning, fired one shot. The bullet entered Hinckley's chin, passed through his throat, and broke his neck. He fell over the washstand and died instantly and the two murderers fled in a panic. The mail carrier sounded the alarm and within an hour a large number of citizens were scouring the countryside for the murderers. Suspicion soon rested on Michael Mooney and he was arrested. At his examination he was held over for action by the grand jury, indicted, tried and convicted of murder in the first degree. He was sentenced to hang on January 20, 1882, but the execution was stayed while an appeal was argued before the supreme court. When the justices affirmed the lower court's decision Governor John B. Neil reprieved Mooney to December 29, 1882, allowing time to consider a petition for commutation, but the petition was denied.

Mooney slept well the night before his execution and ate his usual breakfast. At 10:00 A.M. the correspondent of the *Blackfoot Register* was admitted and Mooney, at first, seemed penitent when he said he wished he had it to do over again but then continued: "If I did that Barnes would never squeal." He said he would have nothing to say on the scaffold, observing, "It would not do anyone any good," and he kept his word. The barber arrived to shave Mooney, seating him facing toward the window for light, and from the chair the scaffold could be seen, as it had been assembled only a few feet from the jail door. At 11:00 A.M. Mooney bathed and put on the suit of new clothes and linen shirt provided by the sheriff. At noon the prisoner returned to his cell with Judge J.W. Morgan, who tried to encourage conversation and disclosure, but Mooney would say nothing of his history, his family, or his crime. At 1:45 P.M. Sheriff Horner read the death warrant and ten minutes later announced that Mooney's time had come. The procession to the gallows was brief and the prisoner needed no support ascending the stairs. He took his place on the trapdoor and told the sheriff, "Do it as quick as Christ will let you, that is, if there is any Christ. I do not care any more for dying than I do for going to a dance." The sheriff and jailor worked quickly but carefully to prepare him and his last words before the black cap was pulled on was to thank the jailor for his kindness. The trap was sprung at 1:58 P.M. and Mooney broke his neck in the fall. Dr. Drake pronounced him dead in ten minutes and then the body was cut down, placed in its coffin, and buried that evening.

Moscow (ID) Blackfoot Register: January 6, 1883; *Salt Lake City (UT) Daily Tribune*: October 29, 1881.

Pierson, George
August 1, 1884

George Pierson was living at Hailey, Idaho, when he entered into a joint venture with John T. "Johnny-behind-the-rocks" Hall. Pierson was going to convert his place into a saloon and Hall was going to provide cigars and whiskey, and they estimated they would need one box of cigars and five gallons of liquor for a start. When the time came to stock the saloon, Hall balked and asked Pierson to obtain the stock on credit; but Pierson refused and walked out, turning the entire operation over to Hall.

Pierson then went to work at the Mountain King Mine. While on a spree, he became enamored of a saloon girl named "Banjo Nell" and they agreed to marry, not in legal form but, in their drunken condition they drafted an "affidavit of marriage" and had all the barroom patrons witness it. Nell then moved to Pierson's cabin and she continued to ply her trade as a prostitute.

Hall was unable to operate the saloon since his credit was bad and he swore he would get even with Pierson for abandoning the venture. Hall made a number of threats against Pierson and on August 22, 1882, he confronted Pierson, saying, "George, I've got a gun to get even on a s__ of a b____." He did not show the gun but Pierson told him that the man who had given it to him was no friend. On August 25 Hall went to Sawtooth, showed his .45 caliber Bulldog revolver, and said that he would kill his man that day. Hall could not find Pierson, as he was at Solace Hill looking for work. But at dusk Pierson was returning home and, when within fifty paces of his cabin, he heard two shots and saw Hall step from behind a tree. Hall said, "You s__ of a b____, I'll kill you too!" Pierson hurried into his cabin and the following day began carrying his .38 caliber six-shooter, but he did not see Hall. That evening he found the inside of his cabin in shambles, the stove broken down and kicked over, and Nell beaten black and blue. Nell told him, "He has beaten me and he'll kill you when he sees you." Pierson went to deputy sheriff Ether to have Hall arrested but the deputy told him, "George, go home and protect yourself, but don't have a fight in the street.... Johnny is getting to be a bad man of late."

Pierson took Ether's advice and returned home, but just as he got to his door Hall stepped out and said, "You s__ of a b____, I am ready!" Pierson asked, "What's the matter with you?" just as Hall fired twice, missing his mark. Pierson drew his pistol, returned fire, and killed Hall. Pierson was arrested and held for the grand jury, indicted, tried at the fall term before Judge Broderick, and found guilty of first degree murder. His sentence to hang originated an appeals process which lasted two years, based on his claim that he had a right to defend his home, his wife, and his life, but the testimony did not support him. His "marriage" to Banjo Nell was a pretense to operate a bordello; he was not actually "in his home" defending it when the killing occurred so it was determined that the killing was not justifiable. The date for execution was set at August 1, 1884.

At 1:30 P.M. on the fatal day the church bells began to toll as a closed carriage drew up to the jail carrying Bishop Tuttle, the Rev. I.T. Osborne, and defense attorney Alanson Smith. Sheriff Furrey brought Pierson out and they entered the carriage while deputies mounted and rode alongside. A crowd of nearly one thousand men and a few women followed the slow moving procession one and a half miles to the gallows, arriving at 2:10 P.M. The entire party walked to the scaffold but Pierson asked to be allowed to ascend alone, and after he was on the platform the others followed.

Pierson made a speech which lasted twenty-three minutes and recounted his entire defense, then claimed he was an old pioneer and called on all other old pioneers to avenge his death; blamed the practice of carrying firearms and warned against it; and blamed his lawyer for using Latin terms at the trial rather than plain language. This tirade was followed by a prayer conducted by Bishop Tuttle, joined by the condemned man. Pierson said good-bye to everyone as he stepped onto the trapdoor, but his knees buckled and he had to be supported while Sheriff J.P. Campbell pinioned his wrists and ankles, adjusted the noose, and pulled on the black cap. The trap was sprung at 2:40 P.M. and Pierson dropped eight feet, breaking his neck. The bottom of the gallows was enclosed from view but the officers allowed those few who desired to climb the steps and view the remains through the trapdoor. At 3:00 P.M. C. Jacobs, photographer, preserved the tragic scene on film. Then Pierson's body was cut down, placed in the plain coffin provided by the county, and buried that evening.

Boise (ID) Democrat: July 6, 1884; *Boise Idaho Tri-weekly Statesman*: August 5, 1884; *Virginia City (NV) Territorial Enterprise*: August 7, 1884.

Kuok Wah Choi
September 18, 1885

In 1883 Chinese doctor Tot Kee, whose real name was Tai Fat, was practicing his profession at Atlanta, Idaho. On October 30 Kuok Wah Choi, alias Ah Sam, murdered Tot Kee by shooting the doctor twice, both bullets striking Kee in the head. Choi was arrested, tried, convicted of first degree murder, and sentenced to hang but the appeals process dragged on for months. The high court finally affirmed the lower court's decision and all hope was lost when the application for commutation was denied by Governor William M. Bunn. Deputies Thomas Bell and Campbell were then sent to select the place to build a gallows, and they chose the second gulch, north of Quigley Gulch, and nearly opposite Treat's ice house. The gallows parts, the same on which Pierson was hanged, had been stored behind the jail and the men arranged to have them taken to the gulch and erected. As the day of execution approached Choi accumulated small pieces of glass. They were discovered, and it was thought he intended to swallow them to commit suicide. Many of his Chinese friends predicted he would never hang, so thereafter he was watched very closely so he could not cheat the hangman. On Thursday night all Choi's clothes were taken, to be sure he had nothing sewn in them with which he could kill himself, and he spent the night dressed in his burial suit. He was taken out of his cell and placed on a cot in the corridor so that he could be watched more closely.

As the church bells tolled at noon a closed carriage drew up to the jail. The sheriff brought Choi out and they entered the carriage while deputies mounted horses and rode alongside. A small crowd followed the slow moving procession one and a half miles to the gallows, arriving at 12:50 P.M. The party walked to the scaffold, ascended, and Choi took his place on the trapdoor. His wrists and ankles were pinioned with straps and, when he was offered an opportunity to speak, he declined. The noose was adjusted, the black cap pulled on, and the trap was sprung at 1:00 P.M. Choi dropped, breaking his neck, but the bottom of the gallows was enclosed from view, so he fell from view of the witnesses. The attending physician was within the enclosure and monitored Choi's vital signs until he pronounced him dead, and then the body hung a few more minutes before being cut down and placed in its coffin. Choi's remains were turned over to his friends and he was buried that evening.

Idaho City Idaho World: November 6, 1883; *Boise Idaho Daily Statesman*: September 19, 1885; *Hailey (ID) Wood River News*: September 17, 1885.

Warlick, Theodore
June 9, 1886

Theodore Warlick murdered Henry C. Savage on January 28, 1886, on the south fork of the Salmon River. He was tried at the spring term of the district court at Mt. Idaho and claimed self-defense but the jury could not accept his version as there was substantial circumstantial evidence contradicting his story. The case was submitted to the jury on Monday evening, April 12, at 9:00 P.M. and the following morning at 10:00 he was convicted of first degree murder. Judge Buck sentenced Warlick to hang on June 9, 1886, and as soon as the prisoner was returned to his cell he tried to hang himself with a piece of rope tied to a nail inserted in a chink in the cell lining. However, he was discovered and taken down before death resulted and thereafter he was closely watched at all times to prevent self-destruction.

On his final morning the condemned man threw his mattress on the floor, and himself on top of it, and when the Reverend Hall arrived to console him he cursed his religious advisor. Warlick refused to change into the new suit provided by Sheriff A.W. Talkington, saying that what he wore was "good enough to go to hell in," and he cursed the sheriff for "hanging a poor Dutchman." As the hour of execution neared Warlick lay quietly on his mattress and refused to get up, so he had to be lifted and held while the manacles were removed and the death warrant was read. The condemned man seemed to be in a stupor and had to be carried by deputies from his cell to the building in which the gallows had been constructed.

The small group of witnesses stood quietly as the officers carried Warlick up the stairs and supported him on the trapdoor while his wrists and ankles were pinioned, the noose adjusted, and the black cap pulled on. When the trap was sprung the deputies timed their release of his arms so that he fell straight down six feet. The body was motionless for ten seconds and then there was a single violent contraction that nearly doubled him up, but he slowly relaxed over the next few seconds and hung motionless. Coroner Kirkwood monitored Warlick's pulse and reported that it grew progressively weaker until it ceased at four minutes and thirty-seven seconds, and a few seconds later the condemned man was pronounced dead. The body hung for quite a while before it was cut down and placed in its coffin. The black cap was removed and the witnesses were surprised by his natural appearance, considering the mode of death, and Dr. Kirkwood announced that Warlick's neck had been broken in the fall. Warlick's remains were buried at the Grangeville cemetery at the request of the deceased.

Boise Idaho Statesman: April 15, 1886; April 20, 1886; June 9, 1886; *Lewiston (ID) Teller*: June 10, 1886; June 17, 1886; *Lewiston (ID) Nez Perce News*: June 17, 1886.

Williams, Frank
July 21, 1888

On December 17, 1886, prospectors "Captain" Winn and Charles Reed were at their cabin on the Snake River, twenty-five miles below the mining camp of Cariboo, when Frank Williams stopped for a visit. He told them he had been out hunting, sat down, and laid his single-shot .50 caliber needle gun on the table. Charles Reed was sitting in a chair directly opposite Williams when Williams shot Reed through the head, the bullet entering at the left jaw and exiting at the back of Reed's head. Williams then grabbed the axe and killed Winn with a blow in back of his left ear and a second blow across the left side of his head; both axe wounds crushed Winn's skull. Williams went to the home of Frank Glover, near his cabin, and asked to use his raft to go to Eagle Rock, and inquired of the deputy marshal assigned there.

Glover and his two guests, Mathew Johnson and Simon Sibbletts, listened to the story of the killing but Williams said he handed his gun to Reed for an examination and when Reed passed it back the stock struck a chair and discharged, killing him. Winn then took the axe and threatened to kill Williams, but he warded off the blow. Winn dropped the axe and yelled, "I'll kill you anyway!" and went for his gun; but Williams said he struck Winn with his rifle barrel, then picked up the axe and finished Winn in self-defense. The three men accompanied Williams back to the scene of the killing and found two bodies beneath the bed, firewood stacked around them and ashes spread on the floor to absorb the blood.

They sent for Sheriff Taylor and Coroner Bassett, who came immediately, held an inquest, and arrested Williams. Careful examination of the wounds and the scene showed that Williams' story was fabricated to cover the murders, so he was held for trial at the spring term. On Monday, May 16, the trial began with Williams still claiming self-defense and on Wednesday at 3:00 P.M. the case went to the jury. Twelve men deliberated for an hour and took four ballots before returning a verdict of guilty of murder in the first degree. Williams was sentenced to hang on July 22 but his attorney filed an appeal with the supreme court and the sentence was stayed while the case was being considered. The lower court's decision was affirmed and at the June 1888 term Williams was sentenced by Judge Broderick to hang on July 21, 1888.

Williams rested easily the night before his execution and maintained his composure during the morning hours. The sheriff read the death warrant at the cell door and at 2:00 P.M. the prisoner walked out of the jail onto the scaffold where he made a short, incoherent speech in which he repeated his claim of self-defense and concluded, "I'd rather die than be imprisoned for life." His legs were pinioned as he spoke but his hands were left free, as he had asked to put the noose around his own neck, and this was granted. After the noose was in place and given a final adjustment by the sheriff the prisoner's arms and wrists were bound and the black cap was pulled on. Williams called out, "Let her go!" at 2:12 P.M. and the trap was sprung. The fall broke the prisoner's neck and there was no visible struggle. A doctor monitored the dying man's vital signs and after Williams' heartbeat ceased he was pronounced dead. The body was allowed to hang until 2:57 P.M. before being cut down and placed in the plain pine coffin provided by the county. Williams was buried before sundown in Idaho City's cemetery.

Idaho City Idaho World: December 28, 1886; May 20, 1887; July 17, 1888; July 27, 1888; *Blackfoot Idaho News*: July 21, 1888.

Wood, Alexander
August 17, 1888

Alexander Wood, who had been born into slavery at Springfield, Missouri, lived in Auburn, Illinois, when he met and married a young divorcee. He soon learned that his wife had been unfaithful so he moved her to Denver, then to Colorado Springs, on to Ogden, and in 1884 settled in Pocatello, Idaho. Wood worked as a barber at the Pacific Hotel and built a fine home for his wife; he furnished it nicely and did everything he could to make her happy. However, he again started seeing clues and hearing stories of his wife's indiscretions. There were many men and few women on the frontier so the opportunities were abundant for a woman willing to be unfaithful; but Wood continued to do all he could for his wife in the hope she would change her adulterous ways.

On the night of May 5, 1887, Wood saw his wife with another man and became frenzied. He returned home, took his .41 caliber pistol, searched for his wife and found her. She was alone but still he beat her, shot her once in the head, and hid her body in the sagebrush near the Portneuf River. When Alex Wood and his wife both went missing a search was made and on May 8 Mrs. Wood's remains were found, the body bruised and the skull fractured. She was buried after the inquest found that she had been beaten to death and Alex Wood was named the murderer. Several days later an Indian came forward and reported he had seen Alex Wood shoot his wife, so her remains were exhumed and an autopsy revealed the .41 caliber bullet in her brain.

The murderer was tracked to Corinne, Utah, arrested and returned to Blackfoot on May 13, 1887. He was examined, held to answer to the grand jury, indicted, and tried at the fall term of the court. He was convicted of first degree murder and sentenced to hang but the sentence was stayed while the supreme court considered his case. The justices took months to affirm the lower court's decision but finally July 21, 1888, was set for his execution along with murderer Frank Williams. Before the date arrived the two murderers escaped jail, but Williams was caught within hours and kept his date with the hangman. Wood disguised himself as an Indian and rode the train to Butte, Montana, then walked to Bozeman, where he was recognized, arrested and returned to Blackfoot. Governor Edward A. Stevenson, to avoid the further delay which would occur if they awaited the next term of court to reset the execution date, granted a respite to August 17, 1888. After noon on that final day the death warrant was read to Wood in his cell and he was escorted to the scaffold at 1:30 P.M. He made a brief speech in which he said he held no ill feelings but never thought he had received justice, and his last words were, "I forgive everybody and hope to meet you in heaven." Wood was cool and composed as he was prepared and at 1:57 P.M. the trap was sprung and the fall broke his neck. By 2:12 P.M. his remains were cut down, placed in a coffin and he was buried that evening.

Boise (ID) Daily Statesman: August 21, 1888.

KANSAS

The land that would become Kansas was explored by Francisco Vasquez de Coronado in 1541. He found the land inhabited by the Osage, Pawnee and Kansa Indian tribes. France later claimed the land, ceded it to Spain in 1762, regained possession in 1800, and in 1803 sold the region to the United States as part of the Louisiana Purchase. On May 30, 1854, the Kansas-Nebraska Act established the Kansas Territory. Kansas was west of the Mississippi River in the central part of the country, so situated that it played a pivotal role in settling the West, as it served as a staging area for wagon trains traveling west. The Kansas Territory became the 34th state on January 29, 1861.

Coon, John Jr.
January 18, 1853

On Saturday, November 11, 1852, fifteen-year-old John Coon, Jr. was locked in the Wyandotte jail and charged with murder. On the previous evening Coon and Martin Big-arms had a drunken brawl with Curtis Punch and the two men beat Punch mercilessly; but it was Coon who struck the fatal blow with a fireplace poker. After completing their investigation the Indian sheriffs released Martin Big-arms but held Coon, and six days later on Friday, November 17, the court convened to empanel a jury. Coon's trial commenced two days later with testimony and arguments concluded in one day and, at dusk, following brief deliberations, the jury returned a verdict of "guilty of first degree murder." The prosecuting attorney then argued that the evidence, at most, could only support a verdict of manslaughter but Coon was sentenced to die by firing squad on January 18, 1853. The application for clemency sent to President Millard Fillmore was denied and nothing further would delay the proceedings.

On January 15, 1853, the council met to arrange for the execution of Coon and they settled the matter at 11:00 P.M. At 1:00 P.M. on January 18 the condemned man was brought from the jail and boarded a wagon, where he took a seat upon his coffin. The wagon was escorted by a party of six armed Wyandotte Indians and a small number of witnesses. The six executioners — James Barnet, Thomas Pipe, Isaac Zane, H.C. Long, Louis Lumpey, and Joseph White — marched along in a solemn procession led by Matthew R. Walker and Philip Brown. They proceeded for two hours until they reached the place chosen for the execution and then the condemned Indian was taken out of the wagon and stood up with a clear field of fire behind. The six executioners took up their positions in a line facing the place where Coon stood. The prisoner's wrists and ankles were secured, a handkerchief was tied over his eyes, and a target was pinned to his chest over his heart. At exactly 3:30 P.M. Walker gave the signal, six rifles fired simultaneously, and the condemned man dropped to the ground — dead. His body was lifted into the coffin and it was nailed shut, and Coon was buried on the spot.

Gettysburg (PA) Republican Compiler: February 28, 1853; *Journal of William Walker.*

MONTANA

Eastern Montana, comprising about 80 percent of the state, was acquired by the United States as part of the Louisiana Purchase in 1803. The first Europeans to enter Montana were Meriwether Lewis and William Clark in 1805, and two years later the first fur trading post was established, though the first White settlement was not founded until 1841. The eastern portion of Montana became part of Missouri in 1812, Nebraska in 1854, and the Dakotas in 1861. Western Montana, comprising 20 percent of the state, was acquired along with the Oregon Country in 1846. It became the eastern portion of Washington Territory in March 1853; then it became the eastern part of Idaho when that territory was formed. Finally it was united with eastern Montana when the Montana Territory was organized in 1864. Montana was admitted as the 41st state on November 8, 1889.

Horan, John P.
August 25, 1863

On July 28, 1862, gold was discovered on Grasshopper Creek and miners were already in the area mining near Virginia City, so the rush to the new gold field was on. The town of Bannack sprang forth and, like most boomtowns, Bannack was lawless, so in May 1863 Bannack elected Henry Amos Plummer as their sheriff. On August 23 John Peter Horan and Lawrence Keeley quarreled over a mining claim they shared. Horan pulled his revolver and, without provocation or warning, settled the matter by sending a single bullet through the head of Keeley, who died instantly. Horan was arrested and the prisoner was closely guarded throughout the night, as a notice of a hearing was communicated throughout Bannack.

The following day a people's court convened and Horan was tried and found guilty of murder in the first degree. The presiding judge, after consulting with his two associate judges, sentenced Horan to hang the following day, August 25, and the verdict and sentence were approved by the masses in a unanimous vote. Sheriff Plummer commissioned the erection of a gallows at the edge of town and required it to be of a sturdy construction. On the final morning, Horan was taken to the site under heavy guard and hanged with the usual ceremony pertaining to such an entertaining and exciting event.

W.A. Clark, U.S. Senator, *Contributions to the Historical Society of Montana*, vol. 1., *List of Early Settlers* (Helena, MT; Independent, 1876).

Wheatly, William W.
August 13, 1875

Sterres, William H.
October 28, 1875

Franz Warl, born in Leibach, Austria, in 1825, migrated to America and settled at Colorado Gulch a dozen miles from Helena, Montana, where he had engaged in the coal-burning business for many years. Warl was an industrious and frugal man and by 1875 he had saved a considerable sum of money, with which he planned to return to Austria. A number of people knew of the large sum Warl had accumulated and knew he kept his money on his person. Among those interested in Warl's fortune was William H. Sterres and Fred Shaffer. Sterres, a black barber, ran a Helena barber shop on Main Street at the foot of Broadway in partnership with Fred Shaffer, a white barber.

On April 9, 1875, Sterres met William W. Wheatly, an old acquaintance, and introduced him to Shaffer. Three weeks later Sterres invited Wheatly to accompany him on a walk into the country to "do a little hunting." They walked toward Ten Mile Gulch and continued to a point on the side of a mountain. It was dusk when Sterres said, "Its no use talking about hunting any longer; I am after money. There is a man near here who has lots of money—$14,000 or $15,000—and he always carries it with him. I know all about it, the French boys told me so three months ago and I have been after that money ever since. I would have left Helena long before if it had not been for this." Wheatly asked how he planned to get the money and Sterres said he would knock the man down with his slungshot.

Shaffer joined them and they climbed to a point among the rocks overlooking Warl's coal-burning pit. Sterres and Shaffer took several drinks of whiskey and gin and chewed tobacco while they watched Warl work and waited for sunset. "This is the twelfth time I have been here," Sterres said, "and I am going to have the money this time if I have to kill to get it." Shaffer took several masks from his pocket and offered one to each man. Sterres took his, but Wheatly declined so Shaffer became angry and said, "You are a d___ cowardly s__ of a b___," and to Sterres he said, "[W]e will do it ourselves." Sterres drew a six-shooter and made Wheatly kneel and swear that he would never tell anybody and then the two barbers started for Warl, Sterres in advance with his slungshot at the ready and Shaffer behind holding a wooden club, while Wheatly sat and watched.

It was dark but Warl was standing near a bright fire, so the two robbers crept up behind their victim and Sterres, without hesitation or warning, struck him a blow to the head with his slungshot. Warl did not fall so Sterres struck him again; Warl cried out twice, and the two robbers tackled him and struggled with their victim for several minutes. During the melee Wheatly called out, "For God's sake, Fred, come back. I hear someone coming." After the two men finished their work they returned to Wheatly, called him a liar, chastised him for using Shaffer's name, and threatened him again if he talked. They returned to Helena and while crossing the Yaw-Yaw ditch, near the Hot Springs, Sterres threw his slungshot into the muddy water.

On May 2 Jake Schilling found Warl's body lying near his coal pit, Warl's dog savagely guarding the body. Schilling went for William Blackhall, Frank la Brush, George Reed and G. Watson, neighbors of Warl; Blackhall was familiar to the dog and was able to tie him at the cabin. The men then examined Warl and found that the ground around the body showed signs of a struggle. Warl's hands were tied behind his back, a cord was tied tightly around his neck, the body had been searched, and one pocket had been cut out. The men covered the body with hay and sent for coroner C.J. Ingersoll and Sheriff Seth Bullock.

Dr. Ingersoll arrived and found that Warl's skull was fractured, the main wound was eleven inches long and extended from one side of the head to the other, there was a second fracture on the left side of Warl's head, and his neck had been broken. However, it was the cord around his neck which had strangled him to death, though any of the other wounds could have proven fatal in a brief time. The coroner determined that the man had been murdered on April 30. Sheriff Bullock searched the area and found where a party of three men had camped for a considerable time at a place overlooking the coal-burning pit. The sheriff found two empty liquor bottles, several quids of tobacco, the lining from a hat, and a number of boot and shoe prints, all of which he carefully documented. He questioned everyone in the neighborhood and this resulted in many leads, but one by one these were eliminated through further investigation until finally suspicion rested upon twenty-five-year-old William Wheatly, who was arrested on Monday, May 3, and lodged in jail.

A search of his camp produced the identities of the other two murderers, Sterres and Shaffer. Wheatly later claimed that when he heard of a murder in Colorado Gulch, and believing they had been at Ten Mile Gulch, he was convinced that they were different events. However, when he learned the truth he called for Sheriff Bullock and told him that Sterres had thrown the murder weapon in the Yaw-Yaw ditch. The sheriff took Wheatly to the ditch at a point three quarters of a mile beyond Kessler's Brewery where a path led to a plank bridge; the water was drained, and they found the slungshot. On Sunday, May 9, Wheatly provided a detailed confession and offered to turn state's evidence.

On May 5 Shaffer had left Helena by stagecoach bound for Benton and five days later he and George Henderson built a skiff, laid in food supplies and, with Louis Duncan, set sail down the river. Deputy sheriff John Quirk was sent from Helena to arrest Shaffer but he arrived at Benton twenty-eight hours late, so he formed a posse of two citizens and two soldiers and they started after the fugitive on horseback. They gained ten hours when they reached Fort Clagett so they purchased a boat and continued their pursuit on the river. They were only four hours behind Shaffer when they reached Carroll but the fugitive had boarded the steamer *Josephine*. The posse refitted their boat but now the fugitive was well ahead of them, traveling on a fast steamer, and made it to Bismarck in the Dakota Territory. Sheriff Bullock wired ahead to the Bismarck police and on May 24 police justice P.M. Davis of Bismarck sent a dispatch to Sheriff Bullock saying that Shaffer was in jail.

The following day William Pierce, who carried a warrant from Fort Peck, sent a dispatch requesting a requisition. Governor Benjamin F. Potts authorized the requisition on the governor of the Dakota Territory, but over the next ten days every obstacle was put in the way of Pierce. He left Shaffer in the custody of the city marshal while he sent a telegram to Helena and, while he was occupied, Shaffer was released from custody and made his escape on the steamer *Western*, never to be seen or heard of again. Back in Helena Sheriff Bullock, with deputy J.H. McFarland, found Sterres at work in a ground-sluice and arrested him. As soon as Sterres was in jail he gave a full account of the murder. At trial he recanted his confession and denied any part in the murder, but Sterres' alibi did not hold up and he was convicted of first degree murder. Wheatly was also convicted of first degree murder but was not given credit for turning state's evidence, as he had done so without any agreement or inducement. Both prisoners returned to court on June 29, 1875, when each was sentenced to hang on August 13, 1875. Sterres won a retrial on appeal so a special term of the district court was convened; but he was again convicted of first degree murder and on September 16 he was sentenced to hang on October 28, 1875. Finally all hope was lost for Sterres and he resigned himself to his fate but, while he was awaiting his second trial, Wheatly was hanged.

On the morning before his execution Wheatly was baptized into the Catholic religion by Father Palladino. After the jail closed Wheatley spent hours in prayer and writing letters to his family and retired after midnight. He arose early on his last day and spent the first hours with his religious advisor, then received a reporter. He told as much of his life story as time permitted and he seemed penitent, crying like a child at times as he talked of his early life. After 11:00 A.M. he prayed continuously with Father Palladino and at noon Sheriff Bullock took him from his cell and sat him in the vestibule of the jail, where the death warrant was read. Wheatly was then conducted into the jail yard and onto the scaffold.

The gallows had been erected within an enclosure but over one thousand people found vantage points on rooftops of houses and sheds; the invited witnesses were within the enclosure. After the prisoner's arms and legs were pinioned he knelt with Father Palladino, who offered a prayer for the salvation of Wheatly's soul. When the prisoner arose he asked permission to address the crowd, which was granted, and he blessed and forgave everyone and then said, "[I]f I were sure of all the wealth of the world, and without fear of the law and punishment it inflicts for wrongdoing, it would be no temptation for me to commit the crime for which I am now about to offer up my life. I make this statement to show you how unfortunate I am and as a warning to you all — just as I go to that awful future, to meet my God. May God bless you all." The prisoner knelt again and prayed and, upon rising at 12:20 P.M., he was positioned on the trapdoor and the black cap was pulled over his head and the noose adjusted. He cried out, "I am ready! God have mercy on my soul!" As he spoke his last word the trap was sprung. Drs. Reece and Holmes monitored Wheatly's pulse and pronounced him dead a few seconds after 12:30 P.M. The prisoner was allowed to hang a half hour more before his remains were cut down; it was determined that his neck had not been broken in the fall and that he had died of strangulation. His body was placed in a plain wooden coffin and given to Father Palladino for burial in the Catholic cemetery.

When the final day arrived for Sterres he was also attended by Father Palladino. At noon the condemned man, followed by his religious advisor, left his cell and walked to the entrance of the iron cage, where he sat in a chair and listened to the death warrant. Sterres then arose and followed the sheriff onto the platform, where he knelt on the trapdoor, crossed himself, and recited the Confiteor, the Lord's Prayer, Hail Mary, and the Act of Contrition. Finally he stood but continued praying loudly. As soon as Sterres was standing his wrists and arms, knees and ankles were pinioned, and when asked he declined to address the witnesses. The black cap was drawn over his face and the noose adjusted at 12:10 P.M. and the trap was immediately sprung. Drs. Reece and Bullard stood beneath the gallows monitoring his vital signs and in ten minutes he was pronounced dead from strangulation, as the fall had not broken his neck. His remains were cut down, deposited in a coffin, and buried in the Catholic cemetery that evening.

Helena (MT) Daily Herald: May 3, 1875; May 14, 1875; May 17–21, 1875; May 24, 1875; June 2, 1875; June 14, 1875; June 29, 1875; August 13, 1875; September 16, 1875; October 29, 1875; *Sioux City (MT) Journal*: June 5, 1875.

McAndrews, Michael
March 1, 1878
Robert, Frank
October 31, 1878

See Addendum, pages 206–207

Koble, Joseph K.; Marsh, Orlando H.
October 6, 1879

Joseph K. Koble, Orlando H. Marsh and a trooper named Frenzler, privates in Company A, 3rd Infantry, at Fort Benton, planned to steal a string of government horses and desert. A teamster named Campbell and a civilian agreed to assist them. Private Patrick Farrell, a close friend of Marsh but not one of the conspirators, was told all the details after he had sworn an oath of secrecy. One of the deserting privates wrote a letter to a notorious lady named Lizzie Clark describing their plans and entrusted the letter to a disinterested party for delivery, but that person delivered the letter to the fort's commander, Colonel Edward Moale. The colonel concealed his knowledge of the plot and, at the time designated, laid a trap at the corral. However, the conspirators did not appear and after waiting a considerable time the colonel removed his forces and assigned a sergeant to watch for and arrest the deserters if they should appear later. The colonel gave his double-barreled shotgun to the sergeant, who carried it to his home to prepare for a long surveillance.

Farrell, a friend of the sergeant's family, was visiting and, seeing the sergeant with the colonel's gun at that particular time, suspected his purpose and offered to go along. Soon after reaching the corral the deserters appeared and Farrell arrested the civilian, so that the soldiers were alerted and fled. Koble and Marsh saw Farrell at the corral and suspected that their friend had violated his oath and informed on them. Marsh was determined to kill Farrell and induced Koble, Campbell and Frenzler to assist him; Campbell obtained a pistol and a straight razor and gave them to Marsh.

On the evening of February 6, 1879, a ball was held at the home of Ellen Martin, which Farrell and the four conspirators attended. Koble retired early and was in bed asleep when Marsh woke him after midnight and told him they were going to kill Farrell that night. Campbell and Frenzler remained at the ball, so they were not present when Koble and Marsh found a hiding place along the route Farrell would take. Sometime before 2:00 A.M. on February 7 Farrell, in an intoxicated condition, started for his quarters. Koble and Marsh attacked suddenly, Koble first cutting Farrell's throat with the razor and then Marsh finishing him by beating him on the head with the pistol, unable to fire the weapon because it would have alerted the post sentry. Campbell and Frenzler were close behind Farrell and, when they came upon the scene, they helped dispose of the body. They first attempted to throw the body into the river through a hole in the ice but this failed, so Campbell, a teamster, took his employer's team and wagon and drove the body twelve miles from the fort, where the four men threw the remains into the brush near Highwood Road.

The circumstances of Farrell's disappearance pointed to the four conspirators and suggested foul play so they were arrested, and under close questioning Campbell and Frenzler confessed, and Campbell stated positively that the body had been deposited in the river through a hole in the ice. All four prisoners were tried and convicted of first degree murder, the two accomplices receiving life sentences at the prison in Deer Lodge, while Koble and Marsh were sentenced to hang on September 5. The body of Farrell was found before the date of execution so Governor Benjamin F. Potts granted a respite of thirty days to allow further investigation. This only served to fasten the guilt more strongly upon the doomed men so the governor declined to intervene, and the date for execution was set for October 6, 1879. The two murderers were an escape risk so they were heavily ironed, but Koble removed his and Marsh's chains no matter how the sheriff secured them, and on October 2 they almost managed to escape.

The gallows had been erected in the jail yard a short walk from the cells of the condemned men, and on the final morning the death warrants were read to both prisoners in their cells before they were escorted onto the scaffold. Once in position on the trapdoor the sheriff asked if they had anything to say and Marsh spoke briefly, claiming he was innocent. But Koble said, "I wish to deny the report that I intended to make a confession upon the gallows, or that I requested a commutation of sentence." Koble then shook hands with the sheriff and deputies and thanked them for their kindness during his confinement. Marsh also shook their hands but said only, "Good-bye." The wrists and ankles of the condemned men were bound and the black caps pulled over their faces. When the sheriff positioned the nooses Koble requested that his be drawn "pretty tight," and when this was done he called out, "Slap it to me!" The trap was sprung in the next moment and both men died without a struggle. The bodies hung thirty minutes before they were then cut down and Dr. Wheelock determined that both men had broken their necks. Both bodies were deposited in plain coffins provided by the county and buried that afternoon.

Butte (MT) Daily Inter Mountain: October 9, 1879.

Pelky, Peter
February 4, 1881

On the evening of September 2, 1880, Peter Pelky was visiting the ranch of Charles Tacke on the Bozeman Road, four miles from Helena, when his host opened his trunk for the purpose of depositing money. Pelky saw a large sum of money in the till of the trunk and resolved to murder and rob Tacke. He went to the stable, saddled Tacke's horse, and got an axe. Tacke followed in a few minutes and as soon as he entered the stable Pelky struck him in the forehead with the axe, knocking him to the ground, and then struck a deadly blow to Tacke's head. The murderer later said he immediately felt remorse, but he had the presence of mind to place Tacke's body and the bloody axe in a manger and cover them with lime before he went into the house, broke open the trunk, and stole $240. Pelky fled but the horse sensed something was amiss and at times turned and tried to bite his rider; several times he refused to travel and had to be led. After Pelky reached Benton he abandoned the horse and acquired a skiff, which he used to drift downriver to Cow Island; after he landed he went to Duvall's wood yard and bought a horse and struck out for Judith's Gap.

Henry Tacke was working in lower Prickly Pear Valley when he was told that his brother had not been seen since the previous Tuesday, and a search provided no clue to his absence. Henry went to town and reported his brother missing, so Sheriff Jefferies went to the Tacke ranch, made a careful search, and noticed that a barrel and a half of lime had been emptied into a manger. This aroused his suspicion so he got a pick, pried off the front board, and discovered the badly decomposed body of Charles Tacke. The sheriff left the remains undisturbed and summoned Coroner Steele, who convened a jury at the ranch. The jurymen found that Charles Tacke was dressed in night clothes, the right side of his skull had been broken in two places and the bloody axe, the murder weapon, had been laid next to the body before the lime was poured on.

Pelky was immediately suspected and a $1,000 reward was posted by Governor Benjamin F. Potts for the capture of the fugitive. Soon after Pelky left the wood yard, Duvall learned of the murder and reward so he started in pursuit, and at Big Spring Creek his two man posse was joined by John J. Bowles. When they reached Burrows & Allis' sawmill on Roberts Creek, six miles above Judith's Gap, they saw Pelky among the workmen breaking for dinner. Duvall immediately ordered Pelky to halt, but he started to run so Duvall placed his gun at his head and warned, "You murdering s__ of a b___, throw up your hands or I'll shoot." Pelky answered, "Yes, Mike, I am a murderer, shoot me through the heart." The three man posse then started back with their prisoner and Bowles read the newspaper account of the murder to Pelky, who readily confessed the crime. The next day while the party was stopped for dinner Pelky made a sudden grab for a gun, placed it in his mouth and snapped it three times; but the gun was of the Burgess patent and, owing to Pelky's ignorance in working it, he had not filled the chamber with a cartridge. Sheriff Rader of Meagher County met the posse on the trail and accompanied them into Helena, where Pelky was lodged in jail, and the three men who captured him shared the reward.

Peter Pelky was indicted, tried at the fall term of the district court, and convicted of first degree murder. He was sentenced to hang on Friday, February 4, 1881, and neither appeal nor application for executive clemency caused a delay. Pelky's cell adjoined the large enclosure surrounding the cells, which gave him the opportunity to talk with the other prisoners; J.H. Kennedy, another prisoner, read the Bible to Pelky daily as the condemned man could not read English.

The scaffold had been erected in the jail yard several days before the execution and on Thursday the coffin was stored beneath it. On the morning of the execution a crowd began to assemble at an early hour and before 11:00 A.M. every rooftop of every house, shed and other elevated place was crowded with curious spectators. At 10:00 A.M. Father L.B. Palladino arrived to read from a prayer book and offer consolation, and several times the priest and prisoner knelt and prayed only to rise and continue their discussions. Pelky said he deserved to hang and wanted to die, and conceded that his trial had been fair and the sentence just; and he thanked the sheriff, undersheriff Charles M. Jefferies, and jailor Peter Tone for their kindness. At 11:45 A.M. the sheriff stepped in front of the cell door and asked, "Father, the time approaches; how soon can you be ready?" and the priest replied, "We are ready any time." The prisoner, dressed in a new alpaca coat, light pantaloons and sandals, was taken from his cell by constable J.H. McFarland and conducted to the door of the cage. When he was seated, undersheriff Jefferies entered and said, "Pelky, I will read to you the warrant of the Court which is my authority for executing you this day," and the prisoner responded by nodding his head. Jefferies read the death warrant and when he concluded, Pelky responded, "That is all right."

The procession formed with Jefferies leading, Pelky and the priest next, followed by constable McFarland. They entered the jail yard and the prisoner ascended eight feet and knelt upon the trapdoor just under the noose. The sheriff, undersheriff, constable, and priest were the only persons on the platform but the scaffold was surrounded by those few people authorized to be present at the execution. A brief prayer was offered by the priest and he shook hands with Pelky; still kneeling, the priest offered a crucifix for him to kiss. The prisoner arose when the priest retired and the officers pinioned his wrists and arms, ankles and knees, and while this was being done he shook hands with the officers and said goodbye. The noose was adjusted by McFarland and then Jefferies pulled the black cap over his face. At a signal the undersheriff cut a small cord and the trap was sprung at 12:01 P.M., but as the body fell five feet the noose slipped to the back of Pelky's neck. The body hung motionless for a few seconds before a quivering of the hands and feet became visible and continued for four and one half minutes. Drs. Morris and Madden monitored his vital signs and in fourteen minutes pronounced him dead. After the body had been suspended twenty-two minutes it was cut down and placed in a coffin, and an examination confirmed that Pelky's neck had been broken in the fall. He was buried that evening.

Helena (MT) Daily Independent: September 3, 1880; September 20, 1880; February 3–5, 1881.

Douglass, John
May 27, 1881

Mrs. Celestia Alice Earp moved to Bozeman, Montana, in 1878 and had, by honest industry and toil, accumulated several hundred dollars. As a soldier's widow she was entitled to, and had filed for, a claim on one hundred sixty acres of land near Flathead Pass and, to prove-up on the claim, had made improvements to her property. John Douglass was recommended to her as a farmhand and she hired him to do some fencing and other work. Douglass soon became infatuated with the young widow and made earnest proposals of marriage, but he was repeatedly rebuffed. His requests soon became demands, which finally degenerated into threats of murder if she would not marry him. In order to gain time she promised marriage at a later date but she feared Douglass, so she made secret plans to return east.

Mrs. Earp hired a private hack to take her to Red Bluff but Douglass was suspicious and kept a close watch on his fiancée's movements. Soon after Mrs. Earp left the ranch he followed on horseback and they arrived in Red Bluff at the same time. He confronted her and again threatened to kill her, but was finally induced to abandon his purpose and return to Bozeman. On March 24, 1880, Mrs. Earp boarded the stagecoach and left Red Bluff, taking a seat on top beside the driver. Douglass, who had reneged on his promise to return to Bozeman, overtook the coach on the road between Red Bluff and Sterling and rode past the coach several times, each time slowing to allow the coach to pass him. The third time the coach overtook Douglass he pulled his revolver and, without hesitation or warning, sent a single bullet into Mrs. Earp's back, which passed entirely through and exited above the nipple. He fired twice more and, when Mrs. Earp showed the slightest sign of life, he fired his last three bullets at her.

The coach hurried into Sterling, where Mrs. Earp languished, suffering terribly from her wounds, until relieved by death the following day. After shooting Mrs. Earp, Douglass rode into Sterling brandishing his revolver and threatening to shoot any man who interfered with him. Dave O'Brien was not put off by his threats and he disarmed and arrested Douglass and took his prisoner to Virginia City, where he was lodged in the county jail. When news came that Mrs. Earp was still alive he broke down, but when word later confirmed her death he exulted in the news. The grand jury met the following Monday and indicted Douglass, and before week's end he was tried and convicted of first degree murder. There were delays of nearly a year from appeals and Douglass tried the "insanity dodge," but never convincingly. Finally the appeal failed and on May 11, 1881, Judge Conger sentenced the prisoner to hang on May 27, 1881. Neither appeal nor application for executive clemency would delay the proceedings further.

At 11:30 A.M. on the final day, the witnesses to the execution, consisting of several officers, the physicians and clergyman, a coroner's jury, and a few spectators, gathered inside the small enclosure. A few minutes before noon Sheriff Platner brought the prisoner into the jail yard and the condemned man ascended the scaffold. The sheriff read the death warrant and offered the prisoner an opportunity to speak, but he declined, so his wrists and ankles were pinioned, the black cap was pulled on, and the noose adjusted. The Rev. W.A. Shannon offered a prayer for divine mercy and when he concluded, at noon precisely, the drop fell and Douglass' neck was broken in the fall. In five minutes Drs. Yager and Smith pronounced him dead and fifteen minutes later the body was cut down and buried that afternoon.

Butte (MT) Daily Miner: May 28, 1881.

Fohrman, Heinrich
May 2, 1883

Seventy-year-old Heinrich Fohrman treated his son-in-law Jacob C. Kenck with great malignancy over the years, and on a number of occasions tried to kill him. On December 22, 1882, Fohrman was sitting by the stove in his son-in-law's saloon on Main Street when Kenck went to the front door to talk with a friend. Fohrman slipped up behind Kenck, placed the muzzle of his revolver close to Kenck's head and shot him once, the bullet entering his son-in-law's brain but not exiting. Kenck was removed to his home, where he died a few hours later. When asked about the crime Fohrman said he had chosen to kill his son-in-law at that particular time so the body could be given to his grandchildren as a Christmas present. He was tried at the March term of the district court and convicted of first degree murder, and on April 1, 1883, he was sentenced to hang on Wednesday, May 2. During his last week several attempts were made to provide the prisoner religious services but he refused, saying he believed in the transmigration of souls and told an *Independent* reporter that he expected his soul to pass into some bird, beast or plant.

The gallows had been built in the jail yard and by 11:00 A.M. the small party of witnesses had gathered at the foot of the scaffold within the enclosure. In a half hour the prisoner was brought into the cage surrounding the cells, where he expressed no regret for the death of Kenck or himself. The prisoner was seated in a chair and the death warrant was read in English, and Ig Miller translated it into German. At 11:50 A.M. Fohrman was escorted into the enclosure, where he acted as if he did not understand any English, smiling and nodding to anything said to him as his wrists and arms, knees and ankles were pinioned and the noose cinched around his neck. At 11:56 A.M., as he uttered in German "Now Chris Kenck will laugh," the trap was sprung and the prisoner dropped six and one half feet. Drs. Cole and Brown monitored his vital signs and at 12:05 P.M. they pronounced him dead. Six minutes later the body was lowered into its coffin, and Fohrman was buried that afternoon. Fohrman made a will just prior to his death bequeathing his remains to the surgeons, as there had been some question of insanity and many thought he should have been sent to an asylum. An autopsy was conducted and, in addition to confirming that the fall had broken his neck, Drs. Cole and Brown reported in the May 5 edition of the *Daily Miner* that "nothing was found to indicate that Fohrman was otherwise than perfectly sane."

Helena (MT) Daily Independent: April 1, 1883; May 2–3, 1883; *Butte (MT) Daily Miner*: May 3, 1883; May 5, 1883; *Virginia City (NV) Territorial Enterprise*: May 5, 1883.

Ah Young
August 16, 1883

Ah Young, alias Ah Kee, took six sticks of giant powder explosives and tried to blow up a tent occupied by several Chinese men at Horse Plains. He believed that this would scare them away and give him enough time to break open and go through their locked trunk, which he knew contained money and other valuables. The sticks exploded but they did not destroy the tent so the occupants were not scared off, but instead rushed out and spotted Ah Young. They called his name, whereupon he pulled his revolver and murdered one of his intended robbery victims and wounded another.

He was arrested, tried and convicted of first degree murder, and sentenced to hang on August 16, 1883. Neither appeal nor application to Governor John S. Crosby for executive clemency delayed the execution. On the day before the execution the gallows was tested several times and it worked perfectly. It was constructed within a high fenced enclosure, as required by law, and after 1:00 P.M. on August 16 one hundred invited witnesses were admitted, and they gathered at the foot of the scaffold. Just before 2:00 P.M. Ah Young was removed from his cell and led into the enclosure; he walked boldly up the stairs onto the platform. He had declined to speak to the witnesses so once on the trapdoor his wrists and arms, knees and ankles were pinioned, the noose adjusted, and the black cap pulled on, preparations that took only one minute. The trapdoor was sprung at 2:00 P.M. and Ah Young's neck was broken in the fall. His pulse could not be detected after ninety seconds but he was allowed to hang thirty minutes before being cut down. His remains were lowered into the plain coffin provided by the county and buried in a pauper's grave that evening.

Butte (MT) Daily Miner: August 17, 1883.

Clark, John A.
December 27, 1883

Thomas Rogers and Peter Lyman had been working on the railroad near Bozeman and had accumulated $800, which Rogers carried. On Wednesday, June 27, 1883, they started for the mines at Clarke's Fork with a wagon, camping outfit, and a fine team of horses. They stopped at the railroad camp in Rocky Canyon and bought some liquor, Rogers paying for it from the large roll of bills he carried. John A. Clark was loitering about the camp, saw the money, learned that they were new to that country, and offered to guide them. This was agreed and when they reached Pine Creek, a small tributary of Trail Creek five miles from Yellowstone Valley, Clark said this was the best and only camping site for miles around.

After camp was set up Clark suggested that he and Rogers go fishing, and also suggested that Rogers take along a rifle in case they happened across some black tailed deer. They had not been gone long when Lyman heard three shots in rapid succession and he started up the trail where he met Clark, who sent him back to camp for a knife or axe to cut up the deer he said they'd killed. But Lyman suspected foul play and, when he got to camp, he pinned a note to the tent which read, "T. Rogers. Stay in camp till I get back. Peter Lyman," then went up Trail Creek to the cabin of Congers Smith and spent the night. The next morning Lyman returned to their camp and found Rogers' bed undisturbed and the horses gone. He and Smith went up Pine Creek, where they found the dead body of Rogers hidden in the brush. Two shots had killed him: one bullet entering near the point of Rogers' chin, and the second wound under his jaw. Rogers' suspenders had been taken off, tied around his neck, and used to drag the body sixty paces off the trail. A roll of currency totaling $500 had been taken but another package containing more than $250 had been overlooked.

The men went for help and filed a complaint with Justice Davis, so a warrant was issued and given to Constable Hineman for service. The pursuing party went down the Yellowstone and found that Clark had stopped at Andy Kingoldsby's at midnight and at 2:00 A.M. someone had knocked on the door of another saloon, but no one would answer. A short distance beyond that second saloon Rogers' team was found where it had been abandoned. White Calfee joined the posse and immediately recognized the description of Clark as a man who had worked for him, and said Clark had a strong attachment for Miss Haxsays, who lived with her parents near Livingston. Calfee was sure they would find Clark there, so the posse went directly to the Haxsays' farm and captured Clark; the fugitive still had Rogers' $500 with him when arrested.

Clark waived examination and was taken to Bozeman where Judge Wade issued a venire for a special grand jury, and Clark was soon indicted and arraigned. He pled not guilty and trial was set for the fall term of the district court. At trial Clark testified that he, Rogers and Lyman met two other men on the trail and, when Clark left with them at 2:00 A.M., Rogers was still alive. He said he went on to Livingston while Lyman and Rogers were going to Clarke's Fork, but on cross examination he could not explain how he had come into possession of Rogers' money. The jury did not believe the defendant's story so he was convicted of first degree murder and sentenced to hang on December 27, 1883. Neither appeal nor application for executive clemency delayed the proceedings.

On his last night Clark wrote a note to the *Chronicle*, three letters to relatives, and composed a song before he lay down to sleep. He awoke at 1:00 A.M. and began singing but soon retired again and slept soundly until aroused by his jailor. The Reverend Stevenson arrived at an early hour and the two men spent the morning praying, singing, and conversing about religion and the hereafter. The sturdy scaffold had been built a year earlier but the man then condemned to death, Carl Adolphson, had been respited. The rope was of "manella," about ¾ of an inch thick, and allowed for a drop of seven feet. Every detail was carefully arranged before the prisoner was led out by Sheriff Blakeley at 11:30 A.M. He had been bound by straps around his arms and wrists, and the legs straps were in place but loose. The prisoner walked up the stairs unaided and took his place on the trapdoor, where the lower straps were tightened and the noose adjusted. When the black cap was presented Clark cleared his throat and said, "Well, gentlemen, I suppose you all know what I am here for — at least you say that I am here for the murder of Thomas Rogers. Gentlemen of Bozeman, I stand here to meet my God, and I say here today that I am an innocent man. I am innocent of the crime and I know nothing about it whatever. The man that testified against me has sworn falsely but I can meet my God an innocent man as far as this crime is concerned...." As soon as the last word was spoken Sheriff Blakeley pulled on the black cap and motioned to deputy sheriff James Ponsford. The deputy touched the spring release, the trap was sprung, and Clark dropped, breaking his neck in the fall. There were two convulsive movements before the body hung motionless. The doctors stepped forward to monitor his vital signs, and in ten minutes pronounced him dead. The body was taken down and delivered to undertaker Semmett, who was standing by with the coffin. Clark was buried that evening.

Bozeman (MT) Weekly Chronicle: June 27, 1883; January 1, 1884.

Harding, Thomas
March 25, 1887

The stagecoach from Melrose to Glendale left town at half past eight on the evening of Saturday, May 22, 1886, with five passengers inside and T.S. Marchant, a San Francisco drummer, on the box with driver George Ferguson. They were several miles out, about halfway up a gulch, when a man sprang from the right side of the road and pointed a double-barreled shotgun. He commanded, "Halt!" but without hesitating fired one barrel at Ferguson from a distance of only a few feet. Five buckshot struck the driver over and under his right eye and several pellets passed entirely through his head; the muzzle was so close that the driver's face was powder burned. Ferguson died instantly and slumped over, dropping the lines. The blast was too close for the buckshot to spread, so passenger Marchant was uninjured as he grabbed hold of Ferguson to prevent him from falling. The frightened horses bolted.

Another passenger had to climb forward to recover the reins and by the time the horses were brought under control they had carried the stagecoach a considerable distance, which took them out of danger from the highwayman. The passengers could not return to Melrose without passing the robber so they continued on to Glendale with Marchant driving. They reported the killing and parties went out from Dillon and from Glendale but they could find no trace of the road agent. His description was circulated and five days later Thomas Harding was arrested at Butte and taken to Dillon, where he was identified as having been in Melrose the day of the robbery and had left town for Glendale just ahead of the coach. Marchant had no difficulty identifying Harding as the highwayman who had killed Ferguson.

Harding was indicted and tried at the October term of the district court at Dillon. He was found guilty of first degree murder and sentenced to hang on December 24; but his attorneys filed an appeal with the supreme court so Governor Samuel T. Hauser granted two consecutive thirty day respites delaying the execution to February 25. The supreme court affirmed the lower court's decision and the matter was next appealed to the U.S.

Supreme Court on a writ of habeas corpus. The basis for the appeal was that Harding claimed to have been thirty-eight miles away at the lime kilns between Melrose and Butte when Ferguson was killed, and he insisted that this could have been proven if a certain witness had been found. Harding's attorney also showed that another man was then in custody charged with the murder, but the writ was denied. An attempt was then made to obtain a further respite from Governor Preston H. Leslie, but when this failed an application for a commutation of sentence was submitted and denied. Harding's only living relative, his mother, tried to persuade President Grover Cleveland to intervene but after carefully considering the matter the president declined to interfere. This action delayed the execution to March 25, 1887.

On Harding's final morning Father Dolls stayed with Harding, but the prisoner made no statement nor a confession of his crime and continued to protest his innocence. He had broken down during the early hours but as the time for the execution approached Father Dolls helped Harding brace up for the ordeal. The counterpoise weight gallows had been erected between the jail and the high fence on the south side and at 2:25 P.M. Sheriff Jones, jailor Rote, guard N. Morgan, Father Dolls and the prisoner emerged from the jail into the enclosure. Harding was hatless, dressed in black broadcloth and carpet slippers as he was led under the crossbeam and the noose adjusted. Father Dolls performed the church rites and then Jones read the death warrant. Harding's arms were strapped to his body at the elbows, each wrist to a leg, the slippers were then removed and his knees and ankles were pinioned, and the black cap was pulled on. A faint "Good-bye!" was heard just before the restraining rope was cut at 2:31 P.M. and the three hundred pound weight dropped six feet, jerking Harding into the air with such suddenness that his neck was broken and when he rebounded his toes were suspended ten inches above the platform. Drs. Peckman and Leason of Dillon were in attendance and they pronounced him dead in six minutes. Harding's remains were cut down and examined; he was found to have dark hollow eyes, knotted veins in his neck, and faint blue decorations of the flesh. The black cap was then drawn over his face in anticipation of his burial, and Harding's remains were placed in a plain pine coffin and taken to the cemetery. He was buried after a brief service by Father Dolls.

Butte (MT) Daily Inter Mountain: March 24–26, 1887.

Hart, John P.
February 10, 1888

In 1883 John Patrick Hart boarded at the Foster House in Elkhorn, and also boarding there was a miner named John Pitts, his wife and his stepdaughter Sarah Starkweather. Hart became friends with them and he thought of Ms. Starkweather as an adopted sister; because of her strong influence he had stayed out of the saloons. Mr. and Mrs. Pitts were having marital difficulties and Mr. Pitts was determined to get a divorce, but he needed grounds before he could file his petition. On November 7, 1885, Hart found Ms. Starkweather crying at the breakfast table and she said that her stepfather had deserted her mother. Hart went to see Mrs. Pitts and learned that her husband had gone to Boulder and was planning to swear out a warrant for Hart's arrest, alleging that he had frequented houses of ill fame in Helena and was now a "debaucher" of Ms. Starkweather. Mr. Pitts would use this allegation, and Mrs. Pitts' alleged approval of the liaison, as his grounds for a divorce from Mrs. Pitts and he would then seek custody of his stepdaughter.

Hart went to Boulder in Jefferson County, Montana, and learned that Pitts had not yet been to the courthouse, so he began searching the saloons. At 10:00 A.M. on the morning of November 8 he found Pitts at Jerry Smith's Saloon and waited outside; and when his accuser came out they talked but Pitts was adamant that he was going to swear out the warrant and file for divorce. He would not listen to Hart's continued insistence that he was innocent of the charge and for the remainder of that day and night the thought of being charged as a seducer of an innocent young lady weighed heavily on Hart, who said later that he believed he would be lynched if the story continued to be circulated. Hart went to the courthouse the next morning, saw Pitts there, and believed charges were being filed against him. Hart shot Pitts and, as the wounded man staggered toward him, he shot him again and Pitts soon died of the wounds. Hart was arrested, indicted, tried three times, and convicted of first degree murder in each trial. The jury, in his third trial held at Helena on a change of venue, could not find that Hart's fear of lynching was justification for the unprovoked killing and Hart was sentenced to hang on February 10, 1888. The duty of officiating fell upon Sheriff Hathaway of Lewis and Clark County and he selected a counterpoise weight design for the gallows.

A high board fence surrounded the scaffold in the little yard at the rear of the jail and by 10:30 A.M. the few invited witnesses had assembled; these consisted of sheriffs from adjacent counties, jurymen, and reporters. A large crowd had gathered outside the jail yard awaiting word that Hart was dead, but they could see nothing of the execution. The condemned man appeared at the jail door at 11:25 A.M., nearly an hour behind schedule, escorted by Sheriff Hathaway and undersheriff Hard with deputies Gibbs and Walker following close behind. Hart walked slowly and deliberately to the platform and took his place beneath the noose. The sheriff asked if he had anything to say and the prisoner replied, "I wish you all a restful conscience and a useful life on this earth. And, I hope when you come through this door you will bring some little child that has no father and mother. This is all I have to say on this earth; Good-bye!" Hart's limbs were bound, the noose was adjusted, the black cap pulled on, and at 11:38 A.M. the rope restraining the two hundred eighty-six pound weight was cut. The weight dropped and Hart was jerked upwards with such suddenness that his neck was broken, and the attending physicians monitoring his vital signs pronounced him dead in minutes. Father V.J. Vonden Broeck, Hart's spiritual advisor, waited until the body was cut down and then took charge of Hart's remains to prepare them for burial.

Butte (MT) Daily Inter Mountain: February 10, 1888.

Scott, Martin L.
February 17, 1888

Martin L. Scott married the widow McCluskey on July 5, 1886, at Butte, Montana. In August Scott went to Granite to chop wood for the Granite Mine and in October his wife followed, but soon it became evident that his wife was being unfaithful and that she stole from their neighbors whenever an opportunity presented itself. In September 1887 the men who occupied a tent near the Scott's house accused Mrs. Scott of stealing a clock, looking glass, and other items. Scott searched their home and found the stolen items, which he returned. He said of his wife, after he returned the items, "She never was the same woman to me after that. She would drink all the whiskey she could get, and when under the influence of whiskey was very abusive. While matters were running along in that way I made up my mind to sell what little I had and send her to her folks, seeing that I could have no peace with her. Mr. Frowen and wife were my near neighbors. He was working on the Granite mine. I asked him to see if he could find me a buyer for my house and what was there. This was in November, on Saturday the 12th."

Later that day Scott was sick and his wife was on one of her sprees, talking loudly and offensively, and when he struck her she rushed out of the house. She was gone all night, staying with the Frowens, but returned home sober and everything seemed resolved until Monday when the constable arrested Martin for wife-beating. Martin was tried and fined \$25, paid \$5 on the fine and was released, and on November 15 he went out to find the remainder of the fine money, taking his rifle with him. According to Martin he returned home at 7:00 P.M. and as he opened the door to a darkened house he was attacked and knocked into a washtub. He was assaulted again and he struck out at his attacker several times with his rifle, managed to rise, but then fainted onto the bed near the door. He was aroused by someone's groans and lit a lamp. He found his wife lying on the floor, her bloodied head lying on some tools stored at the foot of their bed. He tried to lift her but could not because she weighed one hundred seventy pounds and was quite drunk. A quart bottle of whiskey, nearly empty, was on the table and his wife said "Tom the butcher" had brought it, and then she confessed a number of infidelities and other offenses, talking with him until 5:00 A.M.

On Thursday morning, November 16, Constable Thatcher and Justice of the Peace McDonald of Granite went to the Scott home to collect $20 due on the fine for wife-beating. Thatcher knocked but when there was no response, McDonald looked in the window and saw Mrs. Scott lying on the floor. McDonald told Thatcher to have his revolver ready and they forced open the door. Martin was sitting on the bed with his Winchester rifle across his knees and Thatcher ordered him to throw up his hands. The lawmen examined Mrs. Scott and found her dead, her head and clothing saturated with blood; she had a wound between her eyes resembling a bullet hole and her skull was crushed. Martin accused Thomas Beach, the butcher, of killing her but when Constable James Carter arrived Scott was arrested and jailed.

The constable collected evidence at the scene and found that Scott's rifle stock was broken and the muzzle was saturated with blood; a three pound wood-chopper's sledge and a three foot shovel handle were smeared with blood; and the shovel handle had some of Mrs. Scott's hair on it. At the coroner's inquest it was determined that Mrs. Scott had died from a crushed skull and that the wound between her eyes was from a blow, not a bullet, and the jury found Martin L. Scott responsible for her death. The community was so enraged at the brutality of the crime that there was talk of a lynching so deputy sheriff George Hammond took his prisoner to Deer Lodge and placed him in the county jail. Scott was indicted on December 6 and three days later he entered a plea of not guilty. The jury was empanelled on December 23, his trial concluded the following day, and after only one hour of deliberations he was convicted of first degree murder. A motion for a new trial was overruled and the prisoner was sentenced to hang on February 17, 1888. A petition for a commutation of sentence was submitted but Governor Preston H. Leslie refused to interfere.

On Saturday, February 11, the counterpoise weight gallows was erected behind the jail within a twelve foot board fence enclosing an area twenty feet by thirty feet. The gallows consisted of a firm platform below a sturdy crossbeam with two pulleys bolted six feet apart. The rope end opposite the noose was fastened to a three hundred pound lead weight suspended four feet above the ground. The builders conceived the grim idea of building the platform using the murder weapon, the wood-chopper's sledge, and every nail was driven with that blood stained instrument. Scott had remained composed until he heard the craftsman constructing the scaffold and learned of the use of his hammer, and then he began to break down.

On Thursday, the day before his execution, Scott was baptized by Father Deryckerie and afterward he and Father Descrie were with the condemned man constantly. Scott's last night was spent playing cribbage with his death watch guards, George Hammond and Al Cain, and when one hand went against him he raised a hand to Hammond and said, "[N]one of that, I won't have it, play fair." He retired at 11:30 P.M., smoked a cigar, bookmarked his Bible with a ribbon at midnight and slept. He arose at 3:00 A.M. and read his Bible for a while, then slept again until 4:30 A.M. At 7:30 A.M. the priests arrived and a half hour later they held communion, and remained with him in the jail corridor through the reading of the death warrant by Sheriff Coleman at 10:30 A.M. Then Scott returned to his cell for his last hour of prayer. He called for and received stimulants at 11:37 A.M. and then the procession to the gallows formed and started out. Scott took his position beneath the noose, the priests standing on his left while jailor Ross and deputy Holton pinioned his wrists and ankles, and as the men worked Scott whispered to the priests, "I forgive all!" Scott was then given an opportunity to address the crowd of seventy witnesses and he said, "Gentlemen, I have been wronged today, but I forgive all." When the black cap was drawn on Scott said softly, "Jesus, have mercy on me!" The noose was adjusted and at 11:40 A.M. the signal was given and the restraining rope was cut. Scott was jerked up, breaking his neck, and Drs. Douglass and Leisuer of Anaconda stepped forward, monitored his vital signs, and pronounced him dead in five minutes. The body hung a total of twenty minutes before it was cut down and turned over to the undertaker, and Scott was buried in the Deer Lodge Cemetery at 3:00 P.M.

Butte (MT) Daily Inter Mountain: February 16–17, 1888; *Butte (MT) Daily Miner*: February 18, 1888.

Bryson, George D.
August 9, 1889

During the latter part of July 1888, twenty-eight-year-old George Duncan Bryson and forty-five-year-old Annie Lundstrom arrived in Helena and took rooms with Sarah Bennett at 310 Bridge Street. Bryson introduced Lundstrom as his wife and she went by the name Bryson, but while at Mrs. Bennett's boardinghouse the couple quarreled frequently. The quarrels were always about money, with Bryson demanding more while Lundstrom insisted on providing it in small quantities. She told Mrs. Bennett that Bryson would leave her if he got hold of all her money and might even kill her for it. She said she had converted her money into drafts and sewed them into different dresses and other clothing so that, if Bryson found some of the drafts, he would not find all of her wealth. However, though she feared that Bryson would harm her or rob her, she was quite infatuated with him and feared even more that he would leave her.

The couple stayed with Mrs. Bennett two weeks but on August 4 Bryson and Lundstrom moved to the boardinghouse of Mrs. Trunk at 516 Eighth Avenue, Lundstrom paying a month's rent in advance. Mrs. Trunk had two other boarders, a Mrs. Mixture and a Mrs. Hardwick, and the residents all became acquainted with the couple and were soon familiar with their incessant quarreling. Lundstrom developed a close relationship with Mrs. Mixture and told of her fear that Bryson would kill her. On August 21 at 2:00 P.M. the couple left to have dinner, and all the ladies were present and noticed her clothing. Two hours later Bryson returned alone and went to his room, left again and returned late, then spent the night pacing in his room. In the morning he packed his trunks and, at 7:00 A.M., left to get express man Joe Ryan. He explained that Lundstrom had gone on to Butte, and then he moved out.

Mrs. Mixture was immediately suspicious as that morning Lundstrom had asked her to change a $10 dollar bill and had her keep $5 until she returned from dinner. Then Mrs. Trunk disclosed that the rent was paid for two more weeks but there had been no demand for a refund. Still Mrs. Mixture waited three weeks, until she could no longer restrain her fears, and she reported the matter to the police. She had pictures of Bryson and Lundstrom and gave them to the officers; a reporter for the *Helena Independent* newspaper made the public aware of Lundstrom's absence and the possibility of foul play. A search was made for Bryson but he could not be found. However, one day a woman appeared at the post office and asked for Bryson's mail, and left a watch at the post office for safekeeping. The watch was identified as Lundstrom's so, when the woman appeared two days later, lawmen were waiting and followed her to a small hotel near the Northern Pacific Railroad depot.

There they found Bryson living with Flora Thompson, the woman they had followed, and when Bryson was arrested he said Lundstrom had gone to Seattle but refused to say where Lundstrom's trunks were located. The lawmen backtracked and learned that after the fugitive left Mrs. Trunk's home he went to the Lenoir House, registered as J.D. Lundstrom, and had his luggage with him. The following day he moved to the hotel where he was captured and registered under the alias Mr. Barnes from Seattle. A preliminary examination was held and Bryson was held to answer to the grand jury, even though the body of Lundstrom had not been found. A reward of $300 was offered by the mayor for the recovery of the body, but it was not found until October 1 when a blacksmith named Dixon stumbled upon the remains of a woman in a prospect hole northeast of the city. Though in a terrible state of decomposition the remains were identified by the clothing Lundstrom was last seen wearing on August 21, and also by the switch with which she covered her bald spot.

At the inquest the jury found that Lundstrom had died at the hands of Bryson, the grand jury returned an indictment against the prisoner, he was arraigned, and the judge granted a change of venue to Boulder in Jefferson County. Bryson's defense was that the work at the prospect hole, the murder and the concealment of the body, could not have been done by one man; that a hack driver, whose clothes were reportedly covered with blood, disappeared from the country at that time; and that the body found could not be positively identified as Lundstrom's. The trial concluded on March 16 with the jury needing sixteen hours of deliberations to return a verdict of guilty of first degree murder. The motion for a new trial was denied and on appeal the supreme court affirmed the decision of the lower court. Bryson's appeal and application for commutation of sentence were denied and he was resentenced to hang on August 9, 1889.

On the day before his execution Bryson wrote out a statement to be read on the scaffold, and his father was allowed to stay with him until 10:00 P.M., when the jail closed. After everyone left he talked with his guards and the county sheriff, who agreed to sit with him during the night, and the prisoner sang comic songs with fellow inmates for several hours. Bryson expected a message from Governor Benjamin F. White granting a commutation of sentence or at least a respite, but when it had not yet come he retired at 1:00 A.M. and slept soundly for five hours. When the prisoner arose he dressed in the light suit he had worn throughout his trial. After breakfast his father returned and was with him when, at 9:00 A.M., a message arrived saying that the governor saw no grounds for interference.

Earlier that morning the Reverend Guiler had conducted religious services with members of the Salvation Army in attendance. After they retired the prisoner talked with his father in French and left a letter for his six-year-old daughter, in which he proclaimed his innocence. At 9:30 A.M. the sheriff read the death warrant in the presence of local educator Louis de Lestry and deputy Jerry Ellis and when this was done they sent for the Rev. T.A. Wickes, who was joined by Leonard Bom, captain of Helena's Salvation Army post, at 10:00 A.M. After prayers and songs concluded at 10:30 A.M. the procession formed. Bryson was conducted to the gallows, where he read his carefully prepared statement while the straps were being applied to his wrists and ankles. He repeated the elements of his defense, accused the witnesses of perjury, berated the officers for laying traps, and blamed the newspapers for creating prejudice against him, protested his innocence, and finally accused the territory of judicial murder. As soon as he finished his harangue the noose was adjusted and he said, "May God have mercy on my soul!" The cap was quickly pulled on and at 10:52 A.M. the axe fell, cutting the restraining rope. The heavy counterpoise weight fell, jerking Bryson into the air so suddenly that it broke his neck in two places. There followed several convulsive movements before the body hung limp and motionless. Three doctors were in attendance and in nine and one half minutes they pronounced him dead. Twelve minutes after the weight fell Bryson's remains were cut down and placed in a plain wooden coffin and he was buried in the Boulder cemetery, at county expense, at 4:00 P.M.

Helena (MT) Daily Independent: August 10, 1889.

Roberts, Harry
August 23, 1889

In 1869 Harry Roberts came from Wales to Montana, where he worked as a teamster for Emanuel Corea. In January 1889 Corea promoted Roberts to wagon boss. He pushed the men hard, and some felt he worked them too hard and resented him; but he never asked any man to work harder than he did. J.W. Crawford, a large and unusually powerful man, was a teamster on Roberts' crew and by March Crawford's resentment had turned to hostility. The men ate dinner together at the Silver Bow boardinghouse and as Roberts walked to the stable after dinner, according to Roberts, Crawford struck him on the head with a pitchfork, without any provocation or warning. Dr. Bovet intervened and Roberts then challenged Crawford to meet outside the city limits and settle their differences, but Crawford declined.

On May 13 the two men met uptown and at first seemed less combative, almost reconciled, but soon quarreling resumed. The scar on Robert's head was still quite visible and, as they parted, Crawford said, "I'll put a worse scar than that on you." On May 14, shortly after noon, Roberts walked into the Silver Bow boardinghouse with his .38 caliber six-shooter in hand and found Crawford washing his hands. At close range, without warning or hesitation, he shot him once, the bullet entering Crawford's right arm between the shoulder and elbow, and nearly passing through his body. The wounded man ran into the backyard and bled to death in less than a minute as Roberts said, "I got that s__ of a b___ that time!" Roberts raised his gun as Emanuel Corea rushed into the room but Joe Fortin caught the pistol and took it away from him. Roberts and Fortin then started uptown on Park Street and, when they were between Main and Montana streets, they met undersheriff Frank B. Thomas, who arrested and jailed Roberts.

The district court was in session so the grand jury was reconvened and on May 18 they indicted Roberts, and on Monday, June 4, his trial began. The prosecution depended upon witnesses to the shooting and threats made by the defendant, which were all documented in the transcript at the inquest; and the defense was insanity, relying on expert testimony that the wound inflicted to Roberts' head by Crawford made him "subject to mental aberration." The case went to the jury on June 5 and on the first ballot Roberts was convicted of first degree murder. A motion for a new trial was denied and two weeks later Judge de Wolfe sentenced Roberts to hang on August 16. The territorial supreme court considered the case on appeal and affirmed the decision of the lower court.

On August 8 Roberts was removed from his cell and placed in the "box car," the name given the cell reserved for insane prisoners. This cell, in the southeast corner of the jail, was exceptionally large and strong and quite a distance from the other cells. The floor of this cell was carpeted and had been outfitted with a new bed and bedding, a table and chairs, writing material, and an ample supply of reading materials. On his final day the prisoner had given up all hope when, at noon, a seven day respite was granted by Governor Benjamin F. White; the governor then examined every aspect and detail of the crime, testimony, and the physical evidence before he declined to intervene. Roberts seemed relieved by the religious counsel of the Reverend Andrews of the Baptist church and Father Van de Ven of the Catholic church, and both clergymen remained with him until he was led out of his cell at 12:15 P.M.

He was dressed in a new suit of black diagonal with a cutaway coat, shirt without collar, and carpet slippers as he listened intently to

Sheriff Lloyd reading the death warrant. He said he had no last request nor any final words for anyone as he had arranged all that a week earlier. People began congregating at the courthouse at 10:00 A.M., as the sheriff had originally planned for the execution to take place at noon, but he delayed until 1:00 P.M. so that Roberts' friends could make the trip from Anaconda. By noon the second floor windows of the district court clerk's office and jail were filled with spectators. The official witnesses gathered around the counterpoise weight gallows, erected east of the jail and north of the courthouse, included several doctors and a number of reporters.

At 1:03 P.M. the sheriff and Roberts appeared at the east door of the jail followed by Tom Richards, Harry Nichols and Sam Reynolds. The procession moved to the platform where a strip of carpet had been spread to mark the spot where Roberts should stand and he took his place beneath the pulley, the noose being tied back to a post. Roberts was asked if he had any statement so he faced the witnesses and said, "I'd have got my reprieve if it hadn't been for W.A. Clark and W.M. Jack. I forgive them and have prayed to God to forgive them and me. I hope that he will answer that prayer." Reynolds and Nichols applied the straps while Sheriff Lloyd untied the noose from the post and placed it around Roberts' neck. Roberts moved his head to assist in its placement and directed, "Make it a little tighter, that's too loose. It will hurt." So the sheriff cinched the noose tighter. The black cap was pulled on at 1:12 P.M. and the sheriff scarcely removed his hands when the restraining rope was cut and the weight fell. Roberts was jerked three feet into the air and fell back until his toes were suspended six inches above the platform. Drs. Howard, Tremblay and Sarchet monitored Roberts' vital signs and at eleven minutes they pronounced him dead. Two minutes later his remains were lowered into a plain black coffin and on examination it was confirmed that Robert's neck had been broken in two places. The body was carried into the courthouse hall so that the crowd could file past for a final look. The body was next taken to the sheriff's office, where friends took charge and delivered the remains to Sherman's Undertaking Parlor. A funeral service was scheduled for 2:00 P.M. the following day, with burial immediately afterward.

Butte (MT) Daily Inter Mountain: August 16, 1889; August 22, 1889; August 23, 1889; *Butte (MT) Daily Miner*: August 15, 1889; August 24, 1889.

NEBRASKA

The first Europeans to see the land that would become Nebraska was the Pedro de Villasur party in 1720, and they found the land inhabited by the Arapaho, Cheyenne, Omaha, Oto, and Sioux Indian tribes. The region was claimed by France but in 1763 those claims west of the Mississippi River were ceded to Spain. In 1800 France reacquired possession and in 1803 sold the region to the United States as part of the Louisiana Purchase. Nebraska became a territory on May 30, 1854, with passage of the Kansas–Nebraska Act. Nebraska remained a relative wilderness until 1860, when the government began granting free land to homesteaders. Nebraska became the 37th state on March 1, 1867.

Tator, Cyrus H.
August 28, 1863

In early June 1863 Horace Wilson, a boy gathering driftwood in the Missouri River bottoms, found a body floating in a stream not far from Sulphur Springs and men working nearby recovered the body. An inquest was held and the remains were identified as Isaac H. Neff. It was determined he had been cruelly murdered two days before being submerged in the stream, weighted down with logging chains wrapped about the arms, neck and legs. Neff had recently arrived in Omaha from Denver, bringing three unloaded wagons to look for freight to return to Denver, in the company of his freighting partner, Cyrus H. Tator. A party of men was sent to examine the area around Sulphur Springs and they found two of Neff's wagons abandoned there, and it appeared they had been standing several weeks. The third wagon was missing and the party determined that a few days earlier Tator had driven that loaded wagon west toward Denver.

Sheriff Thomas L. Sutton was soon on the trail of Tator and captured him in Colfax County, arrested him for the murder of Neff, and took his prisoner to Omaha, where he was lodged in the county jail. The Omaha district court was then in session, with Judge W.P. Kellogg presiding, so rather than delay to the next term of the court a special grand jury was convened and Tator was indicted on June 17. Tator's trial commenced two days later and the evidence showed the motive for the murder was robbery, as Tator wanted to gain possession of their joint property, and after killing Neff he sold two teams to Heber P. Kimball, who was the strongest witness against him. He also tried to sell the wagons but, failing, left them standing where they were found. After several days of testimony and brief deliberations the defendant was convicted of first degree murder and sentenced to hang on Friday, August 28, 1863. The case was appealed to the territorial supreme court, exceptions taken and overruled and a writ of error denied, and the matter was handled with such efficiently that there was no delay in the proceedings.

The gallows was built at Sulphur Springs, right on the spot where it was determined the murder took place; it was a plain framed apparatus of four erect beams with a platform and trapdoor in the center. On the day of the execution a crowd of over two thousand men, women and children gathered at an early hour and, anticipating the large turnout and the need to preserve order, Sheriff Sutton requested and received from General McKean a guard of forty soldiers from Company C, 7th Iowa Cavalry. During the morning, the Rev. T.B. Lemon administered the Holy Communion to the prisoner in his cell and remained with him until 11:00 A.M., when Sheriff Sutton brought the prisoner out of his cell.

Sutton was assisted by City Marshal Thomas Riley and they placed the prisoner in a buggy, drove him to Sulphur Springs, and escorted him onto the scaffold. Tator took his place at the railing and addressed the large crowd, reading a carefully prepared statement that took thirty minutes to complete. He called on God to witness that "I am an innocent man, I did not murder Neff, and I am ignorant of the author of the deed." The Reverend Lemon then offered a prayer while the prisoner was positioned on the trapdoor and the noose was cinched tight by the sheriff. Next the sheriff and city marshal bound his wrists and ankles and pulled the black cap over his face. The trap was sprung at 1:00 P.M. and Tator dropped to his death, breaking his neck in the fall. The attending physician pronounced him dead after several minutes but the body was not cut down for twenty-two minutes. The remains were lowered into the coffin provided and taken away to await a requisition by his friends.

Omaha Daily Nebraskian: August 29, 1863; *Omaha Weekly Nebraskian:* September 4, 1863; *Burlington (IA) Weekly Hawk-eye*: September 2, 1863; Alfred Sorenson. *History of Omaha from the Pioneer Days to the Present Time* (Omaha: Gibson, Miller & Richardson, 1889).

Diercks, Casper F.
August 16, 1866

On August 15, 1866, William Henry Hamilton, an eleven-year-old boy, was herding cattle for his father on their farm in Otoe County five miles from Nebraska City. That evening the boy failed to return home so a search was made and the dead body of the boy was found with his feet buried in the mud of the nearby creek, his body in a stooping position. The boy had been shot three times — in the right eye, under the right arm, and in the right ear — and the cattle were missing. The body was pulled from the mud and carried to the Hamilton farmhouse, where a coroner's jury was convened, and the jurors determined that the person responsible was a man known as "Cash," who had driven Hamilton's cattle to Nebraska City and sold them. A reward of $200 was posted and the search for Cash began; it was quickly learned that he had crossed the river on the ferry into Iowa.

Two hundred armed and angry men started in pursuit and early the following day they captured Casper Frederick Diercks, alias Cash, at Plum Hollow, Iowa. The prisoner was taken back to Nebraska City and would have been lynched if it had not been decided to give him a trial in a "people's court." Two other men thought to be involved were Sebastian Deitch and R.P. Ford, and they had been jailed in the interim. At 10:30 A.M. two thousand men, women, and children assembled in the public square and elected D.J. McCann president of the court and J. Dan Lauer as secretary. A jury composed of old, influential citizens was then empanelled to try the prisoners, while another committee was appointed to guard the jail to prevent escape, suicide, or a lynching. Twenty special policemen were appointed to keep order and attorneys were appointed for the defense and prosecution. The three prisoners were brought forth and the jury heard the testimony of seven witnesses, including Deitch and Ford, which sealed the fate of their partner in crime. The jury then retired to deliberate and they quickly found Diercks guilty of "willful murder," but recommended that Deitch and Ford be held for the regular session of the district court. A proposition to hang Diercks immediately was voted down and it was decided to give him until 6:00 P.M. to put his life in order. Deitch and Ford were later tried, convicted of being accomplices to cattle stealing, and sentenced to long prison terms.

While the condemned man waited his execution he was allowed to consult with Methodist reverend H.F. Davis and, during his last hours on earth, bequeathed all his worldly possessions. When his time came the condemned man stepped from his cell and was escorted onto the platform, where a prayer was offered by the Reverend Davis as the prisoner was positioned on the trapdoor. The prisoner took the noose in his hand and said, "Holding as I do this rope, which is to send me into eternity, I declare that I am guilty of the larceny, but of murder, I am not." He was then questioned and denied knowing who killed the boy, then said, "May God have mercy on my soul!" As he was speaking to the crowd he had been prepared by having his wrists and ankles pinioned and the noose adjusted about his neck. When he finished his plea for God's mercy the trap was sprung and he dropped to his death. He struggled for a few minutes but then hung lifeless and as soon as he was pronounced dead he was cut down, lowered into a cheap pine coffin, and given to the Reverend Davis for burial.

Andreas' History of the State of Nebraska: Otoe Co., Part 5.

NEVADA

The first European to see the land that would become Nevada was Father Francisco Garces, who reached the Colorado River in the late 1700s while traveling through Spanish Mexico. Several other explorers traversed Nevada before emigrants began trekking across the region. The area was a part of independent Mexico until it passed to the United States on February 2, 1848, as a concession in the Treaty of Guadalupe Hidalgo. The Mormons had positioned themselves to populate the entire region and proposed the State of Deseret stretching from Oregon to Mexico, but Congress, more conservatively, established the Utah Territory in 1849, which only included the area that would become Nevada. The current lower portion of Nevada was triangular in form and was a part of the New Mexico Territory in 1850. On March 3, 1861, the Nevada Territory was organized from the western-most portion of Utah. Nevada could not expand westward — and several border disputes with California were resolved by survey or settlement — but it could expand eastward. On October 31, 1864, Nevada was admitted as the 36th state and moved its eastern boundary to increase its land area by a fourth. In 1866 the boundary was again moved eastward to double in size and that same year the southern triangle, then a part of the newly organized Arizona Territory, was ceded to Nevada and annexed in 1867.

Carr, John W.
November 30, 1860

John William Carr was a gambler from Sonora, California, who came to the Comstock in 1860. He sought his fortune, not digging in the hills but on the gaming tables, and he was adept at sleight of hand. He soon became worried that he would be exposed as a cheat so he took the stage to Thousand Wells Station located on the old Overland Trail. At Thousand Wells Carr decided to take a more direct approach to finding his fortune and began waylaying unsuspecting emigrants as they neared the station operated by Bernhard Cherry. After each robbery he would return to the station and remain as long as his plunder lasted, then leave again looking for his next victim.

Cherry soon figured out how Carr was making his living, so when Carr began terrorizing a young Missourian in preparation to ply his trade as highwayman, Cherry intervened and prevented the robbery. Carr, thereafter, harbored a grudge against Cherry for depriving him of his booty. Several months later Cherry became too ill to continue operating the station, sold his interest for cash, and settled at the Ormsby House in Carson City. Carr believed that Cherry carried the proceeds of the sale on his person so he followed and took a room at the same hotel, exerting great effort to befriend Cherry. One evening at 10:00 P.M. Carr asked Cherry to accompany him and his partner, Radsill, on a walk to discuss a business proposition and Cherry agreed, trusting in his new-found friend. They walked toward the western part of the city until they came within a quarter mile of the estimable residence of Dr. B.L. King, where a light burned in a second story window. Carr asked, "Do you see that light?" and when Cherry looked up Carr pulled his pistol and shot him in the back of the head. Carr and Radsill went through Cherry's pockets but found only a twenty dollar gold piece and a silver half dollar. They then fled to Tuolumne County, California.

Cherry was missed and the next morning his body was found; he had been murdered. Several people remembered that Cherry left with Carr and Radsill, and when they could not be found a search began for the murderers. Carr and Radsill were located within a few weeks, arrested by California sheriff Blackburn, and brought to Carson City on November 13. The court had just ended its fall session so a petition was circulated requesting that U.S. district judge John Cradlebaugh hold a special session, and this was granted on November 19. Radsill turned state's evidence and after testifying he was released; he immediately left the region. Carr at first denied everything but, when it became clear that the chain of circumstantial evidence was strong against him, he confessed. The trial took only one day and Carr was convicted of murder in the first degree, and sentenced to hang in ten days, on November 30, 1860.

The sheriff was ordered to build a gallows and chose to erect it within twenty feet of the scene of the crime. On the fateful morning the surrounding area held a crowd of spectators totaling ten thousand, including five hundred women. Colonel T.W. Bonebrake was given the duty of pinioning the wrists and ankles of the prisoner as he stood on the platform. Carr's only comment as he looked up at the second floor window of Dr. King's house was, "Do you see that light? My God! I do, at last!" In a moment after pronouncing these last words Carr's body dropped through the trapdoor and in nine minutes he was pronounced dead. The prisoner hung a while longer and then was cut down and placed in the coffin provided by the county. Within the hour his remains were buried in an unmarked grave outside the city limits.

Salt Lake City (UT) Deseret News: December 12, 1860; December 26, 1860.

Milstead, Allen
January 9, 1863

On October 29, 1862, Allen Milstead became embroiled in some difficulty with Lyon County commissioner T. Varney at Ragtown, Nevada, and killed him. He was indicted, tried, convicted of murder in the first degree and sentenced to hang at Dayton on Friday, January 9, 1863. From the time Milstead was sentenced until the night before his execution, the condemned man seemed convinced that he would find an opportunity to escape. He spoke little but when he did it was with genuine bravado and when alone he sang, danced, and "swore using language unfit for print."

However, on the night before his execution, he gave up all hope and cursed the judge, the district attorney, and all mankind in general. The Reverend Brown, who came to give religious consolation, was subjected to his tirades until shortly before he was to be taken out of his jail cell, and only then did he ask to have some time with the reverend. At 12:30 P.M. a wagon drawn by a single horse pulled up to the jail and in the wagon was a pine coffin, painted red. On seeing the vehicle the crowd of seven hundred men made a mad rush at the jail to get a better look at the prisoner, but the Silver City Guard held them at a distance. Fifteen minutes passed before Milstead appeared accompanied by Sheriff G.H. Moore and deputy G.W. Shaw. Milstead wore a white shirt, drab pants, a pair of slippers, a felt hat, and a blue overcoat, which was thrown over his shoulders.

The handcuffed prisoner had some difficulty boarding the wagon so he stepped back and asked the sheriff if they could walk to the site of the gallows, and the sheriff consented. The procession started at 12:50 P.M. with two deputies in the lead followed by the wagon, then came the prisoner with Sheriff Moore on his right and deputy Shaw on his left. The procession was followed closely by Brigadier General Ford, and the entire party was surrounded by the guard marching in open ranks and holding back the excited crowd.

The gallows had been erected in Gold Canyon, a deep gorge half a mile above the town. Milstead arrived at the place of his execution at 1:30 P.M. and the regiment of Silver City Guards took positions around the scaffold, and continued to hold back the crowd, which now numbered three thousand people. The prisoner cast a glance over the crowd, fixing his gaze on the Reverend Brown, and then asked the sheriff if he could have a half-hour with the minister as this might do him some good, and this was granted. The Reverends Brown and Lane, who had not been included in the procession, were passed through the guard and they mounted the scaffold, where they talked, sometimes with great earnestness. As Milstead looked over the crowd he saw a man named Wilson, who he also asked to have brought up, and though Wilson was on crutches and sitting in a wagon he came forward when summoned. Wilson and Milstead talked for some time and then Milstead took a pencil and paper, wrote out his mother's address, and asked that Wilson write to her about his death. Wilson wept bitterly while Milstead was on his knees writing, but Milstead did not weep until he said farewell to Wilson. He quickly composed himself and continued to talk with the reverends until the sheriff said his time had expired and removed the handcuffs. The Reverend Brown and the prisoner then knelt to pray and several on the scaffold knelt with them and when the prisoner arose he shook hands with everyone on the platform. He moved to the trapdoor and examined the noose, then helped the sheriff place it over his head, and next his wrists and ankles were pinioned while Sheriff Moore read the death warrant.

Milstead was given an opportunity to speak to the crowd and said, "Gentlemen, Mr. Rosenberg, the Assisting Jailor, I want it understood treated me, when I was in jail, like a gentleman. I am going to die like a man. I committed the murder for which I am here to suffer, but I was justified in doing it. If my witnesses had come into Court and sworn to the truth, Milstead would not be here today. I ask no man to forgive me. I ask God to forgive me. I want it understood that the Sheriffs treated me well. I do not blame them for what they are doing. They are only doing their duty. I hope God will bless them and you." He then looked at the district attorney and continued: "There is Frank Kennedy. Oh, you are the gallows duck; you are a gallows duck. He said he wanted to see me die an ignominious death. You are the only man here who wished to see me die. I hope you are now gratified. I am now willing to meet my Maker." The black cap was pulled over his face and the noose was readjusted, the knot placed under his left ear, and the trap was sprung at 2:15 P.M. The drop was eight feet and Milstead's neck was broken in the fall, and in thirteen minutes he was pronounced dead. The body was left suspended a sufficient time to ensure he could not be resuscitated, then the body was cut down, placed in his coffin, and buried before sundown.

Virginia City (NV) Territorial Enterprise: January 9–10, 1863.

Mo-whut
July 28, 1863

During the summer of 1862 a band of Humboldt Indians was raiding throughout Ruby Valley, then located in White Pine County, Nevada. In August the Indians, led by Mo-whut, murdered a party of immigrants at Gravelly Ford, a popular crossing point on the Humboldt River, and drove off their stock. The Indians were not captured and they continued their raiding in the summer of 1863. On July 20, 1863, Lt. Colonel Morris, with companies A, B, and D of the 3rd Infantry, accompanied by a detachment of cavalry recruits under command of Lt. Westbrook, arrived and encamped in the valley. On July 24 Captain Brown commanding Company L, 2nd Cavalry, joined Lt. Colonel Morris and encamped with him. The captain was informed of the difficulty with Indian raids and devised a plan whereby, on July 26, he and four troopers disguised themselves as immigrants and placed themselves in harm's way.

The trap was sprung when the marauding Indians attacked. Though none of the Indians was killed, their leader was captured and taken to Fort Ruby, a post near Ruby Lake consisting of log and adobe barracks. On the morning of July 28 Mo-Whut was examined and he gave all the details of the attack the year past, then told where the rest of his band could be found. He was tried before a military tribunal, having already convicted himself by his confession, and Major F.A. Gallagher sentenced him to hang at 6:30 P.M. The prisoner was held under close guard until fifteen minutes before his execution and then he was brought to the center of the post. A rough gallows had been erected and the condemned man was hung until it was certain he could not be resuscitated. The remains of Mo-whut were cut down and turned over to his Indian friends, thirty of whom were present as witnesses. With the loss of their leader under such horrible circumstances the raiding ceased, at least for a while, and no further action was taken against the tribe.

Post Return — Fort Ruby: July 1863; *Virginia City (NV) Territorial Enterprise*: July 31, 1863.

New Mexico

The first Europeans to visit the land that would become New Mexico were members of the Alvar Nunez Cabeza de Vaca party in 1536. The Spaniards sparsely settled the area over the next three centuries but the region became a part of an independent Mexico in 1821. During the War with Mexico (1846–1848) the region, while still a part of Mexico, was under U.S. occupation. New Mexico was annexed to the United States as a concession in the Treaty of Guadalupe Hidalgo following that war and in 1850 the New Mexico Territory was organized. In 1854 it was expanded through the Gadsden Purchase. In 1863 the territory was divided, with the eastern half comprising the New Mexico Territory. On January 6, 1912, New Mexico was admitted as the 47th state.

Trujillo, Antonio M.
April 16, 1847

When Mexico declared war on the United States the Mexican government appointed certain men north of the Rio Grande River to positions to "protect and preserve their country and shake off the yoke of a foreign government." One of these men was Antonio Maria Trujillo, a respected older gentleman appointed inspector general, or inspector of arms, by "the legitimate commander for the supreme government of Mexico." In a letter dated January 20, 1847, Trujillo was ordered to mobilize his troops for possible action in two days and that letter, along with one written by Trujillo, were intercepted. Trujillo's letter commanded the mobilization of "all the inhabitants that are able to bear arms, connecting them also with persons in San Juan Caballeros, by the morning of the 22nd of the present month.... We have declared war with the Americans and it is now time that we take up our arms in our hands in defense of our prostrate country, that we may try, if possible, to regain the liberty of our unhappy country."

This was determined to be treason against the United States in the occupied territory that would become New Mexico Territory, and Trujillo was arrested. On March 16, 1847, the prisoner was brought before Judge Joab Houghton in the U.S. district court on the federal charge of treason and he was convicted upon the evidence of the letters. Judge Houghton sentenced Trujillo to hang on April 16, 1847. His case was quickly reviewed by the U.S. Supreme Court and the lower court's finding and sentence were affirmed; President James K. Polk considered the matter and declined to intervene. Trujillo was hanged at Santa Fe, New Mexico, on April 16, 1847, but the historical record contains none of the details of that event.

Santa Fe Daily New Mexican: February 18, 1883.

Stanfield, Robert
July 27, 1849

In late July 1849 Robert Stanfield murdered a man named Kane at the village of San Miguel in San Miguel County, New Mexico. He was tried, convicted, and sentenced to hang on July 27, 1849. Neither appeal nor intervention by Governor Charles Bent delayed the proceedings. Stanfield expiated his crime on the gallows on the designated day but, unfortunately, the detailed record of the crime and execution no longer exist.

Wellsboro (PA) Tioga Eagle: September 19, 1849.

Simms, Andrew J.
November 30, 1849

In late 1849 Andrew Jackson Simms murdered John Jackson at Taos, New Mexico. At his examination Simms was held to answer to the grand jury and during the first days of November he was indicted, arraigned, and pled not guilty. He was tried at the fall term of the court and on November 3 the defendant was convicted of murder in the first degree and sentenced to hang on November 30, 1849. Simms was remanded to the custody of the sheriff and the sparse record indicates no difficulties in maintaining custody in the flimsy jails of that period. Neither appeal nor application for executive clemency from Governor Charles Bent intervened to delay the execution.

A trapdoor gallows was constructed and, on the fateful day, Simms was taken from his cell and conveyed to the scaffold, which, in those early days, was usually constructed some distance from the jail to provide the opportunity for a solemn procession to the site. Sheriff C.H. Merritt was in charge and when they arrived at the gallows the prisoner was escorted up the stairs and onto the trapdoor. He was given the opportunity to speak to the crowd but the record does not reflect what he might have said, though newspapers do record that he showed no cowardice. The condemned man was prepared by having his wrists, arms, knees and ankles pinioned, he was blindfolded or hooded, and the noose was positioned neatly behind his left ear. In but a moment the trap was sprung and Simms dropped to his death. After an attending physician pronounced him dead the remains were lowered into a coffin provided by the county and he was buried in the local cemetery later that day.

Sante Fe New Mexican: November 28, 1849; December 8, 1849; *Milwaukee Wisconsin Free Democrat*: February 6, 1850.

Butler, Marcus; Craig, William; Wade, John
January 31, 1851
Young, Alexander
February 12, 1851

During the entire year of 1850 wagon trains bound for California and other western destinations using the southern route passed through Socorro, New Mexico, and "often stopped for weeks to avail themselves of the conveniences presented for necessary repairs and recruiting of animals." On all of the trains were men of doubtful character and fugitives from justice who had taken positions as cooks, servants, or some menial occupation at such a trifling compensation that no check was made into their character or motivation. By the time the trains reached Socorro their bad characters had surfaced and a number of these scoundrels either left the trains or were discharged. As their numbers in Socorro grew they began to congregate and present a threatening force against the inhabitants. By January 1851 bands of ruffians "had been overawing the quiet inhabitants of the town by parading the streets, heavily armed, and committing all manner of lawless acts. They robbed and killed openly, without provocation or remorse. They ranged like wild beasts."

The border commission had arrived in the region and a small party settled at Socorro, many of them young and well armed. These men kept the worthless vagabonds and ruffians in check for a while but as these commission members moved the six miles to San Elizario, where the main body of the commission resided, the ruffians became emboldened. Soon there were less than a dozen commission members in Socorro and the citizens were again at the mercy of the ruffians; many inhabitants packed all their worldly possessions and fled for their lives. The alcalde of the town was a weakling and delegated authority to another man even more timid than himself, so there was no civilian authority to address the crimes of the miscreants.

On Tuesday, January 28, 1851, Alexander Young, leader of a band of ten men, cut the neck of the keeper of a "fonda," and thereafter the entire band began a spree of petty crime and threatening behavior. On the following day, Young stopped a man in front of the same fonda, took his fowling piece, and went in and shot John Wood to death. Young then took a drink, went to where the body lay, positioned the arms of the deceased across his chest, and laughed over the corpse. Later that evening a man was turned away from town at gunpoint, so it was resolved to send an express to San Elizario asking for military assistance. In two hours the express was returned with a notation declining assistance on the plea, and stating that the citizens should apply to the civil authorities.

On the night of January 29 a fandango, or dancing party, was held at the same fonda where the keeper had been wounded and Wood had been murdered. Young and his band — which included Marcus Butler, William Craig, John Wade, Stephen Stanley, Charles Hughes, Charles Ripley, Thomas McCaskey, Alexander McNiven and two other minor players — went to the fonda searching for Edward C. Clarke with the express purpose of "having a fuss with him and anyone who came to his assistance." Sentinels were posted at the entrance to prevent anyone from leaving or entering and all inside were threatened with death if they moved; even the frightened women were prevented from retiring. Young created quite a disturbance but as the evening progressed the violence increased as he shot out a candle, and then Craig shot the clock to pieces. Young pranced about, several times threatening to shoot Clarke, and then finally he did so. As soon as Clarke was shot, Butler, Craig and Wade joined in the shooting, inflicting no less than ten mortal wounds on their victim. When the party of ruffians left, Clarke was carried to a surgeon, but he soon bled to death. The following morning the citizens of Socorro, but especially the few members of the border commission still living in Socorro, responded to the previously returned express which had denied them help:

> Socorro, Texas, Jan. 30, 1851
>
> Captain, commanding San Elizario:
>
> Sir: Your note was received last night. We regret the circumstances which rendered it necessary for American citizens to ask protection from American soldiers.
>
> Though there are good citizens enough in Socorro who may be summoned for the protection of life and property, we yet thought that those who were sent here for the protection of the same, and the establishment of some kind of order, wo'd have the best right to take the business in hand, especially as it is well known, both far and near, of the non-existence of any responsible and reliable authority at this place.
>
> Trusting that the trifling number we have present will be sufficient for the protection of ourselves and the peaceful inhabitants of the village, We remain, very respectfully,
>
> your obedient servants.

In three hours a large force of armed Americans and Mexicans arrived in Socorro, divided into search parties, and went through every house. All the members of Young's band were captured, except for the leader, who had escaped early that morning. The prisoners were taken before Judge Berthold, examined and committed, and the court remained in session until after dark before recessing. During the night Butler, Craig and Wade were placed in jail under the guard of six well armed men, as they had made death threats toward nearly everyone and there were rumors of a rescue. At 10:00 A.M. the court reconvened, empanelled a jury, and the three murderers were tried and found guilty of first degree murder. Judge Berthold sentenced the men to hang in one hour.

The prisoners were escorted to the little plaza in front of the village church, where they were met by the priest "to give such consolation as his office would permit." A large tree with stout limbs was selected and the condemned men, still reckless and defiant, arrived at sunset, where lanterns gave an eerie glow to the scene. The citizens formed a circle around the tree to prevent a rescue, as ruffians had been gathering in small groups and were loitering about the hanging tree watching the proceedings. The small bands of desperadoes took no action and those in authority finally managed to pull up the three men and keep watch as they strangled to death before being cut down. The other members of Young's band had been brought along and returned to jail with the bodies. Early the next morning, February 1, the bodies of the three murderers were removed from the jail and buried in unmarked graves, and that afternoon at 2:00 P.M. the remains of Clarke were interred with all due Catholic and Episcopalian ceremonies. After Clarke's funeral the citizens went to the jail to consider the case of Alexander McNiven and upon his promise to abstain from drinking liquor from that date on, and attributing his criminal behavior to liquor alone, he was discharged. As soon as he was released he made preparations to leave Socorro and by nightfall he was well on his way west.

The citizens then turned their attention to Young and subscribed a reward of $400 for his capture. The reward prompted many parties to take the field in search of the fugitive and word was sent on the morning of February 11 that Young had been captured and would be delivered at Socorro that evening. As soon as he arrived he was heavily shackled and lodged in jail under a strong guard. That night he asked if either of the other three men hung had confessed and, when told they had not, he asked to write a letter, which was granted, and "he confessed the truthfulness of the charges against him, criminating clearly, and in a worse light the three who were hung first, besides many others. He did not think there was any hope for him after death, but would try and turn his thoughts heavenward. He then knelt down and prayed, after which he was left alone." At 10:00 A.M. the court convened, a jury was empanelled, and at the opening of court the letter containing the confession was read publicly, then signed by the prisoner and witnessed by officers of the court. With all testimony before the court it could have called for a verdict but it was deemed advisable to bring in additional evidence, and this was done to clear the name of several innocent men. Then the prisoner was found guilty of the charges and sentenced to hang.

At 4:00 P.M. Young was escorted to the Catholic church, where he prayed and was blessed, and then the condemned man was conveyed to the hanging tree, where he made his final request that he be buried in such circumstance as the gravity of his case permitted. After the noose was positioned he asked to speak to the crowd and begged those younger than him to "take warning from my example, and even older citizens might profit by the warning provided by my case." He said they could see what gambling, swearing, drinking, and an ungovernable temper, with the worst of evil associations, had brought him to; then he related a few facts of his early life to emphasize his warnings. At 4:30 P.M. he was pulled up and the loose end of the rope was tied off, and he hung until his vital signs ceased. The body was then cut down and conveyed immediately to his pre-dug grave, where his remains were buried and left unmarked.

Gettysburg (PA) Adams Sentinel: April 14, 1851; *Fort Wayne (IN) Times*: May 1, 1851.

Garcia, Felipe
May 25, 1852

On April 23, 1852, Felipe Garcia and Thadeus E.C.S. Canter were engaged in an argument at Tome in Valencia County, New Mexico. When the disagreement escalated Garcia suddenly seized a stick and struck Canter on the head twice, knocking him senseless and inflicting two mortal wounds three inches long and an inch deep. While Canter was in a helpless condition Garcia grabbed a case knife and stabbed him, inflicting two more mortal wounds two inches wide and five inches deep. Canter languished in excruciating agony for three hours before dying of his wounds. Garcia was arrested immediately after the attack and when Canter died he was charged with his murder.

Four days later the grand jury convened and returned an indictment for murder. On April 29 Garcia, who pled not guilty at his arraignment, was tried and the entire matter was disposed of in a single day: the jury found Garcia guilty of first degree murder. He was sentenced to hang on May 25; and the writ of execution was signed and delivered to the sheriff at the same time that the prisoner was remanded into his custody. Garcia was held in the Tome jail for the next month without incident and, on the fatal day, Valencia County sheriff Lorenzo Labadi took the prisoner from his jail cell and, just before noon, hung him until he was dead as required by law. The body of Garcia was buried in the Parish Cemetery at noon and the sheriff then submitted to the court his affidavit that the order of the court had been executed.

Edward D. Tittmann, "The Last Legal Frontier," *New Mexico Historical Review* 2, no. 3 (July 1927).

Montoya, Pedro A.
May 18, 1855

Pedro Antonio Montoya, also known as Pedro or Peter Ranado, lived at "fighting corral" near Albuquerque, New Mexico. In early May 1855 Montoya returned home unexpectedly and found a discharged soldier in bed with his wife, so preoccupied that they did not notice when he entered. He slipped quietly out of the house and retrieved his axe, and when he returned he brutally murdered the ex-soldier. His wife, in a panic and fearing for her life, ran from the house and spread the alarm. Montoya was arrested within minutes and a people's court was convened the following day. Montoya was tried, convicted of first degree murder, and sentenced to hang on May 18.

When the fatal day arrived the prisoner's hands were tied behind him and he was placed in the bed of a wagon seated on his coffin. He was driven beneath a tree with a stout limb, where a rope had been prepared with a noose at one end. Once he stood, his ankles were tied with rope, the noose cinched tight, and a handkerchief tied over his eyes, and then the wagon was driven out from beneath the condemned man. There was no "drop" so it took some time for Montoya to strangle to death, but after thirty minutes the body was cut down and turned over to his wife and friends for burial.

West Gilbreath, *Death on the Gallows: The Story of Legal Hangings in New Mexico, 1847–1923* (Silver City, NM: High-Lonesome, 2002). Robert J. Torrez, *Myth of the Hanging Tree* (Albuquerque: University of New Mexico Press, 2008).

Montañes, Ygnacio
April 11, 1856

Ygnacio Montañes committed a heinous murder at San Miguel in San Miguel County, New Mexico, in early 1856. He was tried at the March term of the U.S. district court, convicted of first degree murder, and sentenced to hang on April 11. Acting governor W.W.H. Davis, not wanting to delay the matter, signed the death warrant on March 17, 1856, ordering the sheriff to proceed with the execution. Although the historical record does not give the details of the murder or execution of Montañes, the *Santa Fe Weekly Gazette* of March 29 reported that, as the fatal day neared, Montañes composed verses which were his farewell address to "his friends and all mankind," and these were published in the April 5 edition. The hanging appears to have been accomplished with only one hitch, that the prisoner's neck was not broken in the fall, as the record shows that Montañes died by strangulation and his remains were turned over to Jose de Jesus Lujan for burial on April 12, 1856. The record of the San Miguel District Court of 1849–1860 shows that the charges accrued in the execution of Montañes totaled $29.40.

Governor's Executive Record, March 17, 1856, Microfilm AASF54A, Archives of the Archdiocese of Santa Fe, San Miguel District Court Record: 1849–1860, *Santa Fe (NM) Weekly Gazette*: March 29, 1856.

Trujillo, Jose A.
June 27, 1856

Jose Antonio Trujillo murdered Jose G. Chavez at Socorro in Socorro County, New Mexico, in early 1856. He was arrested and tried in Judge Kirby Benedict's courtroom during the May term and after the jury returned a verdict of guilty Judge Benedict sentenced the prisoner to hang on June 27. The death warrant was issued by Governor David Meriwether on June 12, 1856, ordering Sheriff Jose Apodaca of Socorro County to proceed with the execution. While there is no record detailing the crime nor execution of

Trujillo, the Socorro County District Court Record for November 1856 contains the notation, "Ordered that Jose Apodaca, Sheriff of Socorro County be allowed the sum of fifteen dollars for the execution of the sentence upon Jose Antonio Trujillo made at the last term."

Socorro County Record Book 1, 1854–1856, NM-SRCA, *Governor's Executive Record,* TANM/NM-SRCA.

Sumner, James B.
July 17, 1857

In mid–1857 James B. Sumner, alias James S. Boynton, a soldier and native of New Hampshire, murdered a man named Stuart near Taos, Taos County, New Mexico, at "a wild and lonely spot in the mountains." Sumner had been friends with Stuart and together they had deserted from their army post. On the day of the murder Sumner approached his victim, who was apparently asleep, and without warning or hesitation fired a single bullet from his pistol, the bullet entering Stuart's brain and killing him almost instantly. Sumner was a despicable character described as "a sad picture of vice and depravity—beginning with filial disobedience and progressing in crime until it has found its termination in the deed [for] which he is to expiate with his life."

Sumner was quickly arrested and lodged in jail, and he confessed to the shooting. He was indicted, tried in mid–June, and convicted of the "cold-blooded first degree murder" of Stuart. On June 25 the prisoner stood before Judge Perry Brocchus to hear his sentence and was told that on July 17, 1857, he would hang by the neck until dead. He was remanded to the custody of Sheriff Gabriel Vigil, who had the responsibility of carrying out the sentence. During his time in jail Sumner's religious needs were attended by the Reverend Stoddard, the chaplain at Fort Union. While there is no record to confirm that the hanging occurred, nor any of the details, it is almost a certainty in those times that Sumner expiated his crime on the date set. There appears no delay from appeal nor from applications for executive clemency as the death warrant was issued by acting governor W.W.H. Davis on July 1, 1857.

Santa Fe (NM) Weekly Gazette: July 4, 1857; July 11, 1857.

Sullivan, Thomas
May 22, 1860

In early 1860 Thomas Sullivan murdered Juan de Dios Lucero in Bernalillo County, New Mexico. He was tried at the May term of the district court at Albuquerque and found guilty of first degree murder. Sullivan was sentenced to hang on May 22, 1860, and that final morning Governor Abraham Rencher issued the warrant directing the sheriff to proceed with the execution. The historical record does not contain the details of Sullivan's crime, incarceration, or execution.

Executive record, 1860 (TANM 21).

Rodgers, Thaddeus M.
September 14, 1860

Thaddeus M. Rodgers worked as an engineer for Herach's Mill at the south end of Water Street in Santa Fe, New Mexico. Rodgers had been on a spree all day December 24, 1859, and when sufficiently fortified by liquor he went to Herach's store with six-shooter in hand and announced that he was going to kill Joseph Herach or a surveyor named William White. White was not present but Joseph Herach was present, and he fled toward the rear storage room. Rodgers took aim at Herach but Marcelino Sabiallos, a teamster, intervened as Rodgers fired and Sabiallos was mortally wounded and soon bled to death. Rodgers was arrested and jailed in Santa Fe but he managed to escape to Colorado. His description was circulated and he was recognized, captured, and extradited to Santa Fe, New Mexico.

Rodgers was tried at the spring term of the district court and found guilty of first degree murder; Judge Kirby Benedict sentenced the prisoner to hang on September 14, 1860. His appeal was rejected by the territorial supreme court and his application to Governor Abraham Rencher pleading for a commutation of sentence was denied well in advance of the date set for his execution. The gallows had been built in an arroyo east of the San Rosario Church outside Santa Fe and on the fateful day a large crowd gathered to watch the hanging. The prisoner was brought to the arroyo in a well-guarded wagon and escorted onto the scaffold. Following religious ceremonies the prisoner was prepared, under the close supervision of Sheriff Jesus Maria Baca y Salazar, and dropped to his death. He hanged for several minutes after the attending physician pronounced him dead and then the body was cut down. The remains of Rodgers were placed in the plain wooden coffin provided by the county and buried that evening.

Rio Grande (NM) Republican: November 22, 1895; *Santa Fe Weekly Gazette*: September 15, 1860.

Sandoval, Pablita
April 26, 1861

Pablita Sandoval was born in Mexico in 1835. She moved to the United States with her parents and settled near Loma Parda, New Mexico. When she reached adulthood she entered into the home-based business of dressmaking, drawing upon seamstress training provided by her mother, and Americanized her name to "Paula Angel." When Sandoval was twenty-six years old she met a Mexican man named Miguel Martin and was strongly attracted to him, even though he was married and had five children. A torrid affair followed for a brief period; but Martin soon tired of the relationship with his mistress, informed her that he had no intention of leaving his family for her, and said he wanted to end the affair. Sandoval seemed upset but reasonable and convinced Martin to see her one last time.

On March 23, 1861, they met and each had their say before Sandoval hugged her lover for the last time. As they embraced Sandoval pulled a butcher's knife she had concealed and stabbed Martin in the back; he died within a few minutes. Sandoval was arrested by Sheriff Antonio Herrera and taken before Judge Kirby Benedict that day. Benedict held her over for trial and five days later the trial of "Paula Angel" ended with a verdict of guilty of murder in the first degree. The jury was not swayed by defense attorney Spruce M. Baird's defense that Sandoval was disturbed by her lover's rejection, nor his plea, "Do not be so cold in soul as to demand the death of this fair maiden who has been wronged by an uncaring adulterer." She was sentenced to hang on April 26, 1861, and required to pay all costs of her execution. The condemned woman languished over the next month and lack of sleep and appetite left Sandoval emaciated and haggard.

A cottonwood tree with a stout limb within one mile of the Church of Las Vegas, New Mexico, was selected as the gallows and at 10:00 A.M. on April 26 Sandoval was placed in a wagon. Her coffin was aboard and she sat on it while Sheriff Herrera drove through the crowd, directly beneath the noose, and ordered her to stand. He hurriedly adjusted the noose, jumped onto the wagon seat and whipped up the horses. The wagon lurched forward from beneath Sandoval and only at that moment did the sheriff realize that he had neglected to tie her arms and legs.

Sandoval was struggling to pull herself up so the sheriff ran to her and, using all his weight, pulled down on her legs. Angry spectators rushed in, pushed the sheriff away, and cut down Sandoval. The sheriff then warned them off with his six-shooter while Colonel J.D. Serna read the death warrant, which required that she be hanged until dead, and the rescuers then backed away. Sheriff Herrera backed the team under the limb again and tied a new noose in the rope. He lifted Sandoval into the wagon, pinioned her arms and legs and then held her up until the noose was adjusted, which forced her to remain standing. He took a moment to examine his work before driving the wagon out a second time, and the law was satisfied. After hanging a sufficient length of time Sandoval's remains were cut down, placed in the coffin she had purchased, and driven to the church for a brief service. She was buried in the town's cemetery before sundown.

Peter Hertog. *Legal Hangings* (Sante Fe, NM: Press of the Territorian, 1966).

Tansey, John R.
April 6, 1862
Philbrook, Darius A.
April 8, 1862

See Addendum, pages 208–209

Lopez, Nestor
October 16, 1863

Nestor Lopez and Leonides Esquibel had a disagreement in the town of Alcalde in Rio Arriba County, New Mexico, and the two men agreed to settle the dispute in mutual combat. However, Lopez armed himself with a bladed instrument and in doing so gained an overwhelming and unfair advantage over his adversary, who believed the fight would be hand-to-hand combat. Lopez inflicted a mortal wound and then, with his adversary entirely helpless, mutilated the body. When arrested he claimed self-defense and explained the mutilation by saying that it was done at the request of his victim. He was indicted and held for trial at the September term of the district court. The jury disbelieved the defendant's excuse for the mutilation and dismissed the defendant's claim of self-defense, as he had armed himself while his adversary remained unarmed. They found him guilty of first degree murder and he was sentenced to hang on Friday, October 16, 1863, and neither appeal nor application for executive clemency delayed the proceedings

On the date of his execution Lopez was taken from his jail cell by Sheriff Juan Lopez and put aboard a wagon. He was driven to the site and the wagon made its way through the crowd of over one thousand curious spectators. A path was cleared by soldiers from Fort Marcy dispatched to keep order.

Lopez stood as three priests prayed for his soul, and he began to tremble slightly as he was being prepared by having his limbs bound and the noose adjusted. He braced up when asked if he had anything to say, and related the details of his crime and confessed to two other unsolved murders. He begged forgiveness and said farewell, then gave a slight bow. When he straightened up his eyes were covered and in a moment the wagon was driven out and he dropped three feet, breaking his neck in the fall. A doctor had been summoned to monitor vital signs. After the prisoner's heart ceased to beat he was pronounced dead. The body was allowed to hang until it was certain he could not be resuscitated and was then cut down and lowered into the waiting coffin, and buried that evening.

Santa Fe (NM) El Novo-Mejicano: November 6, 1863; *Santa Fe Weekly Gazette*: October 24, 1863.

Coffield, Joseph
January 19, 1864

See Addendum, page 209

Martin, Jose M.
May 13, 1864

Jose Maria Martin, alias Jesus Martinez, was a handsome man of petite build and dandyish in dress and appearance, but he possessed a bad disposition. Julian Trujillo was a large and brutish man in appearance but gentle and industrious, and an excellent blacksmith who was liked by all who knew him. Martin and Trujillo had some minor disagreement which Martin took personally, and he swore he would have revenge on the larger man. He murdered Julian Trujillo in Taos, New Mexico, under circumstances which were described as "vindictive and wanton." Martin fled into Colorado, where he remained until he felt safe to return; but as soon as Martin reached Taos he was arrested.

The grand jury indicted Martin. He was tried at the spring 1864 term of the district court, and he was convicted of first degree murder. Judge Kirby Benedict reportedly said, in pronouncing sentence, "It is a painful duty for the judge of a court of justice to pronounce upon a human being the sentence of death. There is something horrible about it, and the mind of the court naturally revolts from the performance of such a duty; happily, however, your case is relieved of all such unpleasantness, and the court takes positive delight in sentencing you to death." The date for the hanging was March 22, 1864, but this was delayed to May 13 when Governor Henry Connelly granted a respite. The governor finally denied the application and ordered the sheriff to proceed with the execution.

On Martin's final morning a full company of well armed militia arrived to guard the jail and gallows. A priest visited Martin's cell and provided religious comfort, then he accompanied the condemned man onto the scaffold. Sheriff Aniceto Valdez led the procession with Probate Judge Santes Estevan at his side.

Martin had remained entirely composed until he exited the jail door and saw the gallows, and then he nearly collapsed. He was carried onto the scaffold and supported upon the trapdoor, and the prisoner was in no condition to speak to the large crowd. The condemned man was prepared by several deputies, who pinioned his limbs and adjusted the noose. As soon as the black hood was pulled on, the trap was sprung. The prisoner's neck was not broken by the fall so he had to hang for more than thirty minutes before strangulation was complete and he was pronounced dead. His remains were then cut down, placed in the coffin provided by the county, and delivered to the church for a brief service and burial that afternoon.

Las Vegas (NM) Optic: May 16, 1895; *Santa Fe New Mexican*: May 5, 1864; May 7, 1864; May 21, 1864.

Madrid, Juan d. D.
September 9, 1865

See Addendum, pages 209–210

Martinez, Antonio M.
May 22, 1868

Antonio Maria Martinez knew Luis Suazo and his wife, for whom he had an uncontrollable lust. Martinez had harassed the family for some time with his efforts to seduce Mrs. Suazo but she was faithful to her husband. In September 1867, her husband not present, Mrs. Suazo was suddenly seized by Martinez. By force and threats he tried to convince her to have sexual relations, but she resisted and scolded him. Martinez then threatened the life of her husband, suggesting that if he was murdered there would no longer be an obstacle to his obsession.

The following day Martinez set up an ambush along a trail where Suazo and his son would pass after collecting piñon, and at midnight Suazo came to the place where Martinez lay in wait. Martinez suddenly rose up and aimed his rifle at Suazo but the boy cried out so Martinez fled without firing a shot. Suazo then started for Abiquiu to report the attempted bushwhacking to the authorities, but Martinez had anticipated Suazo's reaction and had gone ahead on the trail to set up another ambush. The next morning the body of Suazo was found with a bullet hole in his neck; he had bled to death where he fell from his horse. Martinez was arrested and tried in Judge Perry Brocchus' courtroom at the April term of the Rio Arriba County district court in Alcalde. The evidence was circumstantial as no one had seen Martinez shoot Suazo; but it was so overwhelming that the jury easily found the defendant guilty of first degree murder. He was sentenced to hang and then he and two other condemned men were taken to the jail at Santa Fe, which was far more secure than the flimsy jail at Alcalde.

As the fatal day neared there was fear that there would be violence or some attempt to rescue the three condemned Mexicans, so thirty troops were dispatched from Fort Lowell to assist Sheriff Luciano de Herrera in executing the death warrants. The troops arrived on May 21, the day before the hanging and the same day Martinez was returned to Alcalde, while the other two condemned men had received a respite and remained in Santa Fe. The gallows had been erected near the jail and on the morning of May 22 the death warrant was read to the prisoner in his cell; then he was escorted onto the platform. He took his place on the trapdoor and was prepared with his limbs pinioned and the noose adjusted. The historical record does not indicate whether he chose to speak to the crowd of spectators, nor does the record contain the details of the hanging. However, the lack of detail suggests that the event passed without any untoward occurrences.

Roberto Torrez. "Rio Arriba's First Legal Hangings," *Salsa!* (January 1995).

French, Roy
September 12, 1870

Roy French, alias Roy Frank, a twenty-three-year-old Negro, was convicted of murder, though there appears no record of his deed. He was tried at the San Miguel County seat of Las Vegas, New Mexico, in early August 1870, found guilty of first degree murder, and sentenced to hang on September 12, 1870. Neither appeal nor the application to Governor William A. Pile, pleading for executive clemency, delayed the proceedings. On the fatal day the prisoner was escorted by Sheriff Juan Romero and several deputies to the gallows, constructed in an open area off a street near the outskirts of town. A huge crowd had gathered to watch the event and they crowded around the hanging contraption, which appeared to have been constructed of scraps. It was a counterpoise weight design with a pole placed on a fulcrum so that two sacks of rocks, used as the weight, were attached to one end and the noose tied to the other. The longer end of the pole with the noose was held down by a rope tied to a stake in the ground.

When the condemned arrived, a path was cleared through the throngs of curious men, women and children; French was escorted through to the platform, which was only a few inches above the ground. His wrists were already tied behind his back when he was asked if he wanted to speak to the crowd, but there is no record of what he said. The deputies quickly tied his arms, knees and ankles, the black cap was pulled on, and the noose adjusted. The Rev. John Annin prayed for the soul of the condemned man and when he announced, "May the Lord have mercy on your soul," the tie-down rope was cut with a hatchet in the hand of deputy Frank Roto. The sacks of rocks fell to the ground with a thud and the slack rope was taken up until French was flung upwards, then fell back to the end of his rope and the lifeless body swung about. French was allowed to hang for some time before the crowd lost interest and dispersed, and then the body was cut down by the Reverend Annin, placed in the coffin provided, and buried.

Santa Fe New Mexican: September 13, 1870.

Wilson, William
December 10, 1875

Robert Casey went from Texas to Lincoln County, New Mexico, to find an investment opportunity and found it on the Rio Hondo between Lincoln and Roswell. Casey brought his wife from Texas and they began to build up their ranch. Casey built a mill and, because of the additional demand upon his time, hired William Wilson to help around the ranch. On August 1, 1875, Casey attended the county convention in Lincoln and took Wilson with him. After a particularly contentious morning session Casey invited Wilson and Edward Welch to lunch at the Worthy Hotel. Wilson left early and at 2:00 P.M. Casey paid the bill and left the hotel. Wilson had obtained a Winchester rifle and a substantial supply of ammunition and hid beside a building on the route he knew his employer would follow. When Casey was within twenty paces Wilson fired once, the bullet striking Casey's hip. The wounded man limped to the side of a vacant building to escape from his assailant but Wilson followed and shot him through the mouth at close range. Charles Myrick was holding a fast horse for Wilson's escape but Wilson had been delayed when his first shot did not kill Casey, and he was surrounded by a crowd. The murderer placed his back against the wall and surrendered to Sheriff Saturnino Baca.

Wilson was taken to Fort Stanton and lodged in the guardhouse to prevent a lynching, while Myrick mounted the horse and fled, never to be heard of again. Casey was treated by Fort Stanton's post surgeon but died of his wounds the following day, and Wilson confessed that he had killed his employer over an $8 discrepancy in his pay.

Wilson was indicted in early October and his trial commenced on October 15. Testimony occupied three days but it took the jury only fifteen minutes to bring in a verdict of guilty of first degree murder. Judge Bristol Warren sentenced Wilson to hang on November 11 but Governor Samuel Axtell immediately stayed the execution for thirty days to allow time for review. Wilson attempted to escape on October 19 and was so seriously wounded during the attempt that he could only await the fateful day and hope for clemency or commutation. For several days before his execution Wilson was consoled by Father Lamy but there was such confidence that there would be some intervention that the gallows was not assembled until just before daybreak on Friday, December 10.

At 11:00 A.M. the condemned man was driven from Fort Stanton to Lincoln in an ambulance and they proceeded directly to the house of Sheriff Baca, where Wilson dressed in his dark burial suit. At the scaffold, Company G, 8th U.S. Cavalry, under Lt. Gilmore formed a line while four troopers dismounted to push back the large crowd which had gathered. Wilson climbed onto the platform with a firm step and found the sheriff and Father Lamy waiting for him. The death warrant was read by the sheriff in English and then translated into Spanish for the spectators. Wilson's dying declaration was read and translated by the sheriff, who then announced that the execution would be delayed one hour. This angered the crowd, including many influential men in the community, and the protest was so compelling that Wilson was immediately prepared for the drop. The lever was kicked and Wilson fell but his neck was not broken. After nine and one half minutes the body was cut down without a doctor's examination, his remains placed in a coffin, and the black cap removed. Spectators were then allowed to file past to have a last look at the murderer when one curious Mexican woman, making a careful examination of the body, suddenly cried out "For God's sake, the dead has come to life." Wilson was quickly examined by post physician Dr. Carballo and found to be alive. A rope was quickly tossed over the crossbeam of the scaffold, an impromptu noose tied around Wilson's neck, and several men from the crowd pulled up the condemned man right out of his coffin. He hanged another twenty minutes until strangulation completed the task required by law, and then Wilson's remains were cut down, returned to the coffin, and buried that afternoon.

Santa Fe Daily New Mexican: September 3, 1875; October 21, 1875; November 3, 1875; December 21, 1875.

Breckenridge, William
May 8, 1877

William Breckenridge, a Negro, used his six-shooter to rob William Maxwell and his son Emmet near Palo Blanco, Colfax County, New Mexico, on March 23, 1876. Breckenridge made no demand but, without hesitation or warning, shot the elder Maxwell three times, causing fatal wounds to his head and breast; then he shot Emmet in the head, killing him instantly. He rifled their pockets and took $58.50 from the elder Maxwell. Breckenridge fled to Trinidad, Colorado, where he was recognized from a descriptive circular and arrested. He was returned to New Mexico and tried at the spring term of the Taos County district court, convicted and sentenced to hang. Appeals and applications for commutation or clemency sent to Governor Samuel B. Axtell were quickly exhausted without relief.

The gallows had been erected a quarter mile west of Cimarron, which required Breckenridge to be driven to the site, and as the condemned rode to his death seated on his coffin a crowd of four hundred men followed closely. At 1:10 P.M. Breckenridge, accompanied by Sheriff Peter Burleson and deputies Goodlett and Beardsley, climbed the stairs and stood upon the trapdoor. The sheriff read the death warrant and then offered Breckenridge the opportunity to speak.

Breckenridge made a detailed confession, all the time chewing a large quid of tobacco. His speech took nearly an hour and closed with a long prayer, which was followed by another prayer led by the Reverend Lougheed. The condemned man's arms and legs were bound as he stood firmly on the trapdoor and the black cap was pulled over his head, but when the noose was being adjusted his knees began to tremble. At 2:31 P.M. the trap was sprung and Doctors Ludium and Tipton monitored the prisoner's vital signs until they pronounced him dead in eight minutes. The body hung another six minutes before it was cut down and placed in the coffin provided by the county. William Breckenridge was buried that evening.

Santa Fe Daily New Mexican: May 14, 1877.

Gaines, Louis; Williams, Charles
August 21, 1880

Louis Gaines and trooper Johnston got drunk at Silver City, New Mexico. The two men had started for Fort Bayard when their conversation turned into an argument, and the situation deteriorated until Gaines pulled his knife and cut Johnston. The trooper managed to make it to Fort Bayard but soon died of his wound. Gaines was arrested and taken into Silver City, it being a civilian affair. In a separate crime Charles Williams murdered a Mexican musician at Georgetown for no apparent reason and was arrested and lodged in jail at Silver City. Both men were tried before Judge Warren Bristol at the spring term of the district court, where they were convicted of first degree murder and sentenced to hang on August 21, 1880. The appeals process and the applications for clemency or commutation submitted to Governor Lew Wallace were denied and the governor issued the death warrant.

Sheriff Harvey Whitehill had the gallows built in a little draw along the road to Pinos Altos, a short distance outside Silver City. A double hanging was grand entertainment, so spectators came from all parts of the territory. For many it was a family outing, so the crowd of four thousand included many women and children.

On the final day the condemned men were taken from their cells at 2:30 P.M., the death warrants were read, and then the men boarded the wagon which would take them to the gallows. The wagon was guarded by sixty men who had been summoned by the sheriff to prevent any attempt at escape or rescue. On the scaffold waited Sheriff Whitehill, the Rev. E.H. Brooks, Father Stagbud, deputy sheriff Dan Tucker and two defense counsels. After Gaines was placed on the trapdoor he made a rambling speech in which he declared that his life had been very wild but he had never murdered anyone. Williams spoke next and said only that his identity would remain a secret as Williams was not his real name, but one of many aliases. At 3:35 P.M. Gaines' wrists and ankles were pinioned and he waited while Williams was prepared. The black caps were pulled over their faces and the nooses adjusted at 3:40 P.M. and, in a moment, the trap was sprung. The necks of both condemned men were broken in the fall and the attending physician pronounced Gaines dead in fourteen minutes and Williams one minute later. Both bodies were then cut down, deposited in the coffins provided by the county, and buried in the valley east of the scaffold.

Santa Fe New Mexican: August 23, 1880; *Silver City (NM) Enterprise*: October 27, 1943.

Remine, Richard
March 14, 1881

Richard Remine and Patrick Rafferty were partners in a mining claim near Georgetown, Grant County, New Mexico. They shared a small cabin and the only bed. Remine was a young man while Rafferty was an old Irishman, well known and liked and a survivor of the charge of the light brigade at Balaklava. Remine had been on a spree the night of March 15, 1877, and returned home after midnight to find Rafferty lying diagonally on the bed, occupying both his and Remine's portion. Remine made no effort to awaken Rafferty but instead picked up a single-jack, a small sledge hammer, and beat Rafferty on the chest, head and face. Rafferty died during the beating so Remine dismembered the body with an axe and disposed of the parts; but in his inebriated condition he did a poor job of hiding the remains.

He returned to the cabin and went to sleep in the bloody bed. The next morning neighbors found Rafferty's remains, and Remine was arrested while still in bed. He was lodged in the Silver City jail to await the action of the grand jury. He was indicted, tried in Judge Warren Bristol's court, convicted of first degree murder, and sentenced to hang. The case was appealed to the supreme court and reviewed by Governor Lew Wallace. The process continued for more than three years and the general impression was that Remine would be released. As time passed Sheriff Harvey H. Whitehill appointed Remine a jail trusty and, as confidence in his impending release strengthened, the prisoner was allowed to leave the jail to visit the local saloons, provided he returned before 11:00 P.M. On March 7, 1881, the sheriff received a telegram from the governor instructing him to proceed with the execution of Remine. When the prisoner returned to the jail that evening he was locked in his cell for the first time in months and told of the decision. Remine's attorney made one final attempt to save his client by applying to the U.S. Supreme Court, but his application was denied.

During the week Remine awaited his execution, he received religious comfort from Father Stagnon. He continued to profess his innocence and insisted that a man named Winterburn had committed the murder, an accusation fully explored and refuted; but Remine persisted, saying, "I hate like hell to die letting everybody believe I am a murderer." As the day approached there was concern about Remine's resolve and he was asked how he felt. He said, "Well, its pretty rough to have to croak so soon, but a good many better men than I have gone the same road and I guess I can stand it." The concern was misplaced, as on the afternoon of March 14 the condemned man walked to the scaffold smoking a cigar, showing no sign of nervousness or fear.

At 2:40 P.M. Remine was positioned upon the trapdoor and he made a brief statement to the large crowd of spectators, again ascribing the crime to Winterburn. He then knelt to receive the last rites of the Catholic church and, upon rising, his wrists and ankles were pinioned, the black cap pulled over his face, and the noose adjusted. The trap was sprung at 2:45 P.M. and the fall broke his neck, but there were a few twitches of his arms and legs and a slight movement of his hands. The attending physician pronounced him dead in ten minutes, but he was allowed to hang another five minutes before being cut down and lowered directly into a coffin. Remine's remains were taken directly to his grave, which had been dug the day before, and he was buried within the hour.

Santa Fe Daily New Mexican: March 15, 1881.

Young, William
March 25, 1881

Henry F. Dwinger was an elderly, wealthy man who became interested in a pretty young woman named Dora, and he married her against all advice. Dora soon conspired with Henry's son William and William Young to kill her husband and in July 1879 William Dwinger, William Young and Dora Dwinger convinced Henry to accompany them to Santa Rita to inspect minerals. When they arrived, Young directed the old man's attention to a prospect hole and, while the old man was peering in, William Dwinger crept up behind his father and shot him in the head. The three conspirators then removed the body from the site and buried it in a shallow grave. Several months passed before the absence of Henry Dwinger aroused suspicion but soon Sheriff Harvey H. Whitehill began to investigate.

Dora and William Dwinger were immediately suspected in the disappearance, though there was not yet evidence of foul play, and they were lodged in jail and questioned. Though they had months to prepare, their stories did not agree and when questioning continued each made inconsistent statements. Soon both weakened and provided a detailed confession and William Young soon joined them in jail. The three murderers were indicted and granted separate trials. Dora was tried first, in March 1880, convicted of murder in a lesser degree, and sentenced to serve ten years in prison. William Dwinger was tried next, convicted of murder in the 2nd degree, and sentenced to life in prison. Dora and young Dwinger were delivered to the Kansas State Prison, as New Mexico had no prison and contracted with Kansas to house their long term convicts. They were both released in 1886 under order of New Mexico's Governor Edmund G. Ross. William Young, alias "Silver Plate Dick," was tried in late April 1880, convicted of first degree murder and sentenced to hang. When all efforts for clemency and commutation failed the governor granted a respite to examine Young's sanity, but when he was found sane the date for his execution was set by Governor Lew Wallace as March 25, 1881.

The scaffold had been assembled within an enclosure in the jail yard and when the moment arrived Young walked up the stairs with a firm step. He stood upon the trapdoor and surveyed the small group of witnesses, but declined to make a speech. He asked Sheriff Whitehill to "[L]et [me] down easy, do not drop me like a beef steer." The trap was sprung at 1:58 P.M. and the condemned man's neck was broken in the fall. He was allowed to hang fifteen minutes before being cut down and given to Dr. Wood for a postmortem examination. The doctor found that Young's skull was particularly thick but there was no silver plate, something Young had convinced everyone had been installed over a skull fracture from years earlier, which had been the reason his sanity was questioned.

Grant County (NM) Herald: March 19, 1881; *Sante Fe Daily New Mexican*: March 26, 1881.

Clark, Frank C.
May 13, 1881

In January 1881 Frank C. Clark had some disagreement with Robert R. "Luint" Mann and killed him. Clark remained angry and bitter after the killing and later said, "I knew Luint Mann well and would kill Mann again under like circumstances." Clark was arrested, held for action by the grand jury, indicted, and tried at the spring term of the district court. The defendant was found guilty of first degree murder and sentenced to hang on May 13, 1881. All efforts to gain a new trial through appeal, or obtain executive clemency from Governor Lew Wallace through a commutation or respite, failed long before the day of execution.

On the final day Clark was taken from his cell after noon and given time to say farewell to his fellow prisoners. He was placed in a farm wagon and driven to the scaffold, which had been built a short distance from the jail. His three sisters, in a carriage, followed the wagon to the site of execution, where he was given additional time to say good-bye to them for the last time. The condemned man, accompanied by Sheriff James Southwick and one guard, climbed the stairs and centered himself upon the trapdoor. Clark asked the Sheriff, "How much drop you got?" and Sheriff Southwick replied, "About three feet." Clark replied, "I think that ought to be drop enough." When the sheriff tied Clark's legs the prisoner complained: "Down a little lower, Jim, it's not necessary to tie them so tight." When the sheriff positioned the noose Clark said, "That's right, put the noose around my ear so that when I drop I don't slip." The sheriff pulled the black hood over Clark's face and had just started down the stairs when he gave the signal to deputy Dave Wood, who cut the cord which released the double trapdoor at 1:24 P.M. Clearly the drop of three feet was insufficient to break Clark's neck, when the drop should have been between six and eight feet, so it took thirty minutes for Clark to strangle to death; one newspaper reported that the condemned man struggled considerably in dying. Clark was pronounced dead at 1:54 P.M. and the body was allowed to hang several minutes more before it was cut down. The remains were taken to the Catholic church, where the body was prepared for burial and then placed in the coffin provided. Following the Catholic service Clark was laid to rest in the church cemetery.

Las Vegas (NM) Daily Optic: May 14, 1881; *Mesilla Valley (NM) Independent*: May 14, 1881; *Messilla (NM) News*: May 14, 1881.

Barela, Santos
May 20, 1881

Santos Barela was born near Messily, New Mexico, in 1860. In 1881 he was employed as a teamster under contract to grade the railroad bed near the town of Colorado, New Mexico. While working at Colorado he met Jose Jojola and through him Jose's wife. Mrs. Jojola was twenty-five years old and so well proportioned that Barela could not control his lust. On the evening of February 18, 1881, the Jojolas visited Barela at his home and at a late hour left to return to their home. Barela stalked them at a close distance. Upon reaching their home Jose Jojola went directly to bed, while his wife went to light a candle. Barela slipped in behind them unnoticed and went to the bed, placed the barrel of his .45 caliber six-shooter next to Jose's head, and killed him with a single bullet.

Mrs. Jojola, upon hearing the shot, ran out of the house screaming for help, with Barela close behind. He overtook the woman, threw her to the ground and pinned her with his knee, but she continued to fight desperately. Help soon arrived, but not for Mrs. Jojola, as a neighbor named Guerena helped hold her down while Barela raped her. When Barela was arrested and questioned about the murder he confessed, "I killed him because I liked his wife." Barela was indicted in April and the trial followed quickly. The jury listened to evidence for two days before finding Barela guilty of first degree murder, and three days later the judge sentenced him to hang. Neither appeal nor application to Governor Lew Wallace delayed the proceedings.

On Friday, May 20, 1881, sixty people gathered at the scaffold to watch the execution, which took place a short distance from the jail. At 12:45 Barela was brought into the jail corridor, where Colonel Albert J. Fountain translated the death warrant into Spanish. Barela had remained composed throughout the morning as he was consoled by Father Morin, then said farewell to his fellow prisoners and rode to the gallows in a farm wagon. As he climbed the stairs to the scaffold his knees weakened and he began to tremble, but he stood firmly upon the trapdoor as he threw down his hat and knelt to receive the last blessing from Father Morin. Upon rising, Barela's wrists and ankles were pinioned but the ties on his wrists were then adjusted so that he could hold his crucifix throughout the affair. When the noose was positioned and the black cap was pulled over his face Barela began to list heavily to one side, and appeared about to tip over. Sheriff Jim Southwick quickly stepped onto the stairs and signaled to deputy Dave Wood, who, with a sharp hatchet, cut the cord restraining the double trapdoor at 12:52 P.M.

The sheriff had learned to use the proper distance for the drop the previous week and Barela's neck was broken in the fall. It took thirteen minutes before he was pronounced dead and the condemned man did not struggle nor appear to suffer, but the body was allowed to hang another seven minutes before it was cut down. The coffin was brought to the scaffold and Barela's remains were deposited in it before being taken to the Catholic church. He was buried in the church cemetery that evening following a brief service.

Las Cruces (NM) Rio Grande Republican: May 21, 1881.

Romero, Damian
February 2, 1883

In 1880 a ranch on which Damian Romero was employed was sold to an Iowa investor; but Romero remained on working for William A. Brocksmidt, son of the new owner. Brocksmidt became a popular figure throughout the county and he and Romero became friends. Romero taught his employer Spanish while Brocksmidt helped his employee improve his English. On January 10, 1882, Brocksmidt went to Springer to pick up a package of money containing $150. Romero knew of the money, so on January 12 he shot his employer in the head, the breast, and right arm, gathered the money and other valuables, mounted Silvertail — Brocksmidt's best horse — and fled toward Rio Arriba County.

On February 5 Romero was captured on the upper Chama by deputy sheriff Pedro Sanchez. Romero was wearing Brocksmidt's coat and hat and carrying his watch. He was taken to Springer to await trial and he soon implicated Juan Antonio Rael, an Indian, in the murder. Rael had been visiting Brocksmidt at about the time of the murder. Romero was indicted at the April term of the grand jury and his trial began on April 5, 1882. The prosecution called a large number of witnesses, and the evidence clearly showed that the murder was accomplished by one man. Rael was among the prosecution's witnesses and his story, straightforward and entirely plausible, withstood withering cross-examination.

Romero was the only witness for his defense and his story had evolved over time: first that he fired the first shot upon the command and threats from Rael; next that he was present when Rael fired all three shots; and then at trial that he was doing chores while Brocksmidt and Rael took target practice and only learned of the murder after it was done and was not present at the killing. Romero said he took the money, valuables, and clothing and fled when ordered and threatened by Rael. It took only one very long day for the trial to conclude and the following day the jury returned a verdict of guilty of murder in the first degree. Romero was sentenced to hang on May 10, 1882, but the appeals process began after the motion for a new trial was denied. The supreme court issued a stay while it considered the case and finally affirmed the decision of the district court. Governor Lionel A. Sheldon declined to intervene and set the date for execution as Friday, February 2, 1883.

On the day before his execution the condemned prisoner was visited by his mother and two sisters. After the visit he requested that his photograph be taken, so Sheriff Mason T. Bowman took him to the courtroom to pose and his mother and sisters joined him for a group photo. Romero, throughout, insisted that he was innocent and continually added minute details to his story of the killing of Brocksmidt. On Friday morning the condemned man arose at 6:00 A.M. and two hours later Father Accorsini administered the last sacraments. After the noon meal Romero dressed in a dark blue coat, black vest, dark pants, standing collar, black cravat, and a light colored broad-brimmed hat. The scaffold, a sturdy structure with a six foot drop, had been erected on the north side of the jail, and by 12:30 P.M. a crowd of over five hundred spectators had assembled behind the rope barricade.

After the irons were removed from Romero's hands and feet at 12:45 P.M. the march to the gallows began. He was accompanied by the sheriff, with deputies Budeson and Deacy behind, and followed by two newspaper reporters. Romero was invited to speak to the crowd and said, "Well, gentlemen, all I have to say is that I am not afraid to die because I am not guilty. Good-bye!" Sheriff Bowman read the death warrant and the priest administered the last benediction; after Father Accorsini withdrew Romero shook hands with everyone on the scaffold. He handed the sheriff his hat and took his place upon the trapdoor, where the condemned man's wrists and ankles were pinioned, the black cap was pulled over his face, and the noose adjusted. A white handkerchief was placed in his hand, an accommodation allowing Romero to choose the exact moment of the drop, and Romero cried out, "Good-bye all! I am going to Mora tonight, but will come back soon." Sheriff Bowman, thinking Romero had forgotten about the agreed upon signal, said, "Damian, are you ready? If so, drop it." Romero immediately dropped the handkerchief and the trap was sprung at 1:07 P.M. The body fell but the prisoner did not break his neck and violent contortions continued for five minutes as he slowly strangled, so it was not until 1:22 P.M. that county physician Dr. North pronounced him dead. The coffin was brought out of the jail as the body was being cut down and the deceased was deposited into it. The black cap was removed to reveal a swollen face, eyes staring and mouth gaping, with a dark purple rope burn around Romero's neck. The body was taken to Canoncito Ocate, where his mother prepared it for burial.

Santa Fe Daily New Mexican: April 9, 1882; February 3, 1883; *Las Vegas (NM) Daily Optic*: February 2, 1883; *National Police Gazette:* March 17, 1883; *Virginia City (NV) Territorial Enterprise*: February 3, 1883.

Yarberry, Milton J.
February 9, 1883

Milton J. Yarberry was well known in Albuquerque, New Mexico, when the tracks of the Atchison, Topeka & Santa Fe Railroad reached that sleepy city on April 10, 1880. With the arrival of the railroad the town "boomed" and the services of a law enforcement officer became necessary, so Yarberry was appointed constable by the county commissioners on February 1, 1881. On the evening of June 18, 1881, a single shot was fired in Greenleaf's Restaurant on Front Street and Yarberry, with gambler Frank Boyd, went to investigate. They saw Charles D. Campbell, a thirty-two-year-old employee of the railroad, walking toward Stover, Crary, & Company's store.

An old man sitting on the sidewalk pointed out Campbell as the shooter so Yarberry and Boyd hurried after him and Yarberry commanded, "Hold up your hands!" Just as Campbell turned three shots were fired and two bullets struck Campbell's back and the third entered his side, each passing entirely through his body. According to coroner Frank Reese, any of these wounds would have proven fatal. Yarberry surrendered to Sheriff Perfecto Armijo but he was lodged in the Santa Fe jail when there was talk of lynching. Yarberry was examined on July 5 and held to answer to the grand jury, indicted, and his trial began on May 18, 1882. Three days later Yarberry was convicted of murder in the first degree and on June 23 he was sentenced to hang. The appeals process commenced but the territorial supreme court affirmed the lower court's decision, and when efforts for clemency failed, Governor Lionel A. Sheldon set February 9, 1883, as the date for the execution.

After noon of the final day one hundred ten witnesses gathered in the enclosure built around the gallows, but more than one thousand men watched from trees and rooftops as the militia marched the condemned man to the gallows. Yarberry was to be hanged on a gallows of the counterpoise weight design, using a four hundred pound weight to jerk him up. His arms were tied at his back and his wrists cuffed and once he was in position beneath the noose his ankles were tied, the noose positioned and cinched, and the black cap pulled over his face. The cord holding the counterpoise weight was cut at 3:00 P.M. and Yarberry's body was jerked into the air, his head almost striking the crossbeam. He fell back to the end of his rope with a jolt, his neck broken. Three doctors in attendance pronounced him dead in nine minutes but the body hung a few minutes more before it was cut down. The remains were lowered into the coffin provided by the county, funeral services soon followed, and Yarberry was buried in the Catholic cemetery.

Frank Boyd, Yarberry's accomplice, after the shooting made his way over the railroad to Holbrook, Arizona Territory, and was staying at Martin's ranch. He avoided notoriety until October 5, when he accosted two defenseless Navajo Indians at 4:00 P.M. and shot one dead. At sundown forty Indians, each armed with a rifle, arrived at the ranch seeking revenge. They found Boyd about to mount his horse, leveled their rifles at him and on command all fired, riddling his body with bullets.

Santa Fe Daily New Mexican: February 3, 1883; February 10, 1883; *Las Vegas (NM) Daily Optic:* February 9, 1883; *Albuquerque (NM) Morning Journal*: February 11, 1883.

Lara, Ruperto
April 30, 1885

On October 17, 1882, Ruperto Lara, a Pueblo Indian, and Maximo Apodaca, a Mexican, went to White River, where they met George Nedsmith, his wife, and Nedsmith's eight-year-old adopted daughter. The Nedsmiths were traveling home to their ranch at Three Rivers and Lara and Apodaca traveled with them. At sundown, according to Lara, he rode up to the wagon and fired a single shot at Nedsmith, who was bending over inside the wagon. Nedsmith straightened to see what had happened and halloed to Lara, but Apodaca jumped onto the wagon seat next to Mrs. Nedsmith and shot George Nedsmith in the breast with a single round from his rifle. Mrs. Nedsmith crawled under the wagon seat for protection but Apodaca placed the barrel of his rifle under her arm and shot her entirely through the torso. The little girl began crying so Apodaca placed the barrel against her head and killed her as well.

Lara said later that, with all the gunfire from Apodaca's rifle, his horse shied and he was unable to fire another shot. Apodaca then drove the wagon some distance off the trail, where the two men took the horses, divided what money they found, and Apodaca took Nedsmith's overcoat. The Nedsmith family was not missed for three weeks but two men traveling the same trail saw wolves and buzzards showing interest in an abandoned wagon and investigated. They found three badly decomposed bodies but were able to identify the Nedsmiths from property left behind. Within days word of the murders spread and residents of the village of Doña Ana recalled seeing Apodaca wearing Nedsmith's overcoat as he traveled in company with Lara. The two murderers had fled to Mexico and remained there for several years but Pat Coghlan, who owned a store in Tularosa and knew the Nedsmiths well, offered Jim Lloyd $500 if he could lure the men onto American soil and arrest them.

Lloyd convinced Lara and Apodaca that he had conceived a profitable cattle rustling scheme in New Mexico, so they crossed the border with Lloyd and were captured. Apodaca turned state's evidence and testified, quite credibly, that Lara had fired all the bullets that killed the Nedsmiths. Lara then tried to mitigate blame for the killings by claiming that Perry Kearney and Coghlan paid him to kill the Nedsmiths. Lara was given the opportunity to pick Kearney and Coghlan from a group of twenty-five men but he positively identified deputy Dave Wood as Kearney and H.J. Cuniffe as Coghlan. Lara and Apodaca were indicted, tried, and convicted of murder in the first degree and both men were sentenced to hang on April 30, 1885; but Governor Lionel A. Sheldon commuted Apodaca's sentence to life in prison in consideration of his testimony.

Wednesday night, April 29, Lara slept comfortably and awoke in good spirits. He spent the day preparing for his death and at 2:15 P.M. he was brought out of his cell and offered liquor. His wrists were bound and the procession proceeded to the gallows, Lara in front between Sheriff Eugene van Patten and deputy Ascarate. Lara took his place on the trapdoor and listened while the sheriff read the death warrant in English and Spanish. The condemned man was given a chance to speak to the crowd of twelve hundred spectators and spent a half hour relating his story of being hired to do the killing and placing blame on Pat Coghlan; then he asked the sheriff to tell the crowd in English that he did not fear death. He answered a question from the priest, saying he had not been asked by anyone to make a confession, and then the priest concluded the religious ceremony. Lara's ankles were bound and a black velvet cap was placed over his face. After the noose was adjusted Lara sighed deeply, just as the sheriff stepped off the trapdoor and signaled, and at 2:44 P.M. the trap was sprung. Within a few minutes Dr. Woods began monitoring vital signs and he pronounced Lara dead at 2:57 P.M. At 3:00 the coffin was positioned below the scaffold, the body was cut down and lowered directly into it, and within the hour Lara was buried. Apodaca outlived Lara by only six months. He suffered anguish and rarely slept through an entire night, complaining that he constantly heard the child crying since she had been murdered. On November 4, 1885, he committed suicide.

Rio Grande (NM) Republican: May 2, 1885.

James, William
June 18, 1886

Twenty-year-old William James, alias Bolt, traveled to New Mexico and in early 1886 met Charles Towner and a man named Denham. The trio traveled about New Mexico searching for criminal opportunities but when the men quarreled James killed Denham. James was arrested and tried for murder at the May term of the district court in the third judicial district, convicted, and sentenced to hang on June 18, 1886. During his final days he was visited by a reporter from the *Lincoln County Leader* and the prisoner provided him with a copy of his written confession prepared on June 14:

> Towner told me that Denham was going to kill me. So when we were riding on the plains, Towner and Denham were riding side by side, and I had been riding a little to one side. I fell behind and shot Denham without giving him any notion. I killed Denham because Towner said that Denham had threatened me. Denham had made propositions to me to poison Grandmother Allen to get her horses. He also had made propositions with me to kill Morgan Livingston, to rob him and to shoot his horse. I believe Denham wanted to kill me because he had made those proposals to me and I had refused him. When Towner told me that Denham was going to kill me it was before we started out on the plains. He told me several times. Towner first proposed to me to go on the staked plains to hunt for water at Mrs. Allen's house, but I did not consent to go so Denham came there, after we started and had reached Campbell's house, then Towner told me again to look out for Denham, and I said that I would go along and try to get the drop on him.
>
> I believe now that Towner wanted Denham killed because he thought Denham had been intimate with his wife.
>
> Towner's wife was a loose character, and I have heard she has since gone off with another man.
>
> The evidence which we told in the trial was fixed up between us. Towner told me at Roswell that if I would plead guilty and get him out of the scrape, then he would help me to get out of jail. I had a good deal of confidence in him as he had said.
>
> After Denham was killed Towner advised me to skip out. But I refused to do this. When I shot Denham, Towner slapped his hand on his six shooter, and I dropped on him and he took his hand off his pistol.
>
> It was Towner's saddle which was burned up; the leggins, which were thought to be Denham's, were a pair of leggins I stole from a house hear Salt Lake at the point of Guadalope [*sic*] mountains; I do not remember the man's name. The hat which was thought to be Denham's was a hat I got from Henry Parker on Rocky Arroyo. Mrs. Allen did the trading and gave my black Stetson hat for it. The Winchester gun which Denham had belonged to Towner. I killed the horse and burned the saddle in order to hide the murder.
>
> I dragged the body off the road on the horn of the saddle, the rope was put on Denham's feet by Charles Towner, and he picked up Denham's hat and coat when I dragged him off, and came on and helped me bury him. Towner tried to get out of helping me bury him but I said if he did not help bury him I would go off and leave him there.
>
> I did not kill Denham to rob him but because of the threats which Towner told me about.
>
> This statement is made with the full knowledge that I am to die in four days from this

> time on the scaffold, that there is no hope for me in this life, and I call on God to witness that it contains nothing but the truth, that my hopes of salvation are lost, if under the present circumstances I should tell a falsehood. I hope that my punishment may be a warning to all persons in the future not to be led off into crime.
>
> William James Bolt

Sheriff James R. Brent assigned a death watch consisting of deputies Ball, A.N. Harp and Wilson McVeigh and they ensured that the prisoner did not commit suicide or escape. During that last week the scaffold was erected within a tall fence enclosing the jail yard. The hour selected by the sheriff was 2:00 P.M., but at the request of the condemned man the time was moved up, so the sheriff appeared at the cell door at 1:00 P.M. He read the death warrant which had been signed by Governor Edmund G. Ross on June 7 and when the sheriff concluded the Rev. Father Garnier performed the functions of his office. The shackles were removed from James' ankles, the prisoner took his place in the jail corridor between the sheriff and the priest, and they proceeded the short distance into the jail yard and onto the scaffold. As James appeared he announced loudly, "I am not afraid to die — good men have died on the gallows." Then he climbed the stairs with a firm step and took his place on the trapdoor. He was asked if he had anything to say and he glanced at the witnesses below and at the spectators in the courthouse windows before saying only, "Young men should take warning by me. That's all I've got to say."

James' wrists and ankles were pinioned, the noose was adjusted, and the black cap was pulled over his face, and then he was asked if he was ready. The condemned man replied loudly, "God bless you — good-bye all!" In that moment the lever was touched by Sheriff Brent, the trap was sprung, and James fell, breaking his neck. In ten minutes the attending physician announced that James' heart had ceased to beat and he pronounced him dead. The body was allowed to hang another eight minutes, eighteen minutes in all, to ensure he could not be revived and then the rope was cut and the body was lowered into the waiting coffin. The remains were given to Father Garnier, who conducted a graveside service at the Catholic cemetery before sundown.

Santa Fe Lincoln County Leader: June 26, 1886.

Johnson, DeWitt C.
November 19, 1886

On June 10, 1886, twenty-three-year-old Dewitt C. Johnson murdered Albert H. Howe. Johnson and codefendant E.G. Greve were tried separately at the October term of the district court in the third judicial district of Lincoln County, New Mexico. Johnson was found guilty of murder in the first degree, while Greve was found guilty of a lesser offense, possibly turning state's evidence. Greve was sentenced to serve ten years in prison but was pardoned by Governor L. Bradford Prince in 1891, after serving only five years. Johnson was sentenced to hang on November 19, 1886, and neither appeal nor application for executive clemency delayed the proceedings. On November 1, 1886, Governor Edmund G. Ross signed the death warrant, which was delivered to Lincoln County sheriff James R. Brent ordering him to proceed with the execution. It had only been a few months since the execution of William James so Sheriff Brent had the enclosure fencing and scaffold removed from storage and erected in the jail yard. A week before the execution Johnson wanted to reaffirm his Christian beliefs so Sheriff Brent, deputy Andy Robinson, Francisco Romero y Lueras, and the Rev. Father Garnier gathered in the jail for services. Afterward the lawmen retired and left Father Garnier to converse with the prisoner, and the priest spent many hours with him over the next week.

On the final day Sheriff Brent appeared at Johnson's cell door after 1:30 P.M. to read the death warrant. The prisoner then stepped from his cell, had the shackles removed from his ankles, and took his place between the sheriff and the priest. The walk to the gallows was short and, after climbing the stairs with a firm step, the prisoner took his place on the trapdoor. When asked if he had anything to say he declined to make a speech. His wrists and ankles were pinioned, the noose was adjusted, the black cap pulled over his face. As Father Garnier prayed for his soul at 1:40 P.M., the trap was sprung. Johnson dropped and hung motionless as Dr. Paden of White Oaks monitored Johnson's vital signs and pronounced him dead in sixteen minutes. Sheriff Brent cut the rope and lowered the body into the waiting coffin. Dr. Paden examined the remains and determined that Johnson's neck had not been broken in the fall, and announced that death had been by strangulation. At 2:00 P.M. Sheriff Brent, assisted by several attendants, lifted the coffin into a wagon and drove it to the grave previously dug in the cemetery east of town. The body of DeWitt C. Johnson was interred before sundown, following a brief graveside service by Father Garnier.

Las Vegas (NM) Optic: November 29, 1886; *Lincoln (NM) Independent*: November 11, 1886.

Anderson, John H.
May 6, 1887

John Henry Anderson, a Negro, was born into slavery at the Hudspeth farm nine miles from Independence, Missouri. Anderson grew to be a burly young man and because of his size he was accustomed to intimidating other men. In 1874 he made his way to New Mexico and in 1885 he was quarrying rock near Socorro. Early on the morning of June 21 Anderson quarreled with fellow worker Alfonso Williams and the situation escalated into a fight, during which Williams bested Anderson. The victor then made several comments which Anderson later claimed had threatened his life. Throughout the rest of the morning the crew kept the two men separated but the fight had taken more out of Williams than he realized, so by late morning he returned to the quarry's lodging house to rest. Meanwhile, Anderson became increasingly bold, loud, and threatening toward Williams and finally swore to kill him, calling again and again for a weapon. As the noon hour approached Anderson offered to pay $25 for the loan of a gun but still he could not find one.

During the early afternoon hours Anderson obtained a six-shooter with one empty chamber and went in search of Williams. He found Williams asleep on a bunk near a window so he leaned in and shot Williams five times. Williams was rushed to the quarry doctors, who did all they could to save him; but the wounds were mortal and he soon died. Anderson was arrested and indicted, and at the fall 1885 term of the Socorro County district court a jury found him guilty of murder in the first degree and the judge sentenced him to hang. Anderson claimed, as his defense, that his life was threatened by Williams and insisted that his victim had died, not because he shot him, but because the doctors failed to save him. During the appeal process, which took more than a year and a half, the territorial supreme court found the murder to be unprovoked and characterized it as "cold-blooded murder." The decision of the lower court was affirmed and the execution was scheduled for May 6, 1887. Efforts to gain executive clemency from Governor Edmund G. Ross were to no avail.

From mid–April Anderson began to prepare himself through prayer and supplication. Father Lestra was his primary religious advisor but on his last night several ministers of the gospel visited for prayer and Bible study, and they remained throughout the night. Anderson made two final requests of the sheriff: first that the execution be delayed to the last possible moment permissible in the death warrant, which was 4:00 P.M.; and second that his brother in Kansas be sent for to take charge of his remains. The sheriff granted the second request, so at 11:00 A.M. Father Courssey visited Anderson in his cell and three black women followed but they stayed only a few minutes. At 11:15 A.M. the condemned man was led by Father Lestra into the jail yard and onto the scaffold, accompanied by Sheriff Charles T. Russell, deputy A.L. Robinson, and deputy

Cook. The death warrant was read after which Anderson said to the dozen witnesses, "It seems hard that I have come to this, but I hope to meet my redeemer in peace." He again blamed the doctors for Williams' death and thanked the sheriff for his kindness. He shook hands with everyone and then his wrists and ankles were pinioned, the noose adjusted, and the black cap pulled on. At 11:25 A.M. all was ready and the trap was sprung. The attending physician pronounced Anderson dead in six minutes and the body was cut down seven minutes later. The remains were placed in a coffin and taken to the undertaker's parlor to await the arrival of his brother. Half the spectators were reporters and one of them was a photographer, who captured on film the scene at the gallows.

Albuquerque (NM) Daily Democrat: May 7, 1887.

Baker, Theodore
May 6, 1887

Frank S. Unruh was a surveyor for the U.S. government but when there were no duties to perform he would work for a cattle company in Colorado. In 1878 he bought a small cattle ranch near Springer, Colfax County, New Mexico, and began exchanging letters with a young lady in Pennsylvania. They wanted to start a family so in 1880 he traveled east and married Kate. She was a pretty twenty-two-year-old woman with light hair and sparkling blue eyes. In 1882 Kate gave birth to their only child, a son. Kate and Frank were quite happy, except for those times when Frank was called away for long periods on business.

In July 1885 Theodore Baker traveled from Arizona to Springer, New Mexico, to purchase a ranch and on the road to Springer he met Frank Unruh, an earlier acquaintance from Arizona. Unruh invited Baker to stay at his home while he searched for a ranch property, and Baker moved in but made no effort to find his new homestead. Instead he began to undermine the Unruh's marital relationship by recounting tales of Unruh's womanizing in Arizona. On Monday, December 15, 1885, Unruh overheard his wife and Baker having a whispered conversation, became angry, and went into the basement, where he overindulged in wine. In this condition he became loud and abusive and yelled that he was going to beat his wife. Kate went into their bedroom and removed Unruh's pistol, which she gave to Baker for safekeeping. At dinner the two men argued and Unruh said to Baker, "I ought to cut your heart out and hang it on a pole," whereupon Baker went to his room but soon returned and continued the argument. The situation quickly deteriorated to a fistfight which Baker manipulated into his bedroom. Baker then pulled out his pistol, which he had positioned for quick access. He shot Unruh twice and the wounded man ran out of the house using both hands to hold back the blood and bile from a serious stomach wound. Baker followed to the door but returned to his room for Unruh's pistol; now armed with two six-shooters, Baker followed the wounded man and found him collapsed in a sitting position a thousand feet from the house. Baker, using Unruh's gun, shot him in the side, arm and head before he returned to the house to tell Kate that her husband was dead. In a few minutes doubt tugged at him so he returned and shot Unruh twice more.

Baker and Kate were arrested and lodged in the Springer jail. On December 23 a lynch mob took Baker from his cell and hanged him but a posse arrived in time to drive off the mob, cut Baker down, and revive their prisoner. Baker was removed to the penitentiary and placed in protective custody to await his trial. The prisoner was tried, convicted of first degree murder, and on September 6, 1886, Judge Elisha Long sentenced him to hang. Kate had exchanged her testimony for her freedom and, after the trial ended, she took her son and returned to Pennsylvania. All efforts for commutation or clemency from Governor Edmund G. Ross failed but the process delayed the execution. Finally the new date for the execution was set for May 6, 1887.

On the evening of May 5 Baker attended a religious service in the jail with four ministers and thirty parishioners. The next day the clergy made a final plea to the governor but by mid-afternoon a telegram from Governor Ross arrived saying he would not interfere. Baker was taken from his cell later that afternoon and walked to the scaffold with a firm step. He took his place on the trapdoor and was prepared. Just before the black cap was pulled over his face he remarked to the sixty-seven witnesses, "Gentlemen, I am sorry it ends thus," and then through the dark cloth yelled, "Let 'er go!" The trap was sprung at 3:53 P.M. and the fall broke Baker's neck. The attending physician monitored his vital signs and in seven minutes he was pronounced dead; after another ten minutes the body was cut down and placed in the plain coffin provided by the county. Baker was buried that evening following a brief service.

Santa Fe Daily New Mexican: April 16, 1886; August 23, 1886; May 6, 1887; *Las Vegas (NM) Daily Optic*: August 20–21, 1886; September 6, 1886; *Las Vegas (NM) News*: May 7, 1887; May 13, 1887; *Albuquerque (NM) Morning Democrat*: May 6–7, 1877.

Perez, Pilar
July 6, 1888

On March 16, 1886, at the Mimbres River a group of Mexicans abducted a pretty young senorita named Reyes Alvarez, who Pilar Perez insisted was his sweetheart. Perez killed Aguilar Santiago when he interfered. Thomas Hall of Pinos Altos, a deputy sheriff and a deputy U.S. marshal, began searching for the young girl; he had more than a professional interest because he was the father of five children, and he empathized with Mr. Alvarez. Hall did not find the girl and was returning to Silver City when he came upon the party riding in the same direction. He gave no sign that he recognized the party and did not know Pilar Perez personally. However, Perez recognized Hall, got behind the deputy, and shot him in the back and arm. A passing wagon found deputy Hall at 10:00 P.M., alive but mortally wounded, and took him to town where Sheriff James B. Woods and Dr. Slough urged him to name the person who had murdered him. But Hall said he did not see which Mexican shot him and died four hours later.

After shooting deputy Hall, Pilar Perez released Reyes Alvarez and she continued into town where she provided all the details of the shooting, including the name of the murderer. Perez fled to Socorro, then to Albuquerque, and finally into Arizona, where he avoided capture for two years. But Sheriff Andrew B. Laird finally developed a lead and hired a friend of Perez to find him. The informant was in Flagstaff, Arizona, when Perez appeared, so the informant contacted a deputy sheriff who devised a plan for Perez' capture. The fugitive attended a baile, a party with Mexican folk dancing, and was captured while preoccupied with dancing.

Once in jail Perez admitted the killing but said Hall had first shot at him twice and he only fired in self-defense, but Hall's pistol had not been drawn nor fired when he was found dying. Perez was tried at the spring 1888 term of the Grant County district court and the testimony of Reyes Alvarez, his admission, and other circumstantial evidence convicted him. The jury deliberated only for a few minutes before finding him guilty of first degree murder and he was sentenced to hang on July 6, 1888. The appeals process was concluded well before the date set and efforts to obtain executive clemency from Governor Edmund G. Ross failed.

During his final days Pilar Perez made light of his pending death and told the other prisoners he would "ride to hell on a black horse." Sheriff Laird issued sixty tickets to witness the execution, some spectators to view from the windows in the courthouse offices and the remainder to watch from within an enclosure. The scaffold had been built by July 4 and was located on the north side of the courthouse, with a high board fence surrounding the structure to obstruct the view from adjacent roofs and hilltops. Perez confessed to Father Girard on Wednesday and received the sacrament on Thursday, so he was able to sleep soundly his last night and awoke with a healthy appetite.

When the time arrived the condemned man walked to the scaffold and stood on the trapdoor without wavering. He was prepared by the deputies and at 9:58 A.M. Sheriff Laird gave the signal, the drop of a handkerchief, and a black trusty named Wilson pulled the rope release. Wilson felt it an honor to perform such a service; still, he was concealed within a box so that he could not be seen by Perez or the witnesses. Perez broke his neck in a fall of seven feet and after his heart ceased to beat he was pronounced dead by the attending physician. He hung a sufficient time to ensure he could not be resuscitated before he was cut down, placed in a coffin, and taken to the grave site for a Catholic service.

Las Vegas (NM) Daily Optic: July 9, 1888.

Falkner, Frederick
August 19, 1892

In the late summer of 1891 James Lannon was driving his wagon to Texas and stopped in Trinidad, Colorado, where he met Frederick Falkner. Lannon agreed to take him along. They traveled into Colfax County, New Mexico, and camped near Trinchera. During the night Falkner crept up on Lannon while he slept and murdered him with an axe; either of the two blows inflicted to his head would have proven fatal. Lannon's body was found the next morning and a posse was organized at Trinchera. Falkner had taken Lannon's wagon and team and entire camp outfit, so his progress southeastward was slow and the trail plain to follow.

By the next morning the posse overtook the fugitive, arrested him without incident, and lodged him in the jail at Trinchera. Falkner was tried at the fall term of the district court in Las Vegas, San Miguel County, on a change of venue from Colfax County and he was convicted of first degree murder. The conviction was appealed and the territorial supreme court rendered its verdict in early August 1892, affirming the lower court's decision. The date for execution was then set at August 19, 1892. Falkner's attorney prepared a petition with three hundred signatures requesting clemency or commutation, but Governor L. Bradford Prince found no reason to interfere.

An enclosure was constructed around the gallows next to the jail and on the morning of the execution a large crowd gathered around the fence, but only the few invited witnesses were admitted to watch the proceedings. The death warrant was read in the jail and Falkner was walked to the platform after 2:30 P.M. He took his position on the trapdoor where his wrists and ankles were pinioned. He declined to make a statement so, without delay, Sheriff Jose L. Lopez pulled the black cap over his face, adjusted the noose, and the trap was sprung at 2:51 P.M. The fall did not break Falkner's neck so it took twenty minutes for him to strangle to death, then he hung a few minutes longer before being cut down and lowered into the plain coffin provided by the county. He was buried that evening.

Albuquerque (NM) Daily Citizen: August 19, 1892.

Maestas, Herman
May 25, 1894

Herman Maestas married Rosa Duran at Los Alamos, San Miguel County, New Mexico, in February 1894 but the justice of the peace neglected to register the marriage certificate with the county clerk as required, and this voided the marriage. Maestas was soon jailed in Las Vegas on a charge of robbery, and strong evidence seemed to ensure a conviction and a long prison term. This emboldened Pedro Romero, who was interested in Rosa Duran, to investigate the marriage and when he confirmed that the union was null and void he proposed to and married Rosa Duran. Romero and his new wife went to the jail to inform Maestas and then returned to their sheep ranch near Los Alamos.

Maestas broke jail with Jesus Vialpando and they started for the Romero ranch, where they found Romero and a young boy tending their flock. Maestas accused Romero of interfering in his marital relationship and Romero countered that Maesta's marriage was invalid.

Maestas wasted no further words and shot Romero once and then, as he lay helpless on the ground, shot him in the back, killing him instantly. The two murderers next discussed what to do with the boy and finally, upon his word that he would not report the crime for twenty-four hours, he was left unharmed. However, as soon as the two murderers left the boy hurried to a nearby ranch and sounded the alarm. Maestas was soon captured, jailed in Las Vegas, tried at the 1894 spring term of the district court, and convicted of first degree murder. The date of his execution, May 25, 1894, was not delayed by the appeals process nor by applications to Governor William T. Thornton pleading for executive clemency. Vialpando was never charged in the murder of Romero but he paid the ultimate price for later crimes (see Chavez, Feliciano, that follows).

The gallows had been built next to the Las Vegas jail and was surrounded by a high board fence. The execution was delayed by a morning storm but by 12:37 P.M. two hundred witnesses were admitted within the enclosure. The death warrant was read to the condemned man in his cell and at 1:14 P.M. he was led out by Sheriff William P. Cunningham of Santa Fe, Sheriff Lorenzo Lopez of San Miguel County, several deputies and Father Grom. Once positioned on the trapdoor Maestas declined to make a statement but prayed with the priest. He was then prepared for the drop and at 1:20 P.M. the trap was sprung. The prisoner broke his neck in the fall and his heartbeat ceased in five minutes, but the body was allowed to hang another five minutes before it was cut down and delivered to his family for burial.

Albuquerque (NM) Weekly Citizen: May 26, 1894.

Barrett, James
September 14, 1894

James Barrett wanted to be known as a bold, bad man so he committed a variety of crimes in Texas in 1892 before fleeing into New Mexico. He settled in the Pecos Valley in Eddy County and found a job as a laborer at a grading camp at Seven Rivers. On the evening of July 23, 1893, Barrett, in keeping with his persona, instigated a fight with John Holehan and James Barnes but after everything quieted Holehan and Barnes retired. Barrett continued drinking whiskey into the early morning hours and once he was sure his adversaries were asleep he obtained a double-barreled shotgun and threatened the night watchman, demanding to know which tent belonged to Holehan and Barnes. At gunpoint the watchman showed the way and, as he held up his light, Barrett fired a load of buckshot into each sleeping figure, then reloaded while backing out and threatened to kill anyone who tried to stop him.

The following morning, when Barrett was arrested by Sheriff David L. Kemp, he offered no resistance. The populace of Eddy County was so incensed that it was believed Barrett could not get a fair trial so the trial was moved to Lincoln County on a motion for a change of venue. In March 1894 Barrett's defense of temporary insanity failed and he was convicted on two counts of first degree murder. The appeals process took many months but finally the decision of the district court was affirmed and the date of execution was set for September 14, 1894; the application for commutation of sentence was denied by Governor William T. Thornton.

Barrett ate a hearty dinner before being escorted to the gallows at 1:15 P.M. He gave a brief speech to the crowd of one thousand and concluded, "I have been told I would die with my boots on. I'll just fool you a trip, so here goes my boots," and he removed them. Deputy sheriff Bush pinioned the prisoner's arms and legs, pulled the black cap over his head, adjusted the noose, and at 2:05 P.M. the trap was sprung. Barrett broke his neck in the fall and he was pronounced dead in ten minutes. At 2:20 the body was cut down, placed in its coffin, and within the hour Barrett was deposited in his grave.

Santa Fe Daily New Mexican: September 20, 1894.

Chavez, Feliciano; Vialpando, Jesus
November 19, 1895

Lorenzo Martinez owned a large ranch at Cow Springs forty miles from Santa Fe in southeastern Santa Fe County, New Mexico. In January 1895 Lorenzo sent his two sons, thirty-two-year-old Tomas and younger brother Maximiliano, to look after his herd. On January 17 Tomas started southward toward Cañon Blanco in search of stray cattle while Maximiliano remained at the ranch house. Tomas was mounted on a good horse, had a first class saddle and bridle, warm blankets and clothing, and his faithful bulldog alongside. On Tuesday, January 22, Tomas' dog returned to the ranch house, starving and cold, and with a wound where a bullet had ricocheted off his skull.

Maximiliano started south to search for his brother but the dog made every effort to guide Tomas' brother eastward, so Maximiliano finally relented and followed the animal. The dog led him directly to the round-up corral at La Muralla eight miles east of the ranch house, where Maximiliano found tracks from many horses, the ashes of an unusually large fire, and part of a steer's carcass. The dog persisted in digging at the ashes so Maximiliano joined him and, raking through the pile, he found a human foot encased in a heavy shoe and overshoe which he recognized as his brother's footgear. He continued digging and found a human pelvis bone, but the rest of his brother's remains had been consumed in the fire.

When Maximiliano got back to the ranch house he sent word to Sheriff William P. Cunningham in Santa Fe and the sheriff, with deputy Juan Delgado, started for the scene. By the time they arrived snow had obliterated most of the tracks, which led toward Las Vegas, so the lawmen traveled to the way station at the railroad; there a peddler reported that he had been robbed. The sheriff arrested four men, who reported seeing four riders with five horses, one the horse of Tomas, pass their house on Sunday evening. They identified Jesus Vialpando and Feliciano Chavez but did not know the names of the other two men. The sheriff released them and paid them for the information, but also secured their promise to contact him when they located any of the murderers. Several days passed without word and Sheriff Cunningham had given up hope when he received a telegram saying that Emilio Encinias, the youngest of the four men, was hiding at Las Vegas.

The sheriff immediately took the train to Las Vegas and found Encinias hiding from the other three men, who intended to kill him. Encinias provided information that led to the arrest of Vialpando, Chavez, and Zenobio Trujillo and once in custody all four prisoners began talking. They said they left San Pedro for Las Vegas on Friday, January 18, but it snowed by the time they reached the round-up corral. They were tired and hungry and decided to camp, drove six steers into the corral, and butchered one. They built a fire and settled down for the night but as their meat sizzled on the spit a rider approached and Vialpando said, "There is a fine horse coming, that will be a nice chicken for us." Tomas Martinez was invited to join them by the fire and he provided them with coffee grounds. Chavez suddenly grabbed Tomas from behind and held his arms, and Vialpando got the drop on him. Then Vialpando told Encinias and Trujillo to ride ahead and wait. After they left, Vialpando took the victim's overcoat and then shot him. Vialpando and Chavez threw the body on the fire and piled on fence posts and loose wood to consume the corpse and Vialpando then shot Tomas' dog, intending to throw it on the fire, but the dog fled into the darkness.

The two murderers took the horse, saddle, bridle and overcoat and caught up with their companions, and when Vialpando was arrested at his mother's house he had everything he had stolen except the horse. Chavez had nothing from Tomas but showed officers where he had buried the horse, which he killed to avoid detection. Only Vialpando and Chavez were tried for the murder of Tomas Martinez. The five day trial commenced on

March 26, the two were convicted of first degree murder, and on April 12 both defendants were sentenced to hang. The appeals process delayed the execution but the date was finally set for November 19, 1895, and the applications requesting executive clemency sent to Governor William T. Thornton were denied.

Deputy Tucker was put on death watch the night before the double execution and in the morning Vialpando asked for whiskey, but was refused. The gallows could only accommodate one man so at 6:00 A.M. Sheriff Cunningham and a small party, including Father Fourchegu, went to the cells. Each prisoner gave San Miguel County's Sheriff Eugenio Romero $3.25 in nickels they had collected from visitors, and requested he give it to their families. Vialpando was then taken from his cell, led out to a waiting carriage, and driven to the gallows, which had been erected in the arroyo near the gas works a half mile north of the town plaza. There were more than one thousand spectators gathered when Vialpando ascended the steps supported by Sheriffs Cunningham and Thomas A. Hubbell, and followed by Sheriff Romero and six others. He stood on the trapdoor and said not a word as he was quickly prepared for the drop, having his wrists and ankles pinioned, the noose adjusted, and the black cap pulled on. At 6:50 A.M. the trap was sprung and Vialpando's feet came to rest six inches above the ground; his neck was broken in the fall. Dr. Diaz monitored vital signs and the pulse was barely perceptible at four minutes, and soon afterward Vialpando was pronounced dead. The body was allowed to hang thirteen minutes before it was cut down, put in a coffin, and placed in Undertaker Gable's wagon.

The gallows was prepared for Chavez while the sheriff and his assistants returned to the jail and the second condemned man arrived at the scaffold just before 7:40 A.M. He climbed the stairs unassisted and made a rambling speech in Spanish lasting eighteen minutes, which was translated by Hill, Cajal and Delgado taking turns. Chavez admitted the crime and then denied it, implicated Trujillo as the second murderer, and claimed that he had tried to stop the crime. He thanked everyone and finally said good-bye to everyone. The condemned man was then centered on the trapdoor and prepared, and when the black cap was pulled on he yelled out, "Adios, Todos!" and at 8:00 A.M. the trap was sprung. Chavez broke his neck in the fall and Dr. Diaz pronounced him dead after the fourth minute. He was cut down at fourteen minutes, put in his coffin, and loaded onto Undertaker Gable's wagon next to Vialpando. The bodies were turned over to Sheriff Romero and in the morning the coffins were taken to the depot for shipment to Romeroville, San Miguel County, where both families resided.

Santa Fe Daily New Mexican: November 19, 1895.

Sandoval, Dionicio
September 24, 1896

A Bernalillo County commissioner owned two flocks of sheep, one flock herded by Victorian Tenorio and the other by Dionicio Sandoval. Sandoval was ordered to transfer to Tenorio's flock a certain number of rams and ewes and the lambs born to the ewes. The rams and ewes were delivered but Tenorio believed that Sandoval had retained a number of the lambs, thus decreasing the size of his flock, and he complained of the shortage. Both flocks were in the vicinity of San Ysidro on the evening of July 29, 1895, so Sandoval took his rifle and went to Tenorio's camp to confront him about his accusation. Pedro Gallegos and Enrique Salazar were in camp when Sandoval arrived and Tenorio invited his fellow sheepherder to sit with them, but he refused and sat on a keg a short distance away.

Tenorio went to Sandoval to ask why he had come and an argument ensued which ended with each calling the other a liar. Sandoval would later claim that Tenorio attacked him and in the struggle for the rifle it discharged accidentally. However, the two witnesses testified that when Tenorio called Sandoval a liar Sandoval immediately shot Tenorio; they denied there was any struggle for the rifle. Sandoval was arrested, indicted and tried at the end of November 1895. He was found guilty of first degree murder and sentenced to hang on January 3, 1896, but the appeals process commenced and the execution was stayed. The district court's record was affirmed on September 22, 1896, and the date for execution was set for two days hence. Sandoval's attorney immediately filed an application with Governor William T. Thornton pleading for clemency based upon mental deficiency, a medical commission was convened, but the three doctors refuted the claim after finding no mental illness.

On Thursday, September 24, Sandoval arose at 6:00 A.M. and spent half an hour in consultation with Father Durant. After breakfast he dressed in the new suit provided, but chose to wear his old sombrero. Sheriff Thomas A. Hubbell read the death warrants, first Governor Thornton's and then the warrant from the clerk of the supreme court, and the condemned man responded, "I am ready to die and have nothing to say." His wrists were bound and he was taken from the jail to a carriage and driven to the gallows, erected one half mile behind the jail on the fairgrounds. Sandoval mounted the scaffold and stood on the trapdoor, and then his arm, knees and ankles were pinioned. The black cap was pulled over his face, the noose was adjusted, and in the next moment the trap was sprung by Sheriff Hubbell. Dr. J.F. Pearce monitored Sandoval's vital signs and in eight minutes he was pronounced dead; four minutes later the body was cut down. Sandoval's remains were laid on a bench, the black cap was removed, and the body was put on display for the public. After more than two hundred people had examined the deceased he was turned over to undertaker Strong, prepared for burial, and that evening was buried in the San Ignacio Cemetery.

Sante Fe Daily New Mexican: November 30, 1895; *Albuquerque (NM) Morning Democrat*: September 23–26, 1896; *Roswell (NM) Record*: September 25, 1896.

Gonzales, Antonio
September 24, 1896

Charles S. van Sickle, foreman for the Seldom Ridge & Pebble Sheep Company, lived alone at the Zubar ranch, which was their Chavez County headquarters. On Monday, February 5, 1894, van Sickle met Eugenio Aragon driving a hay wagon and van Sickle noticed that Aragon had aboard lumber belonging to his employer, so he threatened to prosecute Aragon if it was not returned. On the following Saturday night Aragon went to the Zubar ranch to kill van Sickle, but he found his intended victim entertaining friends so he abandoned his scheme. Aragon felt he needed assistance to kill van Sickle and he recruited Antonio Gonzales to accompany him on Monday evening, February 12. When they arrived at the Zubar ranch Gonzales hid outside while Aragon, who had concealed a pistol, went to talk with van Sickle. Aragon promised to return the lumber and van Sickle agreed that as soon as it was returned Aragon was forgiven and no prosecution would be sought. Gonzales awaited a prearranged period of time and then knocked on the door, but van Sickle was apprehensive and took his pistol to the door, not concerned about an unarmed Aragon at his back. He opened the door and stared into the darkness trying to see who had knocked and, while preoccupied, Aragon drew his pistol and shot him in the back of the head. The bullet passed through van Sickle's brain and exited through the left eye and, though the wound was ghastly and surely fatal, Aragon ordered Gonzales to shoot into the prostrate body.

A week later Mr. Newman went to the Zubar ranch to replace van Sickle but, not finding him, started for the Keyes ranch and met Fred Keyes, Albert Forest and Blentine Garcia on the road. The three men said they were going to check on van Sickle after a guilt ridden Aragon confessed to the murder and location of the body. They sent for Rockwell's deputy, John Legg, who went to the Zubar ranch to bring in the remains of van Sickle as well as the two murderers. Van Sickle was buried at Rockwell and the two prisoners were lodged in jail. At their examination Aragon and Gonzales were held over for the grand jury and indicted, but in October there was a mistrial. At their retrial in Judge Bantz' courtroom in July 1895 Aragon and Gonzales were convicted of first degree murder and sentenced to hang. The appeals process concluded in August 1896 when the territorial supreme court affirmed the record of the lower court; the date for execution was set for September 24, 1896. Aragon continued to be ravaged by guilt and the fear of being hanged so on September 9 he held back a spoon following his evening meal, carefully honed the edge of the handle to razor sharpness, and cheated the hangman by cutting his own throat from ear to ear. Antonio Gonzales was left to face the hangman alone when Governor William T. Thornton refused to intervene.

Gonzales rested quietly during his last night, awoke in good spirits at an early hour, but had no appetite. He washed and dressed in the new black suit provided by the county, waived the reading of the death warrant, and seemed anxious to proceed. Within the enclosure one hundred witnesses waited as the condemned man walked to the gallows at 6:55 A.M. He made a brief speech while his wrists and arms, ankles and knees were being pinioned, the black cap was pulled over his face, and the noose was adjusted. At 7:00 A.M. the trap was sprung and his neck was broken in the fall. The attending physician reported that the pulse ceased in six minutes and pronounced Gonzales dead. The body hung for several minutes more and was then cut down, placed in the coffin provided by the county, and buried that evening

Albuquerque (NM) Daily Citizen: September 30, 1896; *Roswell (NM) Record*: September 25, 1896.

Padilla, Perfecto; Ring, Rosario
September 24, 1896

The Vipond brothers had been successful miners in Butte, Montana, but chose New Mexico as their new land of opportunity. Fifty-eight-year-old John Vipond traveled to Rio Arriba in search of rich mineral deposits. He outfitted with pack burros and supplies at Bland, New Mexico, and joined a small party of prospectors. Vipond soon struck out on his own and on August 6 he camped on the edge of a small park fifteen miles from Copper City. Vipond was asleep in his blankets when Perfecto Padilla snuck up and crushed his skull with a poll pick (a single-pointed miner's pick) handle. Padilla ransacked the camp, taking everything of value, including the burros, Vipond's hat and a $30 watch.

Vipond's party returned to Bland but when they found Vipond had not returned they formed a search party. On October 4 the skeletal remains of John Vipond were found and John's brother, William, spent the next year and $6,000 investigating his brother's death. He learned that soon after his brother was murdered Perfecto Padilla was seen in Santa Fe wearing John's hat and driving the stolen burros; he also pawned John's watch. When Padilla returned to town he was arrested and charged with the murder, but Padilla might have avoided indictment if an eyewitness had not come forward.

As soon as Padilla was safely behind bars Jose de la Jesus Archibeque came forward and said that he had been riding past Vipond's camp when he saw Padilla, with the pick handle in his hand, moving through the brush toward the sleeping figure. Archibeque was unarmed and afraid, especially after he witnessed the brutal murder of the sleeping man, so he hid until Padilla left the scene and was afraid to come forward until the murderer was jailed. The pick handle described by Archibeque had been collected near Vipond's remains and the octagonal end had fit neatly into the dents in the murdered man's skull. Padilla was tried at the fall session of the district court and found guilty of first degree murder. Judge Laughlin set the date of execution for December 15, 1895, but a stay was granted so that the case could be appealed to the territorial supreme court. Months passed before the decision of the lower court was affirmed and the new date of execution was set for September 24, 1896. Governor William T. Thornton, when petitioned, declined to intervene

Celestino Romero and Carlos Ulibarri, who lived at Tierra Amarilla, Rio Arriba County, had a long-standing feud. Romero sent for Rosario Ring to assist him in handling Ulibarri. Ring, it was soon learned, was a dangerous character who was suspected of killing his wife and child in the Colorado Territory. On September 16, 1895, Romero and Ring were on a spree and once both men were sufficiently fortified with liquor they went in search of Ulibarri. They found him in front of his home and broke a beer bottle over his head, but the struggle continued and Ulibarri's mother came to investigate the commotion. When she arrived the men stopped fighting and she convinced her son to return home with her. When the Ulibarris got to the door Ring pulled his six-shooter and shot Carlos once in the back. Carlos died in his mother's arms within a few minutes. Ring and Romero were indicted and tried before Judge Laughlin at the fall term of the district court and Romero was acquitted but, on November 21, Ring was found guilty of first degree murder and sentenced to hang a month later. The execution was stayed pending an appeal to the territorial supreme court but finally the decision of the lower court was affirmed and the new date for the execution was set for September 24, 1896; when petitioned, Governor William T. Thornton declined to intervene.

Padilla and Ring were kept in the Santa Fe jail, so when the time neared for the execution Sheriff Felix Garcia arranged to take the condemned men to Tierra Amarilla and requested a cavalry guard. The sheriff took Padilla and Ring by train to Chamita, where Lt. Coleman and six cavalrymen met them. The escort rode with the wagon containing the prisoners while the sheriff, his deputies, William Vipond and the father of Ring's victim made up the remainder of the guard. When Ring saw Ulibarri's father he sang, "Oh, where is my wandering boy tonight." Once in Tierra Amarilla the prisoners were confined in the Rio Arriba County jail where Father Antonio Jouvenceau heard their confessions and ministered to their religious needs.

The single-trapdoor, single-rope gallows had been erected near town, so when the time arrived the prisoners were taken from their cells and driven to the gallows in a wagon. Padilla was selected to go first and he was asked if he wanted to address the crowd; he made a brief speech in which he professed his innocence and blamed greed and revenge for his predicament. Padilla was moved onto the trapdoor and prepared, but he weakened as his ankles and wrists were bound and had to be supported by two deputies until the black cap was pulled on and the noose tightened around his neck. The two deputies stepped back suddenly and in that instant the trap was sprung. Padilla's neck was broken in the fall and after hanging a sufficient length of time to ensure death his body was cut down, placed in a coffin, and removed a short distance from the scaffold to await the hanging of Ring.

Ring was then brought from the wagon to the gallows and showed no sign of nervousness as he climbed the stairs and stood on the trapdoor. When given the opportunity he made his speech in English and Spanish, blaming his crime on overindulgence in liquor and warned the spectators to "let liquor alone," and concluded, "and may God help me!" Ring's wrists and ankles were pinioned as he spoke and when he finished the black cap was pulled over his face and the noose adjusted with the greatest efficiency. In a moment he was dropped to his death, and his neck was broken in the fall. After hanging a time sufficient to ensure he could not be revived Ring's body was cut down, placed in his coffin, and removed to the place where the remains of Perfecto Padilla waited. Both coffins were then loaded on the wagon and taken to the cemetery, where they were buried later that evening.

Albuquerque (NM) Citizen: September 26, 1896; September 29, 1896; October 30, 1896; *Sante Fe Daily New Mexican*: September 22–24, 1896; September 28–29, 1896; November 14, 1896; November 18, 1896; November 26, 1895; *Albuquerque (NM) Morning Democrat*: November 16, 1895; September 23, 1896; *Roswell (NM) Record*: September 25, 1896.

Garcia, Jesus
November 6, 1896

Jesus Garcia met a beautiful senorita in Mexico and married her, but marital discord quickly followed and Garcia murdered his wife before fleeing into Arizona. It was not long before Garcia was having trouble with another woman but this time he used his knife to disembowel his unnamed victim. Garcia fled to Loma Parda, New Mexico, and on July 26, 1896, found himself at odds with Isabella Montoya. Without warning he fired at her four times with his six-shooter while she was distracted gathering mesquite beans. One bullet struck her in the face while a second bullet lodged in the small of her back, but this time Garcia was arrested and lodged in the Doña Ana County jail. Montoya lingered for several weeks but finally died of her wounds and Garcia was charged with her murder. He was indicted and held for the fall term of the district court and after a brief trial the defendant was convicted of first degree murder, and on October 9 he was sentenced to hang on November 6, 1896. There was no delay from appeals to the territorial supreme court nor from the applications for commutation or respite sent to Governor William T. Thornton.

The gallows had been erected in the courthouse yard and by noon on November 6 a crowd of more than two hundred, including fifty women, had assembled to witness the hanging. Father Lasesigne had provided religious consolation to Garcia for days, and he provided physical support as Garcia made his way to the scaffold. Sheriff Patrick Garrett and deputies James Brent and Rudesill escorted the condemned man onto the trapdoor. Deputy Brent pinioned Garcia's wrists and ankles while deputy Rudesill took his place at the release. Sheriff Garrett pulled the black cap over Garcia's face and adjusted the noose. A moment later, at 1:00 P.M., Garrett gave the signal and the trap was sprung and the condemned man broke his neck in the fall. Dr. E.V. Cowan monitored Garcia's vital signs and pronounced him dead at 1:17 P.M. and three minutes later Garcia's remains were cut down, lowered into the waiting coffin, and delivered to his friends. The body was taken to the Catholic church for a brief service, prepared for burial, and by sundown Garcia was in his grave.

Rio Grande (NM) Republican: July 31, 1896; August 14, 1896; October 9, 1896; November 6, 1896.

Alarid, Lauriano; Gonzales, Antonio y B.; Gonzales, Francisco y B.; Valencia, Patricio
April 2, 1897

Francisco Chavez was sheriff of Santa Fe County in 1890 when he attended a baile where Jose Silvestre Gallegos was a guest. Francisco y Borrego Gonzales suddenly appeared at the dance and without provocation shot and killed Gallegos. Chavez did not witness the shooting but arrested F. Gonzales and placed him in the Santa Fe County jail to await action by the grand jury. F. Gonzales was indicted but his trial was delayed, and legal procedures prolonged his stay in a cell. Jailor Juan Pablo Dominguez had a longstanding feud with the prisoner and he abused him at every opportunity. F. Gonzales complained to Sheriff Chavez but his pleas fell upon unsympathetic ears, and this finally led to a heated argument between the prisoner and the sheriff, which ended when Chavez pistol-whipped his prisoner into unconsciousness, F. Gonzales swore that he would kill the sheriff when he was free.

F. Gonzales was acquitted at his trial for shooting Gallegos, but his friends convinced him that the animosity toward him would lead to serious trouble so they helped him leave the region. During the eighteen months that he was absent Chavez' term of office ended. F. Gonzales returned to Santa Fe in mid–May 1892 and on May 29 forty-two-year-old ex-sheriff Chavez was ambushed and murdered while returning home. Although there was no clear evidence of the responsible parties, jailor Dominguez, the following day, declared that there was "not enough room in Santa Fe for me and F. Borrego." He and two friends went in search of F. Gonzales and found him in the company of his brother Antonio and Lauriano Alarid, so with the odds at three to three it left F. Gonzales and Juan Dominguez to face each other alone. Dominguez reached for his six-shooter first but F. Gonzales was faster and shot accurately, killing Dominguez.

The Borrego brothers and Alarid were arrested, tried, and acquitted, as the killing had clearly been in self-defense. The sheriff of Santa Fe County, William P. Cunningham, continued his investigation into the death of his predecessor and by January 1894 he had enough evidence to arrest six men — F. Gonzales, A. Gonzales, Lauriano Alarid, Francisco Rivera, Patricio Valencia, and Hipolito Vigil. They found F. Gonzales and arrested him and while shackling his wrists saw Vigil approaching. They ordered Vigil to surrender but the fugitive jumped behind a wooden pole and pulled his six-shooter. He was immediately riddled with pistol and rifle bullets and buckshot. The other four men surrendered without resistance and Rivera was soon cleared and released but the Borrego brothers, Alarid and Valencia were indicted for murder. Their trial commenced on April 23, 1894, with jury selection and concluded on May 29, thirty-seven days later. All four defendants were found guilty of the first degree murder of Francisco Chavez and sentenced to hang. The territorial supreme court stayed the execution while they reviewed the case but finally affirmed the lower court's decision. Governor William T. Thornton, at the direction of President Grover Cleveland, granted a respite. When President William McKinley took office he extended the respite for ten days so he could also review the case, but he found no cause for interference. The date for the quadruple execution was finally scheduled for Friday, April 2, 1897.

The gallows was built adjacent to the jail and was covered with canvas so that the seventy-five witnesses would not see the four condemned men until they dropped through the trapdoor. On Thursday night Sheriff Harry C. Kinsell placed a guard at the cell and a death watch of ten men inside the jail, and the following morning these were reinforced with forty troops from Cavalry Companies B and E. Father Fourchegu was given access to the prisoners at an early hour to provide religious support, and was with them when the death warrant was read by Sheriff Kinsell at 7:30 A.M. The priest remained with the men until 9:00 A.M. when the sheriff returned and announced that their time was up. At 9:07 the four condemned men, with wrists bound behind, marched to the gallows, Valencia first to stand on the west end of the trapdoor, then Alarid, A. Gonzales, and finally F. Gonzales in the east. The men stood shoulder to shoulder as their arms, knees and ankles were tied with rope. They declined to make any statements, so the black caps were pulled over their faces and the nooses adjusted, and at 9:09 A.M. the trap was sprung and they dropped six feet. All but Valencia, because he was of lighter weight than the others, broke their necks in the fall. Valencia strangled to death but was the first to be pronounced dead at 9:13 A.M. by Drs. Sloan, Brady and Crosson. The doctors continued to monitor the vital signs of the hanging men and A. Gonzales was pronounced dead at 9:15; F. Gonzales at 9:16; and, Alarid at 9:17 A.M. All four men hung until 9:28 to ensure there could be no resuscitation, and the last man was cut down at 9:35. Their remains were placed in the coffins provided by the county and released to the families of each deceased for burial.

Santa Fe Daily New Mexican: September 24, 1896; April 2, 1897; *Albuquerque (NM) Weekly Citizen*: April 3, 1897.

Ruiz, Jose P.
June 1, 1900

Twenty-four-year-old Jose P. Ruiz, alias Jose Romero, had been loitering around Albuquerque since May 23, 1898. Donacian Garcia came into Albuquerque on May 28 to attend a church celebration. Afterward he and Ruiz went on a spree at Ruberto's and by 6:00 P.M. both men were quite drunk. They bought a bottle and as soon as Ruiz mounted he began waving his six-shooter above his head; the pair then rode down the river road heading for the Mexican camp a mile west of the river. Bunicio Anaya was saddling his horse when the pair of drunken riders approached and Ruiz, who had holstered his pistol, drew and fired twice at Anaya, the pistol misfiring both times. The riders continued fifty yards where seven-year-old Patricio O'Bannon and six-year-old Arturo Garcia were playing marbles beneath a tree in front of the O'Bannon house. Ruiz, who still had his pistol in his hand, fired at them twice and one bullet struck Patricio in the left shoulder, passing through and severing the jugular vein, and the second bullet struck Arturo in the back of the neck, injuring the spinal column slightly. Patricio bled to death within minutes but Arturo survived following a dangerous surgery. Ruiz fired one more shot as he crossed the bridge and on the west side of the river Ruiz fired his last shot at a small child in front of the house of Manuel Jarmillo, the bullet passing through the child's clothing.

Sheriff Thomas A. Hubbell, deputy sheriff Newcomber and deputy U.S. marshal Fred Fornoff were in pursuit within a half hour. Garcia was captured in the Mexican camp while Ruiz was overtaken and captured on the road to Rio Puerco. A posse of nearly fifty men joined in the pursuit of Ruiz and, when the fugitive was captured, they would have executed him on the spot if the officers had not intervened. Ruiz and Garcia were jailed but Garcia could not be charged with the murders as he had not fired a shot nor even drawn his pistol. Ruiz was indicted, tried and convicted at the October term of the district court, and sentenced to hang. The long appeals process commenced but finally all efforts to obtain a new trial, or clemency from Governor Miguel A. Otero, were exhausted and in January 1900 the date for execution was set at June 1. At the fatal hour Ruiz climbed the stairs and stood on the trapdoor without wavering. The noose was adjusted by the attending physician and the black cap was pulled over his face by a deputy sheriff. A black man had been hired to spring the trap and he did his work only a heartbeat after the deputy sheriff completed his task. Ruiz did not break his neck in the drop so it took twenty-three minutes for him to strangle to death. The body of the condemned murderer was then cut down and delivered to his father for burial.

Santa Fe Daily New Mexican: June 1, 1900.

Ketchum, Thomas E.
April 25, 1901

In 1885 Thomas Edward Ketchum joined brother Sam and the two boys worked various ranches from Texas to Wyoming over the next five years. Along the way they became close friends with William R. Carver and David Atkins. In the Arizona Territory the Ketchum brothers were working on the Bell ranch in the New Mexico Territory when Sam had a dispute with the ranch foreman. The boys left but soon returned and stole supplies from the Bell storehouse, and this crime was followed quickly by a burglary of the post office and store at Liberty, New Mexico. Levi Herzstein and Merejildo Gallegos pursued the Ketchums and were shot to death, so the Ketchums fled into the Arizona Territory to avoid a murder charge and joined Carver and Atkins in Graham County.

In 1897, Tom Ketchum, Carver and Atkins headed south to Lozier, Texas, a water stop on the Galveston, Harrisburg & San Antonio Railroad. Just before 2:00 A.M. on May 14 Ketchum and Carver climbed over the tender, covered engineer George Freese and fireman James Bochat with pistols, and took control of the train. They stopped the engine at the next cut, where Atkins waited with horses and explosives. The three men captured express agent W.H. Joyce, blew open the way-safe, and took three sacks of plunder which Wells, Fargo & Company valued at $42,000. Sam joined the train robbing gang and they enlisted the help of a fifth man named Charles Collings and the party of five made their way to the Twin Mountains bend between Folsom and Des Moines.

On September 3, 1897, they stopped the southbound No. 1 Gulf, Colorado & Santa Fe Railroad train and blew the safe, but found less than $3,500. On December 9 Ketchum and Carver took the horses two miles west of Stein's Pass and when the westbound No. 20 train came at 9:00 P.M. the men who remained at the station forced station agent Charles St. John to show a red warning light to stop the train. They captured engineer Thomas W. North and his fireman and required North to pull ahead and stop, and the robbers then approached the express car. Messenger Charles Jennings and two other guards began firing at them and four robbers were wounded, Collings was killed, and the gang was forced to flee, leaving Collings' body behind.

On April 28, 1898, the gang took over Comstock Station on the Galveston, Harrisburg & San Antonio Railroad halfway between Langtry and Del Rio, Texas. At 11:30 P.M. the westbound No. 20 was leaving the station when two masked men climbed over the tender and captured engineer Walter Jordan and his fireman, uncoupled the passenger cars from the rear of the express car, and forced Jordan to take the engine, tender and express car westward to Helmet before they stopped the train. The robbers cleaned out the way-safe and then blew open the through-safe; the plunder totaled $20,000. The gang moved north to Mustang Creek, Texas, and on July 1, 1898, stopped the westbound Texas Pacific No. 3 train, threw a switch and directed the train onto a siding where the passenger cars were uncoupled and the engine, tender and express car were pulled ahead. They blew the safe and took out an estimated $50,000.

In the spring of 1899 the gang split up and T. Ketchum went to Prescott, Arizona, but by July he was heading toward New Mexico to reconcile with Sam. He was unable to find his brother, or any gang member, so he decided to rob a train singlehandedly. On August 16 at 10:20 P.M. Ketchum climbed aboard the blind baggage of the southbound No. 1 Colorado & Southern Railway train when it stopped at Folsom, captured engineer Joseph Kirchgrabber, and had him stop the train at the bend four miles south of the station. The conductor was Frank Harrington and he armed himself with a shotgun while Ketchum was forcing fireman Tom Scanlon to unlock the couplings, but Scanlon cut the air hoses, which locked the brakes. As they worked, Conductor Harrington opened the door to the coach behind the express car and discharged his shotgun at Ketchum. The heavy load of buckshot tore a gaping wound in the robber's right arm just above the elbow and Ketchum stumbled off into the darkness. He managed to make it to his horse but had already lost so much blood he was too weak to mount, so he lay down beside the tracks. The following morning the posse arrived, found the wounded robber, and easily captured him. He was indicted, tried for assault on a U.S. mail agent, and sentenced to a ten year prison term. While at the prison his wounded arm became so infected that it had to be amputated and the following year Ketchum was tried again, this time for an "assault upon a railroad train with intent to commit a felony," a capital offense in New Mexico. He was convicted and sentenced to hang.

As the date for the prisoner's execution approached he was taken to Clayton in Union County and lodged in their jail. A priest came from Trinidad and stayed with the condemned man throughout his last night. After breakfast Ketchum dressed in the new suit provided by Sheriff Salome Garcia. After the death warrant was read to him in his cell he seemed anxious to proceed, but it was still early. At 11:30 A.M. he asked for music and it was provided by a violinist and a guitarist. At 1:15 P.M. Ketchum began his march to the gallows accompanied by the priest, with the sheriff on his right and Harry Lewis of Trinidad on his left. The condemned man climbed the stairs with a firm step, his head down, and took his place upon the trapdoor. His wrists and arms, knees and ankles were pinioned; the noose was adjusted; and the black cap pulled over his face. He had declined to make a speech but when there was a brief delay he called out, "Let 'er go, boys!"

Governor Otero had sent a man to oversee the preparations and ensure that everything went smoothly. The drop had been calculated at five feet nine inches, a few inches longer than required for a man near two hundred pounds, but the governor's man increased the length of the drop and at the last minute Sheriff Garcia, concerned the drop still might not do the work, increased it to seven feet. The hangman's rope had been carefully soaked and stretched with a heavy weight to remove elasticity and the stretching made the rope, already a bit thin for a hanging, almost cordlike. Where fiber crossed fiber it was lubricated with soap to ensure the knot would slide easily. When the moment arrived the sheriff cut the rope releasing the trapdoor and Ketchum's body fell; the thin rope cut through the condemned's neck, muscles and spine, decapitating the prisoner. The body and head fell to the ground separately with blood spurting from the torso's neck while the head, still in its black bag, rolled about beneath the gallows. The bloody rope rebounded high into the air. After photographers were done with their grisly work documenting the worst bungled execution in the history of the western frontier the head and torso were collected by the undertaker and the head was sewn on. The remains of Thomas Ketchum were buried in the town's cemetery the following day.

Santa Fe Daily New Mexican: April 26, 1901; *San Francisco Chronicle*: April 26, 1901.

Huerta, Toribio
April 26, 1901

Toribio Huerta, born in Northern Zacatecas, Mexico, was married and had three children. He was determined to be a good provider so he worked in the fields and occasionally found work on the railroad, but still they merely subsisted. In early 1901 he learned that good paying jobs could be found in Colorado and on February 18, 1901, Huerta took five pesos, a small quantity of food, and his father's revolver and walked into New Mexico, following the railroad tracks. Three days later he reached the Chappel Switch Station between Aden and Cambray and was resting in a culvert beneath a wooden bridge when he met Pablo Rivas, a nineteen-year-old Mexican returning home from Colorado. Huerta shared his food with Rivas while the boy told him of his adventures in Colorado, and Rivas showed him $60 he had earned. The two men slept beneath the bridge that night and in the morning Rivas expressed interest in Huerta's old revolver. Huerta set up several targets and allowed Rivas to take shots at them, without success. Huerta suggested that Rivas throw his hat into the air while Huerta demonstrated his own shooting ability by shooting the boy's hat in flight. Rivas agreed, threw his hat into the air and watched, waiting for the shot. Huerta, however, shot Rivas once in the back, then shot him once more to be sure he was dead. The murderer dragged Rivas' body beneath the bridge, covered it with dry brush, and set the pyre afire. Huerta continued walking toward Cambray; soon a train passed in the opposite direction, and the train's conductor saw him and the smoke ahead. Thinking the bridge was afire he stopped the train to investigate, used dirt to extinguish the flames, and discovered Rivas' body.

The train continued to Aden, where E.H. Mead, section foreman, telegraphed the El Paso Station to be on the lookout for three lone Mexican travelers reportedly making their way along the tracks. The El Paso police chief captured Cruz Vigil, Jose Garcia and Toribio Huerta. Doña Ana County's Sheriff Jose Lucero went to the scene to investigate the killing and on March 2, 1901, a hearing was held before Judge Parker and Cruz Vigil, who had learned about the murder, turned state's evidence against Huerta. On March 16 Huerta and Garcia were indicted for murder, but Garcia was proved innocent and released. Two weeks later Huerta was tried for murder and his explanation was that he had intended to shoot the hat but the gun discharged prematurely, shooting Rivas in the back, and he then shot Rivas again to kill him and tried to dispose of the body. He was found guilty of first degree murder and sentenced to hang on April 26, 1901. The appeals process did not delay the execution and applications for clemency, sent to Governor Miguel A. Otero, were denied.

By Friday morning, April 26, more than five hundred spectators gathered to watch the hanging. The death warrant was read to the prisoner in the jail corridor and the condemned man was brought out at 10:00 A.M.; once upon the trapdoor he gave a thirty-five minute speech. Huerta had asked to be allowed to give the signal to spring the trap so he could be prepared for the drop, but had to be prompted three times with, "Are you ready Toribio?" before he responded, "I am ready!" The trap was sprung by deputy Robert Burch at 10:45 A.M. and Huerta's neck was broken in the fall. The attending physician monitored his vital signs and pronounced him dead fourteen minutes later, and at 11:05 the body was cut down and placed in the plain coffin provided by the county. Huerta's remains were buried shortly after noon.

Doña Ana County (NM) Republican: February 23, 1901; *Santa Fe New Mexican*: April 26, 1901.

Sanchez, Jose
July 5, 1901

Jose Sanchez was a twenty-seven-year-old tramp who stole everything he could lay his hands on. He had earned the nickname Loco Joe because he had a "fierce and violent temper and would break upon the slightest provocation." On Christmas night Sanchez' camp near Santa Rita was robbed of blankets and wearing apparel so Sanchez appealed to the authorities, who issued a search warrant for other camps in his vicinity, but nothing was found. On December 26, 1900, Sanchez accused Catarino Alemandarez of the theft and a heated argument ensued, but ended without a fight. Later that day parties driving along the Georgetown Road found Alemandarez shot three times but alive. They rushed him into Santa Rita and notified the authorities, and the dying man was able to describe his attacker, Jose Sanchez, who had been seen by several men in the vicinity of the shooting when it occurred. Deputy Edwards arrested Sanchez and brought him to Alemandarez' bedside, where the prisoner was positively identified as the assailant; this was recorded as an antemortem declaration. Alemandarez died soon afterward and the prisoner was charged with his murder. Sanchez was tried at the spring term of the Grant County district court and in his defense Sanchez testified that he was a mile away at the time and, "in any case, no one saw me shoot Alemandarez." After only thirty minutes' deliberation the jury found Sanchez guilty of first degree murder and Judge F.W. Parker sentenced him to hang on June 7, 1901. The execution was delayed a month, to July 5, while the case was reviewed but the appeals process was quickly exhausted and Governor Miguel A. Otero refused to intervene.

On the Wednesday preceding the execution Father Augustin Morin was given the unpleasant task of telling Sanchez that all hope was lost. On Thursday evening the condemned man retired at 9:00 P.M. but did not sleep until 2:00 A.M., then awoke periodically until daylight. He arose at 8:00 A.M. and after breakfast he dressed in the neat black suit provided by the sheriff. He also wore a shirt of negligee so that a stiff collar would not interfere with cinching the knot. At 11:45 Sheriff Arthur S. Goodell read the death warrant to the prisoner, and it was translated into Spanish by Perfecto Rodriguez. Thirteen minutes later Sanchez was marched to the gallows, which had been constructed in Silver City's courthouse yard. Father Morin walked on one side whispering words of comfort while the sheriff walked on the other side and several deputies followed. The condemned man stepped onto the trapdoor without prompting and declined to make a statement. He seemed eager to proceed and said he was "anxious to get out into the country." Sanchez was prepared by the deputies and as soon as the black cap was in place the trap was sprung. The drop was five feet six inches, which broke his neck, and the county physician pronounced him dead at 12:15 P.M. The body was then cut down and delivered to undertaker W.S. Cox for burial in a county plot.

Albuquerque (NM) Daily Citizen: May 1, 1901; May 11, 1901; May 24, 1901; *Santa Fe Daily New Mexican*: July 5, 1901; *Silver City (NM) Enterprise*: May 10, 1901; *Silver City (NM) Independent*: July 9, 1901.

Duran, Alejandro
April 3, 1903

Alejandro Duran was born and raised in Messily, Doña Ana County, New Mexico, but when he turned eighteen years of age he went to California. He married and his wife gave birth to three children. When Duran's mother died in late 1900 he returned to Las Cruces with his family, got his father, then brought the family to the Arizona Territory. He found work in Lucino and moved his family into a dugout, but after working only a week he had a disagreement with the section boss, which ended in a shooting affray, and he fled, never to see his family again. Duran found railroad work at various places under the alias Jose Telles and finally settled at Kennedy, New Mexico. One morning Duran and a friend went on a day long spree before cashing in their tickets for the evening meal, but the ticket taker refused them entrance due to their intoxication and finally pushed Duran out of the doorway. Duran pulled his six-shooter but, in the confusion, he shot and killed his friend. He was arrested and lodged in the Santa Fe County jail.

On the evening of January 18, 1903, Duran and fellow prisoner Alfred Hampe decided to escape. Jailor Epitacio Gallegos was away on an errand so the two prisoners overpowered night watchman Victoriano Casados and locked him in a cell. They went to the jailor's quarters and found Gallegos' pistol and Sheriff Harry C. Kinsell's rifle. Duran took the rifle and suggested that they leave but Hampe wanted to wait for Gallegos to return, lock him in a cell, and thereby delay an alarm and pursuit. When the jailor returned Hampe got the drop on him but the jailor grabbed the pistol and they wrestled for possession. Duran stayed back as Hampe fired one shot close to Gallegos' face, causing powder burns, but this failed to deter the jailor so Duran fired a single rifle bullet, which pierced Gallegos' heart, killing him instantly. The exiting bullet wounded Hampe's arm, and after the shooting they both fled.

Hampe was captured on January 23 near Thornton with his feet frozen and his arm wound festering; Duran had abandoned him that morning. On February 7 Duran was captured making his way to Mexico and as soon as he was made a prisoner he insisted that his shot had wounded Hampe and that Hampe had shot Gallegos, but there was no question of the weapons each prisoner possessed and the coroner confirmed that the deceased had been killed by a rifle bullet. Duran was arraigned before Judge John R. McFie on March 5; he entered a plea of guilty, and was then sentenced to hang on April 3.

On the night before his execution Duran retired at 10:00 P.M. and in the morning received Fathers Vincent Thomas and C. Joseph Hintzen at an early hour, and they spent the morning in prayer. At 8:55 A.M. Sheriff Kinsell and Deputy C.R. Huber, with the two priests, accompanied the condemned man onto the scaffold, where he made his last statement in Spanish, translated by John Conway, and concluded, "Please excuse me if I have offended you. I want you to pardon me and help me by praying for me. I pray everybody to be forgiven." He then knelt, repeated the act of contrition, and arose to embrace each priest. The condemned man was positioned on the trapdoor and his wrists and arms, knees and ankles were bound. The noose was carefully placed over his head and, as the black cap was shown to him, he said, "Good-bye, boys!" Just as the cap was drawn down Deputy Huber signaled with, "All Right!" and the sheriff pulled the lever. Duran dropped four feet, breaking his neck, and Drs. J. Diaz and J.H. Sloan grabbed his wrists to steady the body. They monitored his vital signs and in four and one half minutes pronounced him dead, and two minutes later the body was cut down and delivered to undertaker Charles Wagner. A funeral service was conducted at the Catholic church at 8:00 the following morning and afterwards Duran was buried in the Rosario cemetery.

Santa Fe New Mexican: April 3, 1903.

Conley, John
February 26, 1906

E.N. Jordan of Minneapolis was auditor for a company trying to sell six mining claims located at the Guadalupe Placers four miles from Questa in Taos County. The company did not advance the money to assess the claims so Jordan had to pay for the contract out of his pocket, and hired John Conley for $100 to assess the six prospect holes. Conley hired nineteen-year-old James Redding, sixty-eight-year-old Charles Purdy and Jesus Herrera. Herrera was fired after only one day of work and this enraged Redding and Purdy; Redding was already upset by the small payment for the contract, while Purdy insisted Conley still owed him money from a previous job.

Early on the morning of January 16, 1904, Conley collected his crew to go to the diggings and found that Redding and Purdy were drunk and had been up all night at a wake. He finally got them mounted and riding toward the Guadalupe Placers, but just before they left town Redding bought a bottle of whiskey and shared it with Purdy on the trail. Conley refused to drink with them and when they arrived at their camp, which consisted of several tents, Conley ordered them to go to work immediately but both men refused, insisting that they first prepare a meal. After they ate Conley told them to leave the dirty dishes and go to work, but again they refused. Conley later said that Purdy, with the support of Redding, threatened him and ordered him to leave, but when Conley started for his horse Purdy threw an iron skillet at him.

Redding and Purdy then each picked up an axe and Redding went for Conley, who pulled his six-shooter and warned the boy to stop. When Redding continued forward, and was within striking distance, Conley shot him twice, killing him instantly. Purdy then, according to Conley, started for him with his axe and he was shot in the shoulder; but Purdy did not drop the weapon as he ran into one of the tents. Conley went to the tent and, seeing that Purdy was inside lying in wait to kill him, shot him dead. Conley returned to Questa and then rode on to Red River, where, to avoid surrendering to deputy sheriff Pedro Barela, he surrendered to J.M. Phipps. Conley had his examination before the justice of the peace and was taken to Taos to be held for the grand jury. He was indicted at the spring term of the district court and tried first for the murder of Redding. The physical evidence at the campsite did not support Conley's version of the killings, but the jury divided during early deliberations with seven jurors for first degree murder and five jurors split for second and third degree murder. The larger number finally prevailed and Conley was convicted of murder in the first degree and sentenced to hang in two months; but the appeals process dragged on for nearly two years. Finally the territorial supreme court affirmed the lower court's trial record and the date for the execution was set at February 26, 1906. Governor Miguel A. Otero, when petitioned, refused to intervene.

A crude gallows was erected within the adobe walls of the jail yard and guards were placed on the wall and rooftops to prevent uninvited witnesses from viewing the event. On the final morning the condemned man arose early and at 7:30 A.M. took a small pocketknife he had hidden from his guards for some time, opened both blades, and cut his throat from ear to ear. He severed the windpipe but missed the artery, but still he had lost a lot of blood when discovered. He managed to fight off the guards for several minutes before they restrained him and Dr. T.P. Martin was called. The doctor stopped the bleeding and dressed the wound and a priest was then summoned, in case he did not survive. By 9:20 A.M. it was clear that Conley would not cheat the hangman if the sheriff acted quickly, so those who had been invited to witness the execution were summoned and seventeen men hurried to the jail yard. The condemned man was carried onto the platform and seated upon a stool on the trapdoor but he had to be supported as his wrists and ankles were tied. The hood was pulled on and the noose adjusted and, as the attending deputies stepped back, the trap was sprung. Conley started to slump over as he fell, so he did not fall straight, and the length of the four foot drop was shortened by being seated so that the condemned man's neck was not broken. He strangled and struggled for some time but after ten minutes he was pronounced dead by Dr. Martin. The body hung several minutes longer before being cut down and deposited in his coffin, the coffin placed in a wagon, and driven directly to the public cemetery where his grave had already been dug.

Albuquerque (NM) Evening Citizen: February 27, 1906; *Albuquerque (NM) Morning Journal*: February 27, 1883; *Santa Fe New Mexican*: February 26, 1906.

Medlock, John
May 25, 1906

John Medlock, a Negro, was born in Tennessee but moved to New Mexico at an early age and settled at Gardiner in Colfax County. In 1902 he became interested in a Negro woman named Carrie Boyd but she was living with a Negro named McKinley, and she often used his last name. Medlock was persistent and finally convinced Boyd to leave McKinley and move into his home, not an easy task for a man with a horrible scar where he had lost an eye in a mine explosion. Boyd soon became restless, perhaps only having used Medlock as an excuse to leave McKinley, but within a few weeks she left Medlock and moved into a nearby house with friends. Medlock tried to convince Boyd to resume their relationship, but he was not even permitted to enter the house. Later that same night Medlock found Boyd in the saloon and, without a word of warning or a moment's hesitation, he drew his six-shooter and fired a single shot, which killed his paramour instantly. As Boyd's body slumped to the floor a patron reached out to catch her but Medlock waved him off with his pistol saying, "Let her alone, I want to see her drop." He continued to brandish his weapon in a threatening manner until he had cleared the barroom, then rushed out into the night and disappeared in the darkness.

Medlock fled to Oklahoma, where he was arrested on a charge of attempted murder upon another woman; he was recognized from the descriptive circular which had been distributed widely. He was tried, convicted and sent to Leavenworth Prison for three years on the attempted murder charge, and upon his release he was extradited to Colfax County, New Mexico, to stand trial for the murder of Boyd. He was convicted and sentenced to hang on May 25, 1906, and the appeals process was completed before the date set and Governor Miguel A. Otero refused to interfere.

On his final morning Medlock retired at 1:30 A.M. but arose a few hours later and after breakfast joked and sang as the guards collected the dishes. When his time came the death warrant was read to him in his cell and he was led out to the gallows. The scaffold was a single-trap, single-rope affair, so with two men to hang that day (see Arguello, David, below) Medlock had been chosen to go first. He had written out his statement and, while his wrists and ankles were being pinioned, it was read for him as he stood silently on the trapdoor. His statement thanked Sheriff S. Marion Littrell and the Reverend Jacobs for their kindness and warned other men to avoid liquor and bad company. After a prayer from the Lutheran church service, the black cap was pulled on and the noose adjusted, and at 10:15 A.M. the trap was sprung. Medlock's neck was not broken in the fall and it took thirteen minutes for him to strangle to death. The body was allowed to hang another seven minutes before it was cut down and placed in the coffin provided by the county. The gallows was then prepared for the second hanging.

Sante Fe New Mexican: July 23, 1903; May 25, 1906.

Arguello, David
May 25, 1906

David Arguello was a family man living at Bowen, Colorado, with his wife and family, and he had built a reputation as a good husband and father. In June 1903 the Dassart family moved to Bowen and took up residence at house No. 5 across from the saloon. Daughter Celia was a pretty nineteen-year-old who immediately caught the attention of Arguello and he pursued her to the point of harassment and embarrassment. Arguello persisted after continually being rebuffed. Mrs. Dassart was determined to end Arguello's advances, so she called upon Mrs. Arguello. David Arguello returned home while Mrs. Dassart was visiting and Mrs. Arguello berated him loudly, finally striking him on the head with a sugar bowl during a particularly heated moment. He became enraged and grabbed his pistol, but left without using it. Mrs. Dassart, hopeful that the matter was finally closed, returned home but did not notice that Arguello followed closely. Several men in the saloon saw Arguello follow Mrs. Dassart into her house and close the door and then heard three shots fired. Arguello then walked out of the house and into the hills.

Mrs. Dassart's brother was informed and he ran to the house, where he found his sister lying face down in a doorway to a rear room, the one bullet in her back having pierced her heart and killed her instantly. Arguello got his horse and fled, with an armed posse in close pursuit, but he managed to keep them at bay with gunfire and escaped. He eluded capture for two years by using aliases and taking employment in remote locations, but during that time he supported his family and even lived with them for brief periods. In October 1905 Francisco Garcia of Trinidad, Colorado, learned that the Arguello family had moved to Johnson's Mesa in Colfax County, New Mexico, and believed that David Arguello could be found nearby. He was deputized to arrest Arguello and on Thursday, October 19, Garcia went to the Floyd ranch. He went unarmed as he did not anticipate finding the fugitive. However, Arguello was at the ranch and during a struggle Arguello shot Garcia; the deputy died after identifying his murderer. Arguello was arrested in Colfax County, indicted, tried and convicted of the first degree murder of Garcia. He was sentenced to hang and, after a brief appeals process, the date for his execution was set for May 25, 1906. Governor Miguel A. Otero, when petitioned, declined to intervene.

On his last day Arguello retired at half past midnight and awoke at an early hour but remained in bed and refused breakfast. The gallows was a single-trapdoor, single-rope apparatus and Arguello was the second man to hang that day (see Medlock, John, above). A new rope had to be installed, so he was not taken from his cell until 10:45 A.M. He climbed the stairs with a firm tread and took his place on the trapdoor, where his wrists and ankles were pinioned while Sheriff S. Marion Littrell read the death warrant. After the sheriff concluded his part the prisoner's written statement was read to the witnesses. Then Arguello made a short speech, saying, "I am getting ready to meet God today. I am sorry for breaking the law and also sorry for my past." He prayed briefly before the black cap and noose were adjusted and the trap was sprung at 10:53 A.M., breaking his neck in the fall. The attending physician pronounced him dead in seven minutes and the body was cut down five minutes later. Arguello's remains were placed in the coffin provided by the county and he was buried that afternoon.

Sante Fe New Mexican: July 23, 1903; May 25, 1906.

Sais, Carlos
January 11, 1907

In the summer of 1906 John Billingslea, a telegraph operator in Colorado, and his wife decided to spend their vacation prospecting in New Mexico. It was to be an adventure of sightseeing and camping and there was the hope, ever present, that they might actually stumble upon some valuable mineral deposit. They went to the Manzano Mountains and moved about randomly for two months, not always finding good water and wild game that would have made their enterprise carefree. They met William McLaughlin, who had camped and hunted that area for three years. He had mining experience, so they struck a deal whereby the Billingsleas would fund a prospecting venture and McLaughlin would guide them and locate their camps near good water and an ample supply of game.

Reports reached them of rich mineral deposits found recently in the Oscura Mountains and, though McLaughlin was not familiar with that area, they decided to go there and prospect. While passing through the village of Mountainair they met Carlos Sais and Eliseo Valles and hired them as guides. At noon of the second day the party stopped near Red Hill so that the four men could refill the water casks at a spring Sais and Valles said was at the summit; Mrs. Billingslea stayed behind to set up camp. Mr. Billingslea loaned his Luger pistol to Sais while McLaughlin loaned Valles his Winchester rifle, and in twenty minutes Mrs. Billingslea heard several shots but dismissed them as the men shooting at some mark. Sais and Valles returned at 1:30 P.M. with dry canteens and asked if the other men had returned, but when Mrs. Billingslea said they had not the two guides left again, and in ten minutes returned with water. They ate and loitered about the camp until 4:00 P.M. and then took all the horses and left. Mrs. Billingslea remained in camp two days expecting her husband and McLaughlin or the two guides to return, but when no one came she hiked to a nearby village and asked for help.

A search party set out for the campsite and from there followed the trail of the four men less than a half mile. They found the body of McLaughlin shot in the back of the head, the bullet from the Luger pistol exiting above the left eye and killing him instantly. Billingslea, as he ran, was shot in the shoulder and managed some distance before he collapsed from the loss of blood; the helpless man was murdered by a single shot to the back of the head from a Winchester rifle. Carlos Sais and Eliseo Valles were arrested and indicted for first degree murder and Valles agreed to plead guilty to second degree murder at the fall term of the district court, but Sais pled not guilty and his trial took two days. On December 17, 1906, both men were brought before Judge Frank W. Parker for sentencing; Valles was sentenced to ninety-nine years in the territorial prison, while Sais was sentenced to hang on January 11, 1907. There was no appeal nor application for clemency.

The gallows was constructed under the elevated passageway between the jail and the courthouse, which amplified and echoed every hammer blow and unnerved the prisoner during his last days. He was attended by the Reverend Martin, who remained with him only as far as the jail door when he was led out at 3:40 P.M. on January 11. Sais was accompanied by Sheriff Aniceto C. Abeytia and jailor Silvestre Abeytia, and he took his place on the trapdoor, where he spoke briefly to the crowd of twenty witnesses. He said he had done wrong and warned all young men not to follow his example; confessed his crime; said his only regret was that no relatives visited him while he was in jail; and finally asked the sheriff to send his remains to San Juan across the Rio Grande near Sabinal. It took only a few minutes for the jailor to pinion Sais' wrists and ankles, adjust the noose, and pull on the black cap, and at 3:50 P.M. the sheriff sprang the trap. Drs. C.G. Duncan and C.F. Blackington monitored his vital signs and pronounced him dead in five minutes. The body remained suspended several minutes more and was then cut down and placed in the coffin provided by the county. The following morning Remegio Peña drove the wagon containing Sais' remains to San Juan for burial.

Denver (CO) The Daily News: January 12, 1907.

Amador, Martine
January 13, 1908

Cepcion Mendosa was a pretty young Mexican woman who operated a boardinghouse at Victorio, twenty miles west of Deming, New Mexico; her boarders were the unmarried miners from the Bradley and Wyman camps. She was a hard working and industrious landlady and she attended strictly to her own affairs and never mixed business with pleasure. Martine Amador was a young miner who had come from the Bradley Camp and soon after his arrival in Victorio he began to develop a strong attraction for Mendosa, but she repeatedly rebuffed his advances and refused his proposals to live with him. During the early evening hours of July 19, 1907, Amador went to the home of Mendosa to propose a liaison, but he was rejected again. This time, unlike his previous visits, Mendosa's suitor became loud and threatening and Mendosa, believing she was in danger, fled to a friend's house and remained until 11:30 P.M., when she felt confident that Amador had left. However, when she neared her home Amador suddenly sprang from his hiding place and, without hesitation or remark, shot her. The .22 caliber bullet pierced Mendosa's heart, killing her within minutes.

An alarm was sounded immediately after the shot was heard and men scattered in all directions, intent upon intercepting the murderer, but Amador fled directly out of the country and was always a step ahead of his pursuers. Judge Chapman held an inquest on July 21 and the jury named Amador as the murderer. Mr. Wyman of Wyman's camp wired the authorities in Deming, so deputy sheriff J.A. Baker went to Victorio and took up the trail. He learned that the fugitive was heading for the Bradley Camp in the Florida Mountains, so he telegraphed for camp foreman Hathaway to be on the lookout for Amador. Amador arrived at the Bradley Camp at 11:00 P.M. Sunday, July 20, and was immediately captured. He was returned to Deming to await action of the grand jury, and he was indicted and tried at the November term of the Luna County district court. The defendant was convicted of first degree murder and sentenced to hang on December 13, 1907, but Governor George Curry granted a thirty day respite to consider the application for commutation. When the time had elapsed the governor found no further cause to interfere.

By his final hours the condemned man had resigned himself to his fate with the help of Father Morin. The death warrant was read by Sheriff Don Johnson at 10:00 A.M. and then, accompanied by the sheriff and Father Morin, Amador was taken from his cell and walked to the scaffold in the jail yard. Eighteen witnesses had been invited to the hanging, but Amador declined to speak to them. The prisoner's wrists and ankles were pinioned, the noose adjusted, and the black cap pulled on by jailor Jennings, and at 10:30 A.M. Sheriff Johnson sprang the trap. Amador's neck was broken in the fall and the attending physician pronounced him dead in three minutes; the body hung only two minutes more before being cut down and placed in the plain coffin provided by the county. Neither relatives nor friends had made a claim for Amador's remains so he was buried in a county plot that afternoon.

Deming (NM) Graphic: January 17, 1908; *Deming (NM) Headlight*: July 25, 1907; December 5, 1907.

NORTH DAKOTA

Approximately two thirds of the region that became North Dakota was acquired from France in 1803 as part of the Louisiana Purchase. The northeastern part of the region was acquired from Great Britain in 1818. However, to say this vast area belonged to the United States is misleading, as the Indian tribes were well established and strongly defended their lands. In 1812 British colonists tried to establish the Red River settlement at Pembria but it failed; forty years later Charles Cavaler brought settlers to Pembria and established an agricultural colony. The Dakota Territory was established in 1862 and, in spite of the dangers, the territory was opened to homesteading on January 1, 1863. The railroads arrived in 1871 and the period from 1878 to 1886 was labeled the "Dakota Boom." The Dakota Indians fought this intrusion for two decades but were eventually overwhelmed. On November 2, 1889, the Dakota Territory was divided into the states of North and South Dakota and North Dakota became the 39th state.

Miller, George
October 30, 1885

Eighteen-year-old George Miller arrived at the Snell farm in July 1884 and convinced the Rev. C.Y. Snell of his fervent religious commitment; he was hired at $30 per month and was accepted into the family home near Inkster, North Dakota. The two men harvested a fine crop of wheat and Snell sold a portion of his grain for several hundred dollars, then placed the remainder of the crop in storage at the farm. After he had purchased the farm Snell obtained cattle, horses, and improved farming implements, then planted his fertile acres. In early January 1885 Snell sent three of his four children to Grand Forks to attend school. On January 16, 1885, he left his wife, Abbie, and their ten year old son, Herbie, on the farm with George Miller while he "went on an errand of good will to Mayville where he was engaged in missionary labor for his Lord and Master." He took $300 with him but left some money, keepsakes, and the children's savings locked in a trunk in the house.

Shortly after January 16 Miller sold a load of grain to agent Holden for $205 and asked if he could deliver an additional load of wheat, but without Snell's approval Holden refused. On the evening of January 24, while Abbie and Herbie slept, Miller took an axe and crept up on them. He struck each a single blow with the axe to disable them and then finished his deadly work; from the appearance of the bodies when found, they never awoke. He threw blankets over the bodies, placed the bloody axe beneath the bed, and ransacked the house, taking everything of value. After committing the murders he hitched up Snell's best team of horses to their sleigh and in minus thirty degree temperatures started for Grand Forks. On January 25 Miller registered at the Northwestern Hotel, ordered the team put away, and prominently displayed his new-found wealth. He said his brother would arrive on the train and they were going on to Winnipeg.

He then went to the Chicago Clothing House and bought a buffalo overcoat, black valise, pocketbook, and other items intended to disguise his appearance and told the proprietor that he had sold a team of horses and was on his way to Turtle Mountain. He next went to the barbershop, where the barber cut his hair close and shaved him, to further change his appearance, and while being attended he mentioned he was going to Crookston. There was no train until Sunday so he went to Fargo and stayed a few days, and spent a considerable sum of money on "variety women" before continuing on to Brainard, Minnesota, where he lodged at the house of Malcolm McLaren. There he associated with women of loose character and soon had spent all his stolen money.

He tried to find work with McLaren but was not hired, so he continued on to Anoka, Minnesota. Meanwhile Henry Rutherford, who lived alone at Bennett's place about sixty rods from the Snell home, became suspicious when he saw no "stir or animation at the farm." On Friday he investigated and found the stock nearly famished, so he tended the animals before sounding the alarm; then neighbors broke into the home, found the bodies, and summoned lawmen. Suspicion immediately fell upon the absent Miller, so a telegram was sent to Grand Forks from Inkster asking that Miller be arrested, but the fugitive had already fled the city. On the Sunday after the bodies were found the St. Paul newspapers carried the story of the murders and a description of Miller, and McLaren recognized his former boarder as the fugitive and secured a deputization. McLaren went to Anoka and registered at the same hotel as Miller but, realizing the danger of trying to arrest Miller in his room, he waited until the murderer came down to breakfast. Miller went into the washroom and McLaren came up behind him, placed the muzzle of his pistol against the fugitive's back, and took Miller's pistol from his back pocket. Miller then tried several times to make some excuse to get away but the deputy put his man on the train to Brainard.

On the way, Miller confessed to McLaren the details of the murders and said that he had acted alone, but claimed that he was crazed by liquor and had been chided by Mrs. Snell, and therefore was not responsible for his actions. After he was indicted he changed his story, claiming that one of the witnesses against him, Henry Rutherford, was an accomplice but this allegation was not given credence. Miller was tried in August and he pled guilty but Judge William McConnell required that all testimony be taken so that a record of the case would be available if an appeal was filed. On September 4 Judge McConnell sentenced Miller to hang on October 30, 1885.

On the day before the execution C.B. Pratt, Miller's attorney, delivered a message from Governor Gilbert A. Pierce refusing to interfere. Miller then received the sacrament from the Rev. F. Doran. Miller had mentally composed a statement to be made at the scaffold but, fearing he would not be able to speak at that moment, wrote it out and gave it to the Reverend Doran. He retired to his cell at 9:00 and spent ninety minutes with the Reverend Snell trying to convince him that Henry Rutherford was responsible for the murders of his wife and child. During the late hours he received a number of visitors, including Rutherford. Miller said to Rutherford, "You know you had a hand in this thing, as I have said," and Rutherford replied, "It is a lie and you know it. I don't like to be lied about." Later Rutherford was asked about Miller's statement and he said, "[N]o such thing. It was all a dan-g'd lie!" The gallows, designed by Sheriff Jenks, was erected in the northeast corner of the yard and completed on Thursday, October 29. The apparatus was tested using a two hundred pound sack of sand and found to work perfectly.

On his last day Miller retired at 1:00 A.M. and slept soundly until 7:30 A.M.; after breakfast he was taken into the office, where he was attended by the Reverends Currie and Doran. Sheriff Jenks appeared at 1:30 P.M., read the death warrant, and escorted the prisoner to the gallows, where he took his place on the trapdoor. The sheriff asked if the prisoner had anything to say and Miller spoke for fifteen minutes, saying nothing new. Sheriff Jenks stood behind Miller and when the prisoner finished, his wrists and ankles were pinioned with straps. When the sheriff presented the cap of brown worsted Miller began to speak again, and as the noose was being positioned Miller asked the sheriff to say good-bye to his friends. At 1:45 P.M. the trap was sprung and the fall broke Miller's neck. Coroner Roundwell monitored his vital signs and pronounced him dead at 2:00 P.M., and in ten minutes more the body was cut down. Miller's remains were carried to a jail cell, the straps were removed, and undertaker Caswell took charge of the body. He was buried that afternoon.

Grand Forks (ND) Daily Herald: October 28, 1885; October 30–31, 1885.

Cole, James W.
March 24, 1899

Sophronia Ford, at fourteen years of age, was a tall and particularly attractive Negro schoolgirl living in Bismarck, North Dakota. James W. Cole, a burly Negro, was infatuated with the young lady and made his interest known to her, but she rejected his advances. On December 12, 1898, Ford was walking north on 6th Street on her way to the North Ward School when Cole, without warning or hesitation, shot her to death. He threw down several love letters he had scribbled for the occasion and marched directly to the Burleigh County jail and surrendered. Cole was anxious to proceed, so three days after the crime, the court being in session at the time, the murderer pled guilty and Judge Walter Winchester sentenced Cole to hang on March 24, 1899.

During months in jail Cole had refused the services of clergy, stating that formal repentance would avail him nothing, and he desired no minister on the scaffold. On his last night he was moved from his cell to a second floor room at the rear of the courthouse and, though he had been a model prisoner, he was closely guarded by deputies Mason, Weymouth, and Bowman. He retired at midnight but arose at 3:00 A.M. and dressed in a new black suit, white shirt with collar, white tie, and black shoes he had shined until they gleamed. Witnesses began to arrive at 4:00 A.M. and in an hour they were all present in the courtroom awaiting the call to step outside into the enclosure in the courtyard.

After breakfast Cole talked of his crime and his feelings for his victim, and he seemed anxious to join her. At 5:55 A.M. Sheriff Bogue told Cole his time had come and the prisoner shook hands with everyone present, then waived the reading of the death warrant. His wrists were cuffed behind his back, a strap fastened about his chest holding his arms, and the black cap was perched atop his head. Sheriff Bogue led the way, with deputies Mason and Bowman on either side of the prisoner. When the procession reached the center of the courtroom Cole looked around for a place to access the platform and asked, "Where is it?" Sheriff Bogue directed him to a window and he stepped through onto the platform at 6:10 A.M. The scaffold had been erected so that the prisoner walked directly out of the building and to the center of the scaffold, where he leaned against the rail for support. He hesitated, glancing over the crowd in the dim morning light, and finally had to ask if his friends were present.

When he was assured they were among the witnesses he made a brief statement saying he was sorry for murdering his victim and thanking the lawmen who had been good to him while in jail. He stepped onto the trapdoor and called out, "Let her go, Boys!" However, the prisoner was not yet prepared for the drop so Deputy Weymouth applied the straps to his knees and ankles while Deputy Patterson positioned the noose and pulled the black cap over his face. There was a brief delay while every preparation was inspected and the deputies were given time to step clear, and at 6:14 A.M. the trap was sprung. County physician Ballard applied his stethoscope to Cole's chest and pronounced him dead in four minutes; after hanging two minutes more Cole's remains were lowered to the platform beneath the gallows and the noose was removed. A coffin had been stored there and the body was deposited before Dr. Ballard examined the remains of the prisoner and reported that the prisoner's neck had been broken in the fall. The coffin was removed to the undertaking rooms, and from there the body would be delivered to the cemetery and buried by the county as there were no friends or relatives to claim it.

Bismarck (SD) Daily Tribune: March 24, 1899.

OKLAHOMA

In 1541 Francisco Vazquez de Coronado became the first European to see the land that would become Oklahoma, but it was the French who explored the eastern region. France claimed the area but ceded it to Spain in 1763; in 1800 France reacquired the region. Three years later France sold Oklahoma to the United States as part of the Louisiana Purchase, excepting the panhandle, which was acquired by the U.S. from Mexico in 1845. The area was inhabited by the Osage and Quapaw Indians but by 1818 they had ceded all claims to their land. A number of treaties signed by various tribes over the next twenty-five years turned over most of the remaining land, which was then occupied by a number of Indian tribes relocated by the U.S. government under their policy of "relocation and concentration." The Oklahoma Territory was carved out of the Indian Territory on May 2, 1890, and on November 16, 1907, the Oklahoma Territory and Indian Territory were joined to become the State of Oklahoma, which became America's 46th state.

Allen, Jim
September 24, 1894

In 1889 twenty-year-old Jim Allen, a full blooded Choctaw Indian, was arrested in Jackson County, Oklahoma, on a charge of larceny. The principal witness against Allen was another Choctaw Indian named Dixon Hunter. To avoid a prison sentence Allen lay in wait for Hunter and decapitated him with an axe. Sarah Battlesi, also Choctaw, saw the murder but Allen threatened her with the same fate if she reported the crime. Battlesi, after four years, told authorities the details of Hunter's murder. Allen was arrested, brought to trial in August 1894, convicted of murder in the first degree, and sentenced to be shot on September 24, 1894. Neither appeal nor application for clemency sent to Governor William C. Renfrow delayed the proceedings. The prisoner was kept in the Pushmataha jail, a flimsy affair from which he could have easily escaped, but the condemned man believed escape would brand him a coward — a fate worse than death.

On the day of his execution a large crowd, including thirty Choctaw Indians, assembled at the Pushmataha courthouse grounds at an early hour. The early arrivals were rewarded when the prisoner made his appearance at 8:25 A.M. for Christian services followed by Indian ceremonies. After returning to his cell Allen's spiritual advisor explained that he could not expect forgiveness if he did not confess his sins, and the prisoner replied, "I am guilty. I killed Dixon Hunter." At 1:00 P.M. Deputy Robert Jackson placed a lemon crate five paces from the courthouse door and then brought Allen from the jail. When Allen asked if his "tricke" had come — meaning his coffin and burial clothes — he was assured they had arrived. He then knelt to pray and upon rising rolled open the bosom of his shirt, revealing a quarter-sized white mark painted over his heart. He took his seat on the crate facing the courthouse door while Deputy Jackson retired into the courthouse. Staring at his watch and with his .44 caliber Winchester at hand, Jackson waited. Seconds before the designated time of 2:00 P.M. a distant dog barked and Allen, thinking it an omen, was distracted, so deputy Jackson seized upon that opportunity to shoot the condemned man once in the heart. Allen froze for several seconds before lurching backward onto the ground and uttering several loud groans. Blood spurted four feet into the air from the half inch hole in his breast, so two Indian companions stuffed cotton and rags into the wound to stem the gusher. Allen bled to death in eight minutes. The remains were buried that evening.

Logansport (IN) Daily Pharos: September 24, 1894; *Galveston Daily News*: September 25, 1894.

Milligan, John
March 13, 1895

Twenty-one-year-old John Milligan, a Negro, lived with the Clark family, Gabe and Hannah and their six-year-old grandchild Lucy, in a hut in Deep Fork township northeast of Oklahoma City, Oklahoma County. Milligan had lived with the couple for over five years and was treated as an adopted son, but he refused to work so the old man had to support the family. On the evening of November 3, 1893, Milligan attacked the elderly Negro couple with an axe and first struck a blow at the head of the old man, but it was a glancing blow and a terrible struggle ensued. Hannah awoke and rushed to her husband's aid but they were overpowered by the younger man and he crushed their skulls; then he cut their throats from ear to ear. He next turned his attention to Lucy and, though she pleaded, "Oh John, don't hurt me, don't kill me," he hit her on the head with the ax, cut her throat, and left her lying on the bed. He was certain that all three were dead when he ransacked the cabin and stole $200, with which he planned to return to Tennessee.

When found, Mrs. Clark was dead, her husband was in a dying condition and lasted only a few weeks, and it was believed that Lucy would also die of her wounds. However, Lucy was young and strong and finally rallied; she lived to testify against Milligan. As soon as the crime was discovered Milligan's description was widely circulated and published in a special edition of the *Globe-Democrat*, and a reward was posted. The murderer had fled to St. Louis, where he was recognized and arrested on November 6, but he gave the name William F. Odin. The description of Milligan tallied so closely, however, that he was subjected to close questioning and he finally admitted he was Milligan. He then claimed that the couple had first attacked him and he had killed them in self-defense, and insisted that Lucy had been injured in the struggle. Questioning continued and he eventually weakened, confessing every detail, but then he justified the murders by stating it was his intention only to rob the Clarks and when discovered in the act of searching the cabin he felt the only way he could avoid arrest was to commit murder.

Milligan was returned to Oklahoma City and lodged in the county jail, and indicted, and his trial commenced in Judge Henry W. Scott's courtroom in early February 1894. He was convicted of first degree murder and within a few days he was brought into court and the date of his execution was set for April 6, 1894. Appeals and applications for executive clemency delayed the proceedings until November, when the territorial supreme court affirmed the lower court and the date for Milligan's execution was scheduled for January 11, 1895. Then began the efforts of those opposed to the death penalty on general terms, led by Dr. J.R. Furlong, and on the evening of January 10, 1895, acting governor Lowe granted a sixty day respite. The gallows, which had been erected on the fairgrounds, was taken down and stored while Furlong tried to get a bill thorough the legislature abolishing the death penalty; but he failed.

In late November Milligan escaped from jail by crawling through a ventilator, only to be recaptured in two days by Charlie Fightmaster, returned to his cell, and heavily shackled. Milligan then worked the "insanity dodge" and his bizarre behavior apparently worked well enough for the guards to become complacent. On January 1, 1895, Milligan again escaped, this time by jumping through a glass door, but he was bareheaded, barefooted, and in his shirt sleeves as he made his way in two inches of snow. He was easily tracked to a hay mow a few miles from Choctaw City and recaptured by Harry and Jim DeFord. After he was returned to his cell he was rewarded with another delay as Governor William C. Renfrow granted a two month respite to consider the matter. On the day before the execution Dr. Furlong and A.C. Scott went to the governor and discussed the imminent execution of

Milligan, but the governor decided that the enormity of the deed and the heartlessness displayed by the murderer would not permit his intervention. The sheriff was informed to proceed and he then sent out invitations to the jury of twelve citizens, several officers, the county physician and attorney, other appropriate officials, and five friends of the condemned man.

The fairgrounds would no longer work for the gallows site so during Milligan's last week a tall fence was erected around the jail yard and the gallows was constructed within the enclosure. Milligan was weighed and found to be one hundred eighty-seven pounds, so the gallows was tested with a two hundred pound sack of sand. The apparatus worked perfectly. On the morning of the execution a canvas was stretched over the gallows to prevent any view from neighboring buildings. On the day before the execution Milligan's spiritual advisers spent the entire day with him trying to distract him from his impending doom, but he was weakening and it was thought he would have to be carried on to the scaffold; the death watch — James W. DeFord, Tom Owens, and jailor Garver — were on the alert for any attempt to cheat the hangman.

On Wednesday, March 13, 1895, Milligan arose early and paced restlessly until deputy Jim DeFord asked what he would like for breakfast. Milligan replied, "Jimmie, this is the last breakfast I will get to eat, and I will leave it all to you." DeFord went to the Saddle Rock Restaurant and ordered the best breakfast they could prepare and then, at 9:00 A.M., Sheriff Harry DeFord appeared at the cell door and read the death warrant. Milligan was attended by Friar C.C. Calf and the Reverends Harper and Ross, who prayed and sang hymns with the condemned man. Milligan said, "In two hours I will be sitting on the throne with God." He took great pains in dressing and said of his appearance, "I look so nice, I wish my sister could see me now." Dr. Furlong was in the cell with the prisoner and told him, "John, poor boy, I strove hard to save your life. I first strove hard to have the Governor commute your sentence to life imprisonment; and after I failed in that, I then tried hard to have the legislature abolish the death penalty in the territory. I did this because I was and am thoroughly convinced that the infliction of the death penalty is wrong."

The prisoner's arms were bound behind and at 11:55 A.M. the procession formed, with Sheriff DeFord leading with the prisoner, deputy sheriff's in front and rear, and the procession followed by the clergymen. The prisoner was escorted onto the scaffold and positioned on the trapdoor, where his knees and ankles were bound; next came the noose and black cap. The coroner's jury of twelve men and the others invited by the sheriff, and five friends invited by the condemned man, waited patiently beneath the gallows while Sheriff DeFord and several deputies entered the small booth where the release was located. At 12:03 P.M. a sharp blow from a hatchet severed the cord, the trap was sprung, and Milligan dropped to his death. Dr. Feigenbaum waited beneath and monitored vital signs until he pronounced him dead. The body was then cut down and lowered into a coffin in preparation for burial later that day.

Waterloo Iowa State Reporter: March 21, 1895; *Logansport (IN) Pharos*: February 14, 1894; *San Antonio Daily Light*: April 6, 1894; *Logansport (IN) Daily Journal*: December 2, 1894; *Oklahoma City Daily Oklahoman:* March 13–14, 1895; *Fort Wayne News*: January 2, 1895; *Lincoln Nebraska State Journal*: November 7–8, 1893.

Oregon

Oregon was a part of the "Oregon Country" when it was acquired from Great Britain. A dispute persisted over the northern boundary of the Oregon Country between the parallels of 54°40' and 42°, which at the time was under joint control of the United States and Great Britain and consisted of the area between the northern border of California and Russia's southern border of Alaska. Although there was a strong movement in America to claim the 54°40' boundary, President James K. Polk surprised everyone when, on June 15, 1846, he agreed to the parallel of 49° to separate the United States from Canada. His agreement gave the United States sole control over Oregon. The "Oregon Territory," stretching from the northern border of California to the new Canadian border, and including what would become Washington, Idaho, and Montana, was established in 1848. Oregon was admitted to the Union as the 33rd state on February 14, 1859.

Kendall, William
April 18, 1851

William Hamilton leased several acres of land from William Kendall, a successful homesteader in Marion County, Oregon. Kendall had a small number of hogs which ran wild and were often found on the leased acreage, but this was not the cause of any difficulty between the men because it was common practice in those times. When it was butchering time the hogs would be gathered and, because the process of butchering and preserving the meat was labor-intensive and time-consuming, several neighbors would perform the work together. When several hogs disappeared, Kendall accused Hamilton of theft but he denied any knowledge of the missing hogs. Hogs often disappeared, as they could wander into some remote location and die from a number of causes, be killed and consumed by wild beasts, or just walk off into the dense forest. Hamilton decided to vacate the property but honor the lease by having his sister Melissa Taylor and her husband, William, take up residence on Kendall's land, which angered the lessor.

Kendall visited Mary Ann Mott, a thirty-year-old widow with seven children who depended on Hamilton for their livelihood. He told her, "I'm going to give him a round. As mean a man as him ought not to live." On the morning of January 7, 1851, Kendall was at Henry Smith's home and the two farmers were in the process of butchering hogs when John Hamilton arrived and demanded that Kendall meet with William. Kendall could not leave while engaged in the butchering process and this resulted in demands that Kendall go immediately to the Mott farm a mile away, but John finally gave up and left. At 3:30 P.M. Kendall went to the farm of Hiram and Sarah Taylor, expecting to find William Hamilton, but they directed him to the Mott farm. Kendall then went home and Hiram left for the fields; he saw Kendall take out his gun and fire a test round, reload, and start down the road toward the Mott farm. At 5:00 P.M. William Hamilton mounted his horse and left the Mott farm, and had only ridden a short distance when the Motts heard a shot. They went to investigate and found Hamilton dead and sent for the authorities.

The scene of the murder was investigated and boot tracks were found and, though they were not distinctive, they were the identical size and design of Kendall's boots. The distances between key locations that were walked and timed showed that Kendall could have been at the place the shooter took up his position at the moment of the killing. Kendall was arrested by coroner William Gilham and Joshua McKinley at 10:00 P.M. and, at his examination, he was held to await action by the grand jury. On March 27 Kendall was indicted on a charge of first degree murder. At his arraignment he pled not guilty, and selection of a jury was set for March 31. On April 2 the trial commenced before Judge William Strong and the defense tried to prove that Kendall was too far away at the time of the killing to be responsible. The incriminating evidence was all circumstantial but so well linked that the jury deliberated only thirty minutes before returning a verdict of guilty as charged. Kendall was sentenced to hang at Salem on April 18, and was heavily ironed and guarded for the two weeks until his execution. Kendall mounted the gallows with a firm step and took his place on the trapdoor, where his wrists and ankles were pinioned, the noose adjusted, and the black cap pulled over his face. Suddenly the prisoner lunged forward, trying to strangle himself prematurely, so Sheriff William J. Herren grabbed him and stood him up, and a moment later the trap was sprung. Kendall dropped, breaking his neck in the fall, and was allowed to hang long enough to ensure he was dead and then was cut down, put in his coffin, and buried.

Oregon City Oregon Statesman: April 18, 1851; April 25, 1851; *Oregon City (OR) Spectator*: January 14, 1851; January 16, 1851; April 10, 1851.

Turner, Creed
December 4, 1851

Martha Jane Bonser, though only fifteen years old in 1851, was remarkably beautiful and certain to attract the attention of young men in the region around Suavie's Island near Portland, Oregon. The Bonser family — father, mother, three boys and three girls — had been in Oregon for four years. It was common practice for established families to take in new arrivals, at least until they could get settled, and sometimes they even took early settlers as boarders. Creed Turner, a young man who arrived in Oregon before it became a territory in 1848, boarded with the Bonsers. Edward A. Bradbury, the twenty-four-year-old son of a wealthy Ohio mill owner, was a recent arrival in Oregon and a boarder in the Bonser home. Turner had been attracted to Martha for some time but when Bradbury arrived they seemed to have eyes only for each other. Turner became jealous and was determined to see an end to their attraction for one another, so on October 19, 1851, as the family and Bradbury gathered for a quiet evening, Turner entered the room and walked up beside Bradbury. Without comment or provocation he pulled a dirk, a dagger-like knife usually used for stabbing, and slashed at the young man. He gutted Bradbury with five deep gashes to his stomach, and then inflicted more deep cuts to his left side, chest, and arms. A stomach wound, when the intestines or bowels were perforated as in this instance, resulted in a terrible infection and Bradbury lingered for a day in excruciating pain and fever before he died. The next day he was buried in the Portland cemetery.

William H. Bennett, Washington County's sheriff, was summoned to the Bonser home and told the details of the murder, which Turner did not deny. The sheriff arrested Turner and the following day, after Bradbury died, the grand jury met and indicted Turner for first degree murder. The trial followed in three days and after hearing the testimony of eleven prosecution witnesses Turner was found guilty as charged in the indictment, and on November 4 Judge O.C. Pratt sentenced him to hang in one month.

During the last four weeks of his life Turner worked furiously on his autobiography and as the days passed he became more frantic and dedicated to penning the story of his life. When Turner's time was up Sheriff Bennett went to his jail cell and read the death warrant, then bound the prisoner's wrists in back in preparation for the walk to the scaffold. Turner complained: "It need not be tied so tight, I have large hands and it will not slip." He was marched to the gallows, climbed the steps with a firm gait, and took his place upon the trapdoor. He was asked if he had anything to say to the crowd of two hundred fifty spectators so he stepped to the railing and said, "I committed the deed and now I'm paying for it. If I had to do it over again I would. I leave my written words for you all to read." Turner then returned to the trapdoor and, as the Rev. John S. Griffin and Elder James McBride gave brief sermons, the prisoner's legs were pinioned. There was no black cap nor any sort of blindfold present so he was allowed to scrutinize the crowd as he awaited the drop. Once the noose was in place the sheriff descended to the pin holding the trapdoor and, consulting his watch, pulled the pin at exactly 11:00 A.M. as required in the death warrant. Turner broke his neck in the fall and after he was pronounced dead the body was allowed to hang a sufficient time to ensure that he could not be revived. He was placed in a cheap pine coffin provided by the county and buried that afternoon.

Oregon City Oregon Statesman: December 9, 1851; *Oregon City Spectator*: May 7, 1847; October 28, 1851; November 4, 1851; December 9, 1851; *Portland (OR) Weekly Times*: October 28, 1851; October 30, 1851; December 6, 1851.

Wimple, Adam E.
January 8, 1852

In 1845 Adam E. Wimple traveled to the Oregon Country to seek his fortune. He filed a claim on a section of land near Mary's River and worked for three years on improvements, a requirement to "prove-up" on the land, but when he heard of the big gold strike in California he hurried south. He returned in the spring of 1849 with $10,000 in gold, sold his land claim, and moved to Portland, where he opened a boardinghouse with tavern. In the fall of 1850 he started a general merchandise store in Tuality Plains, Washington County. Wimple was looking for a wife and finally settled his attention on a very young girl who lived near his new store. Mary Allen was twenty-two years younger than her thirty-five year old suitor but she was living a terrible life of abuse, as she had been born out of wedlock and was constantly punished by her stepfather for this "transgression." When the wealthy Adam Wimple proposed marriage, Mary jumped at the opportunity to get out of her stepfather's house.

The odd couple married on January 5, 1851, and then a series of difficulties followed, with Mary leaving her husband several times. Wimple moved about the country trying to find just the right place for them to be happy, finally suggesting they move to the East Coast to get her away from the influence of her parents, but she refused and they remained in Oregon. On August 1, 1851, friends were at the home of the Wimples and some remark by Adam angered Mary. After their guests left at 11:00 A.M. Mary threatened to leave her husband and never return and, he would later say to gain sympathy, that she had confessed to adultery but he had forgiven her.

Adam claimed that Mary ran out of the house but he dragged her back as she bit and kicked him and tore his shirt. He said he went into another room to change his shirt when Mary appeared at the door with a pistol and took a shot at him, but the bullet passed through the sleeve of his fresh shirt. They struggled for the gun and, gaining control, Adam struck Mary twice on the head and Mary fell to the ground, begging for her life and agreeing to go anywhere he wanted and never leave him. Adam said he saw that the two wounds he had already inflicted were fatal and he could not bear to see his wife suffer so he administered the coup de grace — a third very heavy blow to her temple. He said that once Mary was dead he dragged her body to the front of the fireplace hearth, removed the boards that covered the entrance to their basement, and threw her body down.

After he gathered the necessities to make his escape he saddled his mare and set the house afire. Neighbors first saw the smoke at 1:00 P.M. and hurried to put out the flames, but the house was nearly burnt down when they arrived. Polk County Sheriff Benjamin F. Nichols was summoned and, after the fire was extinguished, a thorough search was made and the entrance to the basement discovered.

When the men went down they found that Mary had crawled to the northwest corner of the basement, apparently still alive and trying to survive the flames and smoke. All that remained of the young wife was part of a hip, pieces of burned flesh and entrails, and various rings and beads which Mary always wore. Men began searching the region for Wimple, a reward was posted for his arrest, and fourteen days later James Nesmith captured him wandering in the woods afoot.

Wimple then made a great effort to make his first, detailed, self-serving confession to Nesmith as he was being escorted to jail. The prisoner had his examination, repeating the same story he had been practicing for days, but was held to answer to the grand jury. On August 20 Wimple filed off his shackles and escaped but remained free only two days before surrendering, suffering from hunger and exposure. Now the community was up in arms, first over the brutal murder of a young girl and then the possibility that the murderer would escape, and there was strong talk of lynching. There was little doubt of prejudice in Polk County and no chance for a fair trial, so Wimple was moved to the jail at Oregon City in Clackamas County where the trial would be held on a motion for a change of venue. Wimple was indicted in early September and on September 11, 1852, his trial began in Judge Thomas Nelson's Oregon City courtroom. Many witnesses were called to testify to the domestic problems between the married couple and about the threats Wimple had made toward his wife over the previous months. Clackamas County sheriff William C. Dement fancied himself a detective and he made rudimentary scientific examinations of the evidence, and proved that the "powder burns" on Wimple's shirt were actually smeared on and the tear had been done by hand, rather than from a bullet passing through. It was clear to the jury that the entire "confession" of the killing of Mary Wimple was concocted to seek a lesser penalty, or even an acquittal. The trial took two days and soon after the jury retired they asked for one clarification before returning with a guilty verdict. Judge Nelson sentenced Wimple to hang at The Dalles in Polk County on October 8, 1852.

On the final morning the shackles were removed by the blacksmith and then Sheriff Nichols read the death warrant to Wimple in his cell. The prisoner was taken from the jail and put aboard a wagon and driven to the gallows, which had been built on the outskirts of the city near the cemetery. He was escorted through the crowd and climbed the stairs with a firm step, not showing any sign of nervousness. He had written out his confession and delivered it to the *Oregon Statesman* newspaper reporter so, when asked if he wanted to speak to the large crowd, he declined. The condemned man was positioned on the trapdoor and his wrists and ankles were pinioned, the noose adjusted, and the black cap pulled over his face. In a moment the trap was sprung and he fell, breaking his neck. He hung for some time as his vital signs were monitored by the attending physicians but finally they pronounced him dead, and after hanging a few minutes more he was cut down and lowered into a waiting coffin. Adam Wimple was buried that evening in The Dalles cemetery.

Olympia (OR) Columbian: October 3, 1852; *Portland (OR) Oregonian*: August 21, 1852; August 25, 1852; September 11, 1852; September 25, 1852; *Oregon City Oregon Statesman*: October 9, 1852; October 24, 1852.

Everman, Return W.
May 11, 1852

In the fall of 1851 the Everman brothers—Return William and Hiram—arrived in Polk County, Oregon, and took up residence at Goff's boardinghouse. As soon as the two young men arrived the incidence of petty crime noticeably increased, especially housebreaking. Cyrus Hooker's home was one of those burglarized and a valuable gold watch taken, and Hooker finally settled his suspicions upon Return Everman. Hooker openly accused the twenty-three-year-old of the theft but he had no proof, so his accusation served only to infuriate the thief and Everman threatened to shoot Hooker for "slandering my good name." The Evermans were friends with Enoch Smith, who was living in Polk County when the Everman boys arrived, and Smith already had problems with Hooker, which further aggravated the situation.

The Evermans, and by association Smith and David James Coe, were being closely watched, so they had difficulty making their living in petty crime, and for them honest labor was not an option. They decided it was time to leave so on February 12, 1852, Hiram, Smith and Coe packed their belongings and started south toward the gold fields of California, leaving Return behind. Early the following morning Return went to a rail fence around the field that Hooker had been working lately and lay in ambush. He brought along his musket and pistol and had the long barreled weapon loaded with buckshot and ball. Hooker soon arrived with his team and when he was within thirty yards Return fired the musket, the load striking Hooker's lower back and tearing a gaping hole and knocking him to the ground. Hooker was helpless and slowly bleeding to death but Return would take no chance on Hooker's survival, so he walked to his victim and put the ball from his pistol through Hooker's brain. He then fled south, hurrying to catch up with his brother and the others who were to serve as his alibi.

When Return reached the party he suggested they split up, and he and Coe went on at a rapid pace while Hiram and Smith moved more slowly. The body of Hooker was discovered in the early afternoon of the day of his death and the authorities were summoned. The boot tracks at the scene told the story of a man lying in ambush and then inflicting the coup de grace before leaving the scene, and Return Everman was immediately suspected. Men hurried to Everman's boardinghouse but found he had gone, so a posse was quickly organized and outfitted, and they started on his trail. They overtook Hiram and Smith late that evening and arrested the men as material witnesses, and then part of the posse took their prisoners back to Polk County while the remainder continued on the trail of Return and Coe. The two fugitives were moving at such a rapid pace that it took sixty hours for the posse to overtake and arrest the two men. The inquest on Hooker's remains was held on February 14, 1852, and testimony proved that Hiram had been involved as an accessory, having known beforehand that Return was going to kill Hooker and then helping his brother elude capture. Hiram was tried on April 14, 1852, convicted, and sentenced to serve three years of servitude — there being no prison at the time. Coe was tried as an accessory and acquitted but Smith, who had threatened Hooker's life and put up a reward for his death, was tried twice.

The second trial took place in Yamhill County on a change of venue and he was found guilty of murder in the first degree as an accessory before and after the fact. Smith was sentenced to hang on June 18, 1852, but he received a full pardon from Governor J.P. Gaines and was released eleven days before his date with the executioner. The trial of Return Everman was held on April 20, 1852, and he was convicted of murder in the first degree. Judge O.C. Pratt sentenced him to hang on May 11, 1852, and nothing intervened to delay the execution. While in jail Everman wrote out his confession in great detail, which was published in the *Oregon Statesman* on May 25, 1852.

The responsibility for hanging Everman at the Polk County seat of Cynthian fell to Sheriff W.S. Gilliam. When the morning arrived Sheriff Gilliam went to Everman's cell and read the death warrant, then escorted the prisoner to a wagon for his ride to the gallows. The scaffold had been built outside the city and by the time the condemned man arrived it had been surrounded by three hundred spectators. Everman climbed the stairs and stood at the railing as he again confessed, but his second version diverged somewhat from his published confession, and he talked until he finally ran out of words to delay the execution. The reverend read a short prayer as the prisoner was prepared: his wrists and arms, knees and ankles tied; the noose adjusted; and the blindfold tied over his eyes. The trap was sprung in a moment but the fall did not break his neck and he struggled for fifteen minutes before he was pronounced dead. He was then cut down and placed in a cheap pine coffin provided by the county, and that evening he was buried in the local cemetery with a Presbyterian service attended by few.

Oregon City Oregon Statesman: February 28, 1852; March 3, 1852; March 9–10, 1852; April 20, 1852; April 27, 1852; May 4, 1852; May 25, 1852; June 22, 1852; *Portland (OR) Weekly Times*: February 28, 1852; May 1, 1852; May 8, 1852.

Indian George; Indian Tom
February 10, 1854

On October 7, 1853, two Modoc Indians were on the prowl when they came upon miner James C. Kyle. Kyle had done nothing to provoke or threaten the Indians but, without warning or hesitation, Indian George shot him dead. Later the same day the two Indians encountered miner Richard Edwards, and Indian Tom, without provocation or warning, shot him dead. Pressure was put on the tribe and the chiefs determined that Indian George and Indian Tom were guilty of the killings. In order to keep peace with the white settlers they turned over the two murderers to Jackson County Sheriff Thomas Pyle.

Indian George and Indian Tom were lodged in the Jacksonville jail and at their examination they were held to answer to the federal grand jury. Early on the morning of February 6 both Indians were indicted and Indian George's trial commenced immediately. A jury was seated in judge O.B. McFadden's circuit court and testimony was presented, making a strong case against the defendant for the murder of Kyle. The case went to the jury that same evening and, after brief deliberations, Indian George was found guilty of first degree murder. On February 7 Judge McFadden sentenced Indian George to hang on February 10. Then preparations began for Indian Tom's trial for murdering Richard Edwards. Again there was strong evidence of guilt and Indian Tom was convicted of first degree murder on February 8. Before recessing court Judge McFadden sentenced Indian Tom to hang with Indian George.

The two Indians spent their final two days in farewell ceremonies and singing their death songs. On their last morning they painted themselves in gaudy colors, donned the ceremonial clothing provided by members of their tribe, and they walked to the gallows with the typical stoic Indian perspective on death. They had nothing to say to the crowd of whites gathered about the scaffold and took their places on the trapdoor. Their limbs were tied with rope, the nooses adjusted, and the black caps pulled over their faces. The trap was sprung by Sheriff Pyle, and the two bodies dropped, breaking their necks. After both men were pronounced dead, and had hung long enough to ensure they could not be revived, they were cut down and delivered to their tribe for burial.

Oregon City Oregon Spectator: February 1854.

SOUTH DAKOTA

The region that would become South Dakota was acquired from France in 1803 as part of the Louisiana Purchase, with the exception of a small portion in the northwest corner acquired from Great Britain in 1818. The territory had been explored in 1742 and the land was claimed by France, but in 1762 it was ceded to Spain, then returned to France in

1800. The first permanent European settlement was established at Yankton in 1859 and this became the capital of the Dakota Territory established in 1862. On November 2, 1889, the Dakota Territory was divided into the states of North and South Dakota and South Dakota became the 40th state.

McCall, John
March 1, 1877

In 1876 James Butler "Wild Bill" Hickok told his new wife, Agnes Lake, that he was going to the gold fields in the Dakota Territory with "Colorado" Charlie Utter's party to "strike it rich." The Utter party left Wyoming in late June and arrived in Deadwood just after July 4. Hickok spent the next month mining for gold on the poker tables in the many saloons on Main Street, especially the Senate and the No. 10. On August 1, 1876, he cleaned out the pockets of laborer John "Jack" McCall, who was using the name Bill Sutherland. Hickok then offered McCall a dollar so he could eat but this only enraged McCall, who felt the offer was a personal insult. McCall stormed out of the No. 10 and after playing several more hours Hickok returned to his tent.

After a good night's sleep Hickok returned to the No. 10 to resume his poker playing. McCall returned to the No. 10 just after 4:00 P.M. McCall made his way toward the gold scales near the poker table where Hickok was seated and aroused no suspicion, as he would have to weigh-out dust in order to join the game. Hickok had been losing, so when William R. Massie showed his hand Hickok gave it his full attention. At just that moment McCall pulled his six-shooter, stepped to within a few feet of Hickok's back, and sent a single fatal bullet into the brain of the legendary gunfighter. After McCall shot Hickok, he yelled, "Damn you, take that!" and continued to wave his pistol at the other patrons. He fled out the back door and up the alley behind the saloon and in a few minutes men were in pursuit. The murderer was cornered in one of Deadwood's three butcher shops, where he was captured.

Just as McCall was about to be lynched the mob was distracted and responsible people took custody of McCall and held him for a people's court the following day. Overnight he admitted his name was not Bill Sutherland but John McCall, and concocted a story of Hickok killing his brother. He was acquitted but he hurried out of camp to avoid being killed by Hickok's friends. He went to Laramie, Wyoming, where he began drinking heavily and bragging about killing Hickok, including the details of how he had lied his way out of a conviction. Deputy U.S. marshal A.D. Balcombe overheard the bragging and arrested McCall on August 29. Following a preliminary hearing he was taken to the Dakota territorial capital at Yankton on September 5 and indicted for Hickok's murder on October 18.

His trial commenced on December 4 with no defense witnesses called and two days later, at 10:15 P.M., he was convicted of first degree murder. The defense claimed double jeopardy but the circuit court ruled that the first trial, held in an illegal town built on Indian land in violation of federal law, could not be recognized by the U.S. courts, so on January 3, 1877, Judge P.S. Shannon sentenced McCall to hang on March 1, 1877. The motion for a new trial was denied, the appeal to the territorial supreme court failed, and Governor John L. Pennington refused to intervene. McCall's attorneys then petitioned President U.S. Grant, who also refused to intervene.

The Rev. Josiah Ward of the Congregationalist Church and the Rev. J.A. Potter of the M.E. Church of Yankton offered their services but McCall declined. He spent his final weeks in conversation, prayer, and Bible study with Roman Catholic Father John Daxacher and his assistant, J.A. Curry. On McCall's final night he was given the following letter:

> Merchants Hotel
> Louisville KY
> February 25, 1877
>
> To the Marshal of Yankton:
> Dear Sir:

> I saw in the morning papers a piece about the sentence of the murderer of Hickok, Jack McCall. There was a young man of the name of John McCall left here about six years ago, who has not been heard from for the last three years. He has a father, mother and three sisters living here in Louisville, who are very uneasy about him since they heard about the murder of Hickok. If you can send us any information about him, we would be very thankful to you.
>
> This John McCall is about twenty-five years old, has light hair, inclined to curl, and one eye crossed. I cannot say about his height, as he was not grown when he left here. Please write as soon as convenient, as we are anxious to hear from you.
>
> Very respectfully,
> Mary A. McCall

It had been expected that McCall would break down and present a miserable display of emotion as the moment approached, but he maintained his composure to the end. McCall's irons were removed by a blacksmith during the early hours of his last day, after which he dressed entirely in black, which gave him a boyish appearance. At 9:00 A.M. the prisoner was brought out of his cell by U.S. marshal J.H. Burdick and the death warrant was read in the presence of deputies C.P. Edmunds and R.J. Stanley and the priest and his assistant. At 9:30 A.M. McCall said farewell to his fellow prisoners and left the jail for the last time.

The procession to the gallows included L.D.F. Poore representing the *New York Herald*, Mr. Bryant of the *New England Journal*, Dr. Wilson and the Taylor brothers of the *Dakota Herald*, and Phil K. Faulk of the *Press and Dakotian*. There was a long line of carriages and wagons in advance and behind the marshal's procession. Not a word was spoken during the two mile ride to the school section, north of town and just beyond the Catholic cemetery; they arrived at the gallows at 10:00 A.M. The gallows was a framework eight by ten feet square, the platform in which the trap was arranged was eight feet above the ground, and the entire structure from two feet above the platform to the ground was closely boarded up so that it was impossible to observe the death struggles of the condemned man. A deputy sheriff and a deputy U.S. marshal shared responsibility for regulating the spectators on the grounds and had done so well that there was no crowding or unseemly conduct. As soon as his carriage arrived McCall alighted and was escorted to the platform by the marshal, deputy Ash, and the clergymen. McCall took his place in the center of the trapdoor and, gazing eastward, examined the crowd of one thousand men and women. His limbs were then bound, but he managed to kneel and pray with his priest. He turned his face skyward and then kissed the crucifix when it was offered and clenched it in his right hand. When he arose the black cap was pulled over his face. Marshal Burdick arranged the noose but McCall said, "Wait one moment, Marshal, until I pray." The marshal paused and when the prayer concluded McCall said, "Draw it tighter, Marshal," and Burdick cinched the noose a bit tighter.

At 10:15 A.M. the trap was sprung just as the condemned man uttered, "Oh, God!" The prisoner dropped four feet, breaking his neck, and twelve minutes after the trapdoor opened Drs. D.F. Etter and J.M. Miller were admitted to the enclosure beneath the gallows. They reported that McCall's head was inclined in a drooping position toward his breast, his hands were clenched and blue, and his right hand still grasped the crucifix. They examined the body for a pulse and pronounced him dead. After hanging ten minutes longer the body was cut down and placed in a neat walnut coffin. McCall's remains were removed to the southwest corner of the Catholic cemetery and buried following a brief ceremony by Father Daxacher.

Yankton (SD) Press & Dakotian: March 1–2, 1877.

Egan, Thomas
July 13, 1882

Thomas Egan and his wife Mary had been married for fourteen years by 1881 and had three sons ages four, eleven, and thirteen years.

The Egan family moved from Mason City to Minnehaha County, South Dakota, in 1877. Mrs. Egan, who was thirty-six years old, was a hard working woman who frequently went to the fields to plow, help with the harvest, and took in washing in addition to her household chores. Thomas Egan was not a known alcoholic or violent man, though he was abusive toward his wife. On the morning of September 12, 1881, the two younger children and their parents ate breakfast and then their father sent the boys out to tend the cattle. He obtained a length of rope and; when Mary was preoccupied washing dishes, he slipped a noose over her head, drew it tight, and choked her to death. He dragged her around the kitchen for some time to be certain that she was dead and then threw her body into the cellar, which was little more than a hole dug beneath the floorboards. When the boys returned from the pasture he took them to his timber claim and when they asked about their mother he said she had gone to visit a neighbor. When Mary Egan was missed a search was initiated and her body was found in a sitting position in a ghastly, decomposed condition. Egan was immediately suspected, arrested, and lodged in the Sioux Falls jail. Egan was tried at the fall term of the court, convicted of first degree murder, and sentenced to hang, but various appeals and petitions delayed the execution. During his trial and time in jail he spent most of the time reading his Bible and was attended by three priests, who helped him brace up on his last morning.

On the south side of the jail at Sioux Falls a thirty foot square enclosure of sixteen foot boards was erected, and another buffer was provided by a heavy rope stretched an additional thirty feet from the fence to hold back the crowd of spectators; the rope barricade was patrolled by seven special policemen. Inside the enclosure the scaffold had been connected to the jail door by an incline and early that last morning a crew of workers was busy testing the rope and trapdoor release and bringing in the coffin. After breakfast Egan was joined by three priests and one reverend, who administered spiritual consolation.

At 9:00 A.M. the death warrant was read to the prisoner in his cell and an order was given to clear the incline, the prisoners wrists were bound and the procession to the scaffold began. First came Sheriff Dickson of Minnehaha County and Sheriff Dixon of Lincoln County; next came Judge Carter and Sheriff Baker of Yankton County; then Father Lenehan with the prisoner, and behind them were Fathers Marth and Knauff. The procession moved down the incline directly onto the platform and Egan took his place on the trapdoor. The noose was adjusted and the black cap was pulled on by Sheriff Dickson while Egan's ankles were being bound, and the trap was sprung at 9:38 A.M. The one hundred eighty pound body of Egan dropped five feet six inches, breaking the rope. Four men immediately rushed in and carried Egan onto the scaffold while another secured the trap release from below. Those on the platform tied a noose in the rope's end and, in a few minutes, all was again in readiness. Egan was launched once more and Drs. Morgan, LeBlonde and Olney monitored Egan's vital signs and pronounced him dead at 10:00 A.M. They had examined Egan after the first rope broke and all three doctors agreed that Egan's neck had been broken in the first fall, but nevertheless the body was allowed to hang until 10:12 A.M. before being lowered into its coffin. Egan was buried in the local cemetery before sundown.

Sioux Falls (SD) Daily Argus-Leader: July 13–14, 1882; *Yankton (SD) Press & Dakotan*: July 14, 1882.

Ma-to-o-hi-ti-ke
November 15, 1882

Joseph Johnson was a trooper in the regular army and in 1876 he was assigned to Fort Bennett, the military station at the Cheyenne River Indian Agency. When his enlistment ended J.C. Robb, the military trader at the agency, hired him but Johnson received a proposition from his brother to join him in a stock business on the Jim River. After considering the proposition, he decided to join his brother. He settled his affairs, quit his job, and sent word ahead that he would arrive on a certain date. He drew a little over $800 in gold and currency and saddled his horse. He took his Winchester rifle, which had peculiar markings on the stock, and provisions and started eastward toward Fort Sully. Ma-to-o-hi-ti-ke, often call Wa-pe-pe or by his English name, Brave Bear, had been loitering around the agency for some time and knew of Johnson's plans. He appreciated a fine horse and a good rifle, like those of Johnson, and decided he must have them. He knew the trail that Johnson would follow through Indian country so he rode ahead twenty-five miles and waited for the ex-soldier.

When Johnson appeared on May 15, 1879, the Indian rode along, acting in a friendly manner but waiting for his opportunity. At one point the trail narrowed and Johnson let the Indian fall behind him, and Ma-to-o-hi-ti-ke drew his pistol and shot Johnson in the back, killing him instantly. The murderer took Johnson's horse and rifle, his watch, money and clothing and fled north toward Canada to join his father-in-law, Sitting Bull. The distance to Sitting Bull's camp was more than one hundred miles and the murderer did not want to take money into the Indian encampment so he buried it along the way. He left his wife at the agency, afraid to return or even send word until he was across the border. But along the way he met scout Edward H. Allison. Allison knew the Indian so they talked before each continued on, and Allison gave no sign that he recognized Johnson's horse and rifle. When Johnson did not arrive as scheduled his brother organized search parties from Fort Sully and Fort Bennett. Still it took more than a month to find the decomposed, naked remains of Joseph Johnson, and it was then that Allison reported the Indian's possession of Johnson's horse and gun.

In 1881 Allison was instrumental in arranging the surrender of Sitting Bull and, when the Indian Chief came across the border and treated with the U.S. Army, Ma-to-o-hi-ti-ke was still with the band. As they traveled southward Allison made a point of talking with the fugitive and managed to get a detailed account of the murder of Johnson, and even learned where the Indian had buried the stolen money. As soon as the murderer was on American soil he was turned over to civilian authorities and in the fall he was taken to Yankton via Bismarck and St. Paul and lodged in jail. At St. Paul the prisoner tried to poison himself but quick action by his guards, and efficient medical care, saved him for the gallows.

At the November term the accused murderer was indicted for the murder of Johnson based on the testimony of twenty-three witnesses. The defendant was tried in December, found guilty of first degree murder; and on January 9, 1882, Judge Alonzo J. Edgerton sentenced Ma-to-o-hi-ti-ke to hang on March 9. The motion for a new trial was denied but a supersedeas was granted when an appeal was filed with the supreme court. The high court affirmed the lower court's decision on May 8 and two weeks later Judge Edgerton sentenced the prisoner to hang on July 20, 1882. There soon followed an application to President Chester A. Arthur praying for a reprieve; the president granted a respite of sixty days, but when nothing had been done on the case another application resulted in an additional sixty day respite. Efforts to obtain a commutation of sentence failed and an application for a third respite was denied. On November 13 President Arthur sent a telegram to U.S. marshal Allen saying there would be no further interference on his part.

On November 15, 1882, the prisoner arose resigned to his fate and told jailor Kelly, as he placed a finger beneath his eye, "No water here." He told the jailor he wanted his pipe and his box of tobacco buried with him, and designated a few trinkets to be sent to his wife at Fort Randall. Father Willard arrived at 6:00 A.M. and held mass, taking forty-five minutes for the ceremony, and then Ma-to-o-hi-ti-ke received a visit from two Sisters of Mercy who prayed for the condemned man for an hour. At 10:00 Marshal Allen deployed his deputies to hold back the crowd and an hour later Father Willard returned, accompanied by the two Sisters of Mercy. When a brief session of religious consolation concluded, the blacksmith removed the shackles worn by the prisoner since his first attempt at self-destruction. Ma-to-o-hi-ti-ke said, "I want all White men to come and shake hands — that's good — then I am dead."

At noon the guards and visitors stepped out of the cell to allow the condemned man a few minutes' seclusion with his priest and then the officers descended into the jail and walked down the corridor to the cell. The prisoner had been talking freely and laughing, but suddenly he froze in place as the death warrant was read and interpreted. The prisoner showed nervousness for the first time. When the reading concluded deputy marshal Weed indicated he was ready to escort the prisoner to the gallows and the Indian took the priest's arm and started down the corridor. When they reached the marshal's office his wrists and arms were bound and the prisoner did all he could to hurry the process. He asked for an interpreter and then spoke with him for several minutes, neither confessing nor denying the crime. He asked that no attempt be made to avenge his death nor that any horse be killed, and to omit all other customary mourning ceremonies. It was then but a dozen steps from the marshal's office to the platform, the prisoner surrounded by a detail of U.S. deputy marshals and followed by the coroner's jury.

The prisoner climbed the few stairs and took his place on the center of the trapdoor. One hundred witnesses were in the enclosure and a large crowd was outside, but those excluded could see nothing. The prisoner's knees and ankles were bound with straps and the noose adjusted about his neck, but after the black cap was pulled over his face he began to weaken so two deputies stepped forward to support him. The drooping rope swung within his reach and he grasped it tightly, so one of the deputies had to pry it free from his grip and hold it out of his reach. The officer in charge pulled a cord which rang a bell in the marshal's office and the executioner, concealed there, jerked the rope release at 12:30 P.M. The trap fell and when the body reached the end of the drop there was a loud cracking sound as the Indian's neck broke. In fifteen minutes he was pronounced dead and after another fifteen minutes the body was cut down and delivered to the undertaker. Ma-to-o-hi-ti-ke was buried in the Catholic cemetery the following day.

Bismarck (ND) Tribune: June 26, 1882; *Deadwood (SD) Black Hills Daily Times*: October 14, 1882; November 13, 1882; November 16, 1882; *Yankton (SD) Press & Dakotan*: September 28, 1882.

Gilmore, James L.
December 15, 1882

On June 14, 1879, James Leighton Gilmore, alias Leighton, and Bisente Ortez, bull whackers for an outfit on their way to Pierre on the old Fort Pierre–Deadwood trail, had a heated argument. Gilmore pulled his revolver and, without hesitation or warning, shot Ortez; witnesses said the motive "seemed to be no more than to see which way the Mexican would fall." Gilmore was detained for a few hours but released when Ortez lingered for a day. Gilmore made himself scarce, so when Ortez died of the wound Gilmore was not to be found. At the time of the shooting there were no officers in that part of the country so the murderer easily eluded recapture for two years while working on the Rosebud Reservation.

Gilmore was finally arrested in early August 1881 and on August 9 deputy marshal Charles Gray brought his prisoner before Commissioner Washabough on a charge of murder, and he was held to answer to the grand jury. Gilmore was tried at the fall 1881 term of the court and pled self-defense, claiming that Ortez had previously threatened to kill him with a knife and had threatened him again on the day of the murder. Witnesses refuted his testimony and the jury refused to believe Gilmore's story, so they found him guilty of first degree murder. The prisoner was sentenced to hang but appeals quickly followed and the sentence was stayed. When the U.S. Supreme Court affirmed the lower court's decision the case was appealed to President Chester A. Arthur asking for a reprieve, commutation or pardon. On November 13, 1882, deputy marshal A.A. Raymond received the following telegram from U.S. marshal Harrison Allen: "The president refuses to further respite or pardon Leighton. Prepare for execution Saturday. Have telegraphed the attorney general for instructions. Answer."

The gallows, erected at the rear of the jail, was a rough but sturdy structure twelve by twelve feet, enclosed on all sides by a fence of rough pine boards completely shutting out any view that might have been obtained from housetops and hillsides. To reach the gallows the prisoner had to wend his way through various parts of the building, but this route was entirely inside and therefore secure from observation. The prisoner had received a new suit of clothes on Thursday night which consisted of pantaloons, a white shirt and vest, and a necktie; he spent the evening brushing his coat and smoothing the wrinkles so he would look his best. The Reverend Pelton and Mrs. Early, Tracy and Chiniquy had been with the prisoner for days praying and singing with him and through their efforts he had become reconciled to his fate. After his last supper Gilmore dictated his dying statement and denied accusations that he was a desperado who had killed others, said that Ortez was the only man he ever killed, and blamed bad associations for his fate.

At noon of the last day the marshal received a telegram from one of Gilmore's brothers giving instruction on the disposition of the remains. Marshal Raymond read the death warrant at 2:00 P.M. and as the procession formed Attorney Plowman took his client's hand and said, "Jim, be brave, try and hold up, do not weaken," and Gilmore responded, "I depend on God above for strength." The Marshal asked, "Are you ready?" and Gilmore said he was. The Reverend Pelton led the procession, followed by Gilmore's attorney, then came the prisoner and jailors, and last came the physicians and their assistants. The condemned man, after negotiating the circuitous route to the platform, took his place in front of the trapdoor with the reverend on his right and the marshal on his left.

The reverend prayed and then Gilmore was asked if he had anything to say. He said,

> I have to say Gentlemen, that I was fetched here by my own fault. I don't know what is the reason, but when I was small I always had a bad temper. I was not such a wayward child, but I was born with a desire to ramble all the time. Before my mother died I think I was a good child in everything. She died when I was young, and after that I did not appear to have much pleasure at home. My father was a man willing, perhaps, to do everything to take care of me, but I wanted to wander away from home, and left home three or four times, and my father fetched me back, and I went to California. Still my heart has not been bad. I killed this Mexican, and he is the only man I ever killed. I did shoot another man, but I did not want to kill him or anything like that. The gun went off accidently when I was fooling with it. I have only to say this, I put my trust in God. I know I have been bad. I put my trust in God, even now, if it is too late. All I can say is, I put my trust in God. That is all.

The reverend prayed and then Gilmore continued: "I wish to say I have no hard feelings toward any one. It is the saying I have been a man to kill people, but it is not in my heart. Everybody felt hard against me; but I have not been that kind of a man at all. And I can only ask God to let death be short and speedy. That is all I can ask. Father, receive and forgive me as thou didst the thief on the cross. Goodbye, Fa...."

Between the prisoner's remarks and the prayer Gilmore had taken his place on the trapdoor and his knees and ankles were strapped. The black cap was perched on his forehead and the noose was positioned and cinched. The black cap was pulled down when he said "Good-bye," and thinking this was the end of his speech the trap was sprung midword at 2:45 P.M. Gilmore's neck was broken in the fall and the body hung motionless for seven minutes before Dr. Babcock, who had been waiting beneath the scaffold, pronounced him dead. The body was cut down at 3:05 P.M. and examined and then Coroner Smith placed the remains in a coffin and took charge. He drove the remains to his offices to be held until Monday when relatives would decide upon the final disposition.

Deadwood (SD) Black Hills Daily Times: November 2, 1882; November 16, 1882; December 14–16, 1882.

UTAH

While the United States fought the War with Mexico from 1846 to 1848 Mormons were battling religious persecution in Illinois. In the spring of 1847 a large party of Mormon pioneers headed west and in July found their "promised land" in the Great Salt Lake Valley of what would become Utah. This put them in the enviable position of inhabiting the region when it passed to the United States on February 2, 1848, as a concession in the Treaty of Guadalupe Hidalgo. The Mormons were quick to propose to Congress the State of Deseret, a vast region stretching from Oregon to Mexico, to be under Mormon control. The United States Congress acted more conservatively and divided the region in 1850, establishing the Territory of Utah in the northern portion of the new land and New Mexico in the south. In 1861 Utah was decreased in size by the organization of the Nevada Territory, a rectangular tract of land cut from the western-most part of Utah. In 1864 the Nevada Territory was admitted as the 36th state and was granted additional land from Utah. In 1866 more of Utah's land was ceded to Nevada, and Nevada then outsized Utah by nearly 70,000 square miles. In 1890 Utah finally renounced the practice of polygamy, a source of conflict with the federal government for three decades, and six years later on January 4, 1896, Utah was admitted as the 45th state.

Antelope; Long Hair
September 15, 1854

In 1853 and early 1854 the settlers in the Cedar Valley area of Utah had difficulties with the Ute Indians living in that region. They resolved the conflicts to the satisfaction of the majority of the tribe but a dozen young bucks left their camp, declared war on the whites, and vowed to take revenge. The renegade Indians set up their camp near the mouth of a canyon that held a stand of young trees ideal for poles, which was frequented by the white inhabitants of Cedar Valley. On August 8, 1854, Allen Weeks, a farmer, sent his two sons to the canyon to harvest a load of poles. When William F. and Warren D. Weeks did not return by nightfall a search was organized and the bodies of the Weeks boys were found at the mouth of the canyon. Each had been shot once, the bodies had been horribly mutilated, and they had been scalped.

The murderers might have escaped justice if a party of friendly Ute Indians had not been nearby and witnessed the attack. The friendly Indians, which included Natsab, Yantan and White Weasel, feared reprisals by the whites so they chased the guilty Indians and captured Antelope and Long Hair, the two Indians who had fired the shots.

The two prisoners were charged with murder and tried by a people's court. Five witnesses were called, including the three friendly Utes, Allen Weeks, and Ian Fitch. Antelope and Long Hair were convicted of first degree murder and sentenced to hang on September 15, 1854, and the two condemned men were held under close guard until the date set for their execution. On the final morning the party proceeded to the Jordan River Bridge, leading the two condemned Indians with their hands bound behind them. At the bridge, ropes were tied to beams while the prisoners' legs were bound. They were stood up on the edge of the bridge and blindfolded, and the nooses were placed around their necks and cinched tight. Two men lifted each Indian and dropped him straight down, and each condemned man broke his neck in the fall. After the bodies hung a time sufficient to ensure death their remains were pulled up, the ropes were cut, and the bodies were delivered to the Ute Indians for burial.

Washington (DC) Daily Globe: October 20, 1854.

Ferguson, Thomas
October 28, 1858

Twenty-six-year-old Thomas Ferguson, a cobbler by trade, arrived in Salt Lake City, Utah, in late 1858 and found a job with shoemaker Alexander Carpenter. On September 17, 1858, Ferguson demanded wages he believed were due from Carpenter and, when he was refused, he stormed out of the shop. He went to the nearest saloon and began drinking whiskey, and sometime during the evening hours returned to the shoe shop. He could not, or would not, say if there was any discussion and later claimed he remembered nothing; but at some point he drew his six-shooter and shot the unarmed Carpenter to death. Ferguson was captured and tried before Judge Charles E. Sinclair, convicted, and sentenced to hang. His defense attorney filed an appeal with Governor Alfred Cummings, who granted a respite to Friday, October 28, so he could review the case, but after careful reflection he refused to interfere.

On the day of the execution a wagon pulled up to the jail at 11:00 A.M. and Ferguson was brought out by U.S. marshal Peter K. Dotson, assisted by his deputies and city marshal J.C. Little. Ferguson boarded the wagon and sat upon his coffin as they drove to the gallows. A detachment of militia had been ordered out by Lieutenant General Daniel H. Wells at the request of Governor Cummings, and they formed up on each side of the wagon as an escort. Marshal Dotson, his deputy, J.F. Stone, county sheriff Robert T. Burton, city marshal Little and the executioner led the procession to a bench about a quarter mile north of the entrance to the city cemetery. Ferguson climbed the stairs, took his place on the trapdoor, and was asked if he had anything to say to the crowd of nearly three thousand spectators. Ferguson spent an hour complaining about every aspect of the legal proceedings, at various times pausing to catch his breath or to overcome an emotional upheaval, and each time he hesitated the marshal took the opportunity to perform one of the tasks of preparation — binding his arms and legs and placing the noose. After Ferguson's tirade concluded he asked that a prayer be said for his soul, so guard Jacob Henry knelt and prayed with the prisoner. All that remained was placement of the black cap, but before his face was covered he cried out loudly, "Gentlemen, I bid you all farewell." At 12:38 P.M. the rope securing the trapdoor was cut, the trap was sprung, and Ferguson dropped to his death. His neck was broken in the fall and after hanging a time sufficient to ensure death his remains were cut down. The coffin was brought from the wagon and the body deposited. A grave had already been dug near the scaffold and within the hour he was buried.

Salt Lake City Tribune: November 21, 1903.

Cockcroft, William
September 21, 1861

William Cockcroft and Robert Brown owned lots which shared a common water source. Both men planned to farm their property and needed all the water for irrigation, especially during the dry summer months; the men quarreled loudly and publicly on several occasions. On July 31, 1861, Robert Brown was walking toward his house when Cockcroft fired at him twice from behind his house, but missed his target. Brown turned around and started for town, which required him to pass in front of Cockcroft's front gate. When he was about a rod past it, Cockcroft came out, leveled a double-barreled shotgun at him, and discharged one barrel. He missed again and Brown, who was not armed, turned to face his assailant, raised his hand, and shouted, "Don't shoot!" Cockcroft laid the gun barrel on the gate to steady his aim and fired the second barrel, the entire load of buckshot entering Brown's breast. Brown fell mortally wounded and died in three quarters of an hour.

Cockcroft was arrested, lodged in jail at Salt Lake City, Utah, and on September 11 he was tried for murder. Several eyewitnesses to the killing testified for the prosecution and four witnesses appeared for the defense, but the testimony of the latter only strengthened the allegations. The jury quickly returned a verdict of guilty of first degree murder and on Friday, September 13, at 4:00 P.M. the judge asked, "Do you have anything to say why the sentence of death should not be pronounced?" Cockcroft replied: "I do not think I could benefit myself if I were to talk till tomorrow. I see which way the tide goes, and it is no use talking. I guess, Judge, I will have to take what you have to lay upon my shoulders." The court informed the prisoner that the laws of the territory gave him a choice as to the manner of his execution but he replied, "I do not know that I have any choice." When no election was made death by shooting was mandated. The Judge then sentenced the prisoner to be shot on Saturday, September 21, 1861.

Sheriff Burton decided it would not be in the best interest of the county to transport the prisoner several miles for an execution so he had an enclosure erected around the courthouse yard. On the final day several hundred people waited in the street outside the jail expecting to follow the procession to the place of execution, but they were disappointed by the private affair. Inside the enclosure were only a few persons, most of whom were lawmen. Cockcroft was brought out of the jail into the courthouse yard at 2:00 P.M. and seated in a wooden chair, the paper target already pinned to his chest over his heart. The prisoner was asked if he had anything to say but he declined to make any statement to the witnesses, and then he was bound. At 2:50 P.M. five lawmen from Salt Lake County, who had volunteered for the task, discharged their rifles at the prisoner. Four bullets, one being a blank, inflicted fatal wounds and the attending physician immediately pronounced him dead and the body was buried before sunset.

Salt Lake City (UT) Deseret News: September 13, 1861; September 27, 1861.

Luce, Jason R.
January 12, 1864

On December 7, 1863, Samuel R. Bunton, who had recently arrived in Salt Lake City from Bannack, Montana, was on his way to the Townsend Hotel. When he reached the door Jason R. "Jace" Luce confronted him and asked if he was Bunton. When he said he was, Luce replied, "Well, we have an account to settle, and may as well settle it right here." He attacked Bunton with his Bowie knife and nearly beheaded his victim, then ranted and bragged for a quarter hour while waving his bloody knife in the air. He was arrested and quickly brought to trial. His defense was that while he was mining in Bannack, Montana, Bunton had beat and stabbed him because he was a Mormon, and he said that when he met Bunton a second time his victim had threatened his life. However, Luce had not recognized Bunton at the hotel and Bunton had not recognized him, which refuted his testimony and his justification for the killing. Luce was found guilty of first degree murder and sentenced to be shot on January 12, 1864, and neither appeals nor applications for executive clemency sent to Governor James D. Doty delayed the execution.

On his final day Tuesday, January 12, 1864, Luce confessed all his sins and asked for God's forgiveness, then was taken from his cell and seated in a wooden chair situated in the courthouse yard. He was bound and a paper target was carefully pinned over his heart. As he sat facing the five marksmen the sheriff asked if he had anything to say, but he declined. At noon exactly the order to fire was given and four bullets struck the target, the fifth being a blank, and the condemned man died instantly. Outside the enclosure a large crowd had gathered but they were only able to hear the crack of the rifles. The body of Luce was deposited in a plain wooden coffin and given to his family for burial.

Salt Lake City Tribune: November 21, 1903.

Sutton, Robert
October 10, 1866

Robert Sutton was employed as a hostler for Faust's Overland Stage Station in Tooele County, Utah, where, on October 2, 1866, he had a disagreement with Frederick White, a discharged trooper from Company F of the Nevada Cavalry. Sutton won the argument but fostered a grudge because, during one particularly heated exchange, White had called him by a very offensive epithet. After dark Sutton searched for White and found him asleep in a wagon box; without hesitation or warning, he shot the ex-soldier dead. Sutton was immediately arrested and taken into the town of Tooele where he was kept under close guard in a house on Main and Vine streets because the town had no jail. The following day he was tried, convicted of first degree murder, and sentenced to be shot on October 10; as soon as he was sentenced he was put in leg irons and manacles.

Sheriff Gillespie chose a place outside town for the execution. Early on the morning of October 10 the sheriff pitched a tent to house the firing squad to keep their identities a secret, and positioned a wooden chair sixty yards in front of the tent. He had a grave dug nearby and hired a local carpenter to build a coffin. The sheriff had called out a company of cavalry to hold back the crowd and keep them from any vantage point where they could see the executioners. As expected, a large number of citizens began to assemble at the site by mid-morning. When the fatal hour arrived Sutton was brought from the house which served as his jail and was seated on top of his coffin in the bed of a wagon. He had a "red, white and blue rosette" pinned over his heart as he was driven to the place of his execution and bound into the chair. The prisoner was asked if he had anything to say and he replied only, "[T]o hell with your little Jesus!" When all was in readiness Sheriff Gillespie pulled back the tent flaps and the condemned man, for the first time, saw the five rifles pointed at him, one loaded with powder only. At the sheriff's signal the five rifles fired simultaneously and Sutton died immediately as four bullets pierced his heart. He was removed from the chair, placed in his coffin, and deposited in his grave. The crowd was then dispersed by the troopers and after night fell the sheriff returned and dismissed the firing squad.

Salt Lake City Deseret News: October 5, 1866; October 12, 1866.

Millard, Chauncey W.
January 29, 1869

On December 11, 1868, eighteen-year-old Chauncey W. Millard was riding in the wagon bed behind freighters Harlem P. Swett and Chauncey Mayfield on the west side of Utah Lake, not far from Lehi. Suddenly, without warning, Millard shot Swett in the back, killing him instantly; then he shot at Mayfield as well but the freighter put up his hand in defense and deflected the bullet. Mayfield jumped from the wagon and ran toward the nearby town while Millard fled in the opposite direction, afraid to take the time to rob the dead body of Swett.

The fugitive went to Cedar Valley and hid in a cabin for five days before he fled again. Deputy sheriff Henry Heath and Orrin Porter Rockwell were close on his trail and on December 17 they captured Millard and lodged him in the jail at Provo. Millard was indicted, tried, convicted of first degree murder, and sentenced to die on January 29, 1869; he chose the firing squad as his means of death.

On the date of his execution Millard, with irons on his wrists and ankles, was escorted to the west side of the courthouse and seated in a chair. Four hundred people gathered to watch the young murderer die and, after a few minutes, the condemned man arose and read the seventh chapter of Matthew. He made no further remarks and sat down again, but spoke softly to the sheriff and Dr. Roberts as the manacles were removed from his wrists. Dr. Roberts pinned a paper target over the youngster's heart, then stepped away. The sheriff bound the condemned man to the chair and, after taking several steps away, gave the signal and three rifles reported, two bullets passing through Millard's left breast and killing him instantly. He reflexively raised his right hand a few inches and the testament, from which he had read, fell to the ground. Millard had showed no remorse or repentance but in his last moments of life he had bequeathed his remains, all he had in this world, to Dr. Roberts.

Salt Lake City Deseret News: February 3, 1869.

Lee, John D.
March 23, 1877

In 1850 John D. Lee moved to the southern part of the Utah Territory and over the next seven years built up the town of Parowan in Iron County, Utah. In August 1857 a California-bound wagon train of one hundred forty emigrants, led by Captain Charles Fancher, paused at Salt Lake City to resupply. They could not get provisioned so they swung south, stopping at each Mormon settlement for the same purpose and with the same result. On September 5, 1857, the Fancher train camped at Mountain Meadows. At daybreak two days later Indians attacked the camp, murdered and mutilated twenty adult members of the party, and drove off their stock.

Fancher appealed to the Mormons for aid, so Mormon elder Lee, accompanied by a regiment of Parowan's militia and Indian auxiliaries, agreed to escort the wagon train fifty miles to Cedar City but required that the Fancher party surrender their arms. The emigrants were nearly out of ammunition so they agreed and loaded their wagons. They had not gone more than a few hundred yards when the Mormons and Indians turned on the Fancher party, murdering and mutilating all who were old enough to one day testify against them, and sparing only seventeen very young children. One particular incident characterized the savagery and blood-thirsty nature of the attack: in the midst of the melee, two beautiful young sisters escaped together from the camp and concealed themselves in a thicket. An Indian chief discovered their hiding place and captured them, and an Indian boy who saw the girls captured brought Elder Lee. Lee found the trembling girls with the Indian chief, who asked what was to be done with them, and Lee replied, "They are too old to live." The Indian responded, "They are too pretty to kill," and at that moment the older of the two girls threw herself on Lee's breast, wound her arms about his neck, and cried out:

> Oh, Sir, for God's sake, for your mother's, for your wife's, for your sister's sake, please let us live! Don't kill us; I can't bear to die. Oh, Sir, I'm too young to be put to death so cruelly! If you will let me live I promise to be your faithful servant; to tend upon you, to see to all your wants, to be everything you could wish a poor girl to be, all your life long. And poor Ella, sir, she is younger than I. For the love of the Savior, don't let the Indian do her harm. Please, Sir, as you hope to rest beyond the grave, let us have our lives.

The Indian, not understanding a word that was spoken, again asked Lee, "What shall we do with them?" Lee looked down at the girl whose arms were wrapped around his neck and said, "It is beyond my power to save you. I am acting under orders." At this the younger girl pulled her sunbonnet down over her eyes and the Indian chief, overawed by Lee's authority, took aim and shot her in the forehead, killing her instantly.

At the same moment, Lee untwisted the older girl's arms from around his neck and, grabbing her hair, drew her head back across his breast and cut her throat from ear to ear with his hunting knife.

Soon after the massacre Lee was rewarded with a seat on the Utah legislature and moved to Salt Lake City. After nearly two decades it was decided that someone had to pay for the terrible crime so Lee was arrested by a deputy U.S. marshal. He was indicted for the murders of the emigrants, convicted at trial in July 1875, and sentenced to be shot. The usual appeals were filed, which stayed the execution, and Lee was confident that Brigham Young, at some point, would intervene and save his life. But all efforts to obtain a new trial or a commutation of sentence failed.

The place chosen for Lee's execution was the site of the Mountain Meadows Massacre, where a monument to the event had been erected ninety miles due south of Beaver. The trip from Salt Lake City required nearly thirty hours, so Lee was taken from his cell at Fort Cameron on Wednesday afternoon, placed in a closely covered carriage, and driven southward. A company of soldiers formed an escort for the prisoner and shortly after Lee's caravan left three other wagons left Beaver with instructions to be at the monument by 10:00 A.M. on March 23. Lee was silent during the entire trip and the party arrived a mile from the monument at 8:00 P.M. on Thursday and made camp. On his final morning Lee broke his silence and talked freely, and admitted to personally killing five people but would not confide their sex or age; but then as the hour drew near he again professed his innocence.

At 10:30 A.M. Lee's coffin was placed one hundred yards east of the crumbling monument, about twenty-five feet in front of a corral formed by three government wagons drawn into in a semicircle. The wagons were covered with blankets and behind the coverings stood nine men armed with needle guns. All spectators were kept on the west side of a ravine where they could not identify the executioners. As soon as everything was in place Lee was brought forward, leaning on the arm of his religious advisor from Beaver, and seated on the end of his coffin. At 10:34 Marshal Nelson read the order of the district court commanding Lee's execution and then asked Lee if he had anything to say to the small crowd of witnesses, and Lee said he was not afraid to die; believed in the mercy of God; believed that Brigham Young was leading the people astray; and concluded, "I did everything in my power to save all the emigrants, but I am the one that must suffer. I ask the Lord my God to extend his mercy to me and receive my spirit. My labors are done."

Lee then asked the executioners to spare his limbs and hit his heart, while a photographer set up his equipment and photographed the scene. Lee asked that copies of the photograph be sent to his three wives. Pastor Stokes offered a prayer while Lee knelt by his coffin and then everyone, except the marshal, retired to a safe distance. The marshal tied a handkerchief over Lee's eyes but left his arms unbound at the prisoner's request and directed him to place his hands on his head. The marshal stepped back a few paces and at exactly 11:00 A.M. gave the command: "Ready! Aim! Fire!" Nine guns discharged simultaneously. Lee dropped back upon his coffin, instantly dead, and an examination showed that three rifle balls had pierced his heart, one ball had struck his sternum and a fifth ball had struck his shoulder; all the rifle balls passed entirely through. The body was placed in the coffin and tipped up for another photograph, and then Lee's remains were loaded into a wagon and taken to Cedar City to be forwarded to Panguitch for burial by his family.

Salt Lake City Deseret News: March 28, 1877; *Salt Lake City Tribune*: May 23, 1877; November 21, 1903.

Wilkerson, Wallace
May 16, 1879

In 1877 Wallace Wilkerson lived at Payson, Utah, and worked with his brothers in Homansville. He frequently went into Eureka, three miles away, where he met saloon-keeper William Baxter. Baxter had once referred to Wilkerson as a "California Mormon," which was a terrible slur. On another occasion Wilkerson attended a dance at Baxter's saloon where one patron boasted that he was the best dancer present, so Wilkerson challenged him to a dance contest. When the man refused and called Wilkerson a "s__ of a b___," Wilkerson replied that he would teach the braggart an "entirely new waltz." Baxter then intervened with his six-shooter in hand and threatened Wilkerson.

On June 11, 1877, Baxter went to Homansville on business and stopped at James Hightower's saloon, where he and Wilkerson began playing cribbage for money. Baxter accused Wilkerson of cheating and Wilkerson countered that Baxter had demanded money he had not won. Wilkerson sprang from his chair and took off his coat as if preparing for a fistfight, but Baxter said he wanted no trouble. Wilkerson, without hesitation or warning, pulled a pistol from beneath his vest and shot Baxter in the forehead, killing him instantly. The murderer then grabbed Baxter by the hair, turned his head to one side and shot him through the temple, then fled.

Baxter's body was guarded until the arrival of the coroner the next morning and it was determined that Baxter was unarmed. Wilkerson was captured shortly after the shooting so officers took custody of the prisoner and transported him to Goshen, where they had to use every means at hand to prevent a lynching. Wilkerson had his preliminary hearing before Justice Edwards and was held to appear before the grand jury, and then lodged in the Utah County jail. On September 29, 1877, the defendant pled not guilty to the charges and his trial was set for November. The trial commenced on November 22, 1877, and two days later the jury found Wilkerson guilty of first degree murder. On November 28 Judge P.H. Emerson sentenced the prisoner to be publicly shot on December 14, 1877, but Wilkerson's attorney was working on an appeal and it was filed in time to stay the execution. When the lower court's decision was affirmed by the territorial supreme court an appeal was filed with the U.S. Supreme Court in January 1879. The high court also affirmed the lower court's decision and Wilkerson's execution was scheduled for May 16, 1879.

On the day before his execution the prisoner was transferred from the Salt Lake City jail to the jail in Provo. His wife came from Tintic and other relations came from Payson to visit him on his last night but he refused visits from any clergy. The prisoner remained in a cheerful mood, conversing with his wife until 12:30 A.M., then they undressed and retired but kept up a steady conversation until the prisoner fell asleep at 3:40 A.M. He awoke at 6:00 A.M. and resumed his conversation with his wife, and the couple finally arose at 7:30 A.M. when breakfast arrived. The prisoner dressed in black serge slacks and coat, serge gaiters and a white hat, and had a handkerchief in his right breast pocket. Over his left breast was a button-hole bouquet.

After he was dressed in his burial clothes his friends and relatives were admitted and he began talking excitedly and incoherently, referring often to his distressed wife, who was sobbing in the corner of his cell; it appeared he might break down completely, so stimulants were administered. At 11:20 A.M. Marshal Shaughnessy cleared the cell so that the condemned man and his wife could say their final farewell, and after Mrs. Wilkerson left the marshal told the prisoner he had only a few moments to live. Before noon the prisoner was escorted into the jail yard by the marshal, Sheriff John Turner and a deputy sheriff and seated in a chair. The paper target was pinned over his heart and he was asked if he had any remarks for the small number of witnesses, which included only physicians, reporters and several invited guests. Wilkerson arose from his seat and stated that his time had come. He thanked all the officers, then concluded, "I am ready to die and shall soon be with my God. Good-bye." He shook hands with the marshal, sheriff and deputy, sat down and called out loudly, "[A]im for my heart, Marshal!"

The executioners had been concealed in a small building in the northeast corner thirty-three feet from the chair. At a given signal, a single rap on the wall of the building, the rifles would be put through portholes and at the second signal, two raps, the rifles would discharge. When the first of two raps was heard the condemned man straightened in his chair, threw his chest forward, and raised his head erect. This had the effect of raising the paper target more than an inch. With the second rap the rifles discharged simultaneously and three bullets struck their paper target precisely while a fourth bullet struck the prisoner's left arm, the fifth charge being a blank. The three bullets exited approximately from a single hole and were imbedded in a wooden barricade erected behind the chair. The condemned man raised up on his feet, turned to the south, pitched forward two steps, fell and said, "My God! My God! They missed it!" Wilkerson groaned and gasped for breath as Drs. J.M. and F.D. Benedict of Salt Lake City and Drs. Walter R. Price and Robertson of Provo hurried to his side and comforted him until he died. They reported that he was wholly conscious and clearly demonstrated sensation until seconds before his death. Wilkerson's remains were carried into the courthouse, placed in the justice's office and washed and his bloody clothes were changed. The body was then deposited in a plain board coffin covered in black cloth and, when all was in readiness at 2:00 P.M., Mrs. Wilkerson was taken into the room to see her deceased husband. The following day his body was taken to Payson for burial.

Salt Lake City Daily Tribune: May 17, 1879; November 21, 1903.

Hopt, Frederick
August 11, 1887

Frederick Hopt, alias Fred Welcome, was arrested on July 1, 1879, for stealing a horse. Sheriff John W. Turner of Utah County held him for trial, but when the complaining witness moved to Montana the sheriff petitioned for Hopt's release. This was granted in October and Hopt, who was without funds, was hired by the sheriff to do light work and odd jobs. In mid–December Hopt said he wanted to go to Park City so Turner gave him money, blankets, and other necessities and bid him farewell. Hopt did not leave town but instead went on a spree, was arrested, and the following day was fined $10. Upon his release Hopt left for Park City, after making threats against Sheriff Turner and his family.

John F. Turner, the sheriff's twenty-four-year-old son, had been teaming in various mining camps for three seasons and had been successful in that line of work. He had two good wagons, two span of fine horses, a general camping outfit, and a ton and a half of chopped barley. Some of the grain was in unmarked sacks, while some was in sacks imprinted "John F. Turner, Provo." On June 28, 1880, he left Provo for Park City and on July 1 met Hopt who, being familiar with the area, escorted young Turner through the various camps surrounding the town. Hopt stayed with Turner the next two days and on July 3 he was seen driving one of Turner's teams. He told W.H. Hook that he was going to Wyoming to sell two teams and asked Hook to drive one team. Hook agreed and at 9:00 P.M. Hopt and Turner met Hook and Jack Emerson in Creek & Dodge's Saloon and Hopt left Turner with Hook, who kept the young man occupied with conversation.

Turner then returned to his camp alone, but meanwhile Hopt went to the local druggist and tried to buy strychnine "to kill the rats which are eating my grain at camp." The druggist would not sell him the poison. Hopt was next seen after 10:00 P.M. with blood staining his shirt front and when questioned he said he had a fight "with a s__ of a b___ and struck him and struck him hard." Early Tuesday morning, July 6, Hopt and Emerson drove the two outfits eastward with Turner's dead body covered up in the bed of the front, open wagon. They stopped at Wanship a dozen miles from Park City where Hopt sold some of the grain from the rear wagon, careful to sell only the sacks which had no imprint. Twenty-nine miles from Park City they reached the mouth of Echo Canyon and turned in and proceeded nine miles before they made camp.

The next day they continued on to Evanston, Wyoming, where Hopt sold the grain with Turner's imprint. At Piedmont he sold one span of horses and a wagon to W.H. Moss for $200, signing the bill of sale and having

Emerson witness the transaction, and at Green River he sold the second team and wagon to a Mr. Hall for $225. With money weighing heavily in his pockets he went to Berry's Saloon in Green Valley, argued with the saloon's owner, drew his pistol, and was immediately subdued. He said, "I wouldn't kill anybody, I never did," but he paused for a moment and then said, "Yes I did. I killed a young man in cold blood, and I killed him with an axe." He was not taken seriously and two days later Hopt took the train for Rawlins, Wyoming. On July 14 Hopt went to Cheyenne, took a room at Dwyer's Hotel, and spent lavishly on hired livery teams and sporting women. By July 23 he had spent nearly every stolen dollar and was indebted for board and livery fees.

On July 11 the Phillips boy was fishing with his father in Echo Canyon when he found the body of a young man lying on the side of a mountain behind a large rock. The corpse was rolled up in a tent and covered with large rocks weighing from ninety to one hundred pounds, and lucern leaves and brush were piled on top. When the tent was unrolled it was found that the murderers had tried to cremate the body, but failed. The body was clothed in a shirt, undershirt, drawers, and pantaloons, with one sock turned down as if he was struck dead while removing it. The left side of the dead man's head was crushed in from a blow with an axe and the under-jaw was broken by a glancing blow from the same kind of weapon. A coroner's jury was convened and on July 20 they went to Echo Canyon to hold an inquest. On July 19 Sheriff Turner received a telegram asking if Hopt's title was valid for the team he had sold to Moss at Piedmont so the sheriff started for that place; but when he arrived in Park City he learned of the inquest in Echo Canyon and changed his destination to Coalville. He went with Summit County's sheriff to Echo, where he identified his son's body and made arrangements to have it shipped to Salt Lake City.

The two sheriffs pursued Hopt and took the train to Piedmont where they found the stolen covered wagon and team. At Green River they found the open wagon with lucern leaves and clotted blood in the bed and the murder weapon, the blood stained axe, still in the wagon bed. They continued on to Rawlins but did not find Hopt so the next day they took the train to Cheyenne. When Sheriff Turner stepped onto the depot's platform he saw Hopt standing fifty yards away. Hopt was immediately arrested. Sheriff Turner could not control his anger and attacked the prisoner, screaming, "You murdered my son!" as he strangled the prisoner; but he regained his composure and they soon started on the return trip.

The sheriff prevented several attempts at lynching along the way and at Salt Lake City Hopt was lodged in jail to await the action of the grand jury. On December 14, 1880, Fred Hopt and Jack Emerson were indicted for first degree murder. Emerson, who turned state's evidence, was tried on October 20, 1881, and sentenced to life in prison in consideration of his testimony against Hopt, but he served only a little more than five years before he was pardoned. Hopt was tried on February 16, 1881, convicted, and sentenced to be shot; but the decision was reversed by the U.S. Supreme Court. The second trial began on March 2, 1883, and Hopt was again convicted but this time he was sentenced to hang. The conviction was again reversed by the U.S. Supreme Court so Hopt's third trial began on April 29, 1884, and the defendant was again convicted and sentenced to be shot. The case was appealed to the territorial and then the U.S. Supreme Courts and in April 1886 the U.S. Supreme Court once again reversed the conviction on a technicality. The fourth trial of Fred Hopt began on September 21, 1886, and the defendant was convicted and sentenced to be shot on November 24, 1886. The case was appealed but this time the lower court was affirmed and on June 24 the court rescheduled Hopt's execution for August 11, 1887. Several men and numerous women circulated petitions requesting a commutation of sentence on the grounds that "the poor, persecuted murderer had suffered enough," but on August 1 Governor

Caleb W. West informed Hopt's counsel that he would not interfere.

On the day preceding his death Hopt discussed the manner of the execution and the disposition of his remains with marshal Frank H. Dyer. Hopt presented a written request to the penitentiary physician to spare his remains from dissection and asked to be buried near the prison until his friends could move his remains to a more sacred place. A reporter was admitted and Hopt explained all the details that proved him innocent; when asked, he said he objected to photographs of the execution, and then refused to speak further with the reporter. The prisoner passed a sleepless final night and a Catholic priest, Father Kelly of All Hallows College, arrived early and was with Hopt the entire morning of August 11, providing spiritual consolation and administering the sacrament.

After the dinner meal the other prisoners were locked in their bunkhouses with the north windows sealed to prevent them from watching the event. The prison physician then gave Hopt final instructions on how he was to sit in the chair, and meanwhile the five members of the firing squad were brought to the penitentiary and placed in the Warden's apartment. Each member of the firing squad was covered head to ankle in black cambric and at 12:20 P.M. they were sent to the twelve foot by fourteen foot tent pitched in the northeast corner of the prison quadrangle. Two deputies had delivered five .45–.70 Winchester rifles to the tent earlier, and a bench along the north wall accommodated the executioners as each sat in front of one of five 3 inch square holes cut in the north side of the canvas. Thirty feet away, fifteen feet south of the north wall, a blanket was spread on the ground and a common chair was positioned in the center. At 12:30 P.M. U.S. marshal Dyer escorted Hopt into the yard, followed by the priest, the prison physician and another doctor who was assisting him; next came his friend Royal B. Young, who had stayed with Hopt to the last; then came three deputies marching with the procession.

Hopt sat in the chair and, when asked if he wished to make a statement, he arose and said, "Gentlemen, I have come to meet my fate. Had justice been done me at my first trial, I would not be here today for this purpose. I have no ill-will toward any man living, and am prepared and ready to meet my God." Hopt sat down but refused to be blindfolded, and then the prison physician pinned a one and one half inch paper circle over the prisoner's heart. Hopt placed his hands on his legs, took a deep breath, relaxed, and waited patiently. Everyone stepped back some distance while Marshal Dyer took his place at the corner of the firing tent and asked, "Are you ready gentlemen?" When they replied that they were ready the marshal closed the tent flaps as he said, "Be very careful, now." He then announced, "Make ready!" followed quickly by "Aim!" and at 12:40 P.M. he ordered "Fire!" and five rifles discharged simultaneously.

The condemned man fell over backwards, dead instantly. The bullets had entered in a line eight inches long and exited in a line four inches long, with the top two piercing Hopt's heart, and each of the bullets breaking a rib entering or exiting. Father Kelly stepped forward and administered extreme unction to the dead man's lips before the undertaker deposited the remains in the redwood coffin, which was carried by four deputies and two guards into the prison vestibule. It was afterwards taken into the city where a crowd of over two thousand people viewed the murderer's remains at Skewes' Undertaking Parlor on Third South Street. The following day Hopt was buried in the Catholic cemetery, following a brief service by Father Kelly.

Salt Lake City Tribune: August 12, 1887; November 21, 1903; *San Francisco Chronicle*: August 12, 1887; *Beatrice (NE) Republican*: April 9, 1887.

Davis, Enoch
September 14, 1894

Enoch Davis settled in Wasatch County, Utah, where he married and fathered nine children. During the next twenty years his marriage was marked by terrible quarrels, threats by Mrs. Davis to leave, and counter threats to murder her. On June 5, 1892, the couple quarreled violently and Mrs. Davis wrote a letter to her sister in Heber saying she was coming to live with her. Enoch flew into a rage and made his usual threats but peace was restored. That night Mrs. Davis slept on the bed with the two youngest children, Enoch slept on the floor with the four next oldest, and the two oldest sons slept outside in the corral. After his wife and children were asleep Enoch arose, took his heavy revolver off the wall peg, and crept to the bedside. He struck his sleeping wife a heavy blow on the temple and then carefully pulled her to the side of the bed and struck her a second time; either blow would have proven fatal. He waited until blood stopped flowing and then carried her body to their vegetable garden and buried her in a potato hole. He cleaned the blood and returned to bed, and in the morning he told his children that their mother had flown into a rage during the night and left for Heber. However, that evening he could no longer bear the horrible secret and told the second oldest boy that during the night his mother had committed suicide and had asked him to bury her in a field three miles from the house. The boy had seen too many quarrels, and heard too many threats, and he feared that his mother had met with foul play, so he informed the authorities.

As soon as the son was missed Davis mounted his horse and fled into the Uintah reservation, where he was captured three days later and returned to Ashley. A search for Mrs. Davis was organized and her body was discovered beneath the ooze and slime of the potato hole. The following day the prisoner was moved to Provo, tried in October, and convicted of first degree murder without a recommendation for mercy. Davis was sentenced to death and he chose the firing squad. He was taken to the state prison while the case was appealed, first to the territorial supreme court and then to the U.S. Supreme Court, but the judgment of the lower court was affirmed each time and Davis was finally sentenced to die on Saturday, September 14, 1894. The prisoner's petition to Governor Caleb W. West, pleading for clemency, was denied and U.S. marshal Nat M. Brigham told the prisoner," Well, Davis, it has gone against you. The Governor says the law must take its course." The marshal asked what he wanted during his last hours and Davis requested "good whiskey," which was supplied in ample quantities. A deputy marshal and a deputy sheriff were assigned to convince the curious that the execution would take place in town, so on Thursday afternoon they pitched a tent in the jail yard.

On Friday night lawmen secured a common covered road wagon and loaded a large square tent, some bedding, two inch by six inch planks, a common congress chair, a plain board coffin, some carpenter's tools, and six .38–.90 caliber Winchester rifles. Six "crack shots" chosen from the many applicants climbed aboard; each executioner had a long black alpaca shroud fitted to cover him from head to foot and protect his anonymity. Before 7:00 A.M. several wagons pulled up in front of the prison and Davis and his guards climbed aboard. The place selected for the execution was an isolated spot, commonly called Dry Hollow by the people of Lehi, two miles beyond the county line. The tent had been pitched in the bottom of a wash with the entrance to the west and in the east end were cut six portholes three inches in diameter and two feet apart. Inside the tent were planks on which the executioners could rest the muzzles of their guns. The deputy sheriff stepped off thirty paces and positioned the chair, which was fastened to the ground with stakes, and on the back was lashed the two inch by six inch planks to stop the bullets. The six executioners then practiced firing their weapons simultaneously, with the deputy marshal commanding, "Make ready; Aim; Fire," and the deputy sheriff seated as their target. A little before 10:00 A.M. the deputy marshal rode out to the point on the mountain to watch for the wagons and twelve minutes later the first wagon arrived with reporters. A crowd of two hundred curious spectators, those few who had learned of the ruse at the jail yard, also arrived and took positions on the high ground some distance away. Among those who arrived early were James Davis, Enoch's brother, and two of Enoch's sons, Berlden, aged seventeen and Archie, aged fourteen.

At 10:40 A.M. the prison procession arrived and Davis, who was drunk, greeted everyone. Davis, worried that he would not be allowed to talk, was assured that he would have time to make a speech, and then he launched into a tirade of profanities, several times calling loudly for prostitutes to step forward. His behavior was so bad that the *Tribune* reported as follows:

> Enoch Davis is dead. He died like a dog in fact, the most despicable mangy canine whelp that ever met an ignominious fate could not have whined itself out of existence in a more deplorable, decency-sickening state than was Enoch Davis' last hour.... He could not utter five words during his last hour on earth that were not coupled with obscenity, blasphemy, vulgarity, and profanity.... His own cowardly tears fell through the foulest of breaths during his last hour, his complete lack of nerve, which under the circumstances might have won him a little human sympathy if it were not for his vile and lying tongue, reiterating the lie that his wife's death was an accident and claiming his own execution to be murder. Finally, with death only a few minutes off, he repeated again and again, in his whining, maudlin way, always and ever hoping to the last that a reprieve would arrive at any moment to save him, that he was innocent, even denying his own confession at the trial.

At 11:25 A.M., while Marshal Brigham was reading the death warrant, Davis asked for something to eat and a large cup of coffee but there was no coffee so he was given a sandwich and more whiskey. The condemned man was escorted to the chair by Andy Burt and Dr. Witcher. Davis said, "Say, boss, this is no fair shake. This is altogether too close to them guns." Davis objected to having his hands bound and Marshal Brigham asked, "You will sit like a man, will you?" Davis replied, "I'll set, you bet I will, but take them things off." The cuffs were removed but Davis was too drunk to sit straight so straps were brought, and he yelled, "No, you don't put them on me." He tried to fight off the guards but his torso was tied to the planks on the back of the chair and his wrists were tied to the chair arms. Dr. Witcher pinned, over his heart, a prescription blank with a black mark the size of a silver dollar, and the doctor then tied on a blindfold.

Marshal Brigham ordered everyone to move away while the deputy marshal, who had practiced with the shooting party, moved to the tent and gave the commands. At "Make ready" six rifle muzzles poked through portholes, at "Aim" the guns steadied, and at "Fire" all six weapons discharged as one. Four rifle bullets hit the prescription blank, one went to the side and one was just below, and Davis' body gave a sudden twitch. Dr. Witcher and Dr. Samuel H. Allen of Provo, with Traughber from the *Tribune*, rushed to the chair. The doctors felt for a pulse while the reporter recorded their conversation. At 11:44 A.M. Davis was pronounced dead, but Davis' face presented such a ghastly appearance Marshal Brigham covered it with a black silk handkerchief before the body was placed in the coffin. The entire party then started back to the penitentiary, arriving late in the afternoon, and the body was taken in charge by the prison warden. Davis' body lay in one of the prison apartments until the following day, Sunday, and then was taken to the prison chapel, where the prisoners were allowed to view the remains. That afternoon he was buried in a grave outside the prison walls until relatives could call for it.

Salt Lake City Tribune: September 14–15, 1894.

Washington

Washington was a part of the "Oregon Country" when it was acquired from Great Britain in 1846. In March 1853 a proposal for a "Columbia Territory," to be created from the northern half of the Oregon Territory, was passed by Congress but by amendment the name was changed to the Washington Territory. Washington was admitted to the union as the 42nd state on November 11, 1889.

Kussuas; Quallahworst October 5, 1849

Settlers began arriving in what would become Washington Territory before it came under U.S. control, and several Indian tribes were concerned about these "invaders." Chief Patkanim of the Snoqualimichs became determined to drive them out. He devised a plan whereby he would enter Fort Nisqually of the Hudson Bay Company, pretending to be there to have a gun mended, but he would signal to attack when he saw that there was an opportunity to overcome the forces inside. He believed that he could secure the region for his tribe with the arms and ammunition in the fort's armory. He gave the signal but when the Indians attacked they were confronted by a party of Americans trying to get inside the fort.

The gates to the fort were closed, leaving the Americans outside and shots were exchanged. Leander C. Wallace was killed instantly, while another man was mortally wounded and a third man was wounded but recovered. Once the fort was secured, and shots rained down on the Indians from the safety of the post, they retired and gave up their plan. The Indians then sent word that the Americans in the fort would be allowed to leave but had to leave behind their property; this offer was declined.

Governor General Joseph Lane, hearing of the affair, started for the fort with arms and ammunition, a lieutenant, and five troopers but en route he learned that the propeller ship *Massachusetts*, with Companies L and M of the First Regiment of Artillery, was bound for Puget Sound so he turned back. He sent word that he was ready to punish the guilty Indians and requested that the Hudson Bay Company cease giving ammunition to the Indians. However, efforts at punishing the guilty parties could not commence until arrival of a rifle company recruited at Leavenworth, Kansas, and they did not depart for the "Oregon Country" until May 10, 1849. The company consisted of six hundred men commanded by thirty-one officers and led by Colonel W.W. Loring; they brought along one hundred sixty wagons of supplies and herds of horses and mules totaling two thousand.

J.Q. Thornton had been appointed Indian agent for the area north of the Columbia and for several weeks he investigated the killing of Wallace and offered a reward of eighty blankets, valued at $500, for the surrender of the guilty Indians. The Snoqualimichs in September 1849 delivered five Indians for trial — Stuharrai, Labrina Whyeek, Quailthlumkyne, Kussuas, and Patkanim's brother Quallahworst and they appeared before Judge William P. Bryant on October 4. Testimony and a careful re-creation of the scene exonerated the first three Indians while clearly showing that the two fatal wounds inflicted on Wallace were fired by Quallahworst and Kussuas. The jury found these two Indians guilty and Bryant pronounced the sentence of death by hanging.

The *Massachusetts* had brought lumber to the fort, a small portion of which was commandeered to build a crude gallows. The two Indians spent a restful final night and the following morning the entire company was assembled to watch the execution. The two men marched to the gallows showing no fear, climbed the steps without assistance, and took their places side by side on the single trapdoor. Neither man had anything to say so the order for their execution was read while they were being prepared, their wrists and ankles bound and handkerchiefs tied over their eyes. The nooses were drawn forward and positioned with the knot behind the left ear and without delay the trap was sprung. The men dropped to their deaths and in a short time, after they were pronounced dead, they were cut down and delivered to Chief Patkanim for burial.

Records of the Military Department (89A-12), Adjutant General's Correspondence, 1847–1968. Journal entry: Thurston County Clerk's Office, Steilacoom, WA, October 25, 1849. Frances F. Victor, *The Early Indian Wars of Oregon: Compiled from the Oregon Archives and Other Original Sources: with Muster Rolls* (Salem, OR: F.C. Baker, State printer, 1984). W.P. Bonney, *History of Pierce County Washington* (Chicago, IL: Pioneer Historical Publishing, 1927).

Clokomas; Isiaaskiluckas; Kiamasumkin; Tilakite; Tomahas
June 3, 1850

Dr. Marcus Whitman and his wife, Narcissa, with the Rev. Henry Spalding and his wife, Eliza, led the first wagon train into the "Oregon Country" in 1836 and established the Whitman Mission at Waiilatpu, not far from what would later become the city of Walla Walla, Washington. The Indians in the area were not hostile toward the small incursion and the Cayuse and Umatilla Indian tribes had members living at the mission. In 1842 Marcus Whitman went east and convinced one thousand settlers to follow him back to the Oregon Country, and the arrival of this large party the following year caused immediate conflict. The settlers violated several tenets of life among the Indians: first, the tribe expected payment for crossing their lands and consuming their wild plants and game but the settlers drove off the contingent sent to collect the tribute; and second, the Indians believed that plowing in mother earth permanently hurt the spirits that resided there, but the settlers were farmers and plowed their plots of land.

Over the next several years there were difficulties but no major outbreaks. Among the settlers that had come to the mission in 1842 was a man named Joseph Lewis, a French-Canadian; he instigated conflicts and aggravated the Indians, which was not difficult as the settlers had brought with them measles and the Indians had no immunity when facing an epidemic. Half the Cayuse tribe, already diminished in numbers and influence, would eventually be wiped out in spite of treatment provided by Dr. Whitman. One of the beliefs of the tribe was that a medicine man who could not cure a disease should be killed for his failure, and Lewis played upon that belief. He even suggested that Whitman had poisoned the Indians to take their land and he encouraged the Indians to exact revenge upon the Whitmans.

On November 29, 1847, seventy-two people were living at the mission when a large band of Cayuse Indians attacked, led by Joe Lewis. Dr. Whitman was badly wounded and lay unconscious for hours before being murdered and mutilated. John Sager, recovering from measles, was in the kitchen and went to the aid of Dr. Whitman but was shot to death. Frank Sager hid in the schoolroom loft, but when he saw his sisters terrified by the carnage he came out of hiding to comfort them and was shot dead. Narcissa Whitman was shot in the chest by Lewis but she managed to get to the second floor of the mission and barricaded herself with Andrew Rodgers and others. Later she was coaxed into surrendering on the promise of medical treatment and safety, but she and Rodgers were shot numerous times and died. Judge L.W. Saunders, the mission teacher, was in the schoolroom when he saw the Indians rampaging so he ran toward his house to protect his wife, but he was intercepted and hacked to death. Crockett Bewley, ill with measles, was beaten to death with the slats from his bed and two days later Amos Sales met the same fate. Jacob Hoffman had been butchering a steer and tried to defend himself with an ax but he was shot to death. Nathan Kimball was assisting Hoffman and was wounded while running away, then later that day disguised himself as an Indian and tried to get water for the children but he was discovered and murdered. Isaac Gilliland, a tailor, was taken entirely by surprise and killed while sewing, and Walter Marsh was shot to death while running from the grist mill. The day following the outbreak James Young brought a load of lumber to the mission and was murdered. The remaining residents were held captive for a month before their release was bartered for goods, though a few died while in captivity from illness or wounds.

It seemed that little could be done against the guilty Cayuse Indians so Governor George Abernathy authorized the forming of companies of volunteers to protect the settlers. He organized the "Oregon Rifles" and armed them, and by January the force had grown to over five hundred men. Faced with the probability of extinction the Cayuse chiefs sued for peace and agreed to turn over the Indians guilty of leading the Whitman massacre: Clokomas, Isiaasheluckas, Kiamasumkin, Telakite, Tomahas, and Isholhot (the spelling here is from the indictment). These six Indians were indicted for murder on May 13, 1850, and held for trial in Judge O.C. Pratt's circuit court, though Isholhot was cleared and released before the trial commenced.

The trial of the five guilty Indians began on May 22, 1850, and after two days of testimony the case was submitted to the jury, with this instruction: "[T]he [Cayuse Indian] nation knowing best who those murderers were could be considered prima facie evidence of the murderers' identities." The jury found all five defendants guilty of first degree murder and the date of their execution was set for June 3, 1850.

On their final morning the five condemned Indians marched to the scaffold with typical Indian stoicism, as they were merely "traveling to that happy place beyond this one." Responsibility for the executions fell to newly appointed U.S. marshal Joseph L. Meek, who had lost his daughter Helen to illness while she was held captive by the Cayuse tribe. The five condemned men were marched up the stairs accompanied by Catholic Father Veynet and were positioned upon the single trapdoor, where their wrists and arms, knees and ankles were pinioned and the nooses adjusted. When asked if they had anything to say to the large crowd Kiamasumkin stated that he had not come as one of the murderers but only as one who could give testimony, and had cooperated under orders from his chief. While Father Veynet prayed, the eyes of the condemned men were covered, to prevent fidgeting, and in the next moment the trap was sprung by Meeks. The five men fell to their deaths and, after hanging a sufficient time to ensure they could not be revived, they were cut down and given to members of the Cayuse tribe for burial.

Oregon City Oregon Spectator: December 10, 1847; January 20, 1847; January 20, 1848.

Leschi
February 19, 1858

Leschi, a chief of the Nisqually tribe, had been friendly to the Americans settling the Washington Territory during the 1850s, but he signed the Medicine Creek Treaty of 1854 under protest. He objected to the two square mile reservation set aside for his tribe, which had no access to the Nisqually River. In 1855 and 1856 there were a number of skirmishes by the Nisqually with United States troops and with the settlers. Leschi led a band of three hundred warriors and during one encounter Colonel A. Benton Moses was killed and a reward posted for Leschi's capture.

In early 1858 Leschi's nephew Sluggia turned him over to military authorities and collected the reward money. Leschi was charged with the murder of Col. Moses and tried before a military tribunal, and his attorney argued that there was no evidence he was the one who killed the colonel and it was just as probable that any one of Leschi's three hundred warriors could have fired the fatal shot. The attorney argued that the killing was not done in the course of warfare, which required that his trial be held before a civilian court. Both arguments were rejected and Leschi was held responsible but the jury could not reach a decision. At the appeal trial before the supreme court he was found guilty of murder and sentenced to hang on February 19, 1858. He said of the second trial, "I do not know anything about your laws. I have supposed that the killing of armed men in wartime was not murder; if it was, the soldiers who killed Indians are guilty of murder too. I went to war because I believed that the Indian had been wronged by the white men, and I did everything in my power to beat the Boston soldiers but, for lack of numbers, supplies and ammunition, I have failed. I deny that I had any part in the killing [of Moses]. As God sees me, this is the truth."

When the final day arrived three hundred spectators gathered about the gallows erected at Steilacoom and a few Nisqually Indians gathered at the edge of the crowd. Indian drums beat in the distance as Leschi was marched from the guardhouse to the scaffold. Charles Grainger bound the chief's wrists and ankles, adjusted the noose, and tied a handkerchief over Leschi's eyes, and in a moment the trap was sprung. The chief's neck was broken in the fall and he appeared to die instantly. The traitorous Sluggia was killed by Leschi's lieutenant Wa-he-lut, also known as Yelm Jim, soon after Leschi died but he was not charged in that killing. Yelm Jim was tried and convicted in 1859 of the brutal killing of William White in March 1856. He was sentenced to hang but was reprieved on the day of his execution and released at midnight to avoid a lynching; he returned to his people, where he lived for many years.

Olympia (WA) Pioneer and Democrat: April 29, 1859.

Ely, Francis
March 11, 1864

See Addendum, page 210

Lung Yow
August 15, 1873

On Monday, November 11, 1872, Lung Yow, a twenty-year-old Chinese man, told countryman Ching Nun that a man on a farm two miles north of Walla Walla was hiring Chinese laborers to dig potatoes and convinced Nun to go with him to apply for work. Nun had just returned from the mines and was carrying a substantial cache of money he had saved to book passage for his return to China. Nun agreed to go along and apply for the job digging potatoes, even though there was six inches of snow on the ground. After traveling less than a half mile Yow slowed his gait until he was behind Nun and, without hesitation or provocation, pulled his revolver and shot Nun in the back. The bullet entered to the right of Nun's backbone about four inches above the shoulder blade and passed through to the lower part of the breast. As Nun turned to face his attacker he was shot a second time, and this bullet entered just to the right of the navel and ranged downward and backward. Nun, though mortally wounded, still had the strength to resist and managed to scratch Yow's face, so Yow pistol-whipped Nun into submission.

Yow then went through Nun's pockets, stealing $250 in gold dust and some gold coins before he fled. Nun recovered sufficiently to stagger into Dr. Shiel's stable, summon help, and name his attacker. By the time Tom Tierney arrived with a carriage to bring in the wounded man four Chinese men were on the scene and prepared to pursue the robber. When word of the attack was received in town Justice Oliver P. Lacy issued a warrant for Lung Yow. The following morning at 10:00 A.M. deputy sheriff Thompson overtook the fugitive on the road to Pendleton, arrested him, and found in his pockets a pen knife and two keys, but no money or pistol. Yow claimed self-defense, saying Nun had attacked him with a knife and cut his thumb. Yow showed a minor cut less than a half inch long similar to one made by a smoker cutting tobacco to fill a pipe. The scratches on his face were exactly as described by Nun in his antemortem statement. The prisoner was taken into town and lodged in jail and later that day, when Nun died of his wounds, he was charged with his murder. At the autopsy Dr. C.J. Taft removed the bullets from the breast and stomach and later testified that either wound would have proved fatal.

Lung Yow had his examination on Thursday, November 14, and was held over for action by the grand jury, and in May 1873 he was indicted and tried for murder. The evidence was circumstantial, as no one actually saw the defendant shoot Ching Nun, but every item was so carefully linked there could be no reasonable doubt as to his guilt. Lung Yow was convicted and sentenced to hang on July 11, 1873. A petition was quietly circulated which resulted in a respite to August 15, and this gave certain parties time to organize an effort to campaign for a pardon or commutation. The interested parties offered a $2,000 reward if a pardon was granted and $1,000 if the sentence was commuted to life in prison, and this brought forth a small army of men willing to ride the region getting signatures on another petition. However, when it was presented to Governor Elisha P. Ferry he declined to intervene and on August 13 the governor telegraphed Sheriff Griffin to proceed with the execution.

Lung Yow was certain he would escape death but after the governor's refusal he became despondent and desperate, so the sheriff assigned a death watch to prevent suicide, a rescue, or an escape. On the evening of August 14 Father Duffy spent every minute with Lung Yow. At one point they heard a dog howling, which, in the prisoner's superstitious culture, he took to be his death knell and he gave up all hope. The gallows had been constructed near the jail, where thirty witnesses gathered including county officials, a number of physicians, the press, and several others invited by the sheriff. The prisoner was taken from his cell at 9:15 A.M. and escorted onto the scaffold by Sheriff Griffin and Father Duffy. Lung Yow took his place on the trapdoor and the noose was adjusted around his neck, and then his limbs were pinioned. The death warrant was read to him and he was allowed to kiss a cross before the black cap was pulled over his face. While he was in darkness the sheriff and priest shook his hand to distract him, the trap was sprung at 9:22 A.M., and in fifteen minutes the attending physicians pronounced him dead. Ten minutes later the body was cut down and lowered into a "plain but decent coffin." He was buried in the Catholic cemetery later that day, Father Duffy officiating, with a number of Chinese friends in attendance.

Walla Walla (WA) Statesman: August 16, 1873.

Neuana, Joseph
March 6, 1874

The house of Captain James "Harry" Dwyer was situated at about the center of San Juan Island, Washington Territory, in a valley at the foot of Mount Dallas. The Dwyer's nearest neighbor was the Terrells, who lived two miles distant. On Friday morning, May 23, 1873, Dwyer's cow wandered into the yard of the Terrells and Mrs. Terrell decided to go to the Dwyer house and inform them. As Mrs. Terrell approached the Dwyer property she saw the team standing in the field in front of the plow with Mr. Dwyer lying in a furrow. She thought he might be asleep but when she came near she realized he was dead, so she ran for home and told her husband. Mr. Terrell gathered a party of neighbors. They went to the Dwyer farm to investigate and unharnessed the team, which had been standing there overnight.

They found that Dwyer had been shot from behind at close range, the bullet passing through the spinal column at the base of his neck and coming out under his right eye. He had died instantly and apparently never knew there was anyone behind him; the murderer had been so stealthy he had not left any tracks, so it was immediately suspected an Indian was responsible. The party next hurried to the house and found Mrs. Dwyer lying in a pool of blood on the floor of her bedroom. She had received a full load of buckshot in her side and arm and it had passed entirely through her body and through a middle door, and lodged in a log at the back of the kitchen. She was still wearing a sunshade on her forehead and the men determined that Mrs. Dwyer had been sitting on the front porch sewing a baby's dress for the infant she expected soon; she heard the shot and saw her husband fall so she ran into the house, bolted the door, and threw the key on the floor; then she got a pistol and waited as the murderer approached the house; the murderer shot her through a window, and as she fell her pistol fired into the ceiling.

Eight months earlier, in late 1872, Indians had killed Samuel Fuller and were arrested at Whatcom but no action was taken against them and they were released. It was suspected one of them was responsible for killing the Dwyers and it was not long before four Indians were arrested. One of these was seventeen-year-old Joseph "Kanaka Joe" Neuana, one of the Indians suspected in the killing of Fuller. At their examination on Monday, June 9, 1873, three of the Indians proved an alibi but Neuana was held to answer to the grand jury and lodged in the county jail. He was indicted and his trial commenced in Judge O. Jacobs' Port Townsend courtroom on December 1 and he was found guilty of murder in the first degree. On December 4 he was sentenced to hang on San Juan Island on March 6, 1874. On March 5, his final night, Joseph Neuana gave a full confession of the killing of Fuller and the Dwyers.

The scaffold had been erected on the beach below Point Hudson and a large crowd gathered by 9:00 A.M. A few minutes before 10:00 the prisoner was escorted onto the platform by Sheriff Boyse of San Juan and Major van Bokkelen of Jefferson County. The prisoner walked with his hands in his pockets, the Rev. Father Mans by his side. Once upon the trapdoor Neuana turned to the crowd and said, "I am very sorry for what I have done. All hands, good-bye." The officers began to prepare him for the drop, pinioning his knees and ankles, and for a moment it appeared he might falter. He had requested that his wrists be left unbound and he promised he would not move them, and this was granted. The noose was quickly adjusted and the black cap pulled over his face and at 10:05 A.M. the trap was sprung. The rope was of a large diameter and did not cinch easily, so it shifted under his chin, leaving the strain on the back of his neck, and did not dislocate his vertebrae. He struggled as he strangled to death, clinching and unclinching his hands, and he had convulsions for several minutes. He finally hung motionless as Dr. J. Bingham monitored his vital signs and found a weak heartbeat at thirteen minutes; but shortly afterward Dr. Bingham pronounced him dead and in twenty minutes the body was cut down. He was buried in the Catholic cemetery later that day.

Seattle Weekly Intelligencer: May 24, 1873; June 14, 1873; December 13, 1873; March 7, 1874; *Seattle Daily Times*: March 6, 1874.

Indian Harry
March 20, 1874

A Bella Bella Siwash Indian acquired $10, a considerable sum for an Indian in 1873. Indian Harry and another Bella Coola Indian were determined to relieve him of his riches so on Sunday morning, June 22, 1873, they lured the wealthy Indian to a spot a half mile back of Port Gamble in Kitsap County. They plied their victim with liquor until he was quite drunk and then Indian Harry cut his throat and took his money. The two Bella Coola Indians were arrested and turned over to Sheriff Theodore O. Williams, who took them before Justice Llewellyn for an examination. Indian Harry's accomplice turned state's evidence and the two men were imprisoned at Port Madison, Indian Harry for trial as a murderer and the other Indian as a witness against him.

Indian Harry was tried and convicted of first degree murder and sentenced to hang, but his defense attorneys were able to delay the execution for several months. But finally the date was set for March 20, 1874. Indian Harry, since his sentencing, had displayed the most stoical indifference to his fate and begged Sheriff Williams to give him a new white shirt, black pants, and shoes, and to invite "hiyu Boston cloochmen" to witness his departure. At 10:00 A.M. Friday, March 20, 1874, a reporter was admitted and found the Indian happily smoking his pipe. The condemned man was very proud of his new clothes and made a point of showing them to the reporter, then admitted to killing three Indians previously but denied he had ever killed a white man. He expressed his anxiety by saying he had a "shookum tumtum," though he displayed no sign of nervousness.

At 12:45 P.M. Indian Harry was brought from his cell and seated in a chair on the scaffold, which had been erected in front of the jail's entrance. A crowd of two hundred whites and two hundred Indians crowded around. The death warrant was read and five minutes later the condemned man was moved onto the trapdoor, where he said "in the Chinook tongue," which was translated for the whites, "I have lived a long time and traveled much, but had never realized the meaning of death until now. I think the present a proper occasion, and the time a suitable one; and I have a 'shookum tumtum,' but I am ready to die." While he talked his wrists and ankles were bound and when he concluded, the black cap was pulled over his face and the noose was adjusted. Indian Harry requested that the noose and hood be removed and the sheriff granted the request. Once his face was uncovered the prisoner said, "All tillicums, goodbye," then he turned to the sheriff and said, "All right, Mr. Williams." The cap and noose were readjusted and the sheriff quickly touched the lever. The trap was sprung, the condemned man's neck was broken in the fall, and at 1:05 P.M. the Indian's heart ceased to beat and he was pronounced dead. At 1:20 P.M. the body was cut down and placed in a coffin, and shortly afterwards the remains of Indian Harry were buried.

Seattle Intelligencer: June 28, 1873, March 21, 1874.

Moos-moos
September 18, 1874

James Corrigle, an old man who lived alone twelve miles from Walla Walla, Washington, was found dead in his bed with the head of an axe entirely buried in his skull. The cabin had been ransacked and a number of recognizable articles had been stolen. The Indian Moos-moos had been seen in the vicinity and was immediately suspected, and when captured he had the items stolen from Corrigle's cabin. Moos-moos was tried at the May term of the district court, convicted of first degree murder, and sentenced to hang. The defendant's attorney managed to obtain a stay of five weeks but finally the date for the Indian's execution was set for September 18, 1874.

The prisoner seemed perfectly resigned to his fate and expressed dissatisfaction only at the law's delays. He requested, and was granted, permission to dress himself for the execution, so he tore up a red blanket and made leggings, decorated his head with feathers, and "appeared a true representative of his race." When the time arrived he shook hands with his fellow prisoners, walked to the scaffold, and climbed the stairs with perfect composure. Once on the platform he stepped and shuffled in a manner reminiscent of an enthusiastic Indian dance and gave a few war-whoops. He then shook hands with those on the platform and took his place on the trapdoor, and his knees and ankles, wrists and arms were bound. The black cap was pulled over his face and the noose adjusted and immediately the trap was sprung. The fall broke the Indian's neck and once he was pronounced dead the body was cut down, placed in a coffin, and buried before sundown.

Seattle Intelligencer: September 26, 1874.

Thompson, John
September 28, 1877

On Sunday, February 4, 1877, at 4:00 P.M. John Thompson, a thirty-year-old Welshman, was playing cards at Agnew's Saloon on Walla Walla Avenue in Renton, a coal mining town. He brawled with William Bennett, a fellow worker at the coal mine, and they exchanged blows but neither gained the advantage. When they were separated Thompson left in a drunken rage, vowing to return and punish Bennett. He went to his cabin a short distance down the railroad tracks and came out with a knife. Two hours later Bennett started down the tracks for his home and Solomon Baxter started off right behind Bennett. Thompson had been hiding along the tracks and attacked Bennett with the knife, and Bennett threw up his arm in defense and received a cut to his wrist. They struggled for the knife, but Bennett saw Baxter coming and called out, "Save me for God's sake; for he has a knife." Baxter hastened to the aid of Bennett, got hold of Thompson, and managed to pull off the attacker. However, Thompson pulled his right arm free and drove his knife deep into the abdomen of Baxter, just above the navel ranging inward, backward and upward. Baxter collapsed, bleeding profusely, and a portion of his entrails "the size of a man's hat" protruded from the wound. Thompson then resumed his battle with Bennett, not concerned with helping Baxter, who lay at his feet moaning and writhing in agony. A large crowd rushed to the sound of the commotion and when Thompson realized that he could not kill Bennett he drove the point of his knife into a railroad tie and broke off the blade. Thompson then leaned over the log behind which Baxter lay, and said, "God forgive me for cutting that man; I didn't mean to do it; I cut the wrong man."

As Baxter was being placed in a wagon he asked Thompson why he had cut him and Thompson replied, "[S]erved you right, damn you! What did you interfere for?" Baxter was taken to the nearby house of John Hodder and Dr. Weed was summoned and arrived at 5:00 A.M. When Baxter was examined it was clear the wound was fatal and the doctor informed Baxter that he was going to die as the knife had cut several arteries, including the iliac artery, which always proved fatal in those primitive times. Baxter said, "It is pretty rough to die this way, but it is all right; I was wounded when I only interfered to prevent a quarrel." The patient lingered in agony until 8:30 the next morning but, as he awaited death, notary public George W. Tibbetts was called and the dying man made out his will and dictated an antemortem statement. He told Tibbetts, "I believe that Thompson cut me willfully and maliciously. It was not accidental. Thompson knew it was me when he struck the blow." Two days after being stabbed Baxter was buried in the cemetery at Renton.

At the scene of the struggle G.W. Driver had stepped from the crowd, taken custody of Thompson, and placed him under close guard until he could be delivered to King County's sheriff. The prisoner was lodged in jail to await the outcome of Baxter's condition and when he died Thompson was charged with murder. On February 16 the grand jury was reconvened and they returned an indictment against Thompson; then he was taken into court, arraigned, and pled not guilty. Thompson's trial commenced on Friday, February 23, 1877, and he was found guilty of murder in the first degree; the following day at 3:00 P.M. he was sentenced to hang. Appeals and petitions delayed the execution until September 28, 1877, but on the day before the execution a party of men led by Clarence B. Bagley spent the entire day pleading with Governor Elisha P. Ferry for a respite or commutation. But at 4:00 P.M. they finally telegraphed that there would be no relief.

During his final days Thompson was visited regularly by D.W. Macfie, and the reverend was with him his final night. Thompson remained awake until 3:30 A.M., engaging in prayer and supplication, then fell asleep for ninety minutes and awoke in a nervous state. A reporter from the *Intelligencer* arrived after 5:00 A.M. and overheard the condemned man praying, "with such a fervor it was appalling." Sheriff Lewis V. Wycoff announced that the execution would take place at 1:00 P.M. and as the hour neared he admitted two hundred men, then closed the gates to the enclosure surrounding the jail yard. When the prisoner exited the jail door the Reverend Macfie was on his right and Clarence Bagley on his left; after climbing the stairs unassisted, he had to be gently pushed into place on the trapdoor. The death warrant was read by the sheriff, then it was Thompson's turn to speak, and he said, "I call God to witness that, though I killed Baxter, I did so merely in self defense. I intended no murder, and if I had been given a fair trial I would not be here. I forgive all my enemies as I pray to be forgiven myself. May God forgive my merciless persecutors and enable them to meet death as I meet it. I believe in the mercy of Almighty God and pray that he will pardon all my sins." The Reverend prayed for Thompson's soul, followed by the condemned man's prayer and the singing of a few lines from a hymn. The sheriff shook the prisoner's hand before he pinioned his wrists and ankles. The black cap was then pulled over the prisoner's face and the noose was adjusted, and just as he called out, "Lord Jesus, receive my soul" the trap was sprung and Thompson fell, breaking his neck. There was a slight groan and his feet moved slightly but he had died instantly and, after hanging a sufficient time to ensure he could not be revived, he was pronounced dead. The body was cut down, placed in a coffin, and the remains given to the Reverend Macfie for burial.

Seattle Weekly Intelligencer: February 10–24, 1877; October 6, 1877.

Ki-pe; Shu-lu-skin
November 22, 1879

Ta-mah-hop-tow-ne
January 12, 1882

On July 7, 1878, the steamer *Spokane*, while patrolling the Columbia River, fired at Indians who were crossing below Umatilla near Long Island. The troops thought they were hostile Snake Indians, but they were friendly Cayuse Indians who lived in the area where they were making the crossing. The Indians lost most of their provisions. Confused by the unprovoked attack the band fled up the Yakima River and camped at Rattlesnake Springs. They met a party of Indians from Cold Creek and related the details, and most of the Indians went to Cold Creek. That night, July 9, seven Indians remained at Rattlesnake Springs.

Later that evening Lorenzo Perkins and his bride, Blanche Bunting Perkins, on their way to Yakima City, stopped at the springs. The seven Indians conspired to murder the Perkins couple and, if discovered, they would claim the Perkins couple shot at them first and that they only acted in self-defense. Lorenzo Perkins picketed their horses while his wife cooked their dinner and then, with food in hand, they had a romantic stroll by the stream. As the newlyweds ate, Ta-mah-hop-tow-ne snuck through the brush and shot Lorenzo in the back, the bullet passing through and wounding his hand as it exited. Lorenzo collapsed but arose and staggered back to camp as Blanche rushed ahead and saddled one of the horses and helped Lorenzo mount; Lorenzo started away on the run. Blanche, an excellent horsewoman, mounted the second horse and, riding bareback and without a bridle, hurried after her husband. Her horse was carrying a lighter load so it soon caught up with her husband's mount and passed him, but in a short distance her horse stumbled and threw her. When Lorenzo reached his wife, Ta-mah-hop-tow-ne — who had run after them — shot but missed and Lorenzo, thinking his bride might be shot, dismounted. This gave Ta-mah-hop-tow-ne the opportunity to close ground and reload as he caught up with them and his next bullet struck Lorenzo under the left arm, killing him. Blanche pleaded for her life, promising the Indians horses and other goods if they would spare her, but the Indians parleyed and, acknowledging that Lorenzo was dead and she would be a witness against them, they decided they must kill her. We-show-ah-ta-ne, better known to the whites as Chuck-chuck, then shot her in the breast. They carried the bodies three hundred yards to a shallow gully and covered them with heavy stones. The Indians then returned to Perkins' camp, divided their outfit, and went to Cold Creek to join the other Indians.

The bodies of Lorenzo and Blanche Perkins were discovered in a badly decomposed condition but were in positions that suggested Lorenzo was dead when buried but Blanche was still alive, as one knee was raised up through the rocks and one arm was thrust outward above her head. The remains were taken to Yakima City for burial. The Indians, particularly Chief Moses, learned of the murders and knew the perpetrators but the actions of the tribe in protecting the renegades delayed their capture. Shu-lu-skin, the first Cayuse Indian arrested, was captured by William Granger and A.L. Thorpe in mid–January 1879 and he was examined before Justice H.F. Smith. He gave a detailed confession filling seventeen handwritten pages in which he named the other Indians: Wi-ah-ne-cat, Te-wow-ne, We-show-ah-ta-ne, Ta-mah-hop-tow-ne, Moos-tonie, and Ki-pe. He testified that Ta-mah-hop-tow-ne fired the shot which killed Lorenzo Perkins and We-show-ah-ta-ne killed Blanche Perkins.

As each of the Indians was captured they were taken to Yakima City and held for trial, until all seven were sharing cells in the county jail. Moos-tonie, who had not fired any shots, turned state's evidence and We-show-ah-ta-ne committed suicide; the remaining five Indians were tried for murder, convicted, and sentenced to hang. The Indians were determined to escape and, during their second attempt, Wi-ah-ne-cat was shot to death. Ta-mah-hop-tow-ne fled the region. In their third attempt to escape, Te-wow-ne was fatally wounded, so when the final day arrived only Shu-lu-skin and Ki-pe remained behind bars.

On their final day the two condemned Indians requested to be attended by an Indian agent, Father J.H. Wilbur, and the Reverend Schofer, and they wanted the two men to act as their interpreters. They were told they could make any statements they desired and Ki-pe spoke first: "Christ came to the world to save sinners; he wrote the good book and left it with the whites; the whites had learned to do right but that the good book did not teach them to stick up sticks to hang people on. God created this world for the whites and Indians alike, and that was a good world. I have lived far from God and when I am hanged I will leave my body here in this world, but I do not know where my spirit will go." Shu-lu-skin said little and refused to comment on the Perkins' murders. The interpreter told the Indians that their time had come, they were taken from their cells, and the procession formed. The prisoners walked out the back door of the jail into the enclosure and climbed onto the scaffold.

They were asked if they had anything further to say now that they faced the witnesses and Ki-pe did not hesitate to say, "You all see me here, and you can hang my body, but you cannot hang my spirit. I have my body here in this world but I don't know where my spirit will go." Shu-lu-skin then said, "Whites and Indians, I greet you all as brothers and sisters. I have a good feeling toward you all. I will leave my body in this world and my spirit will go to a better world." Father Wilbur prayed for their souls as they were positioned on the trapdoor and their wrists and arms, knees and ankles were bound, the nooses adjusted, and the black caps pulled over their faces. In a moment the trap was sprung and the two Indians dropped to their deaths, breaking their necks in the fall. Attending physicians stood beneath the scaffold and monitored vital signs until they pronounced them dead. The bodies hung a while longer, to ensure they could not be revived, then were cut down by the sheriff and given to their Indian friends for burial by the tribe.

In late 1881 Tah-ma-hop-tow-ne was captured and returned to Yakima City. On January 12, 1882, he was hanged.

Portland Oregonian: January 21, 1879; November 26, 1879; January 12–14, 1882; *San Francisco Chronicle*: November 26, 1879.

Thomas, A.J.
January 4, 1881

Early in the spring of 1880 the nude body of a man was found floating in the Touchet River in Walla Walla County, Washington. He had been shot in the head and his face had been mutilated so thoroughly he could not be recognized. Several weeks later the body of a nude woman was found near Big Lake in Whitman County, Washington; she had been shot in the head with the same caliber weapon and her face was so thoroughly disfigured that her identification was difficult. The similarity of the murders led everyone to believe that they were committed by the same person. The bodies were each put on public display for the purpose of identification and the woman was identified by several people as a Mrs. Shanks. The body of the man, after three days, could not be positively identified but there was a strong suspicion he was S.W. Brumfield, a man known by that name in Spokane who had disappeared recently. The identifications provided leads and by tracing U.S. bonds in the name of Brumfield that had been cashed and letters to a man by that name, the murderer was traced to Kansas City, Missouri, where he was known as A.J. "Bud" Thomas. Thomas and his wife were arrested a few weeks after the bodies were identified; and the two were brought back to Walla Walla City and lodged in jail. The grand jury at Colfax, Whitman County, indicted both prisoners for the murder of Mrs. Shanks and the grand jury at Walla Walla indicted A.J. Thomas for the murder of Brumfield.

At trial in the fall of 1880 the jury in the Brumfield murder case, after listening to overwhelming circumstantial evidence, retired only to keep up appearances, and quickly returned a verdict of "guilty as charged in the indictment." The judge concurred in the finding and sentenced Thomas to hang on January 4, 1881. His attorney submitted a motion for a new trial but it was denied, and Thomas then told an official, "I don't see how the jury could have found any other verdict." Neither appeal nor application for a respite or commutation would delay the proceedings.

During his final months Thomas was attended by Father Duffy as he prepared for his death. The husband and wife had been jailed together at Walla Walla for some time, and the officers had to physically separate them when it came time for Mrs. Thomas to be taken to Colfax for trial. As the hour of execution neared for A.J. Thomas a crowd of nearly three thousand men, women and children gathered at the courthouse, where the gallows had been erected thirty-five feet from the north entrance. By noon a corridor of militia, including the Walla Walla Guards and the Walla Walla Artillery, formed a path from the jail door to the scaffold. At 12:30 P.M. the gate to the jail yard swung open and Thomas, arm in arm with Father Duffy, walked out behind Sheriff Thompson. Once the party was on the scaffold the sheriff stepped forward and announced, "The time has now come for the execution of Mr. Thomas. He wants to make some few remarks."

The prisoner then stepped to the railing and said,

> Gentlemen, after serving in jail for six months I come before you to pay the debt that I owe the law and that I owe to my God. I leave my poor wife in jail to suffer her trial for the murder of Mistress Shanks in Whitman county, this Territory. I wish to say that I committed that murder and that she was not present; that I sought an opportunity of doing it in her absence and she was not there. I hope that she will be acquitted at her trial. I ask pardon of God and man, my friends, and bid you all a kind farewell, and ask the prayers of all religious people that they will pray for me after I am gone.

Thomas positioned himself on the trapdoor, where his wrists and arms, knees and ankles were pinioned with straps. When the noose was being adjusted he asked the sheriff "not to spoil my collar," and then asked Father Duffy to take charge of his body and see it was buried in the Catholic cemetery. Just before the black cap was pulled over his head Thomas shook hands with the sheriff and in a moment the sheriff stepped back, touched the secret spring, and the trap was sprung. The body dropped six feet and the attending physician, waiting beneath the scaffold, began monitoring vital signs and in sixteen minutes pronounced Thomas dead. Four minutes later the body was cut down and examined, and it was found that his neck was broken. The body was placed in a cheap wooden coffin provided by the county and given to Father Duffy for burial the following day, following a Catholic service for friends and family.

Walla Walla (WA) Statesman: January 5, 1881.

Teuwepa, Andrew
November 15, 1881

In March 1881 Andrew Teuwepa, a Colville Indian, was hunting and stopped at the ranch of Gotleib "Dutch George" Reimer, who had been Teuwepa's friend for years. The Indian found Reimer at work in his barn and asked him for food, but he was refused. Teuwepa left but after Reimer went back to work the Indian returned, stuck the barrel of his gun through a crack in the barn wall, and shot Reimer dead. He dragged Reimer's body a short distance from the barn, went through his pockets, finding $6, and then ransacked the house, finding only a coat and a pistol worth stealing. Teuwepa was captured and lodged in the Stevens County jail, and he confessed to the killing but never showed remorse. He was indicted in early October and immediately tried in Judge S.C. Wingard's courtroom.

In the judge's instructions the judge gave the jury the opportunity to return a verdict of guilty of first degree or second degree murder, manslaughter, or an acquittal and the jury returned a verdict of guilty of murder in the first degree. On October 25 the *Spokane Times* reported that Judge Wingard sentenced Teuwepa to hang on November 15, 1881, saying, "The sentence of this court is that you be taken back to the place from whence you came [Colville], and from thence to the place of execution, and there be hanged by the neck until you are dead; and may God have mercy on your soul!" Teuwepa's defense attorney tried every legal maneuver to obtain a new trial or a commutation but to no avail. Several members of the Colville tribe tried to buy Teuwepa's freedom from Sheriff Fred Kieling with ponies and other goods, but it was explained to them that such a trade was not possible. They then threatened to shoot the sheriff if Teuwepa was hanged, but never acted on the threat.

During his final days Teuwepa spent much of his time singing songs, especially his death song. He seemed unconcerned for his life except that his children be cared for; he showed no concern at all for his wife. Sheriff Kieling made arrangements for the hanging to be private and was prepared to prevent any type of an outbreak or commotion during the solemn moment. The gallows was built within an enclosure behind the jail at Pinkney City, and Teuwepa was taken there just before the fatal day. When his time came he was taken from his cell and escorted onto the scaffold. "He went to the gallows singing as merrily as though going to a party," according to Tom Graham, who witnessed the execution. Apparently all went smoothly and after he was pronounced dead the body of Andrew Teuwepa was cut down and given to his tribe for burial.

Diary of Tom Graham, Stephens County Historical Society; *Spokane (WA) Times*: October 25, 1881.

Snoderly, Ezra
August 7, 1883

James "Mac" McPherson and Canada Owenby had, for some time, planned the murder of freight agent Eli H. Cummins at his warehouse in New York Bar. McPherson said he would keep posted on Cummins' money and let Owenby know when their victim had accrued a substantial sum. Owenby told Ezra Snoderly what was planned and asked him to go along, and Snoderly agreed. On the day before the murder McPherson told Owenby that he had just delivered $900 to Cummins and told him to bring Snoderly to his house at 10:00 P.M. Owenby told his wife he would be out hunting stock all day and would camp out on the prairie, to explain his absence, then went to Pataha to watch for teams going to New York Bar. He wanted to be sure no witnesses would be at the warehouse and, when no one appeared by 4:00 P.M., he went to McPherson's house. Snoderly did not show so the two men proceeded with their plan. On the way out McPherson tore a board from his fence, to drive into the sand and stake their horses.

The two men arrived at New York Bar at 2:00 A.M. on July 26, 1882, and picketed their animals one thousand yards from the warehouse. McPherson went first and when he reached the warehouse he reached through a knothole to lift the latch. He opened the door, and immediately fired five shots at Cummins. He hit his target three times and emptied his five-shooter before he stepped out, but Cummins was not seriously wounded so he arose and bolted the door. McPherson then grabbed an ax lying nearby and smashed open the door, and when he entered Cummins was seated on his bed and asked, "Mac, what in the world have I done to you?" McPherson replied, "Nothing, G__ D__ you! I'll finish you!" Owenby entered behind McPherson and as Cummins cried out, "My God, don't murder me," he fired three shots, hitting his target with each bullet, and Cummins fell to the floor dead. The two murderers picked up Cummins' limp body and placed him on his bed and Owenby went out, but watched through the window while McPherson mutilated Cummins' body with knife and ax, hacking at his head with the sharp edge of the ax three times before nearly decapitating him with the knife. McPherson covered the bloody, butchered remains with a blanket and searched the room. He found a shot sack containing Cummins' coins and a pocketbook filled with greenbacks and he rifled the cash drawer, finding $1,600 in all. He gave Owenby $50 and a week later gave Owenby another $550. Several days later Owenby told Snoderly what they had done and offered to sell him a horse as his share, giving him the bill of sale but not requiring payment in return, which he felt certain would ensure Snoderly's silence.

Later on the day of the murder, two Pataha City residents went to the warehouse for their freight. They were determined to have it before they returned home so when Cummins did not answer his door they set up camp. By 2:00 A.M. the men became suspicious, as Cummins was a dependable agent, so they returned to Cummins' room, forced entry, and found the bloody murder scene.

Within a few months Owenby was arrested and charged with the murder of Cummins and his trial began on January 10, 1883. After three days of testimony the jury was out twenty-three hours but they could not reach a verdict. However, as Owenby awaited the verdict he informed on McPherson and Snoderly, provided a written confession, and agreed to testify against them. The district attorney then prepared to try all three murderers and their trial began in Judge S.C. Wingard's courtroom in mid–June. Owenby pled guilty and the other two defendants pled not guilty, but all three were convicted of first degree murder.

The sentencing of Owenby was delayed but McPherson and Snoderly were sentenced to hang on August 7, 1883. There followed an aggressive appeal on behalf of McPherson, but neither Snoderly nor Owenby appealed the decision. The supreme court justices found error in McPherson's trial and, a week before the fatal day, granted a reprieve pending a new trial. The stay was filed at the county seat on August 3 and as soon as the citizens of Dayton became aware of the injustice they began to discuss lynching. The following day, on August 4 at 10:00 P.M., a vigilance committee of sixty armed and masked men gathered at the public square where the gallows had been erected. A portion of the committee secured the gallows and square while the rest of the party went to the jail and demanded McPherson. Jailor George E. Church refused them entry and fired several warning shots above their heads, but this did not deter the committee and they opened the door with a crowbar. They captured Church, saying, "We are not here to break the law but to fulfill it. That appeal don't go!" They ripped open the cells and took out McPherson, marched their prisoner to the scaffold, and assisted him onto the trapdoor. He said, "Fellows, before God I am innocent, and I die game." He then begged piteously for mercy as the half-inch diameter rope was flung over the crossbeam and tied off. McPherson's wrists were bound and the noose was placed around his neck, and the trap was sprung. His feet touched the ground, so strong hands pulled him up and held him "dangling between heaven and earth," and he slowly strangled to death.

A large crowd had gathered, including women and children, but they were not allowed to see McPherson until all vital signs ceased. The vigilantes then dispersed, jailor Church was released by his guards, and he was given custody of the body. The coroner was summoned and he cut down the body then convened a six man jury who found that "James F. McPherson came to his death by hanging and strangulation, the person or persons causing his death being unknown to the jury." The body was taken to the undertaking establishment of Kimball & Martin and placed in a coffin; the following day, accompanied by his widow and children, he was taken to Pomeroy and buried.

Snoderly had been left in the jail to face his legal end and as the fatal moment neared he asked to enter the cell of Owenby. When admitted, he shook his hand and forgave him. The death warrant was read in the jail and then he was escorted into the enclosure and directly onto the trapdoor. He was asked if he had anything to say to the witnesses and he professed his innocence several times as he was being prepared by having his wrists and ankles pinioned and the noose adjusted. When he finished his brief speech the black cap was pulled over his face and at 11:50 A.M. the trap was sprung. He fell four feet six inches and hung perfectly still, and was pronounced dead in a few minutes. He was allowed to hang until it was certain he could not be revived and then was cut down and lowered into his coffin. He was buried in the local cemetery at county expense.

The authorities were not certain how to handle the Owenby matter, as he had cooperated and turned state's evidence, which often meant the informer went free; but Owenby had been a principal in the death of Cummins and, in fact, fired the fatal shots. They kept him in the Walla Walla jail, unsentenced, until the evening of December 25, 1883, when he and another prisoner attacked the jailor and escaped. A posse took the field almost immediately but the two fugitives eluded capture for a week. Finally, on January 2, 1884, Owenby was found in a barn three miles north of Milton. He was dying from exposure and starvation when he was returned to his jail cell at Dayton, and there was talk of lynching if he recovered. He mustered enough strength to confess, again confirming his previous statements, but no vigilante action was taken as he languished for six days, finally succumbing on January 8, 1884.

Columbia (WA) Chronicle: July 31, 1883; *Dayton (WA) Chronicle*: August 5, 1883; *Seattle Post-Intelligencer*: August 10, 1883.

Elfus, John
January 15, 1884

Thirty-three-year-old John Elfus had been in Walla Walla County, Washington Territory, for eighteen months. During the early evening hours of October 26, 1883, Elfus, a barkeeper in Anderson's Saloon in Prescott, was at his place of employment when he had words with a man named Manning over fifty cents he claimed due him from throwing dice. Later that night there was a dance at Prescott and afterwards fifteen men, including Daniel Haggerty and Manning, retired to Haggerty's Saloon to play cards. While the game was underway Elfus began abusing Manning and said he "wanted to kill the s__ of a b__," but Manning just ignored him. Haggerty told Elfus to behave himself or leave his saloon and then the barkeep on duty, seeing Elfus was bound to have a row, escorted him out.

Elfus began kicking at the door and using "hard language" and finally regained entrance, but then he began freely using profanity toward Haggerty and Manning. Haggerty ordered Elfus out and once again he left without incident; but he hurried to his room at Anderson's Saloon and got a single barreled shotgun loaded with coarse shot. He slipped quietly onto the porch of Haggerty's Saloon and, seeing Haggerty through a glass door, took careful aim and shot him in the neck and the gaping wound resulted in his immediate death. Elfus fled to the farm of E.F. Tice and paid him $10 to take him to the town of Walla Walla. Constable Case of Prescott formed a posse and was soon on the trail, and at Walla Walla, with the help of Constable Gregory, he arrested Elfus. Once in custody the prisoner did not deny the shooting but only seemed curious how long his victim had lived after being shot. He was returned to Prescott and lodged in jail.

The trial of Elfus commenced in Judge S.C. Wingard's courtroom on Monday, November 19, and a venire of twenty-four was sufficient to empanel a jury. After the prosecution closed a strong case Elfus testified and admitted the deed, then told the jury that "I would just as soon hang as not," and said he had nothing against Haggerty "except for putting me out of the saloon." The jury retired for five minutes, just long enough to take one vote, and then returned with a verdict of guilty of first degree murder.

On December 1 Judge Wingard sentenced Elfus to hang on January 15, 1884. On December 10, 1883, the judge signed the death warrant, and Elfus said, "It is all right. I am ready to die." Elfus shared the jail with murderer Canada Owenby and they hatched an escape plan. On Christmas day, as they were about to be served a meal, they attacked the sheriff with bricks and knocked him unconscious. They next attacked the cook and cut his throat, but not fatally. The two men fled and remained free until January 2, when Owenby was captured in a barn, frozen and starved, while Elfus was found in a farmhouse "living off the fat of the land." They were returned to their jail cells and heavily shackled. While Elfus awaited the fatal day he heard from his brother Peter, who lived in Charles City, Iowa. Peter was poor, with a large family, and could do nothing to help his brother, so when the prisoner was asked what reply should be sent he told his attorney, "You tell him not to bother himself about me. I am all right. I got into this trouble and I guess I'll have to stand it." Elfus had resigned himself to his fate with the help of Father Flohr, who did all he could to convince Elfus to embrace the Catholic religion. Elfus allowed the priest free access but said he was "loath to take up a religion I did not follow during my life."

Elfus' last night passed quietly and he had to be awakened for breakfast. At 10:00 A.M. the blacksmith removed his shackles and by 11:00 A.M. Elfus, who claimed to be Lutheran, embraced the Catholic religion, saying he believed that through it he could be saved. Meanwhile a crowd began to gather in the streets all around the courthouse, so a strong guard was deployed to protect the enclosure in the courthouse yard. At 12:15 P.M. Elfus was escorted from the jail to the scaffold by Sheriff James Thompson and Constable Gregory, and one thousand men, women and children were rewarded with a glimpse of the condemned man. When Elfus saw them he called out, "Good bye, boys!" and on the gallows he addressed the witnesses, saying, "I have not much to say, but I will say this much. I ought not to be hung. I did not kill the man in cold blood. I don't understand exactly how I did it; I had nothing against him; I—I—don't know hardly how I did it; it seemed to me when I went to shoot I laid down the gun and it seemed as if somebody told me that if I didn't shoot I would go down and suffer so I did it to save my life. That is the way I made it out. I had nothing particular against him except the man [Manning] owed me four bits and Dan Haggerty protected him. That was not right and made me mad. I have no more to say. God have mercy on me."

Elfus shook hands with everyone on the platform, said good-bye and, turning to the sheriff, said, "When I made the break, Jim, I hope you don't blame me. It was the best thing I ever done in my life. I suppose you forgive me. I tried to save my life if I could. All I wanted to do was to get away." The sheriff did not answer but began pinioning the prisoner's wrists, knees and ankles. The noose was adjusted and as the black cap was pulled over his face Elfus said, "God forgive me," and began to pray in unison with Father Flohr. At 12:22 P.M. the trap was sprung and Elfus dropped five feet and hung motionless while Drs. J.M. Boyd and T.J. Dawson monitored his vital signs. The doctors reported that all sign of life ceased at twelve minutes and at 12:40 P.M. the body was cut down and placed in the plain wooden coffin provided by the county. On examination it was determined that Elfus' neck had been broken in the fall. The remains were taken to potter's field and buried that evening following a brief service by Father Flohr. After the body was removed the crowd surged forward and managed to get the rope, which was cut into pieces and distributed as souvenirs; the crowd also tried to tear down the enclosure and gallows but they were driven back by the officers.

Walla Walla (WA) Union: January 19, 1884.

Timmerman, Jochin H.
April 6, 1888

William Sterling, a teamster from Walla Walla, had taken a load of freight to a logging camp near Ellensburg, Washington, in late September 1886 and started on the return trip when he met teamster Jochin Henry Timmerman returning to Walla Walla. The two men decided to travel together and on the morning of October 3 H.F. Williams and A.C. Ketcham saw the pair of wagons and the two men entering Horse Heaven Hills. The following day Martin Peck, a sheepherder tending his flock in the Horse Heaven Hills, heard two gunshots and soon afterward saw a team of four horses pulling two wagons in tandem driven by one man. The circumstances seemed strange enough to recall but not so peculiar that Peck investigated. Meanwhile Susan Sterling became increasingly concerned when her husband did not arrive as scheduled, so on October 14 she reported him missing to Sheriff A.S. Bowles of Walla Walla County. Six days later, on October 20, 1886, George B. Kintzley was in the Horse Heaven Hills looking for stolen horses when he noticed the tracks of two wagons that mysteriously veered off the road and then back on again five hundred feet further on. He investigated and sixty yards off the road discovered a man's body, fully clothed except that his foot gear was missing and wild animals had disturbed the badly decomposed body. He and the men with him examined the remains and found a bullet hole in the head and in the chest, but there was nothing to identify the corpse. Sheriff D.E. Lesh summoned Susan Sterling to North Yakima, hoping she would be able to identify the body as her husband, but the condition was so poor she could not recognize him at first. However, after dwelling on the matter for some time she eventually said that it was William Sterling.

As a result of Mrs. Sterling's identification the justice of the peace in Goldendale issued a "John Doe" arrest warrant on November 10, 1886, calling for the arrest of the murderer, whose general description was widely circulated. Sheriff Eugene B. Wise thought that the fugitive would try to cross into Oregon and quickly traveled to the Columbia River ferry crossing near Alkali, Oregon. He questioned the ferryman, who confirmed that the wanted man had crossed in early October driving a wagon pulled by a four horse team and towing another wagon; he recalled the wagons because the second wagon's bed and canvas sides were stained with blood. Sheriff Wise crossed the river into Oregon, where he met Sheriff Jim Blakely, who was also searching for the fugitive. Blakely had information that the fugitive was at the Pilot Rock trading post in Umatilla County, Oregon, fifty miles from the Columbia River. The two lawmen organized a posse and went in pursuit but when they arrived they found that their man had become suspicious while drinking in a saloon; he had jumped up and run to the livery stable, where he mounted one of his horses and rode bareback toward Heppner in Morrow County. The posse recovered the wagons, and in the wagon with blood soaked canvas they found Sterling's boots and hat. The sheriff knew a shortcut to Heppner and the posse arrived before the fugitive and captured Timmerman, who surrendered without resistance though he was armed with two pistols.

Timmerman was lodged in the jail at Alkali, Oregon, and insisted he was innocent, but he resisted extradition to Washington Territory. The requisition from Washington's Governor Watson C. Squire was honored by Oregon's Governor Z.F. Moody and on November 22, 1886, Timmerman was returned to Goldendale. He was given an examination by Justice of the Peace John Keats and ordered held to answer to the grand jury, but the one room jail was thought to be too flimsy to keep out lynchers, and there had been talk, so he was moved to the more substantial facility in North Yakima. It took nearly a year to bring Timmerman to trial but on October 25, 1887, his case commenced in Judge George Turner's Goldendale courtroom. The prosecution's case was entirely circumstantial evidence, but every piece was so carefully linked it led to only one conclusion: that Timmerman had murdered Sterling for his team and wagon.

Timmerman testified in his own defense and tried to shift blame by claiming that bushwhackers had fired on the two teamsters and claimed he had killed one of the robbers. He alleged that the decomposed body found was that of the dead robber, a man named George Lester. He said that Sterling had run from the gunfire and he did not see him again, but the defendant could not explain why the body had no boots or hat, nor how his second wagon contained William Sterling's boots and hat. The jury deliberated only briefly before finding Timmerman guilty of first-degree murder. Judge Turner sentenced him to hang on December 15, 1887, but the case was appealed, which stayed the proceedings. On January 28, 1888, the territorial supreme court upheld the conviction and the prisoner was taken three hundred miles to Spokane, where Judge Turner was then conducting court, and he was resentenced to hang on April 6, 1888. The condemned man was returned to the one room Goldendale jail to await his execution and Sheriff William van Vector scheduled it the hour after the mail stage arrived in Goldendale, just in case there was a last minute reprieve from Governor Eugene Semple. The nearest telegraphic office was at Grant, fifteen miles distant, and a rider was stationed there as well, in case a last minute respite came by that means.

On his final day the prisoner was given a quart of whiskey as soon as he arose from a restful night's sleep, and he was allowed to consume the entire contents to brace up for the ordeal. The gallows had been erected directly across from the cemetery and as the hour drew near a crowd of three thousand men, women and children gathered at the foot of the scaffold. The death warrant was read in the jail and then the prisoner was taken out, placed in a wagon, and driven to the gallows sitting on his coffin. When he arrived, he mounted the scaffold unassisted and took his place on the trapdoor. He was asked if he had anything to say and he once again insisted that he was innocent, and his final words were, "All I can say is that, if you ever get caught in a scrape like this, don't let them take you alive."

His wrists and ankles were pinioned, the noose was adjusted, the black cap was pulled over his face and in a moment the trap was sprung. Timmerman dropped to his death, breaking his neck in the fall, and he dangled until the attending physicians pronounced him dead. His body was then cut down, placed in his coffin provided by the county, and buried in the local cemetery across the road from the scaffold. Two years later Timmerman's grave was excavated by a vengeful grave robber and his bones were scattered in the Little Klickitat River. The bones washed up on the riverbank, were collected and identified, and the coroner then ordered the bones buried in the same grave.

Timmerman vs. Territory of Washington, 3 Wash. Terr. 445 (1888); *Seattle Washington Standard*: April 20, 1888.

Wyoming

There were five major land acquisitions by the United States during America's frontier period and Wyoming benefitted from four of these. Eastern Wyoming, comprising about 75 percent of the state, was acquired in the Louisiana Purchase in 1803. In 1845 a tract located in the south central portion of the region was acquired by the annexation of Texas. A northwestern tract of land was acquired when newly elected President Polk resolved the "Oregon Question" on June 15, 1846, and the United States took sole control over the Oregon Country, setting the border with Canada at the 49th parallel. Finally, the southwestern area was added as a concession in the Treaty of Guadalupe Hidalgo on February 2, 1848, following the War with Mexico. There were many explorers, mountain men, fur trappers, and emigrants in Wyoming between 1742 and 1868, the year the Wyoming Territory was organized with land which had previously belonged to the Dakota, Idaho, Oregon, and Utah territories. On July 10, 1890, Wyoming was admitted to the union as the 44th state.

Boyer, John
April 21, 1871

James McClusky was an interpreter at Fort Laramie and William H. Lowry, McClusky's friend, spent a great deal of time at the fort. In late October 1870 the two men visited the home of the Yankton Sioux widow of French trapper Jean Baptiste Boyer and left the widow and her daughter bound and gagged. When John Boyer, the widow's twenty-six-year-old son, returned home he untied them and questioned them closely. They named the men who had made the assault, but would not confirm the son's suspicion that they had been raped. Nothing was stolen, however, and there seemed no other purpose for the attack.

On the evening of October 27 Boyer and several friends were visiting Cuny & Ecoffey's brothel, known as the "six-mile hog ranch," six miles southwest of Fort Laramie on the Baptiste Fork of the Sybille River. The brothel had a front room saloon with gambling, a rear area for dancing, and rooms upstairs where the "soiled doves" plied their trade. House rules required that guns be checked at the bar before anyone could enter the rear dance area. McClusky and Lowry were there and as the night waned they engaged in a heated argument with Boyer. At 2:00 A.M. Boyer called for his revolver and went out to the corral to get his horse, but instead of leaving he rode to the front of the saloon and called out McClusky and Lowry, saying he would "whip them." The two men came out unarmed, expecting a hand-to-hand fight, but Boyer pulled his revolver and shot each man once: the bullet that struck Lowry penetrated his breast, while McClusky was shot in the abdomen. Lowry bled to death in a few minutes but McClusky lingered for several hours in excruciating pain before dying.

Boyer fled to a camp of Sioux Indians and disguised himself as an Indian, which allowed him to avoid arrest for weeks. The authorities applied pressure and the Indians, fearing reprisals, delivered Boyer to Col. F.F. Flint at the fort. On December 13 Boyer was transferred to Fort D.A. Russell near Cheyenne by Sheriff T. Jeff Carr. On March 21, 1871, his trial began and concluded in two days with a verdict of guilty of first degree murder, and he was sentenced to hang on April 21, 1871.

A large crowd was expected to attend the first legal execution in Wyoming so, to ensure some degree of privacy, the old vacant grout building across from the jail was selected as the site for the hanging. The building was too low to build a free standing, full height scaffold so "the scaffold and gallows were erected over a trap door leading to the cellar, through which the man [would pass] in his rapid descent." The drop was estimated at four feet, which would leave the condemned man's head and shoulders visible above the platform and his feet and legs dangling into the basement. Fifteen minutes before Boyer was to march to the gallows the Rev. J.D. Davis and the newspaper reporters were admitted to his cell and he told them he was "going to the happy hunting ground where I will meet my father and brother. Tell my mother I die brave, without a whimper."

At 12:30 P.M. Boyer, wrists and arms pinioned, was brought from the jail to the scaffold by Sheriff Carr and deputy John O'Brien. Only a few spectators were allowed inside the building, including territorial and city officials, newsmen, and several leading citizens, but outside the crowd was large and unruly. Boyer was seated in a chair while the sheriff read the death warrant and then asked if he had anything to say to the witnesses. Boyer said, "Look at me! I no cry; I no woman; I man; I die brave," and concluded that he loved the Great Spirit and was going to see him. The Reverend Davis prayed while the noose was placed around Boyer's neck and adjusted, and the black cap was pulled over his face. In the next moment the trap was sprung and Boyer's neck was broken in the fall. Drs. G.W. Carey and G.H. Russell monitored his vital signs and pronounced him dead in three minutes; after hanging a while longer the rope was cut and the body was lowered into its coffin. Boyer was buried, at his request, in the city cemetery at the north end of Bent Street.

Cheyenne (WY) Daily Leader: October 31, 1870; April 7–8, 1871; April 21, 1871.

Kensler, William
November 19, 1874

Jennie Hogan was born in 1850 and when she came of age she found her way into the brothels of Wyoming. At twenty-two years she was still young and beautiful, but also experienced. In 1872 she was working at Adolph Cuny's & Jules Ecoffey's "six-mile hog ranch," six miles southwest of Fort Laramie on Sybille Creek. The brothel had a saloon with gambling in front, a dance hall in the rear, and rooms upstairs where the girls plied their trade. Twenty-three-year-old William "Toussaint" Kensler lived at Fort Laramie with his seventeen-year-old wife and two children. Kensler, the son of a German father and Sioux Indian mother, had become acquainted with Jennie Hogan and found every excuse to visit the brothel as often as he could. Adolph Penea, a local sheepherder, also visited the six-mile hog ranch and had developed a special attraction for Jennie Hogan. Hogan encouraged Penea to become one of her regular customers, which brought him there often and increased the likelihood of a chance encounter with Kensler.

The inevitable meeting finally occurred on Tuesday, April 9, 1872, when the two men faced off in the bar and began to taunt, then insult, and finally threaten each other until Penea went upstairs and buckled on his revolver. Kensler saw him coming down the stairs and left for the corral. Kensler saddled his horse but, instead of riding off, he drew his Winchester from its scabbard and returned to the outside of the building. He located Penea through a window, took careful aim, and fired one shot. The bullet struck Penea on his left side and passed through his spleen, stomach and liver. The hemorrhaging could not be stopped and the sheepherder died of his wound the following day.

Kensler fled, taking a circuitous route covering many miles over the next several hours, only to arrive at the three-mile hog ranch northeast of the murder scene. He told T.H. Hopkins he had killed a Mexican; after he and his horse had a brief rest, he continued on to

Jose Armido's Ranch where he again confessed. Meanwhile, Hopkins hurried to Fort Laramie to report Kensler's confession but Hopkins brought old news to the fort, because as soon as Kensler had fled the scene of the murder citizens sent for justice of the peace E.E. McCammon. He, in turn, notified the military command. Captain E.R. Wells took the field with one noncommissioned officer, six troopers and a scout determined to capture the fugitive. Kensler, after leaving Armido's Ranch, returned to the three-mile hog ranch and was captured there without incident and lodged in the guardhouse.

Every effort was made to secure Kensler's release but he was tried and convicted at the December term of the district court. Kensler was sentenced to hang but an appeal to the territorial supreme court stayed the execution. While Kensler awaited the decision on his appeal he took matters into his own hands and escaped, then hid among the Indians at the Red Cloud Agency in Nebraska. Every effort was made to have him surrendered to authorities, but on June 13 two lieutenants visiting the agency saw an opportunity to capture the fugitive. They were pursued by the Sioux of Little Wound's Ogala band but managed to make Fort Robinson with their captive. Two weeks later Kensler, under guard of a lieutenant and six troopers, was turned over to Sheriff T. Jeff Carr at Cheyenne. Meanwhile the lower court's decision was affirmed and Kensler was sentenced to hang on Thursday, November 19, 1874. Kensler's attorney then applied to Governor John A. Campbell for a commutation of sentence, which was denied. At the same time an application was sent to President U.S. Grant asking for the same remedy, but at the last possible moment the president decided he would not interfere.

On the day before his execution the prisoner retired at 9:00 P.M. and slept soundly until 7:00 A.M. After breakfast Father McGoldrick arrived and the two men engaged in religious exercises of a fervent nature until noon, but Kensler refused to confess. At 12:15 P.M. Father McGoldrick, the sheriff and his assistants, and Sheriff Dayton of Albany County escorted the condemned man to the old grout building on Twentieth Street. The few witnesses with invitations included reporters, city and county officials, and the city physicians, and they were already assembled when the prisoner's party entered and took seats near the fire. At a signal deputy W. Taylor conducted the prisoner onto the platform, where he took a seat and Sheriff Carr read the death warrant. The sheriff then asked if the prisoner had anything to say and Kensler replied, "I have nothing to say, only to ask permission not to die with my shoes on." This permission was granted. The priest offered a supplication to the Deity, with the prisoner repeating, "Jesus died for me," and "Jesus, I love thee." The priest then closed with "God bless you!" and made the sign of the cross before stepping aside.

The sheriff moved behind Kensler and pinioned his wrists and ankles, then covered his face with the black cap, but Kensler began to tremble so the sheriff called upon one of his deputies to steady the prisoner as the noose was adjusted. The priest stepped forward again and, to brace up the prisoner, said, "Have confidence in your God and He will have mercy upon you." All preparation had been completed with such efficiency that Kensler's request to die with his shoes removed had been forgotten and at 12:28 P.M. the trap was sprung. The prisoner dropped five feet into the cellar below, breaking his neck and in eight minutes, at 12:50 P.M., he was pronounced dead. The body was cut down and placed in the coffin provided by the county but, as there were no friends or family members to take possession of Kensler's remains, he was buried that afternoon at county expense.

Cheyenne (WY) Daily Leader: December 7, 1872.

Donovan, Leroy
January 18, 1884

Thirty-six-year-old William Leighton, a barber by trade, moved to Rock Springs, Wyoming, in 1879 and opened a shop. John

Leroy Donovan arrived in Rock Springs in early 1883. Young and strong, he was fully capable of providing a full day's work, but he worked only when necessary to meet his immediate needs. On more than one occasion he miscalculated and "went broke," but he had befriended Leighton and the barber always helped him out of his predicament. On May 5, 1883, Donovan and George Hunter, the son of his landlady, were repairing a roof using Hunter's tools. The handle of the hammer was broken so Donovan threw it behind some barrels where he could find it later and, when it was dark, he retrieved the hammer. At 10:00 P.M. Donovan snuck into Leighton's barbershop and hid under the bed in the rear living quarters, awaiting the return of his friend and benefactor. Leighton soon returned and went to bed and after a considerable period Donovan, believing the barber asleep, struck a match for light but Leighton stirred so he blew out the match. Leighton arose and checked the room, then returned to bed and Donovan waited some time before striking another match, but Leighton again stirred so he blew it out. When Leighton finally fell asleep Donovan slipped out from under the bed, stood over his victim for a moment, and then struck the barber on the right cheek with the hammer. The wounded man came awake crying out, "Oh, my God! My head!" Donovan then struck him on the right temple with such force that he drove the head of the hammer into Leighton's skull up to the handle. Leighton made a loud, peculiar noise, so Donovan struck him a third blow above the left eye, and when the dying man continued groaning Donovan packed the bedding over the face of the helpless man and smothered him.

Donovan placed the hammer on a table near the bed, took a key from the dead man's pocket, unlocked the dresser drawer, and took out $127. He put the key and the money in his pocket and crawled under the bed, but reconsidered and looked out the window; when no one was seen, Donovan let himself out and took a circuitous route out of town. Donovan reentered the town by the railroad tracks and went to Bill Musgrove's saloon, where he washed off the blood before going about his business. The next day several customers stopped at the barber shop and found it closed at 11:00 A.M. Leighton was known to be prompt but everyone also knew that the barber had a heart condition, so they found an open window and put a small boy inside to check on their friend. The boy returned in a few minutes to report that someone had murdered the barber and the customers then broke open the door and sent for a doctor.

The body, upon examination, had three terrible wounds, the instrument of death lay nearby, two burnt matches were found under the bed, and the drawer where the barber kept his valuables had been opened and rifled. Suspicion soon turned to Donovan as he had been broke the day before the murder but was "flush" the day after. The bartender at Musgrove's Saloon and others recalled him coming in to wash during the early morning hours. This prompted inquiries of Mrs. Hunter, his landlady, who confirmed that he had not slept at the boardinghouse the night of the crime. When she demanded the return of her hammer, the murder weapon last seen in the hands of Donovan, he was arrested and lodged in jail at Green River.

At his examination Donovan said he had been at Musgrove's Saloon the night of the murder and saw Leighton playing cards with a stranger, but the bartender and others refuted his alibi. While the murderer sat in his cell Mr. Tisdel, the superintendent of the coal mines, wrote to the railroad requesting the assistance of a detective. They sent their best man and he was lodged in jail with Donovan under the guise of being a wanted murderer himself. The detective gained Donovan's confidence and obtained a detailed confession, so when the grand jury met in the fall Donovan was indicted for murder. His attorney obtained a change of venue to Carbon County and the trial commenced on October 11, 1883, and took six days. Deliberations took three days, and on October 20 the prisoner was found guilty of first degree murder. On October 23

Judge Parks called Donovan's crime "more an assassination than a murder" and sentenced him to hang on January 18, 1884. Donovan's attorney filed an appeal with the territorial supreme court, and the high court affirmed the trial record and sentence. Next came a petition to Governor William Hale pleading for a commutation of sentence, but the governor refused to interfere. The process was handled with such efficiency that the date of the execution was not delayed.

On the day before his execution the prisoner spent every spare minute reading his Bible. That night he slept well, under the watchful eyes of William Casto and Tom Maloney, and arose at an early hour. After breakfast he was joined by Father Cassidy, but the prisoner took a few minutes from his prayers to thank Sheriff Isaac C. Miller for his treatment while in jail. The enclosure and gallows had been erected a week earlier in the east corner of the jail yard near the courthouse. The death warrant was read in the jail at 11:15 A.M. and the condemned man was escorted to the gallows by Sheriff Miller and the priest; he climbed the stairs and stepped onto the trapdoor without direction. The sheriff asked the prisoner if he had anything to say and Donovan responded, "I have nothing to say, only I did not have a fair trial. If I had I could have proved myself innocent."

The prisoner's wrists and ankles were pinioned with straps, the black cap was pulled on, and the noose of twisted sea grass rope was adjusted. The sheriff asked, "Is the rope too tight?" and Donovan answered, "It is as tight as it can be without choking me." At 11:28 A.M. the trap was sprung and the condemned man dropped six feet, breaking his neck. There was a slight tremor and in three minutes Donovan's knees convulsively pulled up, then slowly straightened and the body hung motionless. At 11:45 A.M. the black cap was removed by Drs. Stover and Woodruff, who were recording Donovan's pulse. They pronounced him dead. Ten minutes later the body was cut down and the coroner's jury, summoned by Coroner Edgerton, signed the death certificate. Donovan's remains were placed in a coffin by undertaker Daly and given to his mother, who took the casket to Hailey, Idaho, for burial.

Rawlins (WY) Carbon County Journal: January 18, 1884.

Cooke, George
December 12, 1884

Mary Ann Cooke moved her family from Worcestershire, England, to Laramie, Wyoming, in 1876. Her son George found permanent employment as a hostler and coal-heaver with the Union Pacific Railroad at their Medicine Bow roundhouse. George's sister Mary Ann married James Blount, a large forty-year-old man who spent a good deal of his time in the many saloons of Laramie. Blount worked as a janitor at one of the public school buildings but relied upon his wife for a substantial portion of their income. Mary Ann bore them a son they named Samuel and on November 25, 1883, Mary Ann gave birth to a daughter.

On Wednesday evening, November 28 George Cooke hopped a freight train from Medicine Bow to Laramie, anxious to see his new niece and spend Thanksgiving with his family. The train arrived before daybreak so Cooke went to a nearby saloon, then moved on to one saloon after another while waiting for the gunsmith to open his shop. He picked up the .45 caliber six-shooter he had left for repair and continued his rounds of the saloons, and by mid-morning he crossed paths with his brother-in-law and brother Albert. The three men continued their drinking with no further thought of family or Thanksgiving dinner. Blount was always a bully but especially when drunk, while Cooke was an inoffensive man when not indulging but rude and contentious when under the influence of liquor.

Blount threatened several times during the day to pummel his brother-in-law, who had never hidden his displeasure at his sister's choice for a husband, and Cooke each time threatened to kill Blount if he tried. The three men parted company at noon, with Cooke and Blount continuing their sprees in separate saloons while Albert went his own way. After nearly a dozen hours of hard drinking Cooke was ready to initiate, rather than fend off, trouble. He went to the railroad's oil room and robbed the workers of their loose change, then went to another saloon to spend his windfall. At 7:00 P.M. Cooke was in J. Fred Hesse's Saloon on Front Street near South A Street and was just leaving to eat dinner.

When Cooke stepped onto Front Street he nearly collided with Blount, who was coming out of Abrams' Saloon two doors away. Cooke loudly insulted and threatened Blount, who tried to calm the situation and even offered to buy Cooke a drink, but finally Blount threatened to pummel his brother-in-law if he continued his harangue. Without warning or further provocation Cooke drew his pistol and pointed it at Blount's head, the muzzle only a few inches away, then fired a single shot. The bullet entered Blount's left cheek just below his eye, the blast burning and blackening the skin around the wound, and the ball ranged through Blount's brain and lodged against the back of his skull, and he died instantly. Cooke fled west on Front Street, threatening pedestrians as he went, and he vanished into the darkness.

A posse was organized and went out in every direction in search of the murderer. Cooke made his way to the railroad tracks and threw away his pistol, which was found by the city marshal during the night, and at 7:30 A.M. the fugitive was found skulking around the railroad tracks trying to find a boxcar in which to hide. He was lodged in the Albany County jail and on December 1 an inquest was held and Cooke was charged with murder. On December 3 he was indicted and four days later his trial began. Cooke did not deny the killing but said he could remember nothing, and stated as his defense that he was too intoxicated to form "malice aforethought" or to premeditate the murder. Nevertheless, the jury found him guilty of murder in the first degree and two days later Justice Jacob B. Blair sentenced him to hang. An appeal followed and the territorial supreme court spent nearly a year considering the request for a new trial before affirming the lower court's decision. The date of Cooke's execution was scheduled for December 12, 1884, and the application for a commutation of sentence to life in prison was submitted, and as quickly denied. Three days before his execution Cooke wrote to Blount's widow, his sister Mary Ann, to ask her forgiveness and at first she refused, but then she reconsidered and forgave him but refused to visit.

The night before his execution Cooke spent hours conversing with his death watch guard, William Tatham, before retiring at 11:00 P.M. He slept soundly and upon arising he dressed in his burial clothes: a white collarless shirt, blue suit pants and new shoes; but he set aside his suit jacket. After breakfast he received the Rev. Father H. Cummiskey, who heard his confession and blessed him, and then the doors of the jail were flung open and more than two hundred curious people filed through to have their last look at the condemned man and bid him farewell. The doors to the jail were closed when Father Cummiskey returned at 10:00 A.M. and the priest spent those last hours in seclusion with the condemned man. A temporary board structure had been attached to the rear of the courthouse building to house the gallows and obstruct public view of the execution. At 11:00 A.M. Sheriff Louis Miller called together the five newspaper reporters and escorted them into the execution building, where a photographer was already in place with his camera set up.

The priest, wearing a cassock and stole, led the procession to the scaffold a few minutes later with the prisoner at his side, Sheriff Miller and deputy James Sterling following closely behind, and then came the jurors and witnesses walking two by two. Father Cummiskey continued his prayers for two minutes after the condemned man was upon the trapdoor but Cooke had taken his position facing the back of the scaffold so the priest turned him to face the crowd, took his hand and said, "Good-bye, George," and the prisoner responded in kind. As soon as the priest left the platform the sheriff stepped forward and asked, "George Cooke, have you anything to say why the sentence of the law should not be passed upon you?" and Cooke replied, "Nothing."

The prisoner's wrists were tied behind his back with a piece of rope, one strap was tightly bound about his chest, another was buckled just below his hips, and a third was secured about his ankles. The sheriff produced a black velvet bag and at the same moment the string tie-back holding the noose was cut and it swung forward behind the condemned man. The noose was put over Cooke's head, cinched and positioned, and the black bag was pulled over his face. Both lawmen stepped back and in a moment, at 11:20 A.M., the supporting post was jerked out, the trap was sprung, and Cooke dropped five and one half feet. City physician Dr. J.H. Finfrock, and Drs. Newell K. Foster, P.F. Guenster and Lewis S. Barnes monitored Cooke's vital signs; in ten minutes his heart ceased to beat and he was pronounced dead. The body hung a total of fifteen minutes before being cut down and placed in its coffin, where an examination revealed that the deceased's neck had been broken in the fall. The lid was fastened and just after noon George Cooke was buried in the city cemetery at the county's expense.

Cheyenne (WY) Daily Leader: December 1, 1883; December 8–9, 1883; December 6, 1884; December 11–13, 1884; *Laramie Weekly Sentinel*: December 1, 1883.

Owens, John
March 5, 1886

John Owens, alias Bill Booth, arrived in Wyoming in July 1884 needing work and a place to live and found both with fifty-six-year-old Jacob Schmerer, a German immigrant and Johnson County pioneer. Schmerer's ranch was on Dry Creek in the Red Hills eight miles south of Buffalo. The unmarried rancher enjoyed the company of the young man, and put him to work haying, hunting, and tending his cows and horses. Schmerer paid off Owens after a month, when the haying was done; but Owens remained in the area and in December 1884 was again working for Schmerer, and agreed to go to Crazy Woman Creek and hunt deer for the rancher. Schmerer, in return, agreed to provide Owens with food and ammunition in exchange for the venison. Owens killed five deer and returned to Red Hills for a wagon and more ammunition, and asked for one hundred cartridges. But after Schmerer went into Buffalo and sold some of the meat he returned with only sixty rounds. They headed to Crazy Woman Creek with Schmerer riding beside the wagon and Owens riding in the wagon but once they arrived Owens, out of spite for being shorted on ammunition, claimed that he could not remember where he left the deer. The old German was furious but could do nothing and returned to his ranch empty-handed.

On Tuesday, March 25, 1885, Owens was in Buffalo buying supplies, then stopped at Schmerer's ranch, and the following day he stopped by Burrill Madden's cabin nearby and had lunch. Owens made a point of telling the coal miner that Schmerer had gone to Crazy Woman Creek to buy chickens and said Schmerer had given him the keys to the ranch house and permission to stay while he was away. At 4:00 P.M. Madden went to the ranch and ate dinner with Owens and then, at the young man's insistence, borrowed supplies he needed badly. Madden returned to the Schmerer ranch two days later and it appeared abandoned, as there were no tracks in the fresh snow, but he reasoned that Schmerer might have returned from Crazy Woman Creek and gone hunting with Owens as the horses and saddles were gone.

When Madden returned a week later the place still had an abandoned look to it so he peered into the ranch house windows. Schmerer's gun and cartridge belt were gone and Owen's gum rubber boots hung from the nail that usually held Schmerer's leather boots. Thinking the old German might have gone on a spree, something he did occasionally,

Madden did nothing for another week. When there was still no sign of his neighbor Madden went into Buffalo but he was convinced to wait yet another week. By mid–April the old German had not been seen for over three weeks, so Madden notified Sheriff Frank Canton. The sheriff, with A.J. McCray, went to investigate but could find no evidence of foul play. Madden remained suspicious and began systematically searching the surrounding hills for Schmerer's body. Finally, on May 2, exactly five weeks after Madden first missed his neighbor, Madden was walking through a canyon two miles from the Schmerer Ranch and caught the scent of a decomposing body. The wind was wrong so he could not follow up the search; he went home, and returned the next morning when he followed the scent to the carcass a dead calf. He was about to give up the search of that canyon when he noticed a swarm of flies hovering over a pile of small rocks beneath a large rock overhang, and thought it strange that the flies were not on the dead calf. He investigated by pulling off a few rocks and as soon as he saw clothing he put the rocks back and hurried into Buffalo.

On Sunday Madden led Johnson County coroner Dr. John C. Watkins, his jury, and Sheriff Canton to the grave and they uncovered Schmerer's decomposed remains dressed in his distinctive plaid trousers, but barefoot. Dr. Watkins immediately recognized his old patient and confirmed his identity from a broken rib he had treated. The dead man's hands had been partially eaten by insects and the head had been wrapped twice. The doctor removed the wrapping and found a cord tied tightly around the dead man's neck; the skull was horribly crushed in three places. He determined that the old man had been killed with a hatchet and that any one of the wounds would have proven fatal.

The jury found that Owens had killed Schmerer, so Sheriff Canton sent descriptive circulars throughout the territory and offered a reward; within weeks Owens was recognized at Miles City, Montana, and arrested. Deputy sheriff McDermott was sent and he returned the fugitive to Buffalo. While en route Owens told of the murder and, as he would at trial, gave a long and detailed account of how he had fought for his life for a quarter hour and finally killed the old man in self-defense. He said he used a hatchet that lay near the stove and described how he had buried the body and returned to clean the cabin's floor and walls. He said he went into Buffalo the next morning to get his pawned pistol and surrender, and only then decided to escape rather than submit to arrest. When asked why he had mutilated Schmerer so brutally he said "Well, you know how it is when a man's excited; he don't know when to quit." He said he was delayed when Madden came for dinner but that evening he packed everything of value and struck out for Montana. Owens was indicted, tried, and convicted of first degree murder when the jury refused to believe his claim of self-defense. He was sentenced to hang by Judge Jacob B. Blair but an appeal followed, which stayed the execution. Finally the territorial supreme court affirmed the lower court's decision and set the date for execution at March 5, 1886.

Owens tried unsuccessfully to escape three times while his case was under review. On his last afternoon he confessed to a reporter of the *Buffalo Sentinel* that he had killed the old man because of a disagreement over a $5 transaction, and admitted he had planned the crime for over a month. Relieved of the burden of guilt Owens slept soundly his last night and arose at 7:30 A.M. After breakfast he dressed in his burial clothes: a black suit, white shirt and socks, and black slippers. At 10:30 A.M. Sheriff Canton read the death warrant. Canton was followed closely by the blacksmith, who removed the heavy shackles. Just before 11:00 A.M. Sheriff Canton, Owen's friend Abe Abrahams, and Father Bex escorted the prisoner from his cell and Owens complained, "I wish you'd hurry up. I want to get to Hell in time for dinner."

The sheriff and priest walked on either side of the prisoner with Abrahams behind holding a large crucifix above Owens' head, at the prisoner's request. The procession was brief as the gallows had been built behind the courthouse in the jail yard and Owens was immediately positioned on the trapdoor and prepared with straps while Father Bex offered a prayer for his soul. Sheriff Canton asked the prisoner if he had anything to say and he declined to speak, so the noose and black cap were quickly adjusted and at 11:05 A.M. the trap was sprung. Owens hung for twelve minutes before he was pronounced dead and after hanging a few minutes more the body was cut down and examined; it was determined that the prisoner's neck had not been broken so he had strangled to death. His remains were placed in a plain pine coffin provided by the county and buried that afternoon.

Cheyenne (WY) Democratic Leader: March 6, 1886.

Carter, Benjamin F.
January 26, 1888

Benjamin F. "Big Ben" Carter was born in Texas in 1850. He grew to be a substantially larger than average man for those times, measuring over six feet tall and weighing more than two hundred pounds, with broad shoulders, thinning blond hair, and piercing blue eyes. Because of his size, or perhaps in spite of it, he developed into a bully who seldom missed an opportunity to upbraid a man smaller than himself. When sober he was surly and vile but when under the influence of liquor he turned into the worst sort of brute, physically abusing anyone unable to stand against him. He called himself the "Badman from Bitter Creek" and made a concerted effort to live up to that sobriquet.

Carter had arrived in Wyoming in 1877 and soon became known as one of the best cowpunchers in the territory and was made "top-hand" for the Charles Herbertz Land & Cattle Company. In early 1886 he was employed by the Hub & Spoke Ranch and was still employed there on October 4 when he left with a wagon and riders for Sweetwater where they were holding their round-up. He separated from the crew and stopped at Jim Averell's road ranch where he took on an ample supply of whiskey before catching up with the men at their campsite, thirty miles from Rawlins. Among the drovers was a small quiet boy of seventeen years, James Jefferies, who had only been with the outfit for two weeks. As soon as Carter arrived he singled out the teenager for abuse and threats and warned the boy to be gone by morning. Carter accused the boy of spying on the outfit and pulled his pistol, and while he had the drop on the youngster he kicked and slapped the boy several times. A short time later he repeated the abuse but no one intervened to help the boy so, to avoid Carter, Jefferies turned in for the night. The rest of the outfit faced an early start so they soon joined Jefferies in the tent and rolled into their blankets.

Carter later said that someone suggested shooting a few holes in the tent and he obliged, then decided to shoot again but his pistol went off prematurely, and this bullet struck Jefferies above the left eye, passing entirely through. The boy never awoke and died in nine hours. After the shooting Carter arose, dressed quickly, saddled a good mount, and fled. Two cowboys rode to the camp of their foreman, who sent riders to warn the other ranchers that Carter might try to swap for a fresh mount from their string. Riders went to the Hub & Spoke Ranch and told Tom Sun, one of the owners, the details of the murder. Carter arrived soon afterward, looking for a fresh mount. Sun disarmed him and sent him into Rawlins under escort. The party arrived at 8:00 P.M. and the prisoner was turned over to a deputy sheriff and lodged in jail.

The following morning, October 6, Carbon County coroner George W. Durant summoned a jury for an inquest and found the killing to be a "willful, malicious and unlawful murder." Durant, also a justice, conducted the preliminary hearing a week later and Carter's attorney successfully filed a motion for a continuance until the May 1887 session of the district court. The trial began on May 21 and lasted only one day, concluding at 9:00 P.M., and the jury deliberated until midnight before returning a guilty verdict on the charge of first degree murder. Carter was sentenced to hang on July 8 but an appeal stayed the execution. The territorial supreme court finally affirmed the lower court's decision and the date of execution was rescheduled for August, but now Governor Thomas Moonlight intervened and granted a respite of sixty-three days, to give him time to consider the prisoner's application for a new trial. The application was denied so Carter's counsel next applied for a reversal of the judgment based upon an error in jury selection, but this was also denied and in July 1887, with all hope lost for a legal remedy, Carter attempted to escape with the aid of a jail trusty. However, the six-shooter and saw blade that were smuggled in were discovered and thereafter Carter was chained to the iron latticework of his cell.

During his final days Carter was baptized by the Rev. R.E.G. Huntington and on the Sunday before his execution Carter took communion in his cell. Deputy L.C. Kelley was assigned day and night as Carter's death watch and he was verbally abused by the prisoner constantly. On Carter's final night he received a reporter and told the newsman that he was ready to die and had attended to his affairs. After the jail closed Carter sat with his forehead resting on his hands, smoked continuously, reading from his prayer book occasionally, and once singing a few lines of the hymn "Nearer My God to Thee." He managed to sleep only two hours before the Reverend Huntington joined him at 8:40 A.M. for an hour of spiritual encouragement. Just before 10:00 A.M. two dozen friends were admitted to bid him farewell and when they left, county physician Dr. T. Getty Ricketts and Sheriff William High appeared and informed the condemned man that he would begin his walk to the gallows in ten minutes. Carter was given whiskey to calm his nerves and then the prisoner asked that the hanging be delayed one hour, and the sheriff said he would grant this final request.

Outside the enclosure a freezing wind and snow flurries reduced the crowd to less than one hundred men, but inside only a few witnesses had gathered. At 10:30 A.M., a half hour sooner than agreed, Sheriff High entered the jail with several deputies and brought Carter from his cell. The procession proceeded to the scaffold, which had been built against the east wall of the courthouse, so that the party stepped through a second story window directly onto the platform, and Carter immediately took his position on the trapdoor. Deputy Thomas Hanks quickly applied the straps pinioning his wrists and ankles while the prisoner was thanking the sheriff for his treatment while in jail. Carter then noticed the attending physicians, Drs. Ricketts and John Osborne, and bid them farewell. The noose of five-eighths inch hemp was heavily lubricated with soap so it was easily cinched tight and carefully positioned by Deputy Kelley, who also pulled the black silk cap over Carter's face at 10:37 A.M. Sheriff High immediately cut the cord which held the trapdoor and Carter dropped four feet, breaking his neck. In only four minutes the doctors pronounced him dead and after hanging several minutes more the body was cut down, placed on a board, and carried into the jail where those who had braved the cold were rewarded with one final look at the murderer. Carter had asked the Reverend Huntington to take charge of his body, and the reverend delivered a simple burial service that afternoon before Carter was buried in the Rawlins' cemetery.

Cheyenne (WY) Daily Leader: October 26–28, 1888.

Black, George A.
February 26, 1890

Sixty-year-old Robert Burnett, also known as "Old Tanglefoot," settled in Wyoming in 1875. Though quite peculiar, he was a likeable sort and described by his many friends as an "eccentric." He wore gunnysacks on his feet tied with wire, ate only with his hands, threw the scraps on the floor of his cabin, and had not bathed in many years. Burnett was feebleminded and terribly superstitious but he was also a litigious old man, and Burnett sued his neighbor George A. Black for harvesting the old man's hay. Burnett won the suit and, when Black could not pay the judgment, the plaintiff was awarded Black's buildings, some hay land, and a few cows. Black had wanted Burnett's far superior land and held a grudge when he lost his property to Burnett. He tried to drive the old man off the land by playing upon the old man's superstitious nature and posting on his cabin door White Cap notices—crude drawings of skulls, cross bones, and coffins. Once, he hid in a clump of sagebrush and fired on Burnett but missed his mark and the old man, instead of turning and running, charged and captured Black. Black said he mistook Burnett for an elk so he was released by the old man without charges being filed.

When Black failed to drive Burnett off the property he moved to Medicine Bow, but soon returned to the Pole Mountain area to live with his brother Benjamin. Black found at Pole Mountain a willing accomplice in Dwight "Roxy" Rockwell, a twenty-eight-year-old man he first met at the JD Ranch. Black explained how Burnett had "stolen" his land and Rockwell agreed to go with Black to help him reclaim his property. Black first went to Laramie and filed a mining claim on Burnett's property and then the two men stocked their wagon with supplies and started out. They arrived at Burnett's cabin on May 28, 1889, and found the old man seated on an overturned pail cutting seed potatoes. Rockwell stood nearby while Black asserted that the land belonged to him and asked, then commanded, that Burnett vacate the property, but the old man refused. Suddenly Black pulled his six-shooter and shot Burnett in the back and when Burnett reached for his rifle Black shot him in the head and then fired once more into the dead body. The two men wrapped the head and then the entire body and hauled it up a remote canyon and placed it at the end of a huge log. They piled pitch pine onto Burnett's remains and set the pyre aflame before returning to the cabin to sleep.

In the morning they scrubbed the wagon and smeared grease on the tarp to cover the bloodstains before returning to the body, where they raked what remained of Burnett into a pile and, with a new pile of tinder, again set it afire before they returned to the cabin and replaced the bloodstained floorboards. That night they returned to Burnett's remains, gathered up the larger bones and remnants and buried them in a gopher hole. Black and Rockwell took possession of the cabin but Rockwell soon left for North Park, Colorado. Burnett was not missed for several weeks but when questioned Black explained that the old man had sold out to him and gone east to spend his final days with his daughter. That story was soon discredited but there was no evidence of foul play. When there was talk of organizing a search party Black threatened to kill any organizer of an investigative committee, so the idea was abandoned.

The Pullman family, Charles and Mattie, with teenage daughter Mary, had recently arrived from Missouri and on August 6, 1889, Mattie and Mary went berry-picking. They were on their way home when they saw a strange pile of ashes covering an area nearly eight feet in diameter, certainly no campfire. They investigated and found small human bones, bits of wire, and small remnants of clothing so they hurried home and told Charles, and the next day the three returned to the site. Charles examined the remains, gathered every bit of evidence into two pails, and carried them into Laramie. He gave the pails to the Albany County attorney, who called in Dr. John W. Harris and his associate, and they identified the remains as human finger bones, part of a skull, teeth, and a rib bone. They also found rivets from overalls like those always worn by Burnett, hobnails from his boots, and bits of bailing wire like that Burnett used to tie sacks over his feet.

Coroner Dr. J.H. Hayford convened a jury, which over five days of testimony and investigation found the remains to be Burnett's. The Black brothers and Rockwell were charged with his murder. George Black and his brother Benjamin were arrested and jailed, but at the preliminary hearing before Justice Charles E.

Carpenter on August 22 George was held for the grand jury and Benjamin was released. Two weeks after the discovery of Burnett's remains Sheriff Charles Yund learned that a check payable to Burnett had been endorsed by Rockwell and cashed in North Park, Colorado, so he deputized J.J. Moore and the two men went in search of the fugitive. Rockwell was working in a field on George Fletcher's ranch when the two officers arrested him and he willingly returned to Wyoming where he confessed all the details of the murder.

In mid–October Black was indicted for first degree murder, while Rockwell was indicted as an accessory after the fact. The trial in the district court commenced on Saturday, November 2, and five days later Black was found guilty of first degree murder, primarily on Rockwell's testimony, and on November 16 Judge M.C. Saufley sentenced Black to hang on January 15, 1890. Rockwell was tried after Black and received a light sentence, in consideration of his testimony, and two years later he was free and living in Montana. The appeal process, financed by his brother Benjamin, began for George Black and the execution was stayed while the territorial supreme court considered the matter, but the respite was only six weeks in duration when the supreme court affirmed the lower court's decision. Governor Francis E. Warren quickly denied the application for commutation of sentence and the date for Black's execution was rescheduled for February 26, 1890.

Black had been a Baptist but a week before the hanging he was baptized into the Catholic faith. On Tuesday evening, February 25, the prisoner was talking with his death watch guards when a reporter from the *Leader* was escorted to his cell. The reporter offered to print whatever the condemned man said and encouraged him to confess but he protested his innocence and persisted in saying Rockwell committed the crime and that he himself was denied a fair trial. Black retired at 12:50 A.M. and spent a restless night and arose at 6:00 A.M.; then Father H. Cummiskey arrived. They were joined by Benjamin Black and their three sisters, and after they left, deputy sheriff Alex McKay visited and pleaded with Black, "for the sake of his soul," to tell the truth but the condemned man continued to insist that he was innocent.

The prisoner braced for the ordeal as he dressed in his new black suit. The scaffold had been erected within a twenty by twenty foot shed at the rear of the jail to provide the condemned man privacy for his execution. At 11:00 A.M. Father Cummiskey started from the cell with the prisoner, a metal cross firmly gripped in Black's right hand, and Sheriff Yund followed closely behind. The distance to the trap was only one hundred feet and the procession stopped a few feet from the trapdoor while the priest offered a prayer, shook hands with Black, and then quickly retired. Fifty people watched as Black stepped onto the trapdoor and his wrists and arms, knees and ankles were pinioned with straps by deputy McKay. The sheriff placed, cinched and adjusted the noose, then asked the prisoner if he had anything to say to the witnesses, but Black declined except to say, "I am not the one who did it."

Sheriff Yund pulled the black cap from his pocket and placed it over the prisoner's face at 11:12 A.M. and in the next moment he turned toward the release, gave the twine a firm tug, and the trap was sprung. The body dropped eight feet, breaking the prisoner's neck, and Dr. Howard T. Ricketts of Carbon and Drs. J.H. Finfrock and Henry L. Stevens of Laramie stood on chairs, one monitoring the heartbeat while the other two each held a wrist and counted the pulse of the hanging figure; in six minutes he was pronounced dead. Black's body was cut down at 11:39 A.M., twenty-seven minutes after he fell, placed in the coffin provided by the county, and slid into a one-horse hearse. He was buried in the potter's field at county expense that afternoon.

Cheyenne (WY) Daily Leader: January 29, 1890; February 26–27, 1890.

Addendum

Shortly before this book went to press, these eight additional executions were discovered.

COLORADO TERRITORY

Smith, George
February 18, 1870

On February 15, 1868, George Smith and Bob Reynolds, Negroes, went to the home of William Hamblin, a milkman in Quartz Valley, where Smith struck Hamblin over the head with a stick of wood, knocking him unconscious. Smith strangled Hamblin to death with a cord from his bed and, using the cord tied around the neck and a wrist, the two men dragged the body to a twenty-foot mine shaft six hundred yards from the house and threw in the body. They ransacked the house, took everything of value, and fled. Soon after the murder a boy, the son of George Newton, was walking with his dog when the animal smelled blood and led the youngster to the mine shaft containing Hamblin's body. He contacted Sheriff Grimes and he suspected Smith and Reynolds, two men thought to have committed a number of crimes in recent weeks, and learned they had started for Denver that morning. Deputy sheriff Brown and Marshal Clark pursued the two men to the Childs' house where Smith and Reynolds were arrested and quickly confessed to Hamblin's murder, and money and property of the murdered man was found in their possession. They confessed to another burglary and Smith was taken to the place they had hidden the plunder, and while away Reynolds convinced his guards that he also knew of a large cache of stolen gold and jewels. The guards removed his shackles and while going after the loot Reynolds escaped. A posse was organized and sent to search the mountains and after a week the lawmen cornered the fugitive. When he resisted he was seriously wounded. Smith had been lodged in jail at Central City, the county seat for Gilpin County, and Reynolds joined him there but he soon died of his wounds. Smith was tried in Judge Hallett's district courtroom at the May term. The defendant was convicted of first degree murder and sentenced to hang in August, but Smith's friends at Central City felt he had not had a fair trial and petitioned the governor for a hearing on the matter. The hearing was granted following a long delay and after listening to arguments from both sides for or against a commutation of sentence or a new trial Governor Edward M. McCook announced that he would only grant a commutation upon the recommendation of Judge Hallett. The judge stated that he felt that Smith had been given a fair trial, and that upon the evidence he would be convicted of first degree murder in a second trial and sentenced to hang, so he refused to make the recommendation. The governor then declined to interfere further and the new date for Smith's execution was set for Friday, February 18, 1870, two years after the murder was committed.

During Smith's final days he was attended by the Baptist reverends Adams and van Voren, and by Father Raverdy. On his final night he asked to be allowed to see the sunset and this was granted, and then he slept soundly until he was aroused at an early hour for breakfast. Father Raverdy then arrived to baptize Smith into the Catholic religion, and following the ceremony the priest administered the sacrament. The gallows had been built on Casto Mountain at the head of Eureka Gulch but a crowd gathered at the jail at 9:00 A.M. to catch a glimpse of the condemned man when he was brought out. At 11:00 A.M. Smith appeared with wrists bound and, with his guards and Father Raverdy, boarded a buggy and was driven to the scaffold, the crowd following the procession at a solemn pace and joined the other at the gallows, totaling two thousand. The prisoner climbed the stairs with a firm step and sat in a chair behind the trapdoor. The death warrant was read and then Smith took his place on the trapdoor, where his arms, knees and ankles were bound and the noose was adjusted. He was asked if he had anything to say but there is no record of a speech. Father Raverdy then prayed for his soul and during the prayer Smith appeared to be on the verge of collapse, but composed himself by the time the priest said "Amen" and, after Smith kissed the crucifix, the black hood was pulled over his head at noon. In but a moment the trap was sprung and the prisoner dropped over five and one half feet, but the fall did not break his neck. There were few signs of struggle as he strangled to death and in fifteen minutes the attending physicians pronounced him dead. The body was allowed to hang another ten minutes before being cut down and deposited in the plain coffin provided. Within a few minutes the coffin was carried to the grave, which had been dug a few feet from the gallows, and the remains were buried.

Colorado Tribune [Denver]: February 24, 1870. *Daily Register [Central City, CO]*: February 19, 1870. *Rocky Mountain News [Denver]*: February 19–20, 1868; February 19, 1870.

MONTANA TERRITORY

McAndrews, Michael
March 1, 1878

In early September 1877 Michael McAndrews and George Mavor were traveling together to Pioneer in Deer Lodge County, Montana. On the night of September 4 they stopped at Captain Cook's place on Boulder Creek and spent the night, and the next day continued on their way. Soon afterward the body of a man was discovered on Boulder Creek and it was clear he had been brutally murdered, but the condition prevented the remains from being identified. Two young men were suspected and they were tracked down, arrested, and taken to Boulder, but they proved an alibi and were released. When the investigation resumed the body was identified as the man seen in the company of McAndrews at Captain Cook's place and he was then suspected. McAndrews was tracked to Pioneer, arrested, returned to Boulder where he disclosed the identity of the dead man, and at his examination on September 17 he was held over for trial in the district court at Radersburg. The trial commenced the last week of

September and concluded on Friday, October 5, when the jury found the defendant guilty of first degree murder. A week later Judge Henry N. Blake sentenced McAndrews to hang on January 25, 1878, but defense attorneys L. J. Sharp and Thomas L. Napton filed an appeal with the state supreme court. Case No. 259 was heard on January 6 and on January 14 the justices affirmed the judgment and sentence of the lower court. However, acting governor Mills granted a respite to March 1 to review the case, but then declined to intervene further.

The execution was conducted within an enclosure erected near the Radersburg jail. The death warrant was read to McAndrews in his cell and he was then conducted onto the trapdoor where he had his wrists and arms, knees and ankles bound and the noose adjusted. There is no record of a statement, so after the black hood was pulled over his head at 2:30 P.M. the trap was sprung immediately. McAndrews broke his neck in the fall and after hanging fifteen minutes the doctors in attendance pronounced him dead. The body was then cut down, deposited into the coffin provided by the county, and prepared for shipment to Helena for burial on Saturday.

Independent [Helena, MT]: September 18, 1877; October 14, 1877; January 14, 1878; March 2, 1878.

Robert, Frank
October 31, 1878

In early September 1877 Frank Robert and his partner, named Morris, camped on Rotten Grass Creek near Clarke's Fork of the Yellowstone on the Crow Indian Reservation in Montana. While Morris slept Robert crept up and crushed his skull with a slung shot. The body was soon discovered and Robert was arrested, and he had all of Morris' money and property with him. Robert made several conflicting admissions about Morris' death before he confessed to killing him, but he insisted that he had shot Morris in self-defense. A more thorough examination of the remains was conducted which showed that Morris had not been shot. All of the circumstantial evidence surrounding the death showed it to be a murder for robbery but various issues, including the case being a federal one because it occurred on an Indian reservation, delayed the proceedings. The trial in Judge Henry N. Blake's U.S. Circuit Court in Virginia City began in early September 1878 and Robert was convicted of murder in the first degree after the jurors deliberated only briefly. On September 16, 1878, Judge Blake sentenced Robert to hang on October 31. The case was quickly reviewed by the U.S. Supreme Court and President Rutherford B. Hayes, but nothing would arise to delay the proceedings.

During his final weeks Robert was attended by Father Kelleher. On his final night he prepared a statement and gave it to the priest to read on the gallows. Deputy U.S. Marshal McFarland was responsible for the execution and he had the gallows erected within an enclosure adjoining the courthouse, and limited the witnesses to a dozen respectable citizens of Virginia City. At 9:00 A.M. the death warrant was read to the prisoner in his cell and then he was conducted onto the gallows. The prisoner took his place on the trapdoor where his wrists and arms, knees and ankles were bound and the noose was adjusted while the priest prayed for his soul. When asked if he wanted to make a speech Robert declined, but Father Kelleher then read his prepared statement repeating his defense at trial, that he had shot Morris in self defense. After Robert kissed the crucifix pressed to his lips, the black hood was pulled over his head and at 9:30 A.M. the trap was sprung. Robert broke his neck in the fall and in ten minutes the attending physicians pronounced him dead. The body was cut down, deposited into the coffin provided by the county, and given to Father Kelleher for burial in the Catholic portion of the cemetery.

Helena Daily Herald [MT]: October 31, 1878. *Independent [Helena, MT]*: September 17, 1878.

NEW MEXICO TERRITORY

Tansey, John
April 6, 1862

On April 4, 1862, Company K of the 3rd Cavalry Regulars was on patrol three miles south of La Jolla, New Mexico, when, just before noon, Captain Joseph G. Tilford placed Pvt. John Tansey in the custody of Sgt. Edward Cullinan and ordered the sergeant to escort the prisoner to their camp near La Jolla. The sergeant, on horseback, followed Tansey closely as he marched him back toward the camp, and they had covered some distance when Tansey collapsed. There were a number of witnesses nearby who heard the sergeant order Tansey to rise and heard Tansey mutter, "I will fix him off." Tansey arose and walked to the head of the horse, pulled his revolver, and shot the sergeant in the lower left area of his chest. The sergeant pulled his pistol and fired two wild shots before he fell from his horse, and a force of men rushed Tansey who was restrained, disarmed, and taken to La Jolla. The prisoner was placed under close guard and a general court martial was convened immediately, and Tansey was tried under the 9th Article of War. The sergeant was still alive when the Dr. B. A. Clements testified that his patient was "in a dangerous condition," and recommended that he not be questioned. Tansey offered no testimony or defense, and after deliberating briefly the officers found the prisoner guilty and sentenced him to be shot in two days — April 6, 1862. At daybreak the prisoner was marched to an open area where the men of the company had assembled, he was placed at the end of a corridor formed by the soldiers, and the officer of the day prepared him for his execution. After the camp chaplain prayed for his soul he was blindfolded and then the firing squad, at daybreak, was ordered to fire. Tansey was killed immediately, placed in the coffin provided by the military, and buried near the camp.

Johnson, Edward C., Gail R. Johnson, and Melissa Johnson Williams. *All Were Not Heroes: A Study of U.S. Soldiers Executed by U.S. Military Authorities During the Late War*. Chicago: E. C. Johnson, 1997.

Philbrook, Darius A.
April 8, 1862

In 1862 the Union forces were gathering at Fort Union, Mora County, New Mexico, preparing to repel an attack from Confederate forces who were intent on occupying the Southwest. The 1st Regiment of Colorado Infantry and the 1st Colorado Cavalry Volunteers were at Fort Union well in advance of the first action, the Battle of Glorieta which raged from March 26 through March 28, 1862. The soldiers had been idle for weeks and this led to restlessness. They were angry because the sole source for many of the necessities of life were available only from the Camp Slough sutler, a scurrilous profiteer. In March the soldiers raided the sutler's store at Camp Slough taking everything of value, including a large supply of whiskey and wine. On March 13 twenty-nine-year-old 1st Sgt. Darius A. Philbrook and other soldiers of the infantry unit became drunk and boisterous inside the sutler's store. Philbrook, as 1st Sgt., was the first to be confronted by Lt. Isaac Gray of Company B of the 1st Colorado Cavalry Volunteers, who was officer of the guard that day, and he tried to quiet the sergeant but Philbrook became verbally abusive and resisted the effort. Philbrook was threatened with arrest and when Lt. Gray turned to walk away the sergeant followed. When ten yards from the door of the sutler's store Philbrook pulled his revolver and fired two shots, missing his mark, and Gray turned around and using the blunt edge of his saber struck Philbrook twice. Philbrook then fired a third shot, which struck Gray between the eyes just above the apex of his nose. Gray collapsed as Philbrook turned and took a half dozen steps before he, too, collapsed. He was quickly disarmed, arrested, taken to Fort Union which was a short distance from the camp, and locked in the guard house. Lt. Gray was rushed to treatment and the bullet, which had struck him at an angle, had deflected downward rather than penetrating and he survived. Philbrook was charged with "striking an officer" during time of war and his court martial convened on March 17. His defense consisted of testimony of his previous good character and service, and he asked for the mercy of the court as he had been drunk at the time. Philbrook was found guilty and sentenced to die by firing squad, and the record of the court martial was reviewed by Colonel Edward Canby, approved, and forwarded to the president. However, more important matters immediately arose as the Union forces were deployed to battle the Confederate forces and, while they were engaged in the fighting, the case was reviewed by President Lincoln, affirmed on April 4, and Philbrook was sentenced to be shot on April 8, 1862. The Union forces were still in the field chasing Confederate forces when word was received that Sgt. Philbrook had been executed.

Hollister, Ovando J. *History of the First Colorado Volunteers*. Denver: Thomas Gibson, 1863. *General Order 25, Dept. of New Mexico*: April 4, 1862. Johnson, Edward C., Gail R. Johnson and Melissa Johnson Williams. *All Were Not Heroes: A Study of U.S. Soldiers Executed by U.S. Military Authorities During the Late War*. Chicago: E. C. Johnson, 1997.

Coffield, Joseph
January 19, 1864

Private Joseph Coffield, *alias* John Coffield, was a member of Company K, 1st New Mexico Cavalry. He had enlisted in July 1862 and a year later he was confined at Fort Canby awaiting court martial for drunkenness. He escaped with a man named Luciano Valencia, but they were soon captured and returned to Fort Canby, where Coffield was convicted and disciplined. He was returned to service by late 1863 when Coffield's unit was engaged in operations against the Navajo Indians, and he was charged with committing a murder and arrested. He was tried by a general court martial and sentenced to be shot. The sentence was affirmed on December 31, 1863, after being reviewed by the general staff and President Lincoln, and Coffield was executed by firing squad at 1:30 P.M. on January 19, 1864.

Alotta, Robert I. *Civil War Justice: Union Army Executions under Lincoln*. Shippensburg, PA: White Mane, 1989. *General Order 33, Department of New Mexico*: December 31, 1863. Johnson, Edward C., Gail R. Johnson and Melissa Johnson Williams. *All Were Not Heroes: A Study of U.S. Soldiers Executed by U.S. Military Authorities During the Late War*. Chicago: E. C. Johnson, 1997.

Madrid, Juan d. D.
September 9, 1865

On July 13, 1865, thirty-two-year-old private Juan Madrid, *alias* Juan Madrill, assigned to Company C, 1st Cavalry, New Mexico Volunteers, was stationed at Fort Union, New Mexico. While on patrol in the Raton Mountains Madrid and two other soldiers, privates Baca and Gomez, were at the one of the tollgate houses drinking whiskey with Corporal Cruz Torrez and one other man in the barroom. Madrid held a grudge against Torrez but did not disclose the source of the ill feelings. Madrid tried to enlist the aid of the other two soldiers in murdering Torrez, but they declined. Madrid followed the corporal and picked up a large stone, put his arm around Torrez' shoulders in a friendly manner, walked with him toward the creek and when the opportunity arose he bashed in the corporal's skull. The three privates then returned to camp and to their separate tents. When Torrez was discovered and rushed to the doctor, gatekeeper Wooltens was summoned while the entire company was being assembled, and he picked out Madrid, Baca and Gomez as the three soldiers in the bar room. Baca and Gomez told the story of the crime and when Torrez died the following day, Madrid was charged with murder. The prisoner was returned to Fort Union on July 27, tried at a general court martial on August 24, convicted and sentenced to hang, though some reports say he faced a firing squad. Madrid's defense was simply that he was innocent and the other two soldiers had lied. Following a review by the general staff and President Lincoln the sentence was affirmed on September 2 and Madrid was sentenced to hang on September 9, 1865. In 1874 the claim of Guadalupe Torrez came before the Committee of the House of Representatives and they granted the widow a soldier's pension.

Alotta, Robert I. *Civil War Justice: Union Army Executions under Lincoln.* Shippensburg, PA: White Mane, 1989. *General Order 23, Dept. of New Mexico*: September 2, 1865. Johnson, Edward C., Gail R. Johnson, and Melissa Johnson Williams. *All Were Not Heroes: A Study of U.S. Soldiers Executed by U.S. Military Authorities During the Late War.* Chicago: E. C. Johnson, 1997. *Report of the Committees of the House of Representatives:* 1874.

WASHINGTON TERRITORY

Ely, Francis
March 11, 1864

Thirty-six-year-old private Francis Ely of Company A, 1st Oregon Cavalry, after two years of exemplary service, deserted from Camp No. 42 on the Port Neuf River near Fort Hall, Idaho, on August 27, 1863. His unit was campaigning against the Snake Indians when Ely took ill for several days in late August and asked the 1st Sergeant to excuse him from sentry duty over the horses and mules, but he was ordered to stand his post. He took his post but deserted and managed to travel sixty-five miles by the following day, when he was overtaken by Lt. John T. Apperson, charged with desertion and theft of his revolver (government property), and arrested. He was lodged in the guard house at Fort Walla Walla and on November 27, 1863, his general court martial began. Ely admitted to desertion but denied stealing the revolver, saying it was hanging on his belt and he had given it no thought. The court deliberated briefly, convicted Ely of the stated charges, and sentenced him to "be shot to death by musketry." The case was reviewed by General Wright's staff and, though Colonel R. F. Maury attached an endorsement requesting a commutation, the sentence was affirmed and forwarded to President Lincoln. The president declined to interfere on February 26, 1864, issued the executive order substituting the death penalty for deserters to imprisonment at Fort Jefferson, Dry Tortugas. Unfortunately word of the order did not reach Fort Walla Walla until after Private Ely was shot to death.

Alotta, Robert I. *Civil War Justice: Union Army Executions under Lincoln.* Shippensburg, PA: White Mane, 1989. *General Order 8, Dept of the Pacific*: February 2, 1864. Johnson, Edward C., Gail R. Johnson, and Melissa Johnson Williams. *All Were Not Heroes: A Study of U.S. Soldiers Executed by U.S. Military Authorities During the Late War.* Chicago: E. C. Johnson, 1997. *Oregonian [Portland]*: March 17, 1864. *Washington Standard [Olympia]*: February 27, 1864.

Bibliography

Adjutant General's Report—1885. *List of U.S. Soldiers Executed by United States Military Authorities During the Late War.*

Alotta, Robert I. *Civil War Justice; Union Army Executions Under Lincoln.* Shippensburg, PA: White Mane, 1989.

Ball, Larry D. *Desert Lawmen: The United States Marshals of New Mexico and Arizona Territories, 1846–1912.* Albuquerque: University of New Mexico Press, 1992.

Bancroft, Hubert H. *History of Nevada, Colorado and Wyoming, 1540–1888.* San Francisco: History, 1890.

Bonney, W. P. *History of Pierce County, Washington.* Chicago: Pioneer Historical, 1927.

Brown, Larry K. *You Are Respectfully Invited to Attend My Execution.* Glendo, WY: High Plains, 1997.

Clark, Walter V.T., ed. *The Journals of Alfred Doten, 1849–1903.* Reno: University of Nevada Press, 1973.

Duff, Charles. *A Handbook on Hanging.* London, UK: Putnam, 1961.

Elman, Robert. *Badmen of the West.* Secaucus, NJ: Castle, 1974.

General Order 8, Dept. of the Pacific: February 2, 1864.

General Order 23, Dept. of New Mexico: September 2, 1865.

General Order 25, Dept. of New Mexico: April 4, 1862.

General Order 33, Dept. of New Mexico: December 31, 1863.

Gilbreath, West. *Death on the Gallows: The Story of Legal Hangings in New Mexico, 1847–1923.* Silver City, NM: High-Lonesome, 2002.

Gillespie, L. Kay. *The Unforgiven: Utah's Executed Men.* Salt Lake City: Signature, 1991.

Grove, Pearce S., et al., eds. *New Mexico Newspapers, a Comprehensive Guide to Bibliographical Entries and Locations.* Albuquerque: University of New Mexico Press, 1975.

Hamilton, Ladd. *This Bloody Deed: The Magruder Incident.* Pullman: Washington State University Press, 1994.

Hollister, Ovando J. *History of the First Colorado Volunteers.* Denver, CO: Thomas Gibson, 1863.

Johnson, Edward C., Gail R. Johnson and Melissa Johnson Williams. *All Were Not Heroes: A Study of U.S. Soldiers Executed by U.S. Military Authorities During the Late War.* Chicago: E.C. Johnson, 1997.

Koestler, Arthur. *Reflections on Hanging.* New York: Macmillan, 1957.

Ladd, Robert E. *Eight Ropes to Eternity.* Tombstone, AZ: Tombstone Epitaph.

Mack, Effie M. "Execution #1." *Nevada* (February 1947).

McLoughlin, Denis. *Wild and Woolly: An Encyclopedia of the Old West.* New York: Barnes & Noble, 1996.

McMillan, Mark. "Lucky Bill Gets the Noose." *Old West* (Fall 1965).

Mencken, August. *By the Neck: A Book of Hangings.* New York: Hastings House, 1942.

Nash, Jay Robert. *Encyclopedia of Western Lawmen & Outlaws.* New York: Da Capo, 1994.

O'Neal, Bill, James A. Crutchfield, and Dale L. Walker. *The Wild West.* Lincolnwood, IL: Publications International, 2001.

Phillips, David R., and Robert A Weinstein. *The West: An American Experience.* Chicago: Henry Regnery, 1975.

Report of the Committees of the House of Representatives: 1874.

Schweikart, Larry, and Bradley J. Birzer. *The American West.* Hoboken, NJ: John Wiley, 2003.

Teeters, Negley, and Jack Hedblom. *...Hang by the Neck....* Springfield, IL: Charles Thomas, 1967.

Thrapp, Dan L. *Encyclopedia of Frontier Biography.* Lincoln: University of Nebraska Press, 1988.

Torrez, Robert J. *Myth of the Hanging Tree.* Albuquerque: University of New Mexico Press, 2008.

Victor, Frances Fuller. *The Early Indian Wars of Oregon: Compiled from the Oregon Archives and*

Other Original Sources: with Muster Rolls. Salem, OR: F.C. Baker, state printer, 1894.
Ward, Geoffrey C. *The West: An Illustrated History*. New York: Little, Brown, 1996.
Wilson, R. Michael. *Crime & Punishment in Early Arizona*. Las Vegas: RaMA PRESS of Las Vegas, 2004.
_____. "Crime & Punishment in Early Nevada" (manuscript).
_____. "Crime & Punishment in Early Wyoming" (manuscript).
_____. *Murder & Execution in the Wild West*. Las Vegas: RaMA PRESS of Las Vegas, 2006.

Index

www.ingramcontent.com/pod-product-compliance
Ingram Content Group UK Ltd.
Pitfield, Milton Keynes, MK11 3LW, UK
UKHW051930100926
8556IPUK00022B/1471

9 780786 448258